Focus and Leverage

The Critical Methodology for Theory of Constraints, Lean, and Six Sigma (TLS)

Bruce Nelson • Bob Sproull

CRC Press
Taylor & Francis Group
Boca Raton London New York

CRC Press is an imprint of the
Taylor & Francis Group, an **informa** business

A PRODUCTIVITY PRESS BOOK

CRC Press
Taylor & Francis Group
6000 Broken Sound Parkway NW, Suite 300
Boca Raton, FL 33487-2742

Visit the Taylor & Francis Web site at
http://www.taylorandfrancis.com

and the CRC Press Web site at
http://www.crcpress.com

To my family and all of those many wonderful people I have learned from, and those who might have learned from me.

Bruce Nelson

To my beautiful and wonderful wife Beverly; Rob, our oldest son; John, our second son; and Emily, our daughter, thank you.

Bob Sproull

Contents

Foreword

Some authors write revolutionary business management books that question industry practices and propose a truly different new and convincing approach. That is true of Bruce Nelson and Bob Sproull's books. Some books are so enticing that you are torn between finishing the book and starting to apply the ideas it presents. This is such a book. Some "business novels" deal with such universal truths that people from all walks of life read them and apply the ideas presented; *The Goal* by Eliyahu Goldratt was probably the first. *Focus and Leverage* is such a novel. Some people are so intrinsically generous that when they write, their obsession is to give you all the knowledge you need to go away and do it, no strings attached. That is the case with this book.

As I write this, the vast majority of organizations throughout the world are trying to improve their performance using approaches inspired from "Lean" or "Lean Six Sigma" (LSS). Very very few are using the Theory of Constraints (TOC). The problem is that the current mind-sets are very sectarian. The Lean community shuns the LSS and TOC communities, the TOC community denigrates Lean and LSS, and so forth. The authors claim that these things are complementary; they call it "TLS"; TOC + Lean + Six Sigma. They could have called it OMOI (Open-Minded Operational Improvement) because the idea is simply to keep an open mind.

In the past 10 years, some people have lectured and written about why and how you should use a cocktail of Lean, Six Sigma, and TOC, but I believe no one has done as well as Bruce Nelson and Bob Sproull. The authors know all about these approaches since they have successfully applied them to Fortune 500 or smaller organizations for decades. They have true expertise in all three components of TLS and they don't suffer from any kind of favoritism.

Their first book, *Epiphanized: Integrating Theory of Constraints, Lean and Six Sigma*, introduced these "TLS" ideas in a traditional manufacturing environment. Both the first and this second book use the same business novel format with, in *Epiphanized*'s case, 100 pages of annexes describing the various tools used in the story. *Focus and Leverage: The Critical TLS Methodology* follows up by applying the same methodology to a helicopter maintenance, repair, and overhaul environment and to a hospital to underline how universal this way of analyzing organizations and improving them is. In this sequel, they add two new ideas: the Interference Diagram/Intermediate Objectives (ID/IO) Simplified Strategy and the Multiple Drum–Buffer–Rope or M-DBR scheduling mechanism. Bruce and Bob are not just aggregators of other people's ideas; they add their own, born of their experience that grows year by year. When they do that, they do it well, blending high-level thinking and a down-to-earth, boots-on-the-ground attitude.

The authors are passionate and experienced "changers" or "improvers." You will sense this throughout the novel. Take, for instance, their emphasis on the crucial active involvement of the people actually doing the job; the SMEs or Subject Matter Experts. You can't help but smile when in the narrative one of the bosses expresses surprise at involving and empowering these people to solve the company's problems. Bruce and Bob not only know it is a key success factor, they show you how you could go about involving the SMEs with tools such as the IO map and Simplified Strategy.

As the narrative unfolds, you will also be introduced to one of the TOC's most powerful operational tools: Critical Chain Project Management. You will learn how you could finish all your projects, whatever they may be, on time and much faster than you thought possible. You will want all your projects to have their Fever Chart.

Focus and leverage is the idea that you should find the constraint or core problem in your organization and focus improvement efforts there. This will have an amazing leverage effect on the overall performance. You can go way beyond Pareto; by working on 1% of your organization, you will affect 99% of its performance. This is because organizations are no longer balanced; they are not homogenous entities. Things move too fast in today's world for you to distribute the work equitably. There are in truth just a few constraints or leverage points—one or two parts of your organizations that are the system constraints—surrounded by "nonconstraints." If you recognize this, you will discover that things are simple, improvements can happen 10 times faster, and you will no longer waste your days in constant inefficient firefighting.

As you will see, this "methodology" takes a global, systemic view. It encourages you to stand back and see the big picture. It is one of its great strengths and it will make you a much better manager. But if you are not yet the big boss, don't use this as an excuse to do nothing. This stuff is viral. Apply it where you are, whatever your level is in the organization. You will see, the others will quickly catch on, because of the extraordinary results, because of the speed of the improvements, and because it is so simple to understand how it works.

I have been mixing Lean, TOC, and Six Sigma together for more than 25 years. I know it works; it works well.

Don't just buy this book … read it, think about it, adapt it to your context, and try to apply at least some of it. You'll see.

Philip Marris
CEO Marris Consulting, Paris, France
Founder and Administrator of the LinkedIn "TLS—TOC,
Lean & Six Sigma" group

Preface

Most books written about continuous and process improvement are written in a textbook format with straightforward information and plenty of graphs and charts to convey the points being made. However, it can happen that some people will read the information presented in the textbook and ask, "How does this apply to me, or my company?" and "How do I apply what this information is asking me to do?" Sometimes, even the best step-by-step instructions can escape even the most adamant of followers for an improvement method in determining exactly "how" to apply what they've learned.

Because of this perceived weakness, we've taken a different approach by writing this book in a novel format. By doing so, it allows the staging of a storyline that many readers will instantly be able to relate to. In fact, many will read this book and wonder, "when did the authors visit the place I work?" A novel format allows for discussion and interaction about "how" the methods that are being implemented combine the expected, and not-so-expected, interactions between people and organizations. This experience is an element that is absent with a textbook. We have used the novel format to incorporate the reality of the workplace; knowing that some people and organizations will buy-in and accept the change, while others will resist it. By being able to explore both the acceptance and resistance, there is a certain amount of realism that surfaces in the conversations and debates.

The storyline of this book weaves some well-known and not-so-well-known thinking tools into the problem-solving sphere and provides the reader with information about how to first discover and then overcome issues not readily known or expected at the beginning of any project. By taking the time necessary to perform a thorough and vigorous *systems analysis* and collecting the right information, the entire improvement process can quickly be reduced from the frivolous many, to the important few. It's the apex of this separation that defines what *must* be done versus what *can* be done, thus allowing the improvement effort to *focus* on the precise system location needing correction and maximizing the improvement *leverage*. Valuable time and resources are not wasted piloting projects that produce little or no value added.

Perhaps, as the subtitle suggests, the most important aspect of this book is the *critical* combination of the three improvement methodologies: the Theory of Constraints (TOC), Lean, and Six Sigma, which we refer to as TLS. By combining the best features from each method, a rigorous improvement approach can be utilized to find the precise system's issue, resolve that issue, and reduce the amount of time required to generate exceptional results.

Another important aspect of this story is an often missing but important segment in many improvement initiatives, which is the active involvement and participation of the shop floor employees. These employees are the true subject matter experts of any system. *Simple* employee involvement is not the same as *Active* employee involvement. Simple employee involvement often implies just a token membership on an improvement team. With Active employee involvement, you go directly to the subject matter experts, on the shop floor, to hear and listen what they have to say. This approach doesn't mean that we don't listen to management; we do! But, clearly when both sides are heard, there will be two different versions and visions about what improvements are necessary and needed. For us, *active* involvement is first, listening to what both sides have to say, forging a new relationship between the groups, and then creating a common goal/objective for the improvement. We have used this method many times and the results have been substantial.

This book is written as a sequel to the second edition, *Epiphanized: A Novel on Unifying Theory of Constraints, Lean, and Six Sigma*. This story focuses on the continuing adventures of Connor Jackson, Joe Pecci, Sam Henderson, and Becky Chen (Jackson). In the sequel, these characters apply their commonsense approach and problem-solving knowledge of process improvement by getting involved in two new industries. First is a company called Aviation Dynamics, which is a maintenance, repair, and overhaul (MRO) facility for commercial helicopters. The company is suffering from poor on-time due date performance, along with a new backlog of repair work that is putting extreme pressure on management and the employees. Because of their previous bad performance, they are fearful of losing some of the new work, some of which is up for contract renewal. Because of past performance, some customers aren't happy. Second, some of the characters get involved with Saint Luke's Hospital after a less than perfect visit to the emergency room (ER). Extended wait times in the ER are a major problem and the team develops and presents a strategy to help the hospital reduce and manage the ever-increasing wait times for several hospital services.

While you might think that these two industries are at opposite ends of the spectrum, both are plagued by the same types of common problems. Both have significant wait time problems defined by delayed completion of services and delivery of products and both are hearing very negative comments from their customers. These problems are, in part, caused by their inability to analyze the system and figure out what to change. Both have "outdated thinking and ideas" about systems management and flow. Both have previously applied the methods and concepts from Lean and Six Sigma but have had very little sustained improvement to show for their efforts. When both are exposed to the TLS methodology, good things start to happen at each organization.

We have emphasized in our writing a stronger push toward understanding the concepts and methods for TOC. This was not done with any bias in mind, but rather from a knowledge consideration perspective. Of the three popular methods, there is probably less known about TOC methods and concepts than Lean and Six Sigma. The existence of this knowledge gap presented an opportunity to increase the exposure, information, and understanding of TOC methods and concepts and then show the practicality when all three methods are combined.

We hope, with this book, that we are able to show the reader the necessary systems thinking best suited to find and analyze what the system issues really are and the negative consequences for not resolving those issues. In the sequel, we have expanded on two concepts first introduced in the Appendix section of the second edition of *Epiphanized*. The first concept is the discussion and application of the Interference Diagram (ID) and Intermediate Objectives (IO) Simplified Strategy, or ID/IO Simplified Strategy. The ID/IO Simplified Strategy is a product of combining several TOC thinking process tools into a single thinking tool. The ID/IO is a comprehensive and combined approach used to discover and analyze prevalent system issues, and in doing so, much less time is required to achieve the desired results. The second concept is the inclusion, discussion, and application of the Multiple Drum–Buffer–Rope (M-DBR) concept and how it applies to both of these industry systems. Also, in the sequel, we introduce the reader to the three *TLS methodology cycles*. The first cycle discusses *which steps to take*. The second cycle discusses *how to take those steps*. The third cycle describes *what the expected results should be*.

We wish you, the reader, an enhanced understanding and success with your continuous improvement journey. We truly believe that if you follow the guidelines and methods we have laid out, your journey will be much easier and, hopefully, more profitable. We wish you much luck in your improvement journey, but, remember, our definition of luck is Laboring Under Correct Knowledge; you make your own luck!

Bruce Nelson and Bob Sproull

Acknowledgments

I dedicated my last two books to my seven wonderful grandchildren and how they truly epitomized my contribution to the world … my legacy, if you will. But my grandkids wouldn't even exist if it weren't for the rest of my family. First, to my beautiful and wonderful wife Beverly, I want to say thanks for supporting me throughout our almost 47 years of marriage. You are my driving force and I love you so much!! Beverly and I were blessed with three wonderful and successful children who married delightful spouses. To Rob, our oldest son, whose brilliance shines through like a beacon of light for the world to see. To Tina, Rob's wife and the mother of two of our granddaughters, whose smile makes the world a much happier place. To John, our second son, whose spirit and financial insight have such a stabilizing impact on our whole family. To Julie, John's wife and mother of our three grandsons, whose mothering skills are a cut above most other mothers. To Emily, our daughter, whose ability to listen to abused children at Child Protect makes the world a much safer place for them. And to Matt, Emily's husband, the world's best Auburn fan and loving father of two of our granddaughters. To all of you, thank you from Beverly and me for giving us seven beautiful and wonderful grandkids who simply enrich our lives.

Bob Sproull

Authors

Bruce Nelson is an independent consultant who, along with Bob Sproull, owns and operates Focus and Leverage Consulting, a management consulting firm specializing in improving the profitability of organizations from all business sectors. Bruce is an internationally recognized expert in Constraints Management and Systems Analysis. He is a certified Jonah, Jonah's Jonah, and Academic Jonah, and is board-certified by the Theory of Constraints International Certification Organizations (TOCICO) in the TOC Thinking Processes, TOC Operations Management, and TOC Project Management. Bruce completed his undergraduate degrees in chemistry, zoology, and allied health from Weber State University, Ogden, Utah, and has an extensive consulting background with numerous Fortune 500 companies and a number of international companies. The primary consulting focus is manufacturing/production, seminars, and workshops emphasizing how to maximize profitability through an integrated Theory of Constraints, Lean and Six Sigma (TLS) improvement methodology.

Bruce is the author of two previous books: *Epiphanized: Unifying Theory of Constraints, Lean and Six Sigma*, second edition (coauthored with Bob Sproull, May 2015, Taylor & Francis/Productivity Press); and *Epiphanized: Integrating Theory of Constraints, Lean and Six Sigma* (January 2012, North River Press).

Bob Sproull is an independent consultant who, along with Bruce Nelson, owns and operates Focus and Leverage Consulting, a management consulting firm specializing in improving the profitability of organizations from all business sectors. Bob is a certified Lean Six Sigma Master Black Belt and a Theory of Constraints Jonah and an experienced manufacturing executive who has served as a vice president of quality, engineering, and continuous improvement for two different manufacturing companies. He has an extensive consulting background in manufacturing, healthcare, and MRO and focuses on teaching companies how to maximize their profitability through an integrated Theory of Constraints,

Lean and Six Sigma (TLS) improvement methodology. Bob is an internationally known speaker and is the author of four books: Second Edition *Epiphanized: Integrating Theory of Constraints, Lean and Six Sigma* (coauthored with Bruce Nelson, 2015, Taylor & Francis/Productivity Press); *Epiphanized: Integrating Theory of Constraints, Lean and Six Sigma* (coauthored with Bruce Nelson, 2012, North River Press); *The Ultimate Improvement Cycle—Maximizing Profits through the Integration of Lean, Six Sigma and the Theory of Constraints* (2009, Taylor & Francis); *Process Problem Solving—A Guide for Maintenance and Operations Teams* (2001, Productivity Press). Bob resides in Kennesaw, Georgia.

1

The Meeting

Joe was sitting at his desk concentrating on his work. The ringing phone broke the silence and his concentration.

"Hello, this is Joe Pecci, how can I help you?"

"Hello Joe, this is Connor."

"Well hello Connor, what's up?"

"Joe, I need you and Sam to meet me at the bar this afternoon. Can you call Sam and see if he's available?" Connor said.

"Sure Connor, I'll call him … what time would you like us to come by?" asked Joe.

"If both of you can be there about 5 o'clock this afternoon, that would be great."

"What's this all about Connor?" asked Joe.

"We have some things we need to discuss," replied Connor.

"Why can't you tell me over the phone Connor?" asked Joe.

"This discussion might require some whiteboard time and could take an hour or so to complete," Connor said.

"OK, I'll get hold of Sam and we'll see you in about an hour," Joe responded.

Joe Pecci was the manager of the Continuous Improvement Office at Barton Enterprises. Barton Enterprises manufactures a series of flexible fuel cells for both military and commercial use in helicopters. Joe has worked for Barton for a little over 3 years now. When Joe first hired on, Barton was a company that was growing rapidly and experiencing an increasing demand for their products, especially from the military. Barton had been a company struggling with some major internal business issues including late deliveries, parts inventory problems, and raw materials availability. Joe had been hired with the specific responsibility of fixing ALL of these problems and getting Barton Enterprises back on the right path to success. During that time, Joe had been able to put together an amazing turnaround effort, but not without the help, guidance, and influence of several other people. Connor Jackson was one of those people. During the turnaround, Joe and Connor had become great friends, so he was rightly concerned when his friend called with what seemed to be such urgency.

It was clear to Joe that Connor had something important he wanted to discuss, and he wanted to do it in person and not over the phone. Remembering back to the day he had first met Connor, it was purely by chance that he had ended up at a local bar one afternoon seeking some lunch during his first week at Barton. The bar was named *Jonah's* and was owned and operated by Connor. Connor had not always been a bar owner. Connor was a semiretired manufacturing/business consultant who had recently been more full-time consultant and less retired. When Joe had first met Connor, he had been very intrigued with his knowledge about business and business systems. Connor had an almost magical way of solving some very complex problems. His approach was logical and always successful.

In his mind, Joe was still pondering Connor's phone call and wondered to himself, "What could be so important that Connor couldn't talk about it over the phone? It couldn't be any issues with the business operations at Barton, because profitability and on-time delivery had never been higher!" Joe continued to trade thoughts with himself wondering what this invitation was all about. Joe refused to think that something bad might have happened and instead convinced himself that whatever it was it had to be business related. "I'd better call Sam and let him know," Joe thought.

Joe dialed Sam's number and waited for the ring. Sam picked up on the second ring.

"Hello, this is Sam," he said in a cheerful voice.

"Hi Sam, I just got off of the phone with Connor and he wants us to come by *Jonah's* this afternoon to talk about something, can you make it?" asked Joe.

"What does he want to talk about?" asked Sam.

"He wouldn't say ... I asked him, but he said he didn't want to talk about it over the phone. He said it would require some whiteboard time," Joe replied.

"What time do we need to be there?" Sam asked.

"He said around 5:00 PM," Joe replied.

"OK, I've got a few things to finish up here, so I'll meet you there," said Sam. "I might be a few minutes late depending on traffic," Sam injected.

"OK, I'll see you whenever you get there," Joe ended the conversation by hanging up his phone.

Sam Henderson was the Vice President of Production at Barton Enterprises and had held this position for some time now. In fact, Barton was the only place Sam had worked since he graduated from college.

Sam had also been an important player in the turnaround effort at Barton. Without Sam's help and internal guidance, the project might not have gone so well. Besides being trusted coworkers, Joe and Sam had also developed an out-of-office friendship as well. They both lived in the same neighborhood and they had shared participation in a lot of the same community and neighborhood activities, including the now famous Saturday afternoon barbecues at Sam's house.

Like Swiss clockwork, Joe pulled into *Jonah's* at exactly 5 o'clock and noticed the all-too-familiar "*CLOSED*" sign on the door. Connor had a habit of closing the bar to conduct meetings, and Joe knew, from past experience, that whenever that sign was posted, it meant that whatever was going on inside was a safeguarded discussion not intended for public consumption. Connor wanted the undivided attention of those inside. Seeing the sign, Joe thought to himself, "Hmm…. I do wonder what Connor is up to?"

As Joe parked his car and headed up the steps toward the front door, he noticed that Becky's silver Mercedes was parked next to Connor's black Hummer. "If Becky is here, it must be some kind of business strategy session, or a business announcement of some kind," Joe said to himself. Joe peeked in the window and then knocked on the door. Becky hurried over to the door and opened it, smiling radiantly, and then gave Joe her traditional hug of endearment.

"Joe, it's so nice to see you," said Becky.

"Same here Becky … it's been a while since I've seen you. You always seem to be out of town working on new deals and we miss you," said Joe.

"Joe, you always seem to know what to say to make me feel special … so thank you," Becky replied.

Becky was the founder and owner of a financial investment firm and had also played a major role in Barton's turnaround. Becky's talents were many, but specifically she understood money! She had a keen ability to undertake the due diligence and analysis of financial reporting and have it all make sense. Her talents were extraordinary and her thoroughness and financial understanding made her an important and exceptional team member. Besides being friends with everyone at Barton, Becky and Connor had grown especially close. In fact, after the turnaround effort, their relationship had developed into marriage between her and Connor.

"Becky, you and Connor are my dearest friends, so of course you're special," Joe replied.

"Where's Connor?" asked Joe.

"He's in the wine cellar getting us a bottle of Chianti," she replied with a big smile.

Minutes later, Connor appeared clutching two bottles of their favorite wine, Chianti Classico. Joe thought to himself, "Two bottles … whatever we're going to talk about must be going to take a while." Since they had all met and become such close friends, Chianti had become the group's "drink of choice," a sort of glue that tied them all together.

"Hey Connor, how's it going?" asked Joe.

"Absolutely perfect," Connor replied.

"How are things with you?" But, before Joe could answer, Connor asked, "Where's Sam?"

"I'm fine and Sam said he might be a few minutes late because of traffic," Joe replied.

"Let's go sit down and have a drink while we're waiting," said Connor.

"I thought you'd never ask," said Joe.

Just as they got to the table and sat down, Sam knocked at the front door.

"There's Sam," Becky said, "I'll go let him in."

Sam came through the door and, without hesitation, gave Becky a big hug. They both walked over to the table and Sam asked, "Where's my glass?"

"Right here in my hand waiting for you," said Connor holding up an empty glass.

"So what's so important that we couldn't do this over the phone?" Sam asked in his customary directness.

"Well, we have a new opportunity that has come our way," Connor replied.

"What is it?" Joe asked.

"Well, Becky received a phone call last week from Ron Parsons at SIMCO. Do you guys remember Ron?" asked Connor.

"Of course we remember Ron," said Joe. Sam was nodding his head up and down signaling that he remembered Ron as well, while he sipped some wine.

Ron Parsons works for SIMCO, a company that builds helicopters for both military and commercial use. His business card says Ron is a Sales Representative, but those who know Ron know that he is much more than just a sales representative. Ron is a very talented person and he has a very acute eye for manufacturing and operations. Ron also has the undivided attention of the executive staff at SIMCO, so when Ron talks they tend to listen. In the past, Ron had focused much of his time on SIMCO's parts and material suppliers. Ron does not like to make delivery date promises to his customers, only to find out later that the order might be delivered late because of supplier problems.

Barton Enterprises is a major supplier to SIMCO for flexible fuel tanks, and at one point, not too long ago, Barton was one of the suppliers that Ron was carefully watching. Barton had a history of late deliveries, which, in turn, had caused SIMCO to be late with some of their deliveries. Ron was told about the changes taking place at Barton, so he wanted to see firsthand what was going on. When Ron arrived for his first visit, he was very impressed with the internal changes that had taken place. In fact, he was so impressed he wondered if the group might be able to implement some improvement changes at SIMCO. Because of all of these interactions that had taken place between SIMCO and Barton, Ron had informally joined this little group and had also spent time learning from Connor, Joe, Sam, and Becky at *Jonah's*. Through these interactions, a strong friendship had later developed between everyone concerned. The people at Barton were people that Ron now trusted, which was why he was requesting their help for his friend.

"What kind of opportunity is it?" Sam asked with suspicion in his voice.

Connor looked at Becky and said, "Becky, why don't you explain it to the gang since this is your brainchild."

"I'd be happy to honey," she replied. "Ron called me yesterday to ask if we might be interested in helping a friend of his. His friend is the General Manager of a company that performs MRO work at a commercial repair facility for the types of helicopters that Ron's company builds and sells," she explained.

"What is MRO?" asked Sam.

"Sorry Sam, it stands for maintenance, repair, and overhaul," Becky explained.

"Maintenance on helicopters?" asked Joe with his eyebrows raised and a certain reservation in his voice.

"Yes, maintenance on helicopters," Becky replied.

"I really know very little about helicopters let alone the maintenance and overhaul of them," said Sam with certain disbelief.

"Me either," Joe interjected.

"The way I see it, you don't have to know anything about the nuts and bolts of helicopters. All you really need is your continuous improvement knowledge, experience, and expertise," said Becky. "It really doesn't matter what the product is with you guys, you always seem to have a way of making things better," she said with a smile.

"Thanks for the vote of confidence Becky, but I'm not sure about this," Sam responded, wondering where this conversation might be headed.

Sam looked at Joe and asked, "How about you Joe, what do you think?" Sam was looking for, and hoping for, an ally to terminate the conversation and hoped he would find it with Joe.

Joe looked at Becky and then Sam and said, "I think Becky might be right! It really isn't a question of having intimate knowledge of the product, because we always relied on the internal subject matter experts to design the solution anyway." Sam was a bit jilted by Joe's response—he had just lost his ally! So, Sam decided to ally with Joe.

"If you're OK with it, then I guess I'm OK also. OK Becky, let's hear more about this idea of yours," Sam said.

Connor sat at the table with his wine glass in hand and smiled at the verbal exchange so far. "This will be fun," he thought to himself.

"Well, as Ron explained it to me, his friend is the GM of an MRO Division that is part of a larger corporation. It seems that there are several contracts for repair service that will be up for renewal soon, and the GM is worried about their current and past performance," she explained.

Sam semiraised his hand and asked, "What's wrong with their performance?"

"As I understand it, several of their customers are complaining about the helicopter scheduled maintenance taking too long and that they can't have their helicopters out of service for that amount of time. Ron told me that the GM has been notified by some of their customers that unless things improve dramatically, they will be looking to take their business elsewhere. In addition to the time, the customers have also noticed an increase in repair costs. This increase is apparently because the repairs rely too heavily on overtime, which they bill back to the customers," explained Becky.

She continued, "The scheduled maintenance repairs are required after an aircraft has flown so many hours and when the hours have been met, the aircraft is disassembled and everything is checked, repaired, or replaced on the basis of the manufacturer's recommendations. The scheduled maintenance is required to meet Federal Aviation Administration requirements and also for insurance purposes. After the MRO process has been completed, the aircraft is reassembled and flight tested before it can be recertified for flight and placed back on the flight line," she explained.

"It sounds complicated," Sam said, this time without raising his hand.

"It only seems complicated because they don't know how to solve the problem!" Becky said, with a certain authority. "And Ron thinks you guys can help them find the solutions to get through the issues. Apparently, about 3 months ago, during a golf game, Ron was explaining to his friend about the transformation he had personally witnessed at Barton and how Barton had gone from one of their worst suppliers to their best supplier. At the time, his friend thought it was an interesting story, but had no real interest in doing more. Ron also told him about the changes at SIMCO and the huge improvements. Back then, Ron's friend wasn't so interested, but times have changed and now his friend has an interest in knowing more about it, so he had Ron contact me looking for some help," said Becky.

Becky took a deep breath, waited for the effect, and continued. "Ron's friend now realizes that the scheduled maintenance performance is sub-par, and with several contracts coming up for a recompete, he's worried they could lose those contracts unless some major changes are implemented to make their customers happy." Becky paused and looked around the table for reaction. Everyone seemed to be waiting for her to continue, so she did. "Each of these customers only has so many aircraft to fly and when the hours are used up, they must be returned for maintenance. The real problem is aircraft availability. If they can't get the aircraft back from scheduled maintenance in a reasonable time, it puts them in a real bind. The only other solution is for their customers to buy more helicopters!" Becky continued with more explanation, "Even though buying more helicopters would help Ron, he also realizes the problem will still exist. If the scheduled maintenance takes too long, and the turnaround time is too slow, and more aircraft are reaching their maximum hours and the aircraft can't have the required maintenance performed quickly, then availability is a real issue." This time, when she scanned the table, she could see the thinking lights turning on.

"And, apparently their performance is not so good for delivering on unscheduled maintenance either," Becky stated. "Even though each of these customers has some aircraft mechanics, what these mechanics do is normally just flight line repairs. In other words, the mechanics deal with those first echelon repairs that can be completed without a tear down or deeper evaluation and testing. When more extensive repairs are required, they send it to the MRO facility for the work to be completed," she explained. "In fact, many of the companies keep their aircraft at the MRO facility. It just makes it easier."

"What makes you think we can do any better?" asked Joe.

"Because I've seen what you guys did with Critical Chain Project Management (CCPM) and Drum–Buffer–Rope (DBR) at Barton and SIMCO's Helicopter Division and I just know you can do the same for this MRO company," she added. "Besides, this is really a systems problem, and nobody is better at systems problems than you three guys!" Her confidence and smile had an impact on both Joe and Sam. Connor already knew he was in the game.

"But, SIMCO was a manufacturing assembly operation, not an MRO-type environment," said Sam. "It's just not the same," he added.

"Wait a minute!" Connor said jumping into the conversation. "You guys are completely missing the point here!"

"What point are we missing Connor?" Joe asked.

"The point is that it is not an issue of manufacturing versus maintenance, repair, and overhaul," Connor said. "Either one of these industries is closely associated with some kind of system," Connor added and, as usual, had piqued their interest.

"What you guys did at Barton was simply phenomenal," said Connor. "The speed at which you turned Barton around was faster than anything I've ever seen," he added. "Joe, you didn't know anything about flexible fuel tanks before you came to Barton, but it was never an issue.

"By changing the system at Barton, you changed the output of the system to the positive. The key point here is a systems analysis and the purpose of the system. Not knowing how to build fuel cells, or helicopters, it didn't really matter! And, you did exactly the same thing at SIMCO by analyzing and changing their system! You still don't have any knowledge about how to build a helicopter, but the guys on the assembly line do," he explained. Now, Connor was scanning the group, Becky was smiling, and Joe and Sam were thinking.

"All you really did was make changes to the system so that they could apply their production skills and knowledge better," Connor explained.

"Thanks for the compliment Connor, but I'm just not sure we can make a difference like we did at Barton and SIMCO," said Sam. "I mean when you're dealing with these kinds of things, there can be so many regulations and policies that you have to follow. It can be a real headache," Sam added.

"You're right about all of the policies and regulations, and all of those are variables in the system that must be dealt with. But, in this case, we won't have any direct dealings with these. Hopefully, those subject matter experts already exist at this company and we'll just be consulting and helping Ron's friend!" Connor said trying to dampen the negativity.

There was still some pushback from Sam. "But, maintenance, repair, and overhaul aren't a product that you can put your hands on and that's what Joe and I are best at."

Connor spoke up almost sternly, but with a partial smile. "Look, you both know and understand DBR and CCPM because you were a part of the implementation at Barton and SIMCO." Connor stressed, "This MRO company is just another system with processes and sequential steps that must be completed. And, there is a product—a refurbished helicopter," he added. "Besides, it's not like I'm not going to be involved with you guys," he added.

"Also, nobody understands and uses the subject matter experts better than you two," said Connor.

"OK Connor, you've almost convinced me," said Joe. "What do Sam and I have to do?" he asked.

Becky jumped back into the conversation and said, "Nothing for now. I told Ron that we would have this meeting, conduct a discussion, and then make a decision." Becky added, "For Ron's friend, there is a certain amount of urgency to start this project and have some good results before those contracts come due again."

"By the way, who is this friend of Ron's?" asked Joe.

"I only partially know that answer," Becky said. "Ron was cautious not to expose too much until we decided if we were in or out. He mostly just referred to him as his friend. If we decide we want to go forward with this project, then I can find out more information," Becky stated.

Becky could sense there was still hesitation and reservation on the part of Joe and Sam, "Think back to when I first met you guys at Barton. You presented me with such a simplistic explanation of the system and it was such an epiphany for me. I can visualize you doing the same kind of thing when it's time to present to the MRO contractor," she said. "Of course, if we decide to move forward with this project, we will definitely need to understand more about the MRO system, but nobody explains what we do better than you and Sam, and please take that as a well-deserved compliment," said Becky.

"You guys need a refill?" asked Connor holding up a new bottle of Chianti. All of them signaled yes, so Connor filled all of the glasses.

"So, Connor, you've obviously thought about this potential project ... have you ever done any work in an MRO organization?" asked Sam.

"Actually, I have," said Connor. "Back in the early '90s, I did some consulting work with the Army," he added.

"What kind of consulting work did you do?" asked Joe.

"The Army was having a problem, or so they thought, with parts availability, similar to the material and parts problems we were having at Barton and SIMCO. So, I showed them how to avoid stock-outs of common parts," said Connor.

"How did that turn out?" asked Sam.

"The results were just like Barton and SIMCO. We were able to achieve about a 40% total reduction in inventory with no stock-outs," Connor explained. "I'm confident this MRO contractor is experiencing similar problems with their maintenance work," he added.

"Was it difficult to get them to accept the new way that you taught them?" asked Sam.

"Of course it was! Change is always difficult for any organization, not just the government," he replied. "But, with some persistence, teaching and mentoring them on the basics of Theory of Constraints, Lean, and Six Sigma, the Army embraced this new concept and saved millions of dollars just on the inventory reduction," Connor added.

"I feel much better knowing that you have experience in dealing with this," Sam said.

Connor smiled and looked at Sam, "But Sam, that wasn't the end of the story!"

Sam looked at Connor with a puzzled look on his face and said, "What do you mean that's not the end of the story. You did help them didn't you?" Sam asked as a question and not a statement.

"Yes, we helped them a lot. But, it turned out that parts were not the only problem they had," Connor replied.

"What other problems did they have?" asked Joe.

"You guys already know the answer, but let me explain," Connor said. "When the parts problem was surfaced and corrected, the system constraint quickly moved to the next system location. As it turned out, even when the parts were available, it still took them way too long for the repairs. The way they scheduled the work had some serious problems. The work sequence was correct, but the time it took to do the work was not correct. There was a lot of wasted time in their system," Connor said.

"You mean just like Barton and SIMCO," Joe said with a smile.

"I mean exactly that!" Connor replied. "By changing the scheduling system from the Critical Path Method to the CCPM system, we actually reduced the number of scheduled maintenance days from 70 days down to 22 days," Connor replied. "Overall, it was just short of a 70% reduction in the time required for repairs.

"The end result was huge for the Army," Connor said. "With these results, there were two ways they could look at what happened. The first way was that they were actually doing the repairs three times faster than they were before. The second approach was this repair depot could actually do three times more work than they did before. Actually, the base commander chose the second approach and put together an internal Army proposal touting the cost and time savings of having more scheduled maintenance repairs conducted at his facility," Connor said. "I only heard about that proposal after the fact and I have no idea what became of his offer. It would certainly make sense for them to do it because of the system's excess capacity that had been exposed," Connor said. "But, I don't know if it ever happened."

Joe was smiling with a big grin. "So, it was the same thing with scheduling, just like Barton and SIMCO," Joe said with a certain understanding that had just hit him.

Sam was still feeling and expressing some reluctance to buying in to the whole idea. "I understand everything you are saying Connor, but we know how to build fuel tanks, not repair aircraft," Sam responded. "Like I said before, comparing manufacturing to performing a maintenance function, to me it's just not the same," Sam added.

Connor looked directly at Sam and narrowed his eyes, "It's exactly the same!" he said, as a slight smile began to appear on his face. "Each of those two functions has their processes tied directly to a system. If the system is not producing what you want, then what part of the system needs to change to give you the results you want?" Connor asked as a direct question to Sam.

Sam thought for a moment and replied, "You'd have to analyze the system and figure out the where the breakdown is—the system constraint."

"Yes, exactly!" said Connor. "And, do you need to know how to repair a helicopter to do that?" Connor asked.

Sam thought for a moment and then answered, "No, you don't." Sam's head slowly started to move up and down signaling a "yes" answer. In his mind, Sam was beginning to understand that because he already knew a lot about fuel cell assembly, because he had worked at Barton for so many years, he had assumed it was a necessary condition to make the transition. In fact, the more he thought about it, the more he realized that the people out on the assembly line had the most knowledge about the fuel cell assembly and not him. He was beginning to formulate the notion that some, if not most, of his fears were unfounded.

After a few more minutes of self-discussion, Sam announced to the group that he understood what was being presented to him. "I think I fully understand what you are saying now," said Sam.

Joe patted his friend on the back and said, "Good, because I can see it too. When Connor talked about the scheduling issues with the Army, my first thought was, that was the same problem we had at Barton and SIMCO as well."

"OK!" said Becky. "Then we are all in agreement that we can help Ron's friend?" she asked.

"I think we can help and it will be a fun adventure," said Joe.

"I'm in," said Sam.

"What about you Connor?" asked Sam.

Connor looked at Becky and blew her a kiss. "Do I have a choice?" he said smiling.

Joe immediately jumped up and started walking toward the whiteboard. "We need to get going on some analysis. There is a lot of information we need and some thinking we need to do!" Joe exclaimed.

"I agree Joe, but that will have to be another day," said Connor. "Besides, we are almost out of wine!" Everyone raised their glass and smiled. Meeting adjourned.

2

Preliminary Strategy Session

Becky called Ron back the day after their meeting and explained that everyone had agreed to try and help solve the issues for his friend. Ron was pleased with Becky's news even though he had expected this would be the outcome. Ron just couldn't imagine they would say "No!" Ron was quick to reemphasize the urgency of what needed to take place. Apparently, Ron's friend had already phoned him a couple of times to see if a decision had been reached. If the answer was "yes," he wanted to get things started immediately. If the answer was "no," he wanted to quickly move to an alternative and get things going.

Becky and Ron decided that a meeting at the maintenance, repair, and overhaul (MRO) facility would be the best way to do it. An on-site visit would allow Connor, Joe, Sam, and Becky to get the visual they wanted and be able to talk with the people who worked there and ask any questions they needed to. Ron said he would set things up with his friend and that a Thursday morning meeting was probably the soonest time they could pull it off. It was already Tuesday morning, so that essentially left them 1 day, knowing that Wednesday would be a travel day.

When Becky finished the phone call, she quickly called Connor, Joe, and Sam to get everyone back to _Jonah's_ for a meeting that afternoon because time was running short. Joe and Sam were at Barton working some tasks for the day and mentally preparing for their first strategy session for the potential MRO contract that afternoon at _Jonah's_.

Joe and Sam had casually met earlier in the day to discuss the best approach but decided they would wait and listen to what Becky had to say first before they actually started mapping it out. There was still some information they were hoping to get from Becky, especially who was this friend of Ron's and where is this place located? They hoped Becky would be able to answer their questions. There were still many items for discussion and all of the players needed to be in the same room to talk about them.

Joe and Sam both arrived at *Jonah's* around 5:30 PM and walked in. Connor had seen them pull into the parking lot and had the customary bottle of Chianti ready with four glasses already filled. Connor motioned for Joe and Sam to come join him at a table in the corner that already had papers laid out and the whiteboard set up on an easel.

"Hey Connor, are you ready to strategize?" Sam asked.

"You bet I am," said Connor.

Joe laughed and said, "That's exactly what we told each other you'd say," and the three of them shared a laugh.

Connor said, "We'll wait a few minutes before we begin. I know Becky has been on the phone with Ron and has gathered some more information." Connor raised his glass and said, "Until she arrives, let's enjoy a glass of wine."

Joe sat down, picked up his glass, and gave it a swirl, sniffing just above the rim. "This wine just keeps getting better and better," he said.

Sam sat down and picked up his glass and took a small sip and asked Connor, "Do you know anything about Becky's new information yet?"

"I haven't seen Becky since we left here yesterday. She's been in her office," Connor said. "The last news I had was when she called and told me everyone was meeting here at 5:30 today."

"We need some input before we start any kind of an analysis," Joe said, still swirling and sniffing his wine.

"So Connor, what do you really think about this MRO stuff? Do you really think we can make it work?" Sam asked.

"Of course we can make it work. If we carefully pick our analysis tools and apply the concepts we know, it will work beyond our wildest dreams," Connor answered.

Just then, Becky came through the front door and headed toward the table. "I'm sorry I'm late, but I was on the phone and got out of the office later than I planned," Becky said.

When she sat down, Connor handed her a glass of wine and she looked around the table and said, "OK, fill me in … where are we?"

"Actually, we've been waiting for you so you could fill us in. We're all very interested in any new information you received from Ron," Joe said.

"I do have some new information," Becky said digging through her file to find her notes. "I've actually spent quite a bit of time on the phone with Ron and I think everyone is ready to get this project rolling," Becky said.

She found her papers, scanned her notes, and said, "I told Ron we had gotten together and decided that we can help his friend," she said. "Ron was very happy with our decision and knows his friend will be pleased," Becky added. "Apparently, this situation is escalating to a new level of urgency, and they really want to move as fast as we can," she said.

"Ron and I had talked about getting together at the MRO on Thursday of this week," she said.

"Holy cow!" exclaimed Sam.

"Like I said, there is a high level of urgency for this project," Becky said.

"Why did they wait so long before they contacted Ron?" Joe asked.

Connor was first with an answer. "It's not atypical for many companies to wait until the very last minute before they decide to do anything," Connor said. "Most often, it's because they don't know what to do. I believe many companies just hope the problem will go away before they actually have to deal with the issues," Connor added.

"Well, whatever the reason is, they want us there on Thursday morning," Becky said.

"So, where is this place?" Joe asked.

"It's in Houston, Texas," Becky said.

"Houston isn't that far away, but it will still take some time to get there," said Sam.

"So, tell us more about this MRO facility," Joe said.

"The company name is Aviation Dynamics. They have a global reach with several foreign locations, but the facility in Houston is probably one of their bigger repair facilities. A very large portion of the work they do is for the oil and gas companies. They maintain the different fleets of helicopters that are used to ferry supplies and people to and from the different drilling rigs, mostly out in the Gulf of Mexico," Becky said. "This also explains why they have such a global reach, because they follow the oil and gas companies around the world to maintain their helicopter fleets," Becky added.

"That makes sense," Joe added.

"With Houston being a major headquarters location for many of the oil and gas companies, this MRO facility is under the microscope a lot. It's the one everyone sees and hears about," Becky said.

"So, what about this friend of Ron's; what's his name?" Joe asked.

"His name is Brad Carter and he's been the General Manager at this facility for about 8 years. Up until just recently, the whole operation had seemed to run very smoothly and no real problems had been encountered," Becky explained.

"However, according to Ron, this all started to change as the price of oil changed and the supply and demand shifted. It seems that the flight hours of the helicopter escalated as well. With more and more flight hours being used, the helicopters were coming back in for scheduled maintenance at a faster rate," she said.

Connor looked around the table and said, "High demand with low capacity." Connor said this almost as a reminder to everyone. "Does that sound familiar to you at all?" Both Joe and Sam nodded their heads, "Yes!"

Becky continued, "The MRO facility first started to sense this situation about 9 months ago."

"So they did know about it and chose not to react?" Joe said, both as a statement and a question.

"Well, yes and no," said Becky. "According to Ron, Brad has some training in the Lean/Six Sigma concepts and at this facility they do collect a lot of data. One of the charts they were specifically looking at was the Statistical Process Control (SPC) data. They used this particular chart trying to measure the system loads compared to the available capacity. The data obviously suggest that the loads were starting to exceed the capacity—on a very regular basis," Becky said. "When they analyzed the data, and the situation, they concluded that they needed to hire more workers and possibly expand their facilities to handle more aircraft," Becky explained.

"We did the same thing at Barton before Joe got there," said Sam. "That's why I was spending so much time at Corporate Headquarters trying to convince them that we needed more people and machines to improve the on-time delivery," said Sam, reminiscing back to those painful days.

"It was kind of the same thing here," said Becky. "Corporate kept telling Brad that he didn't need more people or facilities. His efficiency reports said he had more than enough people, he just needed to get the work done, and get it done NOW!" she added.

Sam nodded his head, understanding now exactly what Brad was feeling. It was a vicious cycle that seemed to have no end.

"When corporate kept saying 'no' to Brad's request for more people, Brad, and his staff, did the only thing they thought they could do, which was increase the overtime to try and get the work done. That's when the customer started to get upset with the increased billings, when the overtime started to increase," Becky said.

"But, that's the wrong way to do it!" exclaimed Joe. "There are other ways to increase capacity and not hire more people," stated Joe.

"That, my dear Joe, is exactly right!" Becky said. "That is precisely the reason why Ron called us when he learned of Brad's situation. We know what to do, and right now Brad doesn't," said Becky.

Connor was smiling, and so far, just enjoying the conversation.

"According to Ron, Brad and his staff also tried to implement some additional cost saving to make the numbers look better. Ron mentioned that they've tried to reduce inventory costs by reducing the parts inventory, which, in turn, has affected the availability of parts," Becky said.

Joe immediately turned to look at Connor. "It's the same thing with parts availability isn't it Connor?"

"We'll look into that when we get there," said Connor, smiling as he answered.

Joe smiled back at Connor knowing he was right, but didn't say anything. He just enjoyed the moment.

"WOW!" said Sam. "This all sounds so familiar. It's just like Barton except with a different name." Sam was shaking his head and smiling.

"Another point Ron mentioned was they have been looking at their processes and trying to reduce the variation in the work cells," Becky added. "So far, they have been able to reduce some variation, but just not enough to overcome the current situation. Right now, Brad is just stymied about how to correct the problem and move forward. He's done what he knows how to do and the problems are still there and causing him an enormous headache," Becky explained.

"It seems they have a very high tendency to focus on cost savings," Joe said almost as a point of fact. "With so much work to do, why would they focus so much time and effort on reducing costs?" Joe threw the question out to the group.

Connor was first to respond, almost with a laugh. "Would you really expect them to do anything different?" Connor asked. "It's an age-old conundrum—reducing costs is the first thing everyone attempts to solve their problem," Connor said.

Sam jumped in. "Having been in Brad's shoes, I can understand why he's doing what he's doing. When the workload increases, you increase overtime to get the work done."

"Correct!" said Connor. "Then what happens?"

"Well, when you increase overtime, the operating expense goes up," said Sam. "And then you get in trouble because the operating expenses are too high," he added.

"Correct again!" said Connor. "So, what do you do next?" he asked to keep the conversation going.

"Next, you try and reduce any cost you can," said Sam. "And you'd want to focus on some of the easier targets, like inventory and overhead, and sometimes laying off people," Sam said remembering back to when his mind was filled with these same thoughts.

"Again, that is the correct answer," said Connor. "So, when you take those actions, then what happens?"

"Well, when you reduce inventory you lose parts availability, especially for the most common parts. When you lay people off, you lose resources to do the work. And when you cut overtime to reduce operating expenses, the work is even slower to get done," Sam said, remembering back to the days at Barton, and being almost saddened.

"So," said Connor, "is it much more understood why Brad is feeling backed into a corner with no way out? Each action he takes is counter to a metric that is already in place. Each action, though it was thought to produce a positive outcome, quickly turns negative after a short period," Connor said in a low, but succinct matter-of-fact kind of voice.

"He's stuck," said Sam. "Just like I was before Joe showed up at Barton."

Everyone sat quiet for a minute. Joe and Sam remembered the time, not so long ago, when they were in the exact same position as Brad.

Becky's voice broke the silence. "By the way," Becky added, "Ron asked me if it would be OK if he is involved with this effort, at least to the point he has time to do it. Apparently, SIMCO has some contracts coming up for recompete and he wants to see if he can learn some new things to make sure they win them." She looked at everyone to see if it was alright.

"It's alright with me," Joe said. "Besides, Ron is a smart guy and I'm sure we'll benefit from his insights."

"Fine with me," said Sam. "It will be nice to see Ron again. I haven't seen or talked with him very much since we got everything straightened out at Barton."

"Fine with me too," said Connor. "The more the merrier." Everyone laughed and took a sip of wine.

"What, if anything, do we need to do before all of this happens?" Joe asked.

"I don't think there is much to do," Becky answered. "We don't have a lot of time to get much done and I think you guys already have a good top-level plan for what needs to happen. The problems they are facing are common problems among many companies. We just need to work out the details and figure out an implementation plan for this facility," Becky said.

"Well, that's partly right," Connor said. "But, I'm thinking the overall strategy might require two approaches that will overlap and materialize in tandem. The first strategy is to help resolve the current issue of performance and scheduling. How do we get them interested in the information we bring to the table to solve the current issues?" Connor asked in the form of an unsolved question; a question that could have many possible answers. Both Joe and Sam were nodding their heads in agreement.

"The second strategy is helping them position to win any new and follow-on contracts," Connor continued. "Many of the elements in the performance improvement need to be in the form of innovative solutions. The best way to do that is to implement what we know, and help them improve the performance, and then convince them to keep using it," Connor said. Again, Joe and Sam nodded their heads in agreement.

"The first thing we need to do is the visual tour of the system and get information from those people working the job. In other words, we want the perspective of the problem from those doing the work. Then, we'll have the discussion with leadership and determine their perspective," Connor said. "What will be very noteworthy is the gap between the two lists and who each side holds responsible for the problems. It's a thought-provoking analysis that you will find most interesting," Connor said with a widening smile.

Becky jumped back in the conversation and said, "OK, we'll leave it at that for the time being. When Ron calls back, I'll get the information for the hotel and the facility address. I'm thinking we need to leave on Wednesday afternoon, or early evening, so we can be ready, bright and early Thursday morning. I'll check into some travel arrangements and see what comes up. This is very short notice, so I'm hoping we can make it all work."

Joe and Sam, almost in unison, said, "Thank you Becky."

"Before we leave this subject, let me add a thought," Connor said. "As I've listened to the information and the conversation, I know we still have many questions, and that's OK!" he said. "What I see going forward is a possible combination of the Interference Diagram and the Intermediate Objectives map, or the Simplified Strategy, as I call it. You are both aware of this, but haven't used it in an actual implementation setting. We first have to get them to agree on the obstacles that block the path, and second, we need consensus on the intermediate objectives to solve the problems," Connor said. "If you spend time thinking about this project at all, these are the two things I want you to think about," Connor said finishing his statement.

Joe and Sam nodded their heads, knowing that they would probably be thinking about nothing except this.

They all stayed at the bar for about an hour, which was enough time to finish another bottle of Chianti. The time passed quickly as they talked about family and how the kids were doing in school, soccer games, and how the kids were looking forward to the upcoming summer vacation.

3

Aviation Dynamics—The First Visit

Becky had been working the Internet trying to find a flight to Houston. So far, she hadn't had much luck. Most of the flights were either full or the departure and arrival times were off from what they needed. At one point, she even called a friend who was a travel agent to see if she could find something available, but her efforts had been no better than Becky's. If it were just her traveling, it would be a lot easier, but trying to find something that worked for all four of them was proving to be a challenge.

Becky was drumming her fingers on the desktop looking at her computer screen when she had an idea. She called her friend back at the travel agency and asked her if she knew how to arrange for a private jet. Liz, the travel agent, said she did and would make a phone call and get back with her. Becky had seen the advertisements before in the airport and remembered the sign from Business Air. Their sign claimed they "could go anywhere, anytime." She thought it was at least worth a try because she was having little success with the traditional airlines.

Liz called Becky back approximately 20 minutes later and said she had found a plane through Business Air that could be available. They talked price and scheduling and Becky decided this was the way to go. All of the problems could be solved and the expense really wasn't that much more for all four of them. Becky told Liz to get everything set up for a departure on Wednesday evening. She also had Liz make the reservations for a hotel and rental car.

Becky called Joe and Sam with the flight information and recommended that they needed to be at the airport about an hour early. She would talk with Connor when he got home.

Wednesday evening, they all met at the Business Air terminal. The terminal was on the opposite side of the airport and located between some of the cargo hangars and maintenance hangars for the airlines.

Becky and Connor arrived to find both Joe and Sam already at the terminal waiting in the small sitting area. Becky came through the door pulling her roller bag with Connor right behind her. "Hey guys!" she said.

Both Joe and Sam stood and Joe said, "Hello Becky, nice to see you."

Before Becky could reply, Sam jumped in and said with a big smile, "This is going to be fun! I've traveled a lot in my day, but never on a private jet."

"Becky, how did you ever decide to do this?" Joe asked.

"Well, let's just say that this single idea solved a lot of other problems," Becky said.

Approximately 30 minutes later, one of the Business Air people walked over to where they were sitting and announced their plane was ready to board. She told them to just leave their bags in the sitting area and they would get them on the plane. They all stood and headed toward the door. When they got out on the tarmac, Sam could see the plane with its door open and the ramp down. "Wow," Sam thought to himself looking at the plane, "I feel like a celebrity." The plane was white and very sleek with two engines in the rear and the big red and blue Business Air logo on the side.

When they got on the plane, there were six captain's chairs with three on each side of the plane. The chairs would swivel so they could face each other and a small table could be set up between if they wanted. They took the four chairs closest to the front and settled in. A few minutes later, the copilot came back to check on them. He gave a short safety briefing about how to use the exit doors and flotation devices, if required. He told them they planned to be airborne in approximately 10 minutes.

Their flight to Houston was just under an hour and totally uneventful except for the fun they all had. Sam was probably the most sorry to see the flight end and he was already looking forward to the flight home. The rental car was waiting for them at the terminal, so they loaded their bags and set out for the hotel. Connor decided he would drive and got the hotel information and address from Becky. She had printed a Google map from the airport to the hotel.

When they arrived at the hotel, they all checked in and then gathered by some chairs in the lobby. Connor suggested that they meet back in the lobby in approximately 30 minutes and they would eat in the hotel restaurant. Joe and Sam agreed and they all got on the elevator and headed for their rooms.

Forty-five minutes later, they were all seated and browsing the restaurant menu. The waitress walked over to the table and asked, "Can I get you anything to drink?" They all looked at each other with a slight smile.

Connor was the first to speak, "By chance," he asked, "do you have any Chianti Classico?"

"We sure do," the waitress answered.

"Great!" Connor said. "Bring us four glasses."

"I'll be right back with those," she said and walked away.

As they waited for their wine, Connor spoke. "I want to go over a little strategy before tomorrow morning. When we get there, the first thing I want to do is get some basic organizational information and then take the tour of the facility. That may seem a bit odd to you, but stick with me on this," he said. "Remember, what we want to do is a systems analysis. We want to see the system for the scheduled maintenance from start to finish. We aren't looking to point fingers or place blame, but we are looking to get a feel for the obstacles that currently exist," he said. "This is precisely the reason I want to do this in two parts. The first part will be talking to the workers on the floor and finding out what they think the obstacles are. Once we have that information, we'll talk with the management team and get their input for what they think the obstacles are." After a thoughtful pause, Connor added, "In order to fix a system, any system, we first have to understand the system, at least at a working level. The details will come later." Connor paused again and said, "I think you will be surprised to hear the range of the perceived obstacles that we get from both sides. Rarely do both sides see the same issues."

"OK," said Joe. "We'll follow your lead as best we can."

"I think it will become obvious very quickly for you why I'm doing it this way," Connor added.

"I hope so," said Sam. "Right now, I'm a bit confused. I thought we were just going to do the same thing here that we did at Barton?"

"We are!" said Connor in a reassuring voice. "However, the situation here is a little different. In order for this to work, it has to be their idea. If we just tell them what to do, they will resist and not do anything. But, if the ideas are theirs, they will own them and make it happen. We just have to point them in the right direction and get them back on track if they veer off course," Connor explained.

They stayed for about an hour more and enjoyed dinner, and two more glasses of Chianti. When they all finished, they agreed to meet back in the lobby at 7:00 AM.

They were all in the lobby early looking for coffee and helped themselves to a travel cup before leaving the lobby. They left the hotel at about 7:10 AM. This time, Becky drove and the drive to the facility had taken approximately

35 minutes. They had arrived approximately 20 minutes early for their 8:00 AM meeting. Connor had wanted to arrive a bit early, just to get a visual on the layout of the facility setting and soak in the surroundings. Over his years of consulting, Connor had developed some rather unscientific methods for conducting a facility evaluation and looking at the buildings; the external surroundings and the parking lot were a few of them. From a usefulness standpoint, most of the things Connor was looking for might not make sense to a lot of people, but he collected the mental data anyway, just to make sure. There were times in his past when it had proven valuable.

At the entrance to the facility was a guard gate. They pulled up to the gate and the guard came out to the car to talk with them. Becky explained who they were and why they were there.

The guard said, "Yes, you are on my list of visitors today. If I could just get you to drive over to that building," he said, pointing with his finger. "And park in one of the visitor parking stalls. Then go inside through those white double doors and that will take you to the reception area lobby," he explained.

"Thanks!" said Becky.

The building the guard had pointed to was built on the backside of the very large hangar that was in front of them. Joe was in the backseat looking out the window and said, "Look at the size of that hangar. It must be at least two football fields on the inside!"

"It's probably more than that," Sam chimed in.

The hangar had the typical rounded roofline with large sliding doors on each side. The building out front was red brick. It wasn't a new building, but it also wasn't that old either. The grounds seemed to be well maintained, with a few trees and bushes and the grass was neatly trimmed. On the left was what appeared to be the employee parking lot and it looked fairly full. "First shift has already started," Connor thought to himself. He also noticed the cars in the parking lot. Most were fairly new, and most were American made.

Most of the unmarked parking stalls closest to the main front door were already full. There were five parking stalls marked for "Visitors" right up front. Connor also noticed that there were no reserved parking stalls for management, at least as far as he could tell; there were no formal signs or markings. He liked that.

Becky parked their rental car in one of the "Visitor" parking stalls. Connor looked over his shoulder at Sam and Joe and asked, "So, what do you think?"

"What do I think about what?" Sam answered.

Sam hadn't noticed a thing yet. Connor smiled and said, "Nothing."

They got out of the car, got their bags from the trunk, and headed for the white double doors and the reception area. When they got to the doors, Connor opened one of them and Becky walked in first and went over to the reception desk and introduced herself and the rest of the gang. The receptionist said, "Yes … good morning! We have been expecting you!"

"Thank you," replied Becky.

"I need you to sign your names in the visitor logbook so that I can issue you a temporary badge," she said. One by one, they stepped up to the desk and filled out the required information and were issued a temporary badge. "Controlled entry and security," Connor said to himself.

"Please have a seat and I'll let Mr. Carter know you are here," said the receptionist.

"Would any of you like some coffee or juice?" she asked.

All of them shook their heads and replied, "No thank you."

The receptionist got on the phone and made a quick phone call to some other location in the building; probably to Brad Carter's administrative assistant to let her know the visitors were here.

Becky, Sam, and Joe walked over and sat down, but Connor continued to walk around the reception area looking at the pictures and other information hanging on the wall. At the far end of the lobby, Connor noticed a hallway approximately 10 ft. long. He started to walk over to the hallway, and as he got closer, he could see that on both sides of the hallway were boards that contained numerous graphs and charts. These boards were approximately 4 ft. × 8 ft. and were completely covered with graphs, charts, and information. Connor walked into the hallway and quickly glanced at both boards. On the left-hand side, Connor noticed a carefully worded "Mission Statement." Most mission statements are very generic in their meaning and application and this one was no exception. This one read: "Satisfy our customer needs with high-quality products." Connor read the statement two more times and wondered to himself, "Is there any company in the world that this statement wouldn't apply to?"

Each board was subdivided into three different sections, and each section seemed to represent a different organization in the plant. He could see a section for "Operations" and another one for "Quality" and one for "Procurement." He turned around and looked at the board behind him. There was a section for "Finance" and one for "HR." The HR section contained job postings for internal positions, of which there were only two. The third section was administrative information and had postings for "Minimum Wage Laws" and "Equal Employment Opportunity." He turned back around to face the other board.

Each organizational section contained graphs and charts that were defining the metrics for each of the areas. Connor thought to himself, "This represents what they think is important to them." In his experience, these display boards were not uncommon. For most businesses, it was a way of displaying the company scorecard. This was where you could see how well the different organizations were doing, or not doing. This information was on display for both employees and visitors alike. In time, Connor had developed quite a knack for looking at these boards and being able to decipher what metrics the company thought to be important. If nothing else, it would help him decide what kinds of questions he should be asking. Connor had also previously determined and observed that most companies seem to measure the exact same things. There had been several times in the past when he had asked different individuals "why" they measured a particular metric. He'd found the most common answer to be "Well, we know our competitor is measuring that, so we thought it would be important for us also." Connor had always found this approach to be just symbolic and classified it as sheep following sheep without any real understanding "why" a particular metric might be important, or not important. Most of this thinking was the fallout of the best practices trend. The assumption being that if someone else was doing it, they should do it also. Connor also knew that many businesses tend to measure many things and not because they *must*, but simply because they *can*. What was going on here seemed to follow the same pattern and trend.

Connor moved closer to see more detail of what kinds of things they were measuring. Under the Operations heading were metrics for *On-time Delivery, Efficiency, Productivity, Standard hours,* and some others. The Quality section had metrics for *Rejects* and *Rework* and some others. The procurement section had metrics for *Total Inventory, Release of Materials,* and *Budget versus Actuals*. All of these subheadings were very interesting to Connor. In his mind, he started to paint the picture of what he would be up against.

Connor turned his attention back to the Operations section and focused specifically on the efficiency measure. The efficiency was being measured in 1-week blocks of time and went back to the first of the year. The weekly efficiencies were summarized to give an average for each quarter. Even though the year wasn't over yet, Connor suspected they would summarize all of the quarterly averages, or an average for the entire year, and determine which one gave them the best results. Connor smiled to himself.

Connor looked over his shoulder to see Joe walking toward him. Becky and Sam were still sitting. Becky was thumbing through a magazine of some sort and Sam was playing with his phone. Neither one of them was paying much attention to what Connor was doing.

When Joe walked up to Connor, he asked, "What are you doing?"

"I'm starting the systems analysis," Connor said.

"What do you mean?" Joe said. "We haven't seen the system yet."

"The metrics of the system, at least the way they see it, and want everyone else to see it, are posted right here," Connor said pointing to the board.

Connor turned to the charts again and noticed that most of the weekly efficiency measures had a stated goal of 100%! Connor smiled and thought to himself, "Good luck with that." On the surface, it appeared they were doing a percentage calculation based on some number of standard hours. The efficiency numbers were down and Connor assumed that the current overtime hours were having an impact. It also seemed to Connor that they were using the efficiency metric as an abstract target because everyone else used it. The primary goal seemed to be high efficiency at every work location. Connor, more than most, understood the fallacy associated with trying to achieve such a goal of 100% efficiency. Next, he looked at the Productivity measure and was surprised again. They were measuring productivity as a percentage! "As a percentage of what?" he thought to himself. Connor looked at all of the other measures on both boards and made some mental notes, smiling as he downloaded the information into his head.

Connor smiled and looked at Joe and said, "There is some good information here, and there is also a lot of nonsense information."

"What do you mean?" asked Joe.

Connor pointed especially to the efficiency chart because he knew Joe would understand and said, "Look at this one."

Joe looked at it and turned to Connor and said, "It's our old friend efficiency."

Connor just smiled with a wide grin. Connor had doubts if the efficiency measure should be used at all in a manufacturing or production environment, except in very specific locations. But, he would hold that thought for the time being. Connor studied the charts for a few minutes longer and concluded that, at Aviation Dynamics, they were dealing with a cost-centric system focused on efficiency and trying to save money.

Joe immediately pointed to the on-time delivery chart. "Look at this, the on-time delivery is averaging 69%!"

Connor smiled and asked Joe, "So, what does that tell you?"

"It tells me they aren't doing well with on-time delivery," Joe replied with a smile. "They are doing the same thing that Barton did, focusing on the wrong metrics and they don't understand the negative relationship between trying to achieve high efficiency and on-time delivery. What does it tell you Connor?" Joe asked.

"It tells me we have our work cut out for us," Connor replied.

Joe quickly scanned his focus down to the procurement metrics. "Connor!" he said, "Take a look at the way they measure inventory." Joe looked at Connor and asked, "Does that seem right to you?"

"It's what they think is important to them," Connor said.

"They seem to be measuring cost savings for inventory purchases on a monthly basis." Joe thought to himself for a minute and then looked at Connor and said, "This type of inventory metric means they most likely have stock-outs and missing parts."

Connor looked and Joe and said, "Joe, I like the way you think."

Just then, the receptionist said, "Excuse me, Mr. Carter is ready to see you now." Connor and Joe walked back over to the receptionist's desk and stood with Becky and Sam.

Connor took the brief lull in the moment to ask the receptionist a question. "Excuse me miss, but can you please tell me what the goal of this company is?" Connor asked.

The receptionist had a somewhat puzzled look on her face as if to say, "What do you mean and why are you asking me?" She finally answered, "Well, I'm not sure, but the mission statement is over there on the wall where you were standing before. Is that what you mean?"

"Not exactly," said Connor. "What I mean is why is this company in business?"

The look of puzzlement on her face became even greater, almost to the point that she started to blush and turn red. "Mr. Jackson, I don't know the answer to that question. Perhaps Mr. Carter can answer it for you," she said.

Connor smiled and thought to himself, "I hope he can."

Joe smiled as well. He was starting to understand what Connor was doing with the systems analysis. Connor was trying to gain data points of the bigger picture. Testing for things he thought should be there. Joe had done similar things in his past and was really starting to get on board with what was happening.

At that moment, another woman entered the lobby from a double glass door and introduced herself. "Hello, my name is Helen, and I'm Mr. Carter's administrative assistant. Would you please follow me to the conference room?"

"Thank you," said Becky. "I'm Becky Jackson and this is Joe Pecci, Sam Henderson, and Connor Jackson," she said pointing to each one as she said their name.

"It's nice to meet all of you. Please follow me," Helen said.

As they started to walk away, Connor glanced back at the receptionist. She was still sitting at her desk and the look on her face was now one of relief. He thought to himself that she must be thinking, "Finally, he's leaving and won't be asking me any more questions …"

Helen guided the group through the double glass door that led back into the administrative area. It was a large room that was sectioned off into cubicles. Each cubicle looked to be approximately 10 ft. square. It was a fairly modern arrangement and the furniture appeared to be fairly new. As they continued to walk, Connor noticed that there weren't many people at their desks. There were papers on the desks and the computers were on, but no people. Normally, that doesn't mean much, but Connor made the mental note anyway.

They continued walking to the far end of the building and entered a conference room that was situated in the corner. The drapes had been opened and there was ample light coming in. In the center of the room was a large conference table with eight chairs down each side of the table and a single chair at each end. There was also the normal array of video and communications equipment. Connor guessed this was the "war room" for the executive staff.

Sitting at the far end of the table were three people. As the group entered the room, all three of them stood up. There was one gentleman sitting at the head of the table and he was flanked by one person on each side. Connor guessed this was Brad Carter and two others were from the management team. The gentleman at the head of the table spoke first, "Good morning. It is a pleasure to welcome you to Aviation Dynamic, Houston Division. My name is Brad Carter and I am the General Manager of this division."

"Good morning," Becky replied. She pointed to each person and introduced them by name. "These are my business associates."

"Good morning to all of you," Brad said.

He then pointed to the gentleman on his right and said, "This is Zeke Evans. Zeke is the Director of Operations." He pointed to the woman on his left and said, "This is Marsha Lopez and she is the Director of the Procurement department and some other administrative functions."

"Very nice to meet you," replied the group almost in unison.

Brad pointed to a side table along the wall and said, "There are doughnuts and coffee, if you would like some before we begin." All four of them walked over to get a cup of coffee.

When they had their coffee, Connor waited for Becky to choose her seat. Becky had chosen to sit next to Marsha. That made perfect sense to Connor. Connor then positioned himself across the table from Zeke, the Operations guy. Joe sat next to Zeke, and Sam was sitting next to Connor.

When everyone had taken their seats, Brad said, "So, let's begin. First, I want to thank you again for coming to our facility on such short notice. I've learned a lot about this group from Ron Parsons and I'm so glad that you decided to have this meeting."

"Thank you for having us," Becky answered.

Joe thought, "Becky is always so politically correct and kind. We're lucky to have her on our team and keep the rest of us in line."

Connor and the others nodded their heads and said, "Yes, thank you for having us." With the pleasantries out of the way, Connor started to move deeper into his analysis mode, which consisted of diligent observation and listening. Connor opened his note pad and prepared to start taking notes.

Brad started the discussion by saying, "Through our mutual friend, Ron Parsons, we have exchanged some previous information. It was because of a golf game and a story that Ron told me about Barton Enterprises, and his own company SIMCO, and the drastic turnaround you had accomplished, that I thought it might be beneficial for us to get together and see if you might be able to do the same thing here," Brad said. His statement was almost a plea for help.

"As you already know," Brad continued, "we are an organization that performs maintenance, repair, and overhaul for commercial helicopters. A large portion of our customers come from the gas and oil industry, many of which are located right here in Houston. The workload from these customers has increased significantly over the last 9 months or so. As a result, we have been having some issues getting these helicopters through our scheduled maintenance process and getting them back to the customer. We also have some contracts that are coming due for recompete, and as you might have guessed, there are some customers who aren't exactly happy with our performance," he said.

"To that end, I hope we can work together and make some changes to improve our performance and better position this division to maintain those contracts, as well as possibly win some new ones," Brad said.

"I've asked each of the different department heads to put together a brief presentation and show some of the numbers and information from each area," Brad said. "That reminds me, Hal Robbins is our Director of Finance, and unfortunately Hal could not be with us this morning. He is trying to get some numbers together for corporate that they needed right away, but he plans on joining us as soon as that is finished." Connor made a note and Becky wrote down "Hal Robbins—Finance" on her note pad.

"So, I'd like to ask Zeke to give his presentation first and talk about the Scheduled Maintenance Operations area," said Brad.

Before Zeke could get up from his chair and position himself at the front of the room, Connor stated, "I'm sure you have some important information and we will want to hear it. However, if it's alright with all of you, I would much rather start with a tour of your facility before we hear this."

Zeke quickly looked at Brad for his reaction and Brad looked puzzled. Brad responded to Connor, "Well, we were hoping to do this first, but if it is important, I guess we can take the tour first."

"Thanks Brad, I really would like to do the tour first and ask questions as we go," said Connor. "Having a visual in my mind will help tremendously in understanding your information better."

4

The Plant Tour

When they left the conference room, everyone left their laptops on the table. As per Brad's request, Zeke escorted everyone out through the building and onto the hangar floor. The first stop was the supply room to get safety glasses for everyone and a quick safety briefing from Zeke. He mentioned how everyone needed to stay within the yellow lines painted on the floor and pointed to the lines he was talking about. He also pointed to the emergency exits on the sides of the building. The huge sliding doors were closed at the moment and the exit doors were marked with the familiar red and white signs.

The group was standing in a small area in front of the supply room counter. Looking straight ahead was a 6-ft.-wide walkway that continued all the way to the other side of the hangar. On either side of the walkway were the repair bays. There were three helicopters on one side, and three on the other side, each one was facing forward. The hangar was huge on the inside and looked even bigger than it had on the outside. The massive sliding doors on either side had Plexiglas windows on the top one-third of the door, which let in ample amounts of light into the work bays.

Zeke started by saying, "This is what we refer to as Hangar 1. This is the hangar where the scheduled maintenance work is done. In front of us, approximately 200 yards that way on the other side of this hangar," he said pointing with his finger, "is another hangar we call Hangar 2. That hangar is used for the unscheduled maintenance and it looks almost identical to this one." Zeke continued, "As you can see," he said pointing down the walkway in front of them, "we have a total of six work bays in this hangar, three on each side."

As the group started moving forward between the painted lines, a gentleman walked up to Zeke and stood by his side. Zeke stopped and introduced him. "Everyone, I'd like you to meet Jim Barnes. Jim is the Hangar 1 Manager and if I can't answer your questions, then Jim can." Everyone nodded their heads in a polite, "Hello."

The group continued walking until they were standing almost in the center of the hangar. Zeke continued his narrative, "Each of these work bays is capable of performing the same scheduled maintenance tasks. We are currently working three shifts a day trying to keep up with the work-loads. We use Saturdays and Sundays for extra shifts and for overtime, if it is mandated and required," he said almost as a matter of pride.

"How many total employees do you have?" Joe asked.

"Right now we have approximately 280 people split between both han-gars. There are six mechanics and one lead mechanic for each bay. There is also a supervisor for each side of the hangar," Zeke said. "The remaining employees are divided between supply and some other specialized func-tions such as avionics and hydraulics. Those crews are smaller and they rotate between all of the work bays as needed." Zeke looked at Joe to make sure that he had answered his question. Joe nodded his head as if to signal, "OK."

"When a helicopter comes in for scheduled maintenance, how long does it take from start to finish?" asked Sam.

"Well, that depends largely on parts availability, and any other issues that might crop up during the process, but on average it's approximately 70 days to complete the cycle from start to finish," Zeke explained.

"Wow!" Sam thought to himself, "That's a little over 9 weeks!"

Sam countered with another question, "Is that the same amount of time it has always taken?"

"Actually no," Zeke said. "Before the big increase in workloads we were averaging approximately 65 days from start to finish."

Joe was thinking back to the charts he had seen in the lobby and was smiling to himself.

Zeke scanned the group for more questions and then continued, "Most of our mechanics come from the military and are fully trained and quali-fied when they get here. The helicopters we work on are used for com-mercial purposes, but it's basically the same type of helicopter used in the military, so the conversion is simple."

Connor looked at Zeke and asked, "Is it possible that we can talk one on one with a few of the mechanics?"

Zeke looked a bit mystified by the question and immediately asked Connor, "Why do you want to talk with them?"

"I consider the mechanics the subject matter experts of the system," Connor replied quite politely and matter-of-factly. "And, their input will not only be necessary, but very important to anything we might decide to do," he added.

Zeke quickly shifted his attention and gaze to Brad looking for some guidance and help. Brad picked up on Zeke's visual request to have him answer the question and Brad responded to Connor, "I suppose we could make arrangements for that to happen."

Connor raised his eyebrows and looked at Brad, "Arrangements?"

"Yes, arrangements," Brad said. "You have to understand this is a union shop, and in order for that to happen, we will need the union steward present," he explained.

"That's fine," Connor said almost smiling.

Brad turned to Jim and said, "Jim, will you please go find Nathan and tell him we need him over here?"

Jim answered, "Sure," and turned and walked away from the group.

Connor noticed Zeke out of the corner of his eye and Zeke still had the panicked look on his face. "I wonder why he looks so nervous," Connor thought.

A few minutes later, Jim came back with a gentleman in tow. The guy looked to be mid-30s, with a very short cropped haircut. His external appearance and swagger suggested military.

Jim introduced him to the group. "Everyone, this is Nathan Brown. Besides being the supervisor of Section 1, Nathan is also the union steward for Hangar 1."

Nathan nodded his head and said, "Hello." Everyone nodded back with a group "Hello."

"So, what's up?" Nathan said.

"These folks here," Jim said pointing to Connor, Joe, Sam, and Becky, "have been invited by Brad to see if they can make some suggestions to improve our performance."

Immediately, Nathan was on the defensive and standing his ground, "What's wrong with our performance?" he questioned, scanning the crowd, but looking mostly at Jim. "We're doing everything the system will allow us to do!"

Connor smiled and thought to himself, "A systems thinker—that's good!"

Connor looked at Becky, who was standing by his side. She had a bit of a surprised look on her face because of the verbal exchange that had just taken place.

Jim immediately countered trying to calm the situation. "No one is questioning your performance, or the union's performance. They are just here to see if we can make some improvements to our on-time delivery numbers. As you know, we haven't been doing a very good job of getting our work out on time," he explained.

"OK," said Nathan. "So, what is it you want to do?"

"Connor," Jim said pointing to Connor, "has made a request to talk with some of the mechanics, and we just wanted you present to make sure no union rules are violated."

"That's good," Nathan said. "Who specifically do you want to talk with?" he asked looking at Connor.

"I have no one specific in mind," Connor said. "So, maybe we can just start in the area that you supervise and go from there?"

"That works. Follow me," Nathan said, as he turned and started walking down the center walkway. The entire group started to follow behind Nathan when Connor turned to Brad, Zeke, Jim, and Marsha and said, "If you don't mind, I think this will just require Joe, Sam, Becky, and me. I'm sure we will be in great hands and well monitored by Nathan."

They all looked a bit surprised and looked at Brad for direction. After a short silence, Brad said, "Of course, good luck with your discussions."

The four of them, along with Nathan, continued walking to Nathan's work cell. When they got there, Nathan explained they could stand behind the yellow line, but they weren't allowed near the helicopters. Everyone agreed.

Connor was looking at the work cell. It was "U" shaped in configuration with some desks along the bottom of the "U" and down the left side about halfway. The other side of the "U" was marked with a 6-in. red line that extended all the way up to the sliding doors. Sitting on the red line were some poles that had straps connected between them, similar to what you might see at an airport check-in counter.

"So, who do you want to talk to?" Nathan asked.

"How about we start with you?" Connor said.

"Great, fire away with your questions." replied Nathan.

Nathan walked over and got some folding chairs stuck between the desks and handed one to each person. "We can just sit here by my desk and that will be fine." They circled their chairs and Connor started, "First, tell me about your process for scheduling a new job."

"OK! First, when we finally clear out a bay and get ready for a new job, we sit down with the scheduler. The scheduler usually knows which job is next based on the amount of time the aircraft has been waiting. But, from time to time, that can change. If there is a particularly upset customer, Jim, the hangar manager, will change the order in which the work is completed. Hopefully, it's the right decision, because once we start tearing it down, we can't just move it out of the way and bring another one in," Nathan added.

"Has it ever happened that they made the wrong decision?" Connor asked.

Nathan chuckled almost to an audible laugh, "It happens a lot more than we want it to."

"When it does happen, Jim is all over the work crew to get it done faster. When I say work crew, I mean me, because if it's one of my crews, he knows he has to go through me first. If it's not me, then it's Olin Smith. Olin is the supervisor of the other three work bay crews on that side of the hangar," he said pointing across the aisle. "I'm sure Jim is being pushed by Zeke, who, in turn, is being pushed by Brad, who, in turn, has probably gotten a call from a customer to get it finished."

Connor nodded his head in agreement with an undeniable smile; almost as if he had predicted that would be the case.

"For each aircraft, the schedule is pretty much the same. In other words, the tasks to be completed during a scheduled maintenance visit are basically the same sequence of tasks depending on which type of aircraft it is. It never changes much, unless there is an engineering modification or change order that is flowed down to do something different. If that's the case, then the tasks will be changed to meet the new requirements," Nathan said.

"Does that happen a lot?" Joe asked.

"Again, it does happen sometimes, but not a lot. Even when it does happen, it's fairly easy to make the necessary changes. It just becomes a matter of making sure the new requirements are implemented and followed. However, sometimes engineering can take an extraordinary amount of time making the decision and coming up with the new specs. If that happens, the aircraft can sit for long periods waiting for engineering," Nathan said. "We take a real schedule hit because engineering changes aren't something we plan for. It just plain stops us in our tracks." It was obvious Nathan was remembering back to such an event because he was slowly shaking his head back and forth.

For the first time since they had been on the shop floor, Becky jumped in the conversation. "Nathan, I'm curious. What kind of improvements have you tried to do in the past to overcome these problems?" she asked.

"Well, that's a little harder to answer. We had some ideas for things we thought would help, but when we presented them to management, most of them were rejected because they cost too much or required too much time," Nathan said. "Since then, we've just kept our heads down and tried to work the issues as they happen. With the workload being what it is, we just haven't had any time to work on improvements. We can't even keep up with what we have to do."

At the same moment Nathan finished his sentence, there was a very loud buzzer that went off. Becky jumped and grabbed Connor's arm. "What is that?" Becky exclaimed, remembering her safety briefing and looking for the nearest exit.

"Not to worry," Nathan said. "That's just the buzzer that tells everyone it's time for the morning break." Sam, Joe, and Connor would never admit it, but they had jumped also. Becky was concentrating on getting her heart rate down. She took a deep breath and smiled as if to say, "OK, keep going, I'm alright now."

Connor looked at Nathan and said, "Listen, we don't want to keep you from your break time, so if you want to take a break—feel free to do so."

"It's OK," Nathan said. "Sitting here talking with you guys is kind of like a break anyway."

"There is one more thing about improvements," he said. "Early on in the improvement process, we did do some Six Sigma Green Belt training. Each work cell, on each shift, was allowed to pick one person to attend the training. Once that training was complete, there were some Black Belts that showed up from an outside company. In fact, there were also a couple of Master Black Belts," Nathan said remembering back to when it all happened.

"We put together some teams in each work cell specifically looking for variation in our processes. We also did some Lean stuff looking for waste and ways to remove the waste and save money. We wanted to reduce the variation and cut costs. We tried to look at all of the maintenance tasks and see if we could improve the time it took to complete an aircraft," Nathan explained.

"What happened with that?" Becky asked.

"Well, I was lucky enough to be picked for the Green Belt training. When I finished the training, I made a request for more training. I could see a benefit in having someone here with at least a Black Belt when the folks that were here left. As you might guess, they told me no!"

"Why?" asked Becky, almost with the tone of a concerned mother.

"Well, it circles back around to cost. Management felt they had spent a lot of money for the Green Belt training and for the people who came in to do the training and help lead some of our projects. They also felt they hadn't really seen a lot of return for the investment. I guess they weren't willing to spend any more money," Nathan explained.

"Anyway, I disagreed with them about not seeing any improvement. We did see some, but just not enough to make them happy. We were able to reduce some of the variation in some of the tasks," he said. "But, I also think we were trying to fix things that didn't need fixing. Some of the Six Sigma projects looked really good, at least on paper, but it didn't necessarily help what we really wanted to do."

"What did you want to do?" asked Becky.

"We wanted to fix it fast and improve the on-time delivery," said Nathan. "And, it just wasn't happening like we wanted. I've thought about what happened and I think we had so many different projects going on at the same time, that we were never sure which ones, if any, were providing good results. I mean, most if not all of the projects claimed some kind of victory for reducing variation and saving money. Yet, the problem was, no one could ever find any real reduction in variation or the cost savings in real money. The predicted savings calculation was there, but the money never was. I was talking with Jim about the projects and he said that Brad kept asking Hal Robbins, he's the finance guy, if we were saving any money. Anyway, Brad kept asking Hal what the impact was to the bottom line. Hal kept telling Brad he wasn't seeing much, if any, of those saved dollars making it to the bottom line. It wasn't long after that they abandoned the whole improvement idea," said Nathan.

"I can remember being at home one weekend trying to figure out where the saved money might have gone," Nathan said. "And, I rationalized an example that helped explain it for me."

"What example was that?" Becky asked.

"Well, I imagined that in my desire to save money on my home utility bill, I turned the temperature down on the thermostat by 5 degrees to save on the gas bill. That action would provide some savings on the gas bill. Any money I thought I had saved from the gas bill was quickly used up by another action to overcome the first action," Nathan explained.

"That's a great example," Becky said. "It makes perfect sense to me."

Connor was nodding his head saying to himself, "This guy is a thinker! We need to make sure he is part of the implementation team when we move forward."

Just then, the buzzer sounded again signaling the end of the break. Becky jumped again, but was better prepared this time because she knew what it was.

"We probably got off track with the last discussion from the things you want to talk about," Nathan said.

"Not at all," Connor said. "It's all good information."

"So what else are you looking for?" Nathan asked.

"I'd like to ask about parts availability," Joe said. "Do you have many issues with the process?"

"We do have problems," Nathan said. "In fact, I would probably rank parts availability as the number one problem!"

"Why is that?" Joe asked.

"Well, again, the parts availability issue goes back to another one of our cost savings ideas," Nathan said. "Approximately a year ago, somebody, somewhere, had the idea that we had too much inventory in our parts system. I guess they saw it as a way to increase profits if we reduced our inventory and I guess that might have worked for a little while, but it quickly caught up with us and now it costs us a lot of time."

"What do you mean it costs you time?" Joe asked, already knowing the answer, but wanting to make sure.

"It costs us schedule time," Nathan said. "If parts aren't available, then the work has to stop. If work stops, the schedule stops, but time on the customer clock keeps ticking and we end up with a late delivery. When they first started this, I was told corporate had come up with some kind of a forecast to estimate how many aircraft might come in for repair during the coming year. There was also some data that suggested which parts were used most often, how many of those parts we might use in a year, and how much each of those parts would cost."

"So what happened?" Joe quizzed.

"What happened was they ran the numbers using that formula and came up with the total parts dollar amount for the year. Then, they divided it by 12 to give us a monthly budget. We ended up with a budget for parts each month with strict orders not to exceed the budget! Even if we needed parts, we had to wait until the next month when money was available to buy them. It wasn't uncommon to be out of money by the first or second week of each month," he said.

"To compound the problem even further they issued a policy, from procurement to the supply room, that the unscheduled maintenance hangar would get the parts first if they needed them. As I understand it, they thought by doing it that way they could get those aircraft in and out faster and still make money. It seems like it should have worked, but it didn't. Even when new parts were ordered, there was a good chance the unscheduled maintenance hangar could beat us to them."

"How have you been able to overcome that problem?" Joe asked.

"We haven't," Nathan said.

"So, they still issue a budget every year?" asked Joe.

Nathan laughed and said, "Yes, but it's even worse than you think."

"How is it worse?" Joe asked.

"It's the exact same budget," Nathan said. "The workload has increased and the demand for parts has gone up, but the budget is the same."

Joe couldn't believe what he was hearing. It just didn't make sense to him.

"And, we have another problem. There are some parts that are required to be completely overhauled. Some of those parts we can do, but most of them we can't. We don't have the right equipment and capabilities at this facility to do some of the overhauls, so it has to be sent back to the vendor to have it done. When we send a part out, we have no choice except to wait for the return. We don't have any in-house parts to replace it with. Procurement told us it was too expensive to do that, so we wait," Nathan finished. The discussions continued back and forth.

Becky was watching the clock wondering when the lunchtime buzzer would activate. She didn't want to be caught off guard again so she asked Nathan when lunchtime was.

"In approximately 30 minutes," he said. "It starts at 11:00 AM and ends at 11:30 AM."

Sam, who had been mostly quiet chimed in with, "Does everyone go to lunch at the same time?"

"I guess so," Nathan said. "At least everyone on the shop floor does. I don't know what the people up front do for lunch. It might vary for them.

"Most people bring their own lunch. We don't have a cafeteria in the true sense of the word; we just have a lunch room. There are some vending machines if you are interested. If you like candy bars and soda for lunch, it's the ideal spot," Nathan added with a laugh.

"Do you all want to go to the break room?" Nathan asked.

"Is it possible we could just stay here for a few minutes and have a huddle?" Connor asked.

"I guess that would be alright as long as you don't talk with anyone else until I get back," said Nathan.

"We promise," said Connor.

Nathan went over to his desk and opened a drawer and got his lunch out. "I'll be back in approximately 25 or 30 minutes. You all be good while I'm gone," he said with a smile and walked off.

"We will," Connor said with an even bigger smile.

When Nathan was out of earshot, Joe looked at everyone and said, "Wow!"

"Wow is right," Connor said. "What a gold mine of information. This usually doesn't happen with the first guy you talk with."

"I was worried right up front that there was going to be a fistfight when Jim mentioned performance," Becky said.

"There is no doubt there is some tension between management and the union. Each side seems to be untrusting of the other side," Joe pointed out.

"This is one of the reasons I like to talk with the workers and management separately. If Brad, Zeke, Jim, and Marsha would have been here, it would have been much different," Joe added.

"Do you think we will hear the same thing from management when we talk with them?" Sam asked.

"I doubt it," Connor said. "But, we'll give each side a chance to tell their story. Remember: we aren't here to point fingers and place blame. We want to understand the system and the effects coming from it."

"I'm beginning to understand a little more about what you mean when you say 'Systems Analysis,'" Sam said. "I'm starting to appreciate that it's much more than just processes and machines—it's the people too!"

"Correct!" Connor said. "People own the system and the only way we can change the system is by having the people who own it, change it. The ideas for change have to come from them, so the proposed solutions have to fit the needs of both management and the union."

Becky looked at her watch and noticed it was about 11:20. She asked Connor, "By chance, have you seen a sign for a restroom?" Connor stood up and looked around and said, "No. I haven't seen one." As he was standing, he noticed Jim at the far end of the walkway on the other side of the hangar. Connor noticed Jim was looking in their direction so he waved his arm with the "come here" signal. Jim walked toward them.

When he got there, Jim asked, "Are you done with the interviews?"

"No," Connor replied. "But if you could direct us to the restroom, that would be a big help."

"Oh, yes, they are right over there in the corner," he said pointing with his finger, back to the opposite side of the hangar.

"Thanks!" Connor said. He turned to Sam and Joe, "Are either one of you guys interested in the bathroom?" Both said "yes."

"OK, let's go before Nathan comes back," said Connor.

"Jim, do you need to escort us over there?" Connor asked.

"No," Jim said. "As long as you stay within the yellow lines you'll be fine. Just follow the walkway and when you get to the end, turn right. It's on your left."

"Is mine over there as well?" Becky asked.

"Yes, right next door to where Connor is heading," Jim replied.

"Thanks!" Becky said, as she got in step behind the other three.

A few minutes later, they were all walking back toward the work cell. Connor noticed that Jim and Nathan were standing and talking. When they reached the work cell, Jim turned to Connor and asked, "How much longer do you think you'll be?"

"There are a couple of more things I want to talk about," Connor answered.

"OK, when you finish, just have Nathan give me a call and I'll come get you and take you back to the conference room," Jim said.

"That works. We might be 2 hours or more," Connor stated.

"That's fine," said Jim and turned to walk back toward the offices.

Becky looked at Nathan and asked, "Is everything OK?"

"It's fine, listen," said Nathan looking at everyone, "I want to apologize for my little outburst this morning with Jim. I was a little testy and it was probably unnecessary to be that way. We've had a bit of a rough patch lately, but it's getting better."

Everyone smiled as if to say, "We understand."

They all sat down again on their folding chairs in the little circle.

"It's just that Jim and I live and work on the FEBA," said Nathan.

"What is the FEBA?" Joe asked.

Nathan gave a little chuckle and then explained, "For those of us from the military, it means *Forward Edge Battle Area*, in other words, the front line," he explained with a smile.

"I still don't understand," said Joe. "This is a commercial company and not the military."

"Yes, that's right, but we use it as a reference to describe the situation. There is a formal separation between a group supervisor and the hangar manager. Jim's side of the line is considered management. My side of the line is considered the union. It's along this line where most of the confrontations take place. Jim gets the requests and orders flowed down to him, which he passes on to the supervisors. On the other hand, the supervisors get the complaints and issues flowed up to them, which we pass on to Jim. It's just the point in the process where the information exchanges sides and we call it the FEBA. Actually, I have kind of a dual role. Not only am I a supervisor, but I'm also the union steward, so I get involved with many of these exchanges," Nathan explained in detail.

"I see," Joe said. "That helps explain a lot, at least for me."

Everyone else nodded their heads as if to agree.

Connor began the conversation again by asking Nathan, "Are there any other obstacles that stand in the way of being able to do your job better?"

Nathan thought for a moment and said, "There are probably a lot of things, but we just deal with them when they happen and keep trying to move forward."

"Let me ask my question another way. Suppose that Nathan was king for a day, is there anything you would change if you could?" Connor asked.

"Yes, I'd change the way we do tools," Nathan replied.

"What do you mean?" Connor asked.

"A while back, I think approximately 9 months or so, there was an issue with some missing tools. It was three crescent wrenches that ended up missing and they had to buy some new ones. It happened with my first shift crew in work cell 3," he said pointing up the line to where work cell 3 was located. "We searched all of the toolboxes to see if the wrenches had just been misplaced, but we couldn't find them. So, the company ended up having to buy three more wrenches. They were approximately $30 each for replacement costs. I remember that because I had to sign the investigation report. Anyway, approximately a week later, they came out with a new policy that each toolbox had to be hand receipted to each mechanic and turned in to the supply room on a daily basis. The justification was accountability of the tools," Nathan explained.

"Accountability is not a bad thing," said Sam.

"No, it's not, but the way we do it is," said Nathan.

"What do you mean?" Joe asked.

"With the new policy also came a new process. Before all of this policy change was implemented, the tools used to remain in each work cell. There were six different toolboxes with one for each mechanic. Those same tools were available for all three shifts. Now, the new procedure requires that each mechanic has to inventory and sign for the tools at the beginning of each shift and then have them inventoried again before they could turn them in at the end of the shift. The tools have to be returned back to the supply room," Nathan explained.

"I'm beginning to see the problem," Sam said.

Nathan smiled. "Good, but let me explain more of the problem. Before the end of the shift, the mechanic starts his tool count for inventory. They usually start approximately 45 minutes to an hour before the end of shift. Most often, many tools are out of the boxes and located on work trays out near the aircraft where the mechanic was working. Those tools are brought back over to the boxes and put where they belong. All of the other tools in the box need to be accounted for. When everything is accounted for, the mechanic has to take his toolbox to the supply room where Agnes does a recount and inventory of the tools. When Agnes is satisfied all the tools are there, she usually slides the toolbox down the counter to Bette. Bette, in turn, opens the box so the incoming mechanic can recount and inventory the tools before he signs for them and takes them back to the work cell," said Nathan as he scanned the group for understanding.

"Holy cow, now I really see the problem," Sam said.

"The outgoing shift stops working an hour or so before the shift ends just to get the tools turned back in. It doesn't take long for the line to start building to return tools. The starting shift can sometimes be 30 minutes late getting to the work area because they are waiting in line to get tools," said Nathan.

Continuing, Nathan said, "Some of the guys have made a formal complaint that they have to come to work 30 to 45 minutes early just to get tools before the shift starts, and they want to be paid for the time standing in line. It's probably a valid complaint." Nathan added, "For the work crews turning in their tools, they sometimes get stuck in line and can end up leaving 30 minutes or so late. They wanted to be paid overtime to stand in line."

"Wow!" Joe said as he leaned back in his chair.

"When management said 'no' to the overtime, the outgoing work crews just started to form the line earlier and earlier so they could leave on time. The incoming crews slowed down coming in early and they showed up on time, but it took them longer to get back to the work areas with their tools," said Nathan.

"So, how much time do you think is involved with this tool transfer on a daily basis?" Connor asked.

"I'm guessing approximately an hour and 30 to 45 minutes every day of lost work time, per work area, per shift," he replied.

"And all of this happened because of $90 worth of wrenches?" Connor asked.

"We're just trying to follow the rules—the policies and procedures that management has established. We don't want to give them anything to come back after us and say we aren't doing what they asked. That's one of the reasons I was a little testy with Jim when he mentioned performance this morning. For an instant, that's why it struck a nerve with me because we're only doing what the system will allow us to do," said Nathan.

Connor's mind was running in high gear. He was mapping the obstacles and negative effects from the system as he currently understood it. Connor looked over at Joe and he appeared to be doing the same thing. This was a major development in the analysis.

"Is there anything else you think we should know?" Connor asked.

"Not really. There are other things, but most of them are just annoyances and we work them as they happen."

"Is it fair to say that these same kinds of things are happening in all of the work bays?" Connor asked.

"Pretty much, we have a weekly supervisor's meeting with Jim and sometimes it includes the hangar manager and supervisors from the unscheduled maintenance side as well. Usually when that happens, Zeke is involved with the meeting as well. It's a fairly common occurrence that we are all facing the same type of issues. When Olin and I meet with Jim, it's usually about scheduling problems. A lot of times, the schedules will overlap with dates and the outside resources become a problem," Nathan explained.

"What outside resource?" Joe asked.

"Things like vendor parts, or the avionics crew, or even the hydraulic crew. The schedules sometimes put the avionics and hydraulic crew in three different locations at the same time. So, we have to figure out where they should start first, where they go second, and so on. Sometimes, by the time we figure it all out, there is another schedule from a work cell that also requires them to be at that location. It just never ends," he added.

Connor looked at everyone else in the group and asked, "Do any of you have any further questions for Nathan?"

They all shook their heads "No."

Connor turned back to Nathan. "We, especially me, want to thank you for your candor and the insights you provided. It will be most helpful."

"Well, let me say I enjoyed my time talking with you. This turned out much differently than I expected. At first, I thought you were just some folks management hired to come out and yell at us and tell us what a bad job we are doing because they were getting tired of doing it," said Nathan.

"Absolutely not!" Connor exclaimed. "We wouldn't do that. We are not here to point fingers, or place blame. Our job is to first seek understanding of the current system and you have helped us do that. Without that understanding, we cannot even come close to recommending good solutions," said Connor in a reassuring way.

"I hope that works out for all of us," Nathan said.

"It will," Connor said with a smile.

Becky looked at her watch. They had been talking for quite a while now and it was almost 3:00 PM. She was getting ready to say something to Connor, when he spoke to Nathan again.

"Nathan, can you do us a favor and call Jim? Tell him we are ready to go back to the conference room."

"Sure," Nathan took out his cell phone and called Jim.

"Hello, this is Nathan. Everyone here is ready to go back to the conference room. OK, I'll see you in a minute." He disconnected. "He'll be right here," said Nathan.

Jim showed up to walk everyone back to the conference room. As they were walking back up the aisle, Joe could see the supply room's counter ahead of them. Sure enough, there were two lines forming. There was one line checking tools in, and the other line checking tools out. Joe turned and looked at Connor and nodded his head as if to point at the supply room counter. Connor smiled and nodded his acknowledgment.

Jim went through the doors to the office area. He held the door open while everyone entered. When they were all inside he said, "Follow me." As they walked, Jim causally asked Connor if he had "Gotten everything he wanted."

"I think so," Connor said, not revealing the cards he was holding.

"Good!" Jim said.

When they passed Brad's administrative assistant, Jim leaned in and asked, "Can you please call Zeke, Hal, and Marsha and tell them we are back in the conference room."

"I sure will," Helen replied.

When they entered the conference room, Brad was already there. He stood when they came in and welcomed them back. "Did you get what you wanted?" he asked Connor.

"I think so," Connor said, again not revealing his hand.

"Great!" said Brad.

Jim spoke up to tell Brad that Helen was making the phone call to Zeke, Hal, and Marsha, and they would be here in a few minutes.

"Fine, please everyone have a seat." Connor kept standing. He didn't want to take a seat yet until he knew where everyone else was sitting. He thought to himself, "This is their conference room and I'm sure they all have their selected seating spot, so I'll wait and fill in behind them."

Five minutes later, they were all sitting at the table. Becky heard the muffled sound of the buzzer going off again, but she didn't jump this time. She looked at her watch and it was 3:30 PM. It was time for the first shift to end and the second shift to start.

Brad took a moment to introduce Hal Robbins, the finance guy, who had missed the morning session.

Brad looked at Connor and asked, "So, what did you find out?"

"We got some of the information we were looking for," Connor replied.

Connor noticed that Zeke shot a glance to Brad out of the corner of his eye.

"Are you ready to share your findings?" asked Brad.

"Not yet. We have some analysis and work to do, before we do that," Connor replied. "Besides, we were all hoping to hear your presentation now," Connor said.

Brad looked at Zeke who responded, "Well, my presentation will probably take longer than the time we have left today."

"In that case, let's plan for it the first thing in the morning. Are you OK with that Connor?" Brad asked.

"That will be fine," replied Connor.

Everyone started to gather their stuff and get ready to head back to the hotel. When they were ready, Zeke walked them back out to the reception area. The same woman was sitting at the desk and she had a momentary look of terror when she saw Connor. "I hope he doesn't ask me any more questions," she thought to herself.

Jim walked over to the reception counter and said, "All you have to do is sign out in the register. You can keep the same badges and use them in the morning. That will save some time."

They all shook hands and walked out the door. Connor looked back over his shoulder at the receptionist. She had a definite look of relief on her face. Connor smiled and kept walking. In the car, Connor announced that dinner would be at 6:00 PM in the hotel restaurant. Everyone nodded and said "OK."

5

Aviation Dynamics—Day 2

Everyone met for dinner at 6:00 PM in the hotel restaurant. When they were seated, the waitress came over and asked, "Chianti?" Connor raised four fingers and she said, "I'll be right back with those."

Joe was first to speak, "What an interesting day this has been. I must admit I was a bit shocked to hear some of the things I heard today."

"You're right!" Sam said.

"I'm convinced they are very focused on trying to save money and saving money will not help their customer performance issues. On the one hand, they have corporate mandating cost saving actions to try and show a profit. On the other hand, their customers want better on-time performance," Connor said.

"But, if the performance was better, and they could get the helicopters back to customers on time, then profits would improve," Sam said.

"That's exactly right," Connor added.

"It's also why we need to shift their focus from saving money to making money. We need to move them from their comfort zone of what they know how to do, into a zone of doing what needs to be done," Connor added almost as if he were thinking out loud.

"Change is always hard for anybody, or any organization," Joe said. "If it lacks urgency, then it probably won't happen."

"I think the urgency is there. They are just looking for the right answers in the wrong place," Connor said. "I also sensed they have been playing the cost cutting card for a while now and any previous benefits are starting to run dry. There really isn't much more to cut!"

"Brad is looking for a way out and he's not sure what to do anymore. All of the old comfortable ways, the ways they've always done it before, are not working," Connor said. "They want the good results, but they keep doing the wrong things."

"I don't think they understand their system very well," said Joe.

"Maybe they haven't looked at their system at all? There does seem to be a big disconnect between the union and management. Talking with Nathan today, I got the feeling the employees really are trying to do the right thing," Sam added.

"We got some good data today, but we need some more. Let's do some good data reduction and analysis and see if we can paint the picture. Joe, I want you to get with whomever you need to and put together a visual flow map, at least top level of how the system appears now. Sam, I'd like you to think about a Pareto chart that shows the effect, in hours, of how much time is lost in a day doing other things, like standing in line for tools," Connor asked.

A few minutes later, the waitress arrived to serve dinner. After she had presented each plate and was ready to leave she asked, "Do you need anything else?" Again, Connor raised four fingers for more wine.

"This looks so good!" Becky said. Heads were nodding and forks and knives were in hand and ready to be used.

After dinner, Becky leaned back in her chair with both hands up to her head rubbing her temples. "That was really good, but I think I'm starting to get a headache."

"Are you OK?" Connor asked.

"I think I'll be fine. I just need some rest."

"Why don't we call it a night and meet back in the lobby in the morning?" Joe said.

"Good idea. We'll meet at 7:00 AM in the lobby," Sam said.

They paid the bill and walked over to the elevators to go up to their rooms. When they got off the elevator, it was the customary "Have a good night, and we'll see you in the morning."

At 7:00 AM, both Joe and Sam were in the lobby waiting for Becky and Connor. Joe could see the elevator doors from where he was standing, and a few seconds later, the doors opened and out walked Becky and Connor. They walked over to Joe and Sam and Sam asked, "How was your night?"

"My night was good," Becky said. "But, I think Connor was up most of the night on his computer. Every time I rolled over, the desk lamp was still on and he was sitting at the desk."

Sam and Joe both looked at Connor as if to inquire "What's up with that?" Connor's only response was "Are we ready to go?"

They all got in the car and headed back to Aviation Dynamics. The drive was about the same time, and when the gate guard recognized them, he just waved them through. They even parked in the same visitor's stall. They entered the building into the lobby and Connor noticed the same woman behind the reception desk. For an instant, she froze as if to say, "Oh no! It's him." They all walked up to the desk to sign in and Connor just smiled and said "Good morning." She nodded her head politely and said "Good morning." While they were all signing in, she got on the phone and called Zeke. Moments later, Zeke appeared through the door to escort them to the conference room.

As they were walking, Zeke threw out a group question and said, "I hope everyone had a good night?" Everyone nodded and answered "Yes."

When they got to the conference room, Brad, Hal, Marsha, and Jim were already there. Brad stood from his chair and greeted everyone, "Good morning, I hope you all had a good night?" Again, the heads nodded and everyone said "Yes."

"I trust you all remember Hal, Marsha, and Jim?" Brad asked as he pointed to them.

"We do," Becky said.

They all took a seat around the table and got their laptops out of their bags. Brad began the meeting with, "Since you spent the majority of the day yesterday out on the shop floor, I thought we would postpone Zeke's production presentation and begin with Marsha to talk about procurement." Everyone nodded their concurrence.

Marsha got up and moved to the front of the room. There was already a white screen pulled down behind her and she walked to the laptop sitting on the table. She pressed a button, or two, moved the mouse around and her presentation appeared on the screen.

"Good morning, my name is Marsha Lopez and I am the Director of Procurement for Aviation Dynamics, Houston Division." Everyone around the table had their chairs turned to see the screen. "I want to give you some background about our procurement process and how it works." She walked up to the computer, pushed a button, and a new slide appeared on the screen. "At AD, we use a minimum/maximum procurement system. This allows us to set the maximum level for the number of parts we want or need. We can also set the minimum number of parts the system is allowed to have before we reorder," she said. All of them were familiar with this type of procurement system.

"We used to carry quite a bit of inventory in our system trying to make sure we had enough of the right parts to keep everyone working, which seemed to work fairly well. Our inventory levels stayed high, but so did the dollars to support it. Approximately a year ago, we got a mandate from corporate to reduce our inventory dollars. They wanted to see less inventory and more profit," she said.

"Did it work?" asked Joe.

"Sure it worked!" Hal said, jumping into the conversation.

"For the next two quarters after that, we were able to show a very nice gain in our profit margins," Hal added.

"Two quarters?" asked Joe.

"Yes! After that, the improvements started to decline because production started to take longer and we couldn't get the helicopters finished and out the door. Our revenue started to fall and the cost savings weren't as noticeable after that."

Joe wondered to himself if they had been able to connect the dots as to "why" that happened. Sam, Connor, and Becky were wondering the same thing.

"It was about that same time that we started looking at our production processes to see if we could make improvements by reducing the variation with the MRO," Hal said.

"You really mean 'save money,'" Connor thought to himself. Hal had already moved himself in to take over Marsha's presentation and we were only on slide three.

"We had a meeting with Zeke to see what the options were. We all agreed that we should do some Lean and Six Sigma training and see if that would help. We thought we should try to improve efficiency and reduce variation. We brought in some Master Black Belts to do the training. We trained at least one person from each work cell to help lead a team for that area. At one point, we had 36 different teams, from all three shifts and both hangars."

"How did that work out?" asked Joe.

"Well, we did make some improvements; at least we thought we did. When the teams were reporting progress every month, there was some efficiency improvements and variation reductions that showed cost savings. But, it just wasn't enough to justify continuing to do it. We abandoned the program after approximately 3 months."

"After that, we started to look for other ways to reduce cost."

"What did you do?" asked Joe.

"We started to look at other budgets like training, travel, and overhead anywhere we thought we could save some more money. We cut training and travel to the bare minimum and even laid off five people on the support staff to help us make up the difference," Hal said.

What had started as a procurement presentation was now squarely in the lap of finance. It seemed as if Hal just couldn't wait his turn. He wanted everyone to know right up front that he was doing everything he could to save money.

"We also implemented some new policies and procedures through procurement about lost tools. We wanted to enforce accountability for the tools. We had some problems with lost tools and I think this new approach has helped a lot," Hal said looking at Marsha for concurrence.

"Yes," Marsha said, "we haven't had any lost tools since then."

"A lost tool is one thing, but lost capacity and revenue is another," Connor said to himself while taking notes.

Joe politely raised his hand and Hal pointed to him, "I have a question for Marsha." Marsha immediately perked up and said, "Yes?"

"When you reduced your inventory levels down on both the maximum and minimum, did that have any effect on parts availability?"

Marsha sheepishly looked at both Brad and Hal and said, "Well, there were a couple of issues. There were some parts that we ran out of. When we started looking at the data, we found that the lead time to order some parts was longer than we wanted, or expected. The suppliers couldn't, or wouldn't, get us parts as fast as we needed them."

"How did you solve the problem?" asked Joe.

"Well, we did take some actions," Marsha said. "I had the buyers start putting pressure on the suppliers. The buyers started telling suppliers if they couldn't improve their on-time delivery, we might have to start looking elsewhere for parts. Of course, that doesn't apply to all of our parts because some of them come from single qualified vendors, and it's the only place we can get them." Marsha stopped for a moment still looking at Joe. "We did find out that, for some parts, we are competing with the military and the suppliers told us they always sell to the military first. Their reason was both patriotic and financial. They said the military will pay a higher price for the same part, and they wanted to help the military first."

Joe nodded his head as if the answer was understood and accepted.

Brad had been unusually quiet during most of the morning conversation. Connor had been keeping an eye on Brad just to gauge his reaction for some of the discussion. Connor deduced that Brad had a good poker face, because there were a couple of times when he exhibited a surprised look. But, Connor also guessed that rather than play his hand in the conference room, Brad wanted to speak with his management team in private.

Just then, Helen, Brad's assistant, stuck her head in the door and announced that the lunches had arrived. Becky looked at her watch and noted that it was 11:30 AM. "Funny thing," she thought to herself, "I didn't hear the buzzer at 11:00 AM."

Brad gestured a thank you to Helen, then explained that he had taken the liberty of ordering sandwiches so they could stay in the conference room and keep working.

During lunch, Becky reminded Connor, and the others, that they had a plane to catch at 5:30.

"Can't they wait if we are late?" Sam asked. "After all, it is a private jet."

"They can wait, but they are just like a taxi cab, which might be missing another fare, only these guys charge a thousand dollars an hour to wait."

Connor smiled and said, "We'll be there on time, don't worry."

Brad started the afternoon by asking if there were any questions for Marsha, or Hal for that matter. No one raised their hand. There was an eerie silence. Finally, Connor spoke and he was speaking directly to Brad.

"Brad, if I might be so bold as to ask, are you a religious person?"

"What?" Brad replied. "I don't know what you mean?"

"What I mean is, are you a religious person?"

Brad had no idea where this kind of question had come from, but he answered. "I guess I am. I'm a good-ole Southern Baptist."

Connor smiled and asked, "What would it take to convert you to another religion?"

"Convert to another religion?" Brad wanted to make sure he understood the question.

"Yes," Connor replied.

"Well, I don't think I would. Being a Baptist is what I am, and what I've always been."

"So, what you're saying is you wouldn't change, because you've always done it that way?" Connor asked, now looking for clarity from Brad.

"I guess that's right," Brad said. "It's the way I've always done it, so I would keep doing it that way."

Everyone was looking a bit puzzled with Connor's line of questioning, but no one said anything. Mostly they were interested to see where this was going and what Connor was trying to do.

"What if there was a better way or in this case a different religion?" Connor asked.

"You mean a better way to be a Baptist? My wife might like that," Brad replied. Everyone smiled. "I'm still not sure I understand what you're talking about."

"What I mean is a better way that's different from the way you've always done it. What if the overall strategy of this operation changed from 'saving money' to 'making money'?" Connor asked in a noncommittal way.

Hal immediately jumped back in. "If we can save enough money, then we'll be making money. I see what you mean."

"That's not at all what I meant. What I meant was if you're making enough money you won't have to worry so much about saving money," Connor said.

Brad narrowed his eyes and looked at Connor, "You've got my attention."

"There's a story," Connor said, "about a guy who is lost in the desert and has no water. As he walks through the desert, he sees a water pump in the distance. As he gets closer, he figures out the water pump is real and not a mirage. Sitting next to the pump, he sees a one-gallon bottle of water. His immediate reaction is to drink the water because he's so thirsty. But, attached to the bottle is a note which reads: '**CAUTION**: *This bottle of water should be used to prime the pump. If you choose to drink the water now, you will gain short-term relief from your thirst. However, if you use the water to prime the pump, you will have ALL the water you want.*'" Connor waited for the effect.

Hal said, "I'd drink half the water now to satisfy my thirst, and use the other half to prime the pump."

"It won't work," Connor pointed out. "Half a bottle is insufficient to satisfy your thirst, and it is also insufficient to prime the pump. You lose short term and long term." This conversation went back and forth for some time with others guessing how best to use the water. Finally, Brad jumped back in and said, "That would be a tough choice. My immediate reaction was to drink the water, but then I changed my mind."

"Why did you change your mind?" Connor asked.

"I started thinking about the long-term need and not just filling the short-term need," Brad answered.

"Now, I'm convinced you can do it another way," Connor said. "You just made that choice."

"You're a clever man Connor," said Brad. "Now I know why Ron Parsons wanted me to talk with you." Brad thought for a moment longer and said, "I can see what you're saying."

"What is he saying?" Hal asked.

"What he's telling us is we drank all the water from the bottle. That water was all of our cost-cutting efforts to save money. We gained some relief, but only for a short period." Connor smiled and Brad continued, "What we should be doing is priming the pump so we can have all we want," Brad said with a smile.

Becky, Sam, and Joe were all sitting in silence as was everyone else. They had never seen this side of Connor before.

"So, Connor, can you help us prime the pump?" Brad asked.

With a confident voice and smile Connor replied, "I think we can."

Becky looked at her watch and noticed it was now going on 3:00 PM. They would need all of that time to get back to the airport before 5:00 PM. She got Connor's attention and pointed to her watch with her finger. Connor nodded his head.

"When can I expect you back?" Brad asked, looking at the group.

"I think in about a week or ten days," Connor replied. "That will give us some time to finish our analysis and get ready."

"Let's see." Brad was looking at a calendar. "Ten days from now will be a Monday—that works for me."

"We'll be here."

This time, Brad walked with the group back to the reception area. When they had all finished signing out and turning in badges, Brad shook everyone's hand. He shook Connor's last. "You made me realize something today about what we've been doing and how it might be wrong—thank you!"

"Here's to priming the pump," Connor said and shook Brad's hand.

As he was leaving the building, he turned around and looked at the receptionist and said, "You were right about Mr. Carter. He does understand what the goal of this company is. I'll see you in about a week or so." Her shoulders slumped a bit as if to say "Good grief, he's coming back."

On the way back to the airport, their spirits were jovial. Sam was happy because he was getting on the private jet again. Everyone else was happy because it had gone so well.

When they were airborne, Sam and Connor were sitting across from each other and facing each other. Becky was across the aisle and Joe was in front of her. Connor looked at Sam and asked, "So, are you still convinced you need to know how to repair a helicopter to do this?"

"Not anymore," Sam laughed. "Not anymore."

Connor noticed Becky was rubbing her stomach and her temples with her eyes closed. "Are you getting a headache again?" Connor asked.

"Yes I think so," Becky replied in a soft voice.

"Well, now you've got the weekend so you can rest."

"For you two," he said pointing to Joe and Sam, "let's get together at *Jonah's* on Monday to start some strategy and figure out what we want to do. Let's say about 5:00 PM." Both nodded their heads in agreement.

Everyone put their heads back in the seat and closed their eyes. A private jet was such a great way to travel.

6

The Hospital Visit

On Monday, Sam and Joe arrived at *Jonah's* to discuss their go-forward strategy with Aviation Dynamics, only to find the door locked and no lights on. This seemed very odd, because Connor was the one who set up the meeting. He was always available for their discussions and strategy sessions. *Jonah's* was closed, which was not unusual, but the door was also locked and it was a surprise for both of them. Even when the closed sign had been in the window before, Connor had always been inside, but not this time.

"What do you want to do?" asked Sam.

"Let's wait a little while longer and see if Connor shows up," Joe said.

The two of them waited in the parking lot, constantly checking their watches.

"Maybe he and Becky decided to just get away for the weekend?" Sam said more as a question than a statement.

"That's possible," Joe replied. "And maybe they're just late getting back. I'll give Connor a call on his cell and see if I can find out where he is," he added.

Joe dialed Connor's number. The phone rang six times before going to voice mail. Joe left a message to call him and then disconnected.

"No answer," said Joe with a concerned look on his face.

"Maybe he had to go visit a new client and just didn't mention it to us," Sam said. Whatever the reason, Sam and Joe were definitely becoming more concerned. This wasn't like Connor to want everyone here and then not show up himself.

"I'll give him a while to call back. If he doesn't, I'll try again," Joe said.

"I've got some reports I need to finish at work, so if we haven't heard anything in the next 20 minutes, or so, I'm just going back to the plant and finish them up," Sam said.

"I've got some things I need to finish as well. Let's just go back to Barton and finish what we need to do and if we haven't heard from Connor before then, we'll give him another call before we leave the plant and go home," Joe said.

"That works for me," Sam replied.

They both walked back to their cars and headed back to Barton. Joe was beginning to get a little more worried about Connor and why he wasn't answering his phone.

About an hour later, Joe walked down the hall to Sam's office. His door was partially closed. Joe lightly tapped on the door and poked his head inside, and asked, "Have you heard anything from Connor?"

"No, I haven't. I was just about to come looking for you to see if you had heard anything," said Sam.

"I haven't either. Let's give him another try on his cell phone and see if he answers," Joe replied.

"I hope nothing's wrong," said Sam. "I'm still thinking that maybe he got tied up with something and he didn't tell us." Joe tried calling again, but still no answer.

It was going on 6:30 PM and they still hadn't heard from Connor. They both decided that, before they went home, they would drive back to *Jonah's* and see if Connor was there. When they arrived, *Jonah's* was still locked and no lights were on. As they stood contemplating what to do next, Butch, one of Connor's employees, pulled into the parking lot. Sam and Joe walked over to talk to him, thinking maybe he knew where Connor was, or at least they hoped so.

"Hi Butch, do you have any idea where Connor is?" asked Sam. "We were supposed to have a meeting with him, but the place is locked up," said Sam.

"No, I'm just getting here for the evening shift," Butch replied. "No one called me and said, 'don't come in today.'" Butch walked to the front door and cupped his hands around his eyes to look inside. "It looks just like it did when I left last night. Have you guys tried his cell phone?" Butch asked.

"Yes, we have, multiple times," said Joe. "We've called and left messages, but so far nothing," he added.

"Maybe you should try Becky's cell?" said Butch. "I know when I've tried to get Connor before, if he doesn't answer his phone, I always try Becky. It's usually a pretty good bet that when you find one of them, you find both of them."

"That's not a bad idea," Joe said. Joe dialed Becky's number. Her phone went immediately to voice mail. Joe just shook his head from side to side, indicating that Becky hadn't answered her phone either.

Sam and Joe were becoming increasingly worried as they stood wondering what to do next. Just then, Joe's cell phone rang. He could see that it was Connor calling and hurriedly answered it, motioning to Sam that it was Connor. "Hello Connor, what's up? Is everything OK?" Joe asked. As Joe listened to Connor's reply, his expression changed dramatically to one of surprise. "OK, so what can we do to help?" he asked, but the phone disconnected.

"There's a problem with Becky!" Joe declared.

"What is it?" Sam said with a look of concern.

"Becky's in the hospital and Connor said she's having severe abdominal pain!" Joe exclaimed. "He said it started earlier this morning. He heard her in the bathroom throwing up and went to check on her. He asked if she was OK and she said yes, but about 3 hours later it all started again. He said he's been at the hospital with Becky since early afternoon."

"What's wrong with her?" asked Sam.

"I don't know. Connor was starting to tell me and then the phone went dead right in the middle of our conversation," replied a stunned Joe, remembering that Becky had complained of headaches and abdominal pains on their last trip to Aviation Dynamics.

"Are they still at the hospital?" Sam asked in a panicked voice.

"He said they're still in the emergency room. Connor said they've been there all afternoon!" Joe added.

"If she's having severe abdominal pain, you would think she wouldn't still be in the ER? Why haven't they admitted her yet? Did he say?" Sam asked in rapid-fire questions.

"Like I said, the phone connection went dead," Joe said. "I'm thinking that the best thing we could do is go to the ER, if for nothing else than to just give Connor some moral support," Joe suggested.

"I agree, let's go!" said Sam.

They both jumped in their cars and hurried toward the hospital. When they arrived, they parked in the visitors' lot, jumped out of their cars and sprinted toward the ER doors. When the doors opened, they entered and stood for a few seconds, just scanning the room. They saw lots of people sitting in chairs, but Connor was nowhere to be seen.

"Do you see him?" Sam asked.

"NO!" was Joe's quick reply.

They assumed he was still with Becky, maybe in one of the curtained exam rooms at the far end of the ER. By now, they were both deeply concerned for Becky and Connor. They tried calling the hospital's main line to see if Becky had been admitted, but were told she hadn't been. They talked to the ER receptionist and she said that Becky was indeed in one of the curtained rooms and pointed down the hall.

"I'm really confused," said Sam. "If Becky is in such pain, why in the world would they keep her in the ER?" Sam asked. They both thought it was very strange that someone with such pain wouldn't be admitted right away.

They both sat for a while, and then paced for a while, walking around the waiting room wanting to find out more information. Both of them had called their wives to let them know where they were and what had happened, with the promise they would call them back the instant they found out any information. Their silence was broken when they heard Connor's familiar voice at the admission desk. "Why can't you people get her admitted?" he said in a very loud and angry voice.

"Calm down Mr. Jackson, we're doing everything we can," was the receptionist's response, obviously one that she had used many times before.

Even from a distance, it was obvious that Connor was clearly upset, but as he turned to walk away from the desk, he noticed Sam and Joe watching and listening. Joe and Sam walked toward him, and Connor walked toward them. The expression on his face told the story and it was obvious he was visibly shaken and blurted out loud enough for the receptionist to hear, "You guys can't believe how messed up this place is! Everything about this place is broken! Their system is absolutely a mess!"

"How long have you been here Connor?" Joe asked.

Connor took a deep breath and said, "I finally convinced Becky that I was taking her to the ER about 2:00 PM and we've been here ever since," he said with a look of frustration.

"Why in the world haven't they admitted Becky yet?" Joe asked, showing his deep concern for Becky.

"I told you, it's all broken here! How they receive new patients, their first look at patients, the time it takes to get test results back, their admitting decision process … everything is broken!" Connor replied in an obviously loud tone. Connor looked at them both and said, "Sorry guys, I have to get back to Becky, but thanks for stopping by." He walked down the long hallway and into one of the many curtained bed areas in the ER.

"God, I feel so bad for Connor. I've never seen him in such a state!" said Sam.

"I wonder if all hospitals have this same problem or just this hospital," Joe rhetorically asked.

"I wish there was something we could do," Sam said.

The two of them continued sitting in the ER watching the other people and seeing the same look of frustration on the faces of the various family members and friends who had brought people to the ER. Sam and Joe sat there for another hour or so, until they finally saw a bed rolling out with Becky in it and Connor right by her side. He was holding Becky's hand with a look of deep concern and anxiety on his face and rightfully so. There was Becky, the woman of his dreams, the love of his life, lying on a hospital gurney with multiple tubes attached to her arms, being wheeled to some unknown location in the hospital. Joe and Sam tried to follow but were turned back by an ER nurse.

When Becky finally got to her room, Connor continued to comfort her. They had only been there a minute or two when the door opened and a man entered and introduced himself. "Hi, I'm Dr. Jules Price and I'm on staff at the hospital," he said.

"I'm Connor Jackson and this is my wife Becky," Connor replied.

"Dr. Branson, from the ER, called me to check on your wife. I'm glad you're here Mr. Jackson, I need you both to answer some questions for me," said Dr. Price. "One of the things I need to do is a good review and workup of symptoms, so I need you to tell me what they are."

"We already answered all those questions with the doctor in the ER," Connor said.

"I know," he said, "but I just want to make sure we've got them all and review what's already here. We need to also understand the progression of your wife's symptoms. I mean, is it getting worse or is it stabilizing?" he added.

Becky started to explain her symptoms to Dr. Price but was quickly overcome with a new onset of pain. Because she couldn't talk, Connor took over.

"As you can see, she is still having a lot of pain that seems to come and go," said Connor. "Can't you give her something for her pain?" he questioned.

"They didn't give her anything for pain yet?" Dr. Price said looking at her chart.

"I don't think so," said Connor. "Look how bad she is still hurting."

He studied the chart for a second and said, "She is getting some pain medication right now. It's part of the IV drip going into her arm. We don't want to give her too much yet, until we figure out for sure what we're dealing with," he explained.

"We first need to understand this situation a little better, so please continue," said Dr. Price. "Becky, can you tell me where the pain is; can you point to it?" asked Dr. Price.

Becky struggled, but managed to point to just beneath her belly button and Dr. Price marked the location on a piece of paper in his notebook that had a drawing of a human outline on it. "What other symptoms has your wife had?" he asked Connor.

Connor replied, "She threw up several times this morning, and threw up again earlier this afternoon before I finally brought her in."

"Has she had any bowel movements?" Dr. Price asked.

Connor looked at Becky, who was still having a pain-filled episode and said, "Honey, have you had any bowel movements?"

Becky grimaced and nodded her head to indicate yes.

"Can you describe it for me?" asked Dr. Price in a business-like manner.

"Diaaaarheaaa," answered Becky, fighting the pain as she tried to answer.

"What about gas?" asked Dr. Price.

"NO!" Becky shouted out.

"What's wrong with her Dr. Price?" Connor asked impatiently.

"I don't know for sure right now. We'll need some more tests and probably some new x-rays to see if we can narrow it down. We might even need a CT scan."

"When are you going to admit her?" Connor asked.

"She is admitted. She was admitted the instant she left the ER and came to this room," Dr. Price explained.

Dr. Price was studying the notes on Becky's chart and finally said, "I'm not exactly sure what's wrong with her, but she is showing signs and symptoms of a possible bowel obstruction."

"What exactly is a bowel obstruction?" Connor asked in a surprised voice.

"A bowel obstruction is a blockage that prevents food or liquids from passing through your small or large intestine," explained Dr. Price. "I'm not exactly sure if this is the case, so we'll need to review the x-rays from the ER and do a possible CT scan to confirm," he explained.

"What causes these blockages to happen?" asked Connor.

"Well, for example, they can be caused by fibrous bands of tissue that might form after having had a surgical procedure," he explained.

"Becky hasn't had any surgeries that I know of," said Connor. "So it can't be that," he added. "What else could it be Dr. Price?" asked Connor.

"Well, it could be a food blockage. Sometimes food can harden in the bowel and it makes it difficult to move through. Think of it as constipation on steroids. There are some other possibilities, and I don't want to alarm you, but it's also possible that she could have a tumor that can block the intestine," explained Dr. Price.

"A tumor!" exclaimed Connor. "Are you saying Becky may have cancer?" Connor asked as he moved Dr. Price away from the bed. "Is that what you're saying?" asked Connor in a very concerned voice.

"No, no, I didn't say she had cancer," replied Dr. Price. "What I said was, if she has an obstruction, it could be a tumor and if it's a tumor, it could be cancerous. However, not all tumors are cancerous. Some can be just abnormal tissue growth, but not cancerous," he explained. "We just don't have enough information yet to make a definitive diagnosis about what it is, or isn't," he explained in a very calm manner.

"How will you know?" asked Connor in a very serious voice. "What kind of tests are you going to do?" he asked.

"The first will be some new x-rays, which should help us find out if her pain is being caused by any blockages that might exist in either the small or large intestine," explained Dr. Price. "She had some x-rays when she first came in and I want to compare them and see if there is a blockage, then we might do a CT scan of the abdomen, which will help us determine if the blockage is partial or complete. We'll do that if the x-rays are inconclusive, or point us in that direction," said Dr. Price.

"What's the difference between a partial or complete blockage?" Connor asked with a look of concern on his face.

"Don't worry about that just yet. Let's just hope that it's partial instead of complete," said Dr. Price. "If it's partial, we should be able to treat it and it will go away on its own. If it's a complete blockage, then your wife might have to have surgery," added Dr. Price.

"Surgery!" exclaimed Connor.

"Yes, but don't get too excited until we see all of the test results first," said Dr. Price in a reassuring manner. "We need to see the results, before we make any decisions on surgery. There are obviously a number of different possibilities that we need to look at and eliminate them as we go," he added.

Connor was beside himself with anxiety, not knowing what was wrong with his beautiful wife. He moved a chair to the bedside and reached out for her hand wishing he could take her pain away. He hoped that, whatever the problem was, it could be treated and resolved without having surgery.

There was a light knock on the door and in walked a nurse and another man in a white lab coat. The nurse said, "Mr. Jackson, we're here to take your wife for some additional x-rays that Dr. Price ordered." The man in the lab coat and the nurse helped Becky onto the gurney and started wheeling her away. As Connor started to follow them, the nurse turned and said, "Mr. Jackson, you need to wait here."

Connor replied, "But why can't I go with her?"

"We have policies that must be followed and this is one of them," she explained.

Connor sat in the room waiting for Becky to return for what seemed like an eternity. As Connor was waiting in the room, he was thinking to himself about the process Dr. Price was using to diagnose Becky's problem. It was really no different from the process he himself used when appraising underperforming or "ailing" companies. One of the tools he frequently used for his assessments was the Current Reality Tree (CRT), so he had a good understanding of how Dr. Price was coming up with his diagnosis. Dr. Price looks for symptoms in his patients and then links them through cause and effect until, ultimately, he narrows them down to a single core problem. Sometimes, just like using the CRT, there are "things" that are hidden, so, sometimes, he has to dig deeper by running other tests to either confirm or eliminate additional missing elements.

As he was thinking about the CRT, the door opened, and in walked Dr. Price, along with the two others guiding the gurney. Connor was happy to see his wife and hoped that Dr. Price had good news for him about her.

"Well, what did the x-ray results show, Dr. Price?" Connor asked, waiting in anticipation for some good news about Becky's condition.

"Good news Mr. Jackson," replied Dr. Price. "The x-ray indicates only a partial blockage and we're pretty sure we'll be able to treat her for a few days and she should be able to return home," he added. "The other good news is, she shouldn't need any surgery," he added.

"So what are you going to do next Dr. Price?" asked Connor.

"We're going to give her some medicine and additional fluids through her IV. Depending on the type of results we get from that, we may have to put an NG tube through her nose and down into her stomach," explained Dr. Price.

"What the hell is an NG tube?" asked Connor in a very negative tone of voice. "Does she really have to have this tube in her nose?" he asked.

"NG is a nasogastric tube. The tube is intended to remove excess fluids and gas and will help relieve pain and pressure," explained Dr. Price. "We may not have to use it, but I wanted to make sure you understood why, just in case we have to," he added. "Please understand, most bowel obstructions are partial blockages that get better on their own, but some people, perhaps your wife, may need this tube," said Dr. Price.

Connor had become so frustrated by this entire experience so far that he decided to have a discussion with Dr. Price and let him know about it. "Dr. Price, I want to tell you something that has really been bothering me about this whole experience," said Connor. "When I brought Becky into the ER, I wasn't sure what I was expecting, but I wasn't expecting what I got! Do you realize it took more than 5 hours to get her admitted?" he asked. "I just don't understand how so much time could elapse before she was admitted," he exclaimed in an almost condescending tone.

"Mr. Jackson, wait time is a problem at almost any hospital in the country and the healthcare industry is trying to find ways to reduce it, but so far we haven't been very successful," said Dr. Price. "First, we need to determine in the ER if the patient needs to be just treated and released, or admitted. In the case of your wife, it took a while to make that determination. Your wife was transferred from Dr. Branson, in the ER, and was admitted to the hospital under my care," he added.

"As far as overall wait times are concerned, we've experienced several layoffs to our hospital staff as a way to save money and become more profitable. We are measured against standards, and as a result, our efficiencies have been considered too low for our accountants, so we've had to make some cuts to compensate," he added.

"Here we go again. Why is it that every organization thinks that improving efficiency and saving money is the answer to all of their problems?" Connor thought to himself.

This was not the answer Connor wanted to hear, especially with his background. He hadn't expected to hear about efficiencies and manpower cuts in a hospital environment, but when he thought about it, it made perfect sense. And the reasons seemed to be the same, because traditional cost accounting has invaded all types of industry segments, including healthcare. As long as this hospital, and every other hospital for that matter, used the same, outdated accounting procedures, their results would be no different from those of any manufacturing company using the same procedures. He could see much more clearly that the reasons for the long wait times and behaviors he had witnessed were in fact related to how the staff at this hospital was being measured.

"I'll make you a deal Dr. Price," said Connor. "You get Becky back to good health and I'll help you solve these ridiculous wait time problems. People should not have to wait for medical care and certainly not in an ER. Waiting for more than 5 hours just doesn't cut it!" he added in a rather loud voice.

"I'm not sure we need your help Mr. Jackson. We have a very extensive and active Lean Six Sigma implementation going on at this hospital, so I feel confident that wait times will be reduced in the future. The extended wait times are such a complex problem and we are trying to work the issues," he added. "We know our processes are full of waste and variation and we're working to remove both," he explained. "Like I said, it's a complex problem that will take time to improve."

Connor listened thoughtfully to what Dr. Price had explained and then said matter-of-factly, "One thing I know for certain Dr. Price is that complex problems can be best solved with simple solutions! Patients, like Becky, can't wait for the future to see improvements; they need them now!" he exclaimed.

"And you think you can fix our wait times without using Lean tools and other techniques?" asked Dr. Price.

"I didn't say I wouldn't be using Lean tools Dr. Price, but Lean by itself is not enough. In fact, if Lean is all you use, you could create more problems than you solve!" Connor replied. "What's missing is a way for you to *focus* your improvement effort on the critical parts of the process and looking only at those areas that truly control and affect your wait times. Those extended wait times are the effect of the system's output, but what is the real causality of those wait times?" Connor directed his question directly to Dr. Price.

"I don't know what you do for a living Mr. Jackson, but we have certified Black Belts and Master Black Belts working on this problem and I assure you that they know what they're doing," said a now defensive Dr. Price.

"How long have they been working on reducing wait times in the ER?" Connor asked.

"I'm pretty sure this project started approximately 6 months ago," replied Dr. Price.

"How much have the wait times been reduced in 6 months?" Connor asked.

"The last report I saw stated approximately 18 minutes have been reduced from the ER process," Dr. Price responded in a somewhat proud manner.

"But how much have the actual patient wait times decreased, with the removal of those 18 minutes?" Connor asked.

"I assume all of it, but I don't know for sure," replied Dr. Price. "If I recall, this improvement took place at the patient check-in at the front end of the process," he added.

"Then there's a very good chance that the actual wait times haven't decreased at all," replied Connor.

"Of course it has Mr. Jackson, 18 minutes is 18 minutes, no matter how you slice it!" replied a now obviously irritated Dr. Price. "What makes you think that patient wait times haven't gone down?" he asked in a sarcastic tone.

"Because what you have done is make a 'localized' improvement," said Connor. "When you focus on local improvements, or isolated parts of a process, there is no guarantee that a system-wide improvement will occur," he added. "Have you actually looked at the measured wait time data to see if they have gone down?" Connor asked.

"No, I haven't, but there is a report that comes out every 2 weeks that I can show you," replied Dr. Price. "Let me go get a copy. I'll be right back," he added.

Connor turned his attention back to Becky who had drifted off to sleep. Even though Dr. Price had given him good news, Connor was still very concerned about Becky. Connor leaned down and whispered in Becky's ear, "Becky, I promise you that I will help this hospital solve their patient wait time problems, so you never have to go through this again."

Dr. Price returned clutching a piece of paper to show Connor. "Mr. Jackson, you were right, there has not been much improvement at all in overall wait times," he said apologetically. "Before we started, our average wait times were approximately 240 minutes and now, 6 months later, our average wait times are 237 minutes," explained Dr. Price. "Three minutes of reduction is nothing!" he said in a somewhat embarrassed tone. "So what do you think we are doing wrong?" he asked. "The hospital is spending a lot of money for training and certifying employees in Lean Six Sigma and it doesn't appear that our return on investment is very good," he added in a humbler tone as he was scanning the report.

"I'll tell you what Dr. Price, let's focus on giving Becky the very best medical attention right now," replied Connor. "You get Becky back to good health and I promise you that I'll show you a better way. Right now I want you to focus on Becky," Connor said.

"We've already started her treatment process and we just need to watch for results," said Dr. Price. "We need to let this IV drip do its thing for a little while longer," he added. "I do want to hear more about why you think our approach to wait times might not be working. I actually sit on the hospital staff for improvements and I'm sure everyone might be interested to hear what you have to say about this matter," he added.

Even though Connor's mind wasn't really on continuous improvement, he replied, "I told you, I will help you with your wait times, Dr. Price. The hospital's problem is really no different from if you were a manufacturing facility trying to produce a physical product," he explained. "In manufacturing, the flow of products through a system process is dictated by the presence of a limiting step, or process, and until that step is identified, improvements in flow will simply not happen. And as I see it, your biggest challenge is improving flow. You see, the problem I have with many Lean implementations is that there seems to be an almost maniacal attempt to remove waste everywhere, mostly in the hopes of reducing cost," Connor said.

"What's wrong with reducing waste and saving money? Our Black Belts and Master Black Belts have gone through extensive training in Lean and Six Sigma, and like I told you, they know what they're doing," he added with a certain confidence.

"I'm not questioning anyone's abilities Dr. Price, but they're missing the true *focus* and *leverage*, like almost everyone does," Connor responded. "Most trainers of Lean Six Sigma haven't heard much about the Theory of Constraints (TOC), so they don't teach this critical phase of continuous improvement," he added.

"Focus and leverage, TOC; what are you talking about?" questioned Dr. Price. "Could you please explain this in terms I can understand?"

Connor decided that Dr. Price was not going to understand what he was talking about without showing him visually, so he pulled out his iPad from his backpack and found a picture of a piping system. "Look at this," he said holding his iPad out for Dr. Price to see.

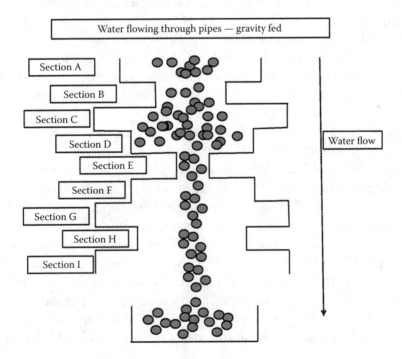

"Here is a simple cross section of a piping system used to transport water through nine different sections of pipe," Connor explained.

"What the hell does a piping system have to do with patient wait times?" Dr. Price asked.

"You asked me to have patience Dr. Price, so now it's your turn, please bear with me on this," Connor replied. "As you can see, this is a gravity fed system. Water enters this system at the top in Section A, passes through Section B, then Section C, and so on until it reaches the receptacle at the base of the system," he explained.

"OK, so what?" Dr. Price questioned.

"Suppose I asked you to increase the flow of water through this system. In other words, you need more water to get through the system; what would you do?" Connor asked.

Dr. Price studied the sketch and replied, "I would increase the diameter of Section E because that section is the smallest."

"How much larger would you make the diameter for Section E; what would you base your decision on?" quizzed Connor.

Again, Dr. Price studied the drawing and replied, "That would depend on how much more water I needed."

"So you would make it look something like this?" asked Connor.

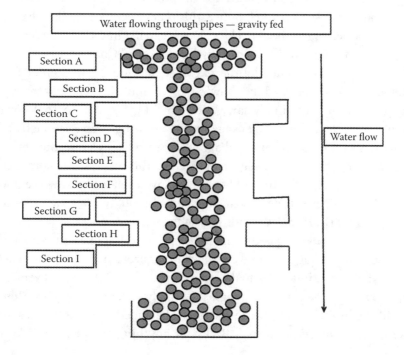

"Yes," he replied.

"Correct, so would it be safe to say that, unless and until you 'fix' Section E, no additional water could flow through the system?" Connor asked.

"Yes, of course, but I still don't understand what this has to do with wait times in the hospital," he asked.

"And if you increased the diameter of any other section of this piping system, would more water flow through the system?" asked Connor.

An obviously frustrated Dr. Price said, "No Mr. Jackson, but could you get to the point of this exercise?"

Connor closed the picture of the piping diagram and opened another one, only this time he showed Dr. Price a simple four-step process with cycle times for each step.

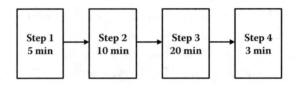

Connor showed the picture to Dr. Price and explained, "So now we have this simple, four-step process, with the time it takes to complete each of the steps. If I asked you to 'speed up' this process, what would you do and why would you do it? If you'll notice, this process looks a lot like what you have explained to me about Becky's blockage in her intestine. You can't get any more through until you open up the blockage," Connor said.

Dr. Price was intrigued by the reference and looked at Connor for a moment and then studied the drawing for a minute longer and then raising his eyebrows, he simply said, "Holy cow! I get it Mr. Jackson! You're absolutely right about the blockage. In this drawing, Step 3 is exactly the same as Section E of the piping diagram, or even Becky's intestinal blockage, meaning that the only way I can speed up this process, or improve the flow, is by reducing the time of Step 3! Remove what is blocking the flow! Now, it makes perfect sense to me," he replied proudly.

"Very good Dr. Price," Connor responded with a smile.

Dr. Price, still looking at the diagram said, "And just like you explained, I can see why having a focused approach for improvements is clearly a better way!" He continued, "It makes no sense at all to make improvements to, for example, Step 1. Making it faster simply won't help, because Step 3 is still the limiting factor in this system," he added confidently. "It's just like it makes no sense to treat Becky for anything except her blockage.

Holy cow!" said Dr. Price. "This explains why we haven't seen substantial improvements in our ER process! They only made the check-in faster, and it wasn't the problem," he exclaimed.

"You're exactly right Dr. Price," Connor said.

"So, if all of this is true, then why in the world isn't everyone teaching this simple, basic ideology?" asked Dr. Price. "This totally explains why when we reduced our check-in steps and process in the ER, we didn't see any real change in patient wait times!" he added excitedly. "It was no different from trying to speed up Step 1 of this process! Can you tell me more about your methodology?" he pleaded.

"Dr. Price, the TOC has been around for nearly 30 years. However, it has not been as widely adopted by many companies, nor is it being taught in most Lean Six Sigma training, or even academia. One reason is that many people believe that TOC was developed strictly for manufacturing and production, so it couldn't possibly apply to industries like healthcare," Connor stated.

"But it's such an inherently simple concept to grasp once you see it," said Dr. Price. "I, and the hospital improvement team, need to know more about this," said an obviously excited Dr. Price.

"I will explain much more to you, but for now Dr. Price, my wife needs your attention," replied Connor. "Like you just learned, any real system improvement comes from focusing on the constraint and I want you to focus on Becky!" Connor said in a serious voice. "Like I told you before Dr. Price, if you can make Becky healthy again and free of pain, I will help your hospital become the 'model' healthcare facility that others will want to copy," he added.

"Thanks for the incentive and I will absolutely take care of Becky," replied Dr. Price. It was clear that this hospital was about to have a new set of eyes looking at its processes, and those eyes were none other than Connor Jackson!

Connor decided to spend the night with Becky in her room. Connor kissed her on her cheek and told her that he loved her. Connor eventually fell asleep in his chair, still holding Becky's hand. One thing was for certain, Connor wasn't going anywhere … at least not without his beloved Becky.

7

Aviation Dynamics—The Strategy

Becky had been in the hospital for 3 days now and Connor had been at the hospital almost constantly for those same 3 days. He had only taken time to go home and shower and get clean clothes. His time at the hospital had gone by slowly and he was mentally exhausted, but also prepared to do whatever it took to get his Becky back.

Sam and Joe had visited a couple of times and even came in one evening with their wives. They had brought some flowers to brighten the atmosphere in Becky's room and add some much needed color. During one of those visits, Sam, Joe, and Connor had talked briefly out in the hallway. They had discussed the upcoming visit back to Aviation Dynamics, and Sam was pushing to postpone the visit.

"I think we should call Brad and let him know what has happened, and see if we can change the date to go back," Sam said.

"I agree," said Joe.

"I don't agree," said Connor. "I think the three of us need to spend a little time going over some data, collect our thoughts, and build a preliminary strategy. You guys need to go back on Monday and get this effort started. Brad and his company are facing some urgency here and we need to help them the best we can," Connor explained.

"But Connor, we can't go back without you!" exclaimed Sam.

"Why not?" asked Connor.

"Because we need to be here with you and Becky," Joe said.

"Why?" asked Connor.

"Because you and Becky are two of our dearest friends and we want to be here with you," Joe answered.

"Look guys," Connor said. "Both Becky and I very much appreciate your friendship and support and I don't think that either one of those will change whether you're here or there. Both Becky and Brad are having some troubles right now and I think we can help both of them at the same time," Connor explained.

"I'm not sure we can give Brad the help he really needs unless you are there," Sam said. "Besides, Brad is expecting all of us to show up next Monday."

"We don't need all of us to be there to make this work," Connor said narrowing his eyes looking at them both. "Both of you guys are much better at this than you think you are. I don't think you'll run into anything that you can't handle and if you do, just call me," said Connor.

"I don't know about this," Sam said.

"I do know about this, and we need to do it, and get it done," Connor said. "Let's plan a meeting tomorrow around noon at the bar. Most of the testing with Becky is already complete, and anything they do always happens in the morning, so that would free up a couple of hours of my time to sit down and talk," said Connor.

"OK," said a reluctant Sam. Joe nodded his head in agreement.

"Now, let's get back in the room before everyone thinks we have abandoned them," Connor said.

They all turned and went back into Becky's room. Joe and Sam's wives were talking with the nurse. The nurse was in the room recording the vital signs and readouts from the various monitors. Connor walked back over to Becky's bed and the nurse looked at him and said, "Everything still looks very good, Mr. Jackson!"

"Thank you," Connor said.

The nurse turned and left the room. Becky was awake and sitting up in bed. The episodes of pain had subsided and she did feel better. She still had the IVs in her arm and looked tired. She was engaged in the conversation, but only at a minimal level. Everyone could tell that she was ready to close her eyes and go to sleep. Finally, Sam's wife spoke. "I guess we better get going. We need to get back home before the kids burn the place down." Everyone smiled. Joe, and his wife, echoed the same thought. As they were all leaving, they offered Connor the reassuring support that if he needed anything, he just had to give them a call. Connor thanked everyone for their concern and support.

When they had all left, he walked back over to his chair and sat down. By now, Becky had already fallen asleep. Connor reached out and softly took hold of Becky's hand and said, "Stick with me babe, we're going to make this right."

The next day, Connor showed up at *Jonah's* about 11:30 AM. It had been an uneventful night and morning at the hospital. No real change—good or bad. Everything seemed to be the same. The charge nurse had his cell number and was left with strict instructions to call him if anything did change.

Connor walked to the front door, opened it, and went inside. The lunch crowd was just beginning to arrive, but it wasn't busy yet. He walked over to his favorite table in the corner. This table had become the informal meeting place when everyone met at the bar. He sat down and took a pad of paper from his bag, all the while thinking to himself, "Everything is going to be alright."

At approximately 5 minutes before noon, both Joe and Sam walked in. They immediately noticed Connor in the corner and walked over to the table.

"How's Becky doing?" asked Joe.

"She seems fine, no real changes yet." Sam and Joe both nodded their heads.

"So, sit down and let's do this," Connor said.

Sam and Joe sat down and Connor started. "OK … let's get a preliminary plan about how we want to handle this. When we were there last week, we gained some great insights into what's going on. They are totally focused on trying to save money and not understanding that the real leverage is making money. Somehow, in their mind, saving money is equal to making money, and they aren't. It's just the traditional way people try to solve the problem and then get very disappointing results. What we need to do is shift their energy and focus to making money." Connor stopped and paused for a moment, thinking back to his conversation with Dr. Price. "You know, the hospital is trying to do the same thing."

"What thing?" Joe asked, puzzled by Connor's comment.

"Save money!" Connor said. "Anyway, we won't worry about that right now. That's a problem for another day," Connor added and continued. "When you get there, the first thing you want to do is build a strong implementation team and surface as many additional obstacles as you can. I'd suggest a strong team composed mostly of the hourly workers, those guys out on the shop floor; they are the true subject matter experts. Make sure that Nathan Brown is part of that team. In fact, it would be good to get some recommendations from Nathan about who else should be on the team," Connor added.

"Second, you need to schedule some time and get everyone together to understand the basic concepts of Theory of Constraints (TOC), Lean, and Six Sigma, and then build the Interference Diagram with the team. The basic discussion about TOC and the piping diagram, four-step process, and the five focusing steps will probably work well for this. Watch out for Hal. If he gets this concept at all, he will immediately see excess capacity in other areas and might suggest more layoffs in order to save more money." Connor warned, "Keep a leash on him! Make sure management doesn't try to intimidate the workers and control the meeting. The last thing we need to have happen is the hourly guys are in the meeting, but afraid to say anything for fear of some kind of retribution from management. You have to sell this concept as a necessary integrated team effort. Everyone's thoughts and recommendations matter," Connor explained.

Joe and Sam were writing notes as quickly as they could. Connor was in his zone and continued to talk. "Third, you need to establish the overall objective. The objective needs to be their idea; the end game as they currently see it. Make sure it's reasonable and fits within what we want to accomplish, as well. It will be the same objective for the Interference Diagram and the Intermediate Objectives map. The overall objective needs to come from an agreement of both sides, between management and the employees, about what the objective really is. This might be a bit tricky. Management will want to achieve corporate objectives and the employees will want to protect the employees. There might be some gray areas, so watch for it," Connor warned.

Connor continued, "When you start defining the system obstacles, filter them as they are brought up and discussed. Make sure it's really an obstacle and not just a grievance or annoyance, or something that someone remembers that happened 10 years ago, but nothing since then. These have to be issues that both sides can agree on; things that stand in the way of achieving the objective," Connor stated. "You'll also need the flow of the system from start to finish. Sequence the tasks as they need to take place. Look at the bigger picture, such as scheduling, procurement, return to vendor, maintenance, repair, and overhaul (MRO), flight test, and so on. Don't worry about the individual tasks to do the actual MRO work, look at the flow. The actual tasks to do the work are pretty much set in place and won't change much," he explained.

Sam was beginning to feel a bit overwhelmed and his confidence was beginning to slide just a bit. He looked over at Joe and Joe seemed to be doing just fine, taking notes and listening intently.

"For any of the obstacles that have a time element associated with them, and most will, make sure you dive down enough to capture the impact. For instance, you already roughly know the time impact for standing in line to get and return tools. Look for those things that steal time from the available capacity," Connor continued. "All of the things they might be doing that take time away from working on the helicopters," he added.

"Fourth, when you have the obstacles, and everyone agrees, then see if there are any obstacles you can stop doing right now. If there are, remove them on the spot. For the remaining obstacles, start to define the intermediate objectives to overcome them. Ask the question: 'What must exist, or be in place, in order for the obstacles not to exist anymore?' Let them provide the answer. The answers to those questions will become the intermediate objectives. When we have that list, we can start to build the Intermediate Objectives map," he added.

"I think this exercise will probably take the full 2 days you'll be there," Connor stated.

"It might take longer than that," Sam said.

"I think you'll do just fine," Connor said with a smile.

Joe was busy going down the checklist he had written and looked up at Connor. "This is a pretty extensive list," Joe said.

"It is," Connor answered. "But, I think you'll be surprised at how fast it will come together. They have an urgency to make something happen and I think we can take advantage of that," said Connor.

"I hope so," said Joe.

"There is no hope involved. I'm confident you guys can make it happen," Connor stated.

"With Becky in the hospital, you guys are going to have to make your own travel arrangements. With such short notice for this trip, I might suggest you use the private jet again. They will probably offer the best means to meet the schedule and turnaround time," Connor added.

"We can use the private jet?" Sam asked, with a half-smile on his face.

"Yes!" said Connor. "Do you have the number for Becky's travel agent?" he asked.

"I do," Joe said. "We've used her before, in fact, several other times."

"Good! Then go ahead and get everything set up. When you get back, we'll review your findings and go from there. We'll also need all of the backup data to support the reasons we're doing some of the things we're doing. They need to understand 'why' these things are happening and what is necessary to overcome them," said Connor.

"If you have any questions, or need something, give me a call, or a text message, or even an e-mail and I'll get back to you as soon as I can. Right now, I'm going back to the hospital and check in on Becky," said Connor.

By then, it was about 1:15 PM. Some of the regular lunch crowd had already filtered in and out. Joe, Sam, and Connor gathered up their stuff and headed out the front door to the parking lot. Connor got in his Hummer and headed back to the hospital. Joe and Sam stopped to talk for a minute.

"What do you think Joe?" Sam asked.

"I think we can do this," said Joe.

"I hope you're right," Sam answered. Sam was glad that Joe's confidence was so high. He also knew that Joe had experience doing this kind of thing. He hoped it would be enough.

They both got back in their cars and drove back to Barton. They had some things they needed to get done before Sunday night.

8

Becky Leaves the Hospital

Becky lay in her hospital bed, asleep, with her IV still firmly in place. Connor was very happy that Dr. Price hadn't had to insert the nasogastric tube, and so far, his pain management plan appeared to be working very well, at least for the moment. He considered himself and Becky to be very lucky that her abdominal pain wasn't being caused by a tumor.

As Connor sat beside her bed, he was reflecting about how Dr. Price had explained that wait times are seemingly a universal problem in all hospitals. Connor was searching his internal memory banks trying to reflect back to similar experiences that were similar to the one he had just experienced in the hospital's emergency room (ER). Connor reasoned that the real problem he had encountered was one of basic system synchronization into and out of the ER. He thought, "It's clearly a flow problem, which was really no different from what I, Becky, Sam, and Joe had recently observed at Barton Enterprises, and other places." Connor also considered that the hospital ER solution he was thinking about might work well with the unscheduled maintenance at Aviation Dynamics.

Connor began thinking through the sequence and process of the ER and unscheduled maintenance. Connor visualized helicopters flying and then landing with an apparent mechanical or electrical problem. When the helicopter lands, a troubleshooter would analyze the aircraft and then perform a sort of aircraft triage. Based on the triage, a preliminary diagnosis is determined, which is based on the observed symptoms or tests, and then a decision must be made as to whether or not the aircraft should be repaired on the flight line, or whether it should be moved into a hangar for repair. "This scenario really isn't any different from a patient coming to a hospital with some kind of ailment or injury, and just like the aircraft triage, an ER physician examines the incoming patient, reviews the symptoms, maybe runs some tests, and then makes his preliminary diagnosis," he thought to himself. "After the data are collected, the doctor then has a decision to make. Do I treat the patient here in the ER, or do I admit the patient into the hospital?" Connor concluded. In concept, it is really the same scenario as the unscheduled maintenance he had discussed already with Sam and Joe. Connor imagined what this scenario might look like and then sketched it out on his tablet.

He thought again about what the actual process might look like in the emergency room. "Let's see," he thought. "Patients arrive at the ER and then are seen by a doctor for the initial diagnosis ... a sort of triage-type scenario just like at Aviation Dynamics," he thought as he continued to sketch it out. "In the triage step, the doctor decides whether or not the patient needs any diagnostic tests to help with the diagnosis. Once the doctor receives the results of the testing, an initial diagnosis is made. And finally, the doctor must decide whether to treat the patient in the ER or admit the patient into a hospital ward," he concluded.

Hospital emergency room Multiple Drum–Buffer–Rope (MDBR)

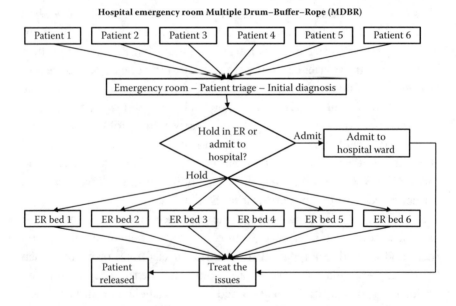

As Connor was studying his preliminary drawing and crystallizing his thoughts, he hadn't noticed that another person had come in the room and was standing by Becky's bed. He quickly tapped the save button with his finger and closed the drawing.

"Hello Mr. Jackson, my name is Dr. Imul Jahata. I'm a gastroenterologist at the hospital and Dr. Price asked me to come by and check your wife to make sure her x-rays looked normal," he explained.

"Does Dr. Price suspect more problems?" Connor asked.

"No, Mr. Jackson, Dr. Price and I have a set methodology that we use together and one part of this is for me to check her latest x-rays," he replied.

"And?" asked Connor.

"Mr. Jackson, everything looks normal at the moment, so there's no need for concern at all," explained Dr. Jahata. "Sometimes, these blockages can move and place stress on the patient, so we always check to be sure," he added.

After Dr. Jahata left, Connor couldn't help but think back to what he and Becky had experienced over the past few days. He reached down and took hold of her hand. He had been amazed by the significant wait times in the ER. "There has to be a simple 'fix' for these wait times," Connor thought to himself. "I must find a way to help overcome the excessive wait times," Connor concluded. "I know that's what you would want me to do sweetheart," he thought as he squeezed her hand. But when he felt a gentle squeeze back from Becky's hand, he smiled and whispered excitedly, "I love you Becky ... did you have a good rest?"

Becky sat up in her bed, stretched with both arms and said, "Yes, I did Connor ... I feel so much better today."

Hours later, Connor was still thinking about the long wait he had experienced, so he decided to walk to the nurses' station and talk with the head nurse on duty. "Excuse me, my name is Connor Jackson ... my wife is in room 262," he said.

"Yes, Mr. Jackson, my name is Sylvia Bonner ... how can I help you?" she asked.

"I was wondering if you've ever worked in the ER?" Connor asked.

"Yes, I worked there for approximately 6 years ... why do you ask?" she replied.

"My wife, Becky, and I experienced a very long wait time there and I was wondering if you had any explanations as to why you think there can be such long delays?" he asked.

She thought for a moment and then replied, "I think there are probably many reasons patients have to wait so long. For example, the time it takes to get test results back can sometimes take an hour or more," she explained.

"An hour or more?" said Connor. "That seems like an awfully long time to me! Why do you think it takes so long for test results?" he asked.

"Stop and think Mr. Jackson. The ER doctor orders the tests and then the Lab Tech is paged to come draw the blood, if blood work is what the doctor wants done," she explained. "The Lab Techs might be busy, drawing other blood samples or maybe they're in the lab running tests, so they may be delayed until they're finished," explained Sylvia. "Eventually, they show up and draw the blood, label it, and then take it to the lab for testing," she added. "And then there's sample preparation in the lab. All of this must be done before the test actually gets run," said Sylvia.

"What happens next?" asked Connor.

"Once the test is run, then the results must be documented and returned to the ER for the doctor to translate," she replied. "Why is it that you want to know about these things?" asked Sylvia.

"I promised Dr. Price that I would help him with the extended wait times in the ER," Connor replied.

"Mr. Jackson, the long wait times are not just in the ER. We have long wait times for patients going to surgery, the oncology clinic, the eye clinic … everywhere!" she exclaimed.

"I suspected as much Sylvia, but can you tell me what else you think might be contributing to the long wait times in the ER?" Connor asked.

"Here's one for you. The time it takes to prepare a room in the ER after it has been used takes way too much time," she said.

"When you say prepare a room, exactly what do you mean?" asked Connor.

"When we've finished with a patient, that's when they are either admitted or sent home, the room has to be thoroughly cleaned and readied for the next patient," she explained.

"How long does that take?" Connor asked.

"It depends," said Sylvia.

"Depends on what?" asked Connor.

"Let me back up a bit," said Sylvia. "Approximately 2 months ago, there was an edict from our parent company, Healthcare International, to cut staff," she continued. "Our leadership team met and decided that cutting the housekeeping cleaning crew was the most logical choice and the easiest to do. And since then, we've had problems all over the hospital with patients waiting because the rooms are not ready and the assigned nurse has to do it," Sylvia explained.

Connor was getting a better mental picture of what was going on at the hospital. How these reduction decisions were being made with little consideration of the impact on the overall system. "Cost cutting is not the way forward to increasing profitability!" he thought to himself. "Even if it does provide some benefits, it's only for a very short time, then what?" he asked himself.

"So Sylvia, what you are saying is that if the hospital had more people to simply clean the rooms, the rate of being able to service more patients would increase?" Connor asked.

"Definitely!" she replied. "And the wait times would decrease," she added.

Connor thought to himself, "How much can housekeeping really cost?"

"What else? What are some other reasons in your opinion?" he asked.

"Well, I know you want to focus on the ER, but I used to work in Surgery and they had their troubles as well. Things like not having all of the surgical equipment in place before the patient arrived has caused unnecessary delays or maybe not having the anesthesiologist available," she replied.

Connor thought, "Hmm, the more I hear, the more I'm convinced this is just like not being fully kitted to perform a repair in aircraft maintenance, repair, and overhaul (MRO). Maybe the solution is not as difficult as everyone thinks it is?" Connor pondered as he evaluated his thoughts. "Maybe if we can solve the ER synchronization problem, we can do the same type of thing at Aviation Dynamics?" he thought.

Connor returned to Becky's room and once again she was sound asleep. Since Becky was asleep, Connor started making more notes and sketching out his ideas and vision. The idea he had presented to Joe and Sam about Multiple Drum–Buffer–Rope was, in his mind, a potential solution to the excessive wait times in the ER. The hospital bed availability is really no different from hangar bay availability, and when he thought about it, the availability of beds in the intensive care unit, or other units, is really the same as well. "In all cases," he thought, "it's simply a matter of synchronizing the flow." It really doesn't matter if it's an aircraft or patients, neither are flowing through the processes in a timely manner. He continued sketching out his thoughts. "I think I'll call Joe and Sam and see how things are going in preparation for the Houston trip." Connor stepped out of the room and conferenced in both Joe and Sam on his cell phone.

"Hi guys," said Connor.

"How's Becky doing, Connor?" asked a concerned Joe.

"She is sleeping right now, but earlier she told me she was feeling much better," replied Connor.

"That's great news Connor … I know how relieved you must be that she seems to be recovering," said Joe.

"You bet I am," Connor replied. "Guys, I was wondering how your Aviation Dynamics trip preparation is going?" he asked. Both Joe and Sam indicated that they should be all set to go on Sunday and they would call and get all of the travel arrangements in place.

Connor then explained his concept about how he believed that the solution for the hospital might also work very well for unscheduled maintenance at Aviation Dynamics. "So I'll be very interested in hearing about what you guys end up finding in Houston," said Connor. "So, make sure you stay in touch with me while you're gone, and thanks again for doing this without Becky and me," he added. Connor disconnected and returned to Becky's room.

As Connor was sitting with Becky, there was a knock on the door. The door opened about halfway and in walked a young man, probably in his mid-30s.

"Mr. Jackson?" asked the young man.

"Yes, that's me, and who are you?" Connor asked.

"My name is Terry Mansfield. I'm the Continuous Improvement Coordinator for this hospital," he replied. "I've been talking to Dr. Price and he thought it would be a good idea if we met. He said something about you helping us solve our problem with wait times here at Saint Luke's Hospital," said Terry.

"Yes, we did have that conversation," replied Connor.

"Dr. Price also told me that you have a radically different improvement methodology," quizzed Terry.

"I'm not sure I would agree that it is 'radical,' but it's probably different from what you have been using," said Connor.

"Mr. Jackson, I came to see you so that we could set up a time to meet and discuss your methods. So when might you be available to chat?" asked Terry.

"Terry, first of all, please call me Connor. My schedule is completely dependent on my wife's condition. She's recovering from an intestinal blockage and she's been here a few days already, so hopefully we'll be checking out to go home later today or maybe tomorrow," Connor explained.

"I remember having pancreatitis a few years back and it was so painful. I didn't think it was ever going to stop hurting, but eventually it did," said Terry.

"I have an idea Terry," said Connor. "I own a bar down on Center Street and if my wife gets discharged in the next day or two, we could meet there for our meeting. It's called *Jonah's* and we have meetings there all of the time," said Connor.

"You want to meet at a bar?" asked Terry, not believing that he had ever been invited to a bar for a meeting before.

Just then, a soft voice from across the room said, "Do you like wine?" It was Becky and she was awake and starting to sit up in bed.

"Yes, I love wine, Mrs. Jackson," said Terry.

"Well then, you will love our bar ... and please call me Becky," she said.

"That sounds great to me, Mr. and Mrs. Jackson," said Terry as he wrote down Connor's phone number and the address for *Jonah's*. He thanked Connor and Becky for their time and told Becky he hoped she feels much better soon, then left the room.

"Sorry Connor, I didn't mean to barge in on your conversation like that," said Becky.

"Honey, don't worry, it was nothing," said Connor.

"Who was he and what does he do?" Becky asked.

"His name is Terry Mansfield and he's the hospital Continuous Improvement Coordinator," Connor said.

"What were you talking about with him?" Becky asked.

"Honey, I promised Dr. Price that if he could make you pain free again, I would help him reduce wait times in the ER," Connor replied.

"That should be fun. Has Terry ever used Theory of Constraints, Lean, and Six Sigma (TLS) before?" asked Becky.

"I doubt it, but he will soon find out more about it and how it can be used to his advantage in the hospital," said Connor. "In fact, Becky, I may even have a solution for them already," he added.

"Great!" Becky said with a smile. Becky and Connor chatted for a while longer. Becky was getting tired again and wanted to sleep. Connor decided to take a nap in his chair.

A short time later, Connor was awakened by noise around Becky's bed. He opened one eye and could see a nurse checking Becky's vital signs. He could see that Becky was awake and talking to the nurse. "So how soon do you think I'll get to go home?" Becky asked the nurse.

"Well, based on your condition and your vitals, I would think that Dr. Price will probably release you tomorrow, but you never know about these doctors around here," she said. "I'm sure Dr. Price will answer that question for you a little later or in the morning," she added. As she was talking with Becky, she also removed her IV, which brought a big smile to Becky's face.

"That would be wonderful," said Becky. "I'm so ready to get home and get into my own bed," she said excitedly. "Please tell all of the nurses that I really appreciate the good care I received on this unit," she added.

"Thank you Mrs. Jackson, you were a model patient for us," replied the nurse with a smile and then left the room.

"Honey, I sure hope that nurse was right … I want to get you home," said Connor. "By the way, I talked to Joe and Sam and they're all ready for their trip to Houston," said Connor.

"Maybe if I get released tomorrow, you can go with them," said Becky. "I think both of them would feel much better if you were there with them," she added.

"Absolutely not!" exclaimed Connor. "There is no way in hell I'm leaving you here in the hospital, or at home for that matter, so I can go to Houston," he said in a very convincing tone.

"OK, it was just a thought," said Becky. "I am feeling much, much better if that might influence you to change your mind," she said.

"I won't change my mind."

The next morning at 7:00 AM, there was a knock on Becky's door and in walked Dr. Price. Connor was asleep in his chair and Becky was resting in bed. Dr. Price shook Connor's leg and Connor sprang to life, sitting up straight. He nudged Becky and she woke up, rubbing her eyes. "Good morning Dr. Price," said Becky.

"Good morning Becky … how are you feeling today?" asked Dr. Price.

"I'm feeling great … no pain whatsoever," she said with a smile and then added, "Can I go home today?"

"Let me just check your chart for the blood work I ordered yesterday," he said as he turned the pages in Becky's chart. "Everything looks great Becky, so it looks like you'll be going home today," he added.

"Yeaaaaaa!" Becky shouted and applauded the good news.

"I do want you to take it easy for the next week or so. Sometimes, there can be a recurrence if you try to do too much, too soon," said Dr. Price.

"Don't worry Dr. Price, she is not allowed out of bed for the next week," said Connor.

"Well, I don't want her to stay in bed, I just don't want her to try and do too much." Dr. Price smiled and then said, "By the way Connor, did Terry Mansfield stop by to see you?"

"Yes he did, and we agreed that one day next week he would come to my bar and we could talk about how we might be able to improve things here," said Connor.

"You're going to have a meeting at a bar to discuss continuous improvement?" asked Dr. Price with his eyebrows raised.

"Yes, it's a unique kind of place where businessmen meet all of the time to discuss business problems. You're welcome to join us if you like Dr. Price," said Connor.

"Based on your description, there's no way you can keep me away. When are you meeting?" asked Dr. Price.

"We haven't set a day and time yet, but when we do, I'll have Terry give you a call and let you know," Connor said.

Then Becky said, "I hope you like Chianti Classico?"

"I don't think I've ever had any, but I'll give it a go," said Dr. Price

Dr. Price left the room and Becky and Connor proceeded to start packing for her release. They were both excited to be going home.

9

MRO Strategy—Day 1

When Joe and Sam returned to Barton, they went to Sam's office to call the travel agent. Sam found the number and they got her on speaker phone. She answered on the second ring. They explained their situation about needing to get back to Houston on Sunday night and wanted to know if the private jet could be available. They could stay at the same hotel and they needed a rental car.

"Boy, you guys are living the dream with all the private jet travel," Liz said.

"Yes we are," Sam replied with a big smile.

"OK, I'll need to call Business Air and see what they might have available, and I'll also need to check the hotel and rental car. What time will you leave on Sunday?" Liz asked.

Sam and Joe looked at each other across the desk. Finally Joe replied, "Around 5:30 PM."

"What about the return trip?" Liz asked.

"Let's plan about 5:30 PM. Tuesday evening," Joe replied.

"OK, let me put all of this together and give you a call back when I have everything confirmed," said Liz.

"That's fine," Sam said and they disconnected.

Sam and Joe talked for a few minutes about the upcoming events at Aviation Dynamics and what they needed to get ready. They went through the list from the notes they had taken during the meeting with Connor and made assignments between themselves about who was going to do what. They decided that Joe would take the lead.

The phone rang and Sam looked at the phone number on the readout. It was Liz from the travel agency, so instead of speaker he picked up the phone and said, "Hello?" A short pause and then he said, "Oh, yes, how are you?" Another longer pause and finally, "Great, we appreciate you getting that all set up for us." Sam disconnected and looked at Joe. "That was Liz, from the travel agency; everything is set up and ready to go. She said to be at the Business Air terminal about 5:00 PM on Sunday. She will e-mail me the itinerary with hotel and rental car information. When I get it, I'll forward you a copy," said Sam.

"Thanks," Joe said.

They worked for a couple more hours on their charts and presentation data and finally decided it was time to go home. They hoped to spend some time with their families before leaving again.

On Sunday evening they both arrived at the Business Air terminal approximately 10 minutes before 5. They parked and went inside, checked in with the clerk, and sat down. Approximately 20 minutes later, they were boarding.

When they landed in Houston, the rental car was waiting and they made the drive to the hotel and checked in. So far, everything was clicking like clockwork, no hiccups, and no issues.

They met in the hotel lobby the next morning at 7:00 AM and made the drive to Aviation Dynamics. When they arrived, they pulled up to the gate. The guard walked to the car and looked in.

"Good morning, I'm Joe Pecci and this is Sam Henderson. We have an appointment with Mr. Brad Carter," Joe said.

"I remember who you are," he said, looking at his clipboard. "It says here, on the list, there was supposed to be four of you?" He was bending down to get a better view of the backseat.

"That's true," said Joe. "But two of our associates were unable to make the trip. Today it's just Sam and me."

"Do you remember where to park?" the guard asked.

"Yes!" They pulled into the same visitor parking stall they used before, got out, got their bags and went into the building. It was the same woman at the reception desk and she recognized Joe and Sam. She was watching the door closely, looking for that "other guy." When Joe announced that only he and Sam had made the trip, she looked visibly relieved. They signed in and got their badges. While they were signing in, the receptionist called Jim. A few minutes later, he was at the door to escort them in. Jim immediately asked where Connor and Becky were. Joe's only response was they had been unable to make this trip.

"So, it's just you two guys?" Jim asked in an almost disappointed voice.

"Yes, just us two guys," Joe responded.

"OK, follow me," said Jim. They headed back to the same conference room they had been in previously. When they entered, Brad, Zeke,

Marsha, and Hal were all there. Brad stood and asked, "Where are Connor and Becky?"

Joe again walked the cautious line for a response. "Well, Becky had a medical issue and she's been in the hospital."

"Oh my goodness, is she alright?" asked Brad showing concern in his voice.

"They were still running some tests to sort things out when we left, so we don't know for sure yet, but every indication so far says she should be fine," Joe said.

"Please, when you talk with Becky and Connor again, please pass on our very best wishes with the hope of a speedy recovery," said Brad.

"I'll do that," said Joe.

"Please have a seat," he said pointing to the chairs around the table. "There is coffee over there," pointing to the side table. Joe and Sam both took the opportunity to get a cup.

When they were all seated, Joe moved to the front of the room and plugged his flash drive into the computer. He moved through his files and found his presentation. He clicked the mouse a couple of times to bring his presentation up on the screen. He then started to speak. "After we left last time, we went back and had some discussions about what we want to do here. On the basis of those discussions and observations, the first thing we need to do is assemble a team," Joe said pointing to the outline on his chart. Joe noticed Zeke was looking around the room. Finally, Zeke spoke.

"I think we have everyone in the room right now that needs to be on that team," Zeke said.

"Not quite," Joe answered.

"What do you mean?" Zeke asked.

"I mean we don't have any of the subject matter experts from the floor," Joe replied.

"Why do we need them?" Zeke asked.

"Because they will be the most important part of what we want to do," Joe said.

Zeke looked puzzled, but didn't respond.

"So, this will be a combined effort of us and them?" Jim asked.

"It will be a combined effort, but not of us and them. Rather, it will be an effort that requires all of us," Joe said. "You see, we are doing a systems analysis. You, the management team, own the system and the workers work within that system. And each side will have a major contribution toward the success of the system," Joe explained.

"You're right," Jim said. "We do own the system and the workers just need to do what we tell them to do," he added sarcastically.

"They have been doing what you asked," Joe said. "And if the system was working like it should be, we all wouldn't be in this room right now. Am I right?" Joe asked.

There was silence. No one wanted to admit that Joe might be right. Finally, Brad spoke up. "OK, you might be right. So, what do we do about it?" he asked.

"The next thing we do is get our entire team assembled to continue the discussion," said Joe.

"Who is it you want from the floor?" Brad asked.

"I don't have any particular names, except one," Joe replied.

"Who is that?" asked Brad.

"We're going to need Nathan Brown," Joe said. "I'm hoping Nathan can suggest who some of the other team members might be."

Instantly, Zeke shot a look at Brad that suggested, "Oh no!" and quickly responded with "Well, we can't have Nathan, or anybody else, in here for very long. They all need to be on the floor helping to get helicopters out the door," said Zeke in a forceful voice.

There was an extended silence, then Brad spoke. "Zeke, the way I see it, Nathan, and the others, can't get any more aircraft out the door until we fix the issues that are stopping us from doing it right now. So, I might suggest we get Nathan in here, and whoever else is suggested, and get this process going," Brad said rather sternly.

Zeke looked at Jim and said, "Could you please go out to the floor and ask Nathan to come join us." Jim left his chair and exited the room.

A few minutes later, Jim returned with Nathan. When they entered the room, Nathan spotted Joe and Sam. He raised his hand and waved. Joe and Sam both waved back. No one else bothered to wave.

There was a bit of a worried look on Nathan's face, like he thought he might be in trouble for something. Brad invited Nathan to take a seat, which he did right next to Sam. Brad then explained what was going on and how they were putting together a team to explore some improvement possibilities. Nathan looked a little more relieved. Brad also asked Nathan if he could recommend some others to be on the team.

"Like who?" Nathan asked.

"What we're looking for are those people who would be most knowlededgeable about any issues on the floor," Joe said.

Nathan smiled and said, "That could be just about anybody. How many people do you want?"

"I think probably yourself and maybe five or six more," Joe said.

"Do you want them from all the shifts, or just day shift?" Nathan asked.

"For right now, just the day shift," Joe replied.

"OK, I think we should have two of the Green Belts from Olin Smith's crews and two from my crews. I also think we need to include Agnes Thompson from the supply room and her supply room assistant, Bette Carson. Do you want anyone from Hangar 2?" Nathan asked Joe.

"Not right now. We'll just focus on scheduled maintenance and Hangar 1 for the time being," Joe answered.

"Do you want me to go get them now?" Nathan asked.

"Not just yet," Joe replied. "OK, we now have five members from management and we will have seven members from the floor. Is everyone OK with these selections?" Joe asked.

Everyone shook their heads "yes," even though none of management team fully agreed. They still weren't sure why Joe thought it was necessary to include the hourly workers.

"OK," Brad said. "Jim, could you and Nathan return to the floor and get the people Nathan has mentioned."

"We sure can," said Jim.

Jim and Nathan left the room and walked back to the shop floor. Nathan talked with Olin Smith and explained what was going on and why they needed two of his people. Olin agreed and assigned his two Green Belts to go with Nathan. Jim walked over to the supply room and talked with Agnes and Bette. Jim and Agnes found someone to watch the supply room while they were gone. Nathan selected two more Green Belts from his other crews. About 10 minutes later, they returned to the conference room with the people. When the hourly workers walked into the room, you could see the apprehension on all of their faces. They came through the door and just huddled in a little group not sure what to do, where to sit, or why they were there. Brad stood and invited them all to take a seat around the table. There weren't enough seats around the table, so some sat in the chairs next to the wall.

"I'm glad you all could make it. I'm sure you've heard about what might be going on here, but let me give you the real scoop," Brad said. He explained some background about the urgency to win some of the upcoming contracts, and keep the current contracts they had, and why Sam and Joe were there now, and why all four of them had been there previously. He explained why they were putting this team together and what they needed to accomplish. Brad then went around the table and had each of the newest team members introduce themselves and what areas they were from. Joe was taking notes on the names and job duties.

"Hi, I'm Bobby Carson from Olin Smith's crew 2," said Bobby.

"I'm Agnes Thompson and I'm the supply room supervisor," she said.

"My name is Bette Green, and I help Agnes in the supply room," said Bette.

"I'm Fred Smith and I work for Nathan on crew 3," he said.

"My name is Jeff Hunt and I also work for Nathan," Jeff said.

"My name is Hector Gomez and I'm the team lead for Olin Smith's crew 3," said Hector.

The management team introduced themselves, as did Joe and Sam. When everyone was finished, Brad turned the time back over to Joe.

Joe quickly did a recap of what the team was going to do including the need for the system analysis, and system flow. "We are going to use a combination of Theory of Constraints, Lean, and Six Sigma methods, or what we call TLS. I'll give you a brief overview of each of those methods," Joe added.

Joe walked back up to the computer and pushed a button and his slide appeared on the screen.

Theory of Constraints (TOC)
The Five Focusing Steps
- **Step 1**—Identify the system's constraint(s).
- **Step 2**—Decide how to exploit the system's constraint(s).
- **Step 3**—Subordinate everything else to the above decision.
- **Step 4**—Elevate the system's constraint(s).
- **Step 5**—**Warning!** If in the previous steps a constraint has been broken, go back to Step 1, but do not allow inertia to cause a system's constraint.

"In our case, we are looking at the entire system to complete the scheduled maintenance repair of an aircraft," Joe said. Joe then went through each of the bullet points and supplied a definition.

"Step 1, identify the constraint. Every system has a constraint no matter what kind of a system it is. If a constraint did not already exist, then the system should be able to produce at infinite capacity. We need to find our constraint," Joe said.

"Step 2, decide how to exploit the constraint. Once we figure out what it is and where it is, we need to figure out how to get the most out of it. Remember: it is possible to find more than one constraint. Not all constraints are equal, so we need to be careful to select the right one first," Joe added.

"Step 3, subordinate everything else to the constraint. What that means is once we find the constraint and we understand that the constraint is the limiting factor for our system, then we need to slow down the other work to the same pace as the constraint. Subordinate the flow."

"Step 4, elevate the system's constraint. If the constraint has been exploited, but it still cannot produce at a level necessary to keep up with demand, then we have to elevate the capacity, which could mean more people, more machines, or whatever," Joe explained.

"Step 5 is a warning about when the constraint moves. If we fix a constraint, it will immediately move, or roll, to the next constraint in the system. In other words, it will roll to the next slowest operation in the system. When that happens, we go back to Step 1 and figure out where it rolled to, and follow the steps again," he explained.

When he finished, he asked the group, "Are there any questions?" No one raised their hand, so he moved on. Joe walked back to the computer and moved to the next slide and said, "Let me show you a simple example of a system's constraint. In this example, we have used a cross section of a piping diagram. You can see that our system is used to transport water from one end to the other. The cross section represents the different diameter of the pipe sizes in our system. The pipe diameters can be thought of as the available capacity at each section," Joe explained.

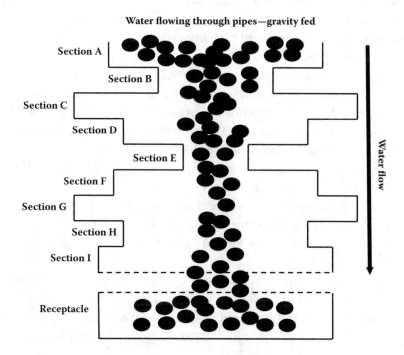

Joe pointed to the diagram on the screen and said, "Here is the simple flow through the system. In this system, can anyone tell me where the constraint is located?" He asked as he turned and faced the group. He was surprised to see almost every hand in the air. "Wow!" Joe thought to himself.

Joe pointed to Jim and asked, "Where is it?"

"Right there at Section E," Jim said, pointing with his finger.

"You mean right here?" Joe asked, using his laser pointer and pointing to Section E. "Why did you pick Section E?" Joe asked.

"Because it's the smallest pipe in the system and it restricts how much water can get through the system," Jim replied.

"What if your demand had increased and you needed to get more water through the system, what would you do?" Joe asked Jim, but basically threw the question to the group as well. Again, he was surprised because almost all of the hands were raised. This time Joe pointed to Hector Gomez and said "Yes?"

"You need to put a bigger pipe in Section E to get more water through," Hector said.

"OK, then how much bigger does the pipe need to be?" Joe asked pointing to Hector.

Hector paused and thought for a moment, "I guess that depends on how much more water you need," Hector said.

"We need a lot of water," Zeke said, trying to hide his statement under his breath, but everyone heard him anyway.

Joe looked at Zeke and smiled.

"I have a question for the group," Joe said. "Look at the example and specifically look at Section H. Suppose we had an improvement effort for Section H and we put in a pipe that was twice the size of the current pipe. My question is this: 'How much more water would we get through the system by making Section H twice as big?'" Joe asked.

Everyone was looking at the diagram, but so far no one had said anything. Finally, Zeke spoke up.

"Not a single drop more would get through," Zeke said.

Joe spun on his heels to face Zeke and said, "Wait a minute! We just made an improvement to the system and you're saying we get nothing in return for doing that?"

"That's what I'm saying. We wouldn't get any more water," Zeke said.

"Why not?" asked Joe.

"Because Section H didn't need a bigger pipe, Section E does. The only way we get more water is if Section E has a bigger pipe," said Zeke.

Nathan raised his hand and asked, "Mr. Pecci, it's getting close to lunchtime now and we were wondering if we could take a break and go to lunch?"

Joe looked at Sam. Sam was supposed to be watching the time and let Joe know when they were getting close to lunch. Sam had been so involved in Joe's presentation and the conversation he had forgotten to look. Sam quickly looked at his watch and nodded his head "yes," it was time for lunch.

Joe told the group, "Lunchtime it is. Make sure you are back in your seats at 11:30. We still have a lot of things to cover this afternoon."

The hourlies, and most of the management, headed toward the door. The hourlies went to the lunchroom and the others headed back to their offices. Everyone had cleared the room except Brad, Joe, and Sam. Brad got out of his chair and walked toward Joe.

"This is fascinating stuff Joe," he said with a smile. "I'm beginning to understand much better that we were looking in all the wrong places for improvements. When I think about it now, I realize that an improvement is not really an improvement unless it helps the entire system. What we were doing was hurting much more than it was helping. We were shooting at everything with the hope of hitting something," Brad said in a much softer voice. Joe just nodded his head up and down as if to say "Yes." Brad did the same head nod.

Brad excused himself and said he needed to go check for phone messages and his e-mails. When Brad walked out of the room, Joe and Sam walked over to refill their coffee cups. "So, how do you think it's going so far?" Joe asked.

"I think you're doing well," Sam said. "I think the message is starting to get across."

After lunch, they started the session again. Joe welcomed everyone back and said he wanted to talk about Lean and Six Sigma next. Joe walked over to the computer and pushed a button. His next slide popped onto the screen.

Lean manufacturing
- Popular improvement method
- Philosophy centered on the "Whole System" approach
- Focus on the existence and removal of non–value-added (NVA) activities
- Removal of "Waste" in the process or system
  - ✓ Take action to remove or significantly reduce waste
  - ✓ Facilitate flow of value through the system
- Save money wherever and whenever possible

"Most of you already know a lot of information about Lean because of the improvement programs you have been involved with in the past. The principles of Lean were derived from the Japanese manufacturing industry and first appeared in America circa 1988. The primary focus of Lean is looking at the entire system to find and remove non–value-added activities. Looking for and finding those steps that add no value to the end product," Joe said.

"Primarily, the outcome of Lean is to improve Quality, cut waste of all kinds, and reap the cost savings that go with it," Joe said walking back to the computer and moving to the next slide.

Lean manufacturing
- Linked to, and sometimes called, the Toyota Production System (TPS)
- Lean tool set
  - ✓ Value stream mapping (VSM)
  - ✓ SMED
  - ✓ Five S (5S)
  - ✓ Kanban (Pull system)
  - ✓ Poke yoke (Error proofing)
- Moderate use of control charting

"The primary tools for Lean are listed here," Joe said, pointing with his laser to the Lean tool set. "For most companies that decide to use Lean, there is also a moderate amount of control charts that they create," Joe said.

"Are you familiar with control charts?" he asked. Most everyone nodded their head "Yes."

"Next, I want to give a brief overview of Six Sigma," Joe said still standing at the computer, while the next slide appeared on the screen.

Six Sigma
- Identify and remove the cause of defects
- Minimize variability in manufacturing and business processes
- Uses primarily statistical method

"Six Sigma is used primarily to control and reduce the variation within processes. The hopeful end result is that the process can make exactly the same part or product each and every time, with minimal, or no variation," Joe said, flipping to the next slide. "As you can see," Joe pointed out, "there are some similarities and some differences between all three of these methods. What we hope to achieve is implementing the best from all three of these to achieve our objective. It's a concept we refer to as TLS," said Joe.

Six Sigma
The DMAIC project methodology has five phases:

1. Define the system, the voice of the customer, and their requirements.
2. Measure key aspects of the current process and collect relevant data.
3. Analyze the data to investigate and verify cause-and-effect relationships.
4. Improve or optimize the current process based on data analysis.
5. Control the future state process to ensure that any deviations from the target are corrected before they result in defects.

"Are there any questions?" Joe asked. Joe scanned the room. No one looked distressed or confused about what they had just heard, so he moved on. "OK then, the next task for all of us is to agree on an objective for this project," Joe said. He opened the question to the group.

Hal immediately raised his hand and said, "We need to make more money! That has to be our objective."

Joe knew Hal's answer was true. It was probably what the management team was thinking about, but he also knew it wasn't what the employees were thinking about. Joe knew that if on-time delivery improved, which was how the employees were measured, then it was also highly likely the revenues and profit would improve as well. He countered Hal's answer with, "That's a fair answer Hal, but what do we need to do to make more money?" Joe asked. His answer was directed to Hal, but open to the group.

"We need to get the repairs done faster," Hal quipped. Joe noticed Zeke and Jim had their fists clenched like they were ready to pound the table. Joe was remembering Connor's comment about not letting management take control of the meeting. Right now, it was looking like management against management. Joe was just getting ready to speak when Brad jumped in.

"I think you're right Hal," Brad said. Hal was beaming like a schoolboy who had just given the teacher the right answer. "However, I think we'll start making money again as soon as we fix our system. Improved revenue and profit will be the outcome of a well-functioning system." Hal's shoulders drooped a bit.

"That's a very good point Brad," Joe said, knowing he had just been saved from having to redirect the group.

"I think we need a system that allows us to deliver the aircraft on, or ahead, of the scheduled due date," Brad said. "If that were in place, then everything else would fall into place," Brad replied as if he were thinking out loud.

"Are there any other ideas from anybody else?" Joe said scanning the group. Nathan raised his hand. "Yes?" said Joe pointing to Nathan.

"I think Mr. Carter is right about the system. If we could just get the system to work for us, and not against us, we could do much better," Nathan said. "As a supervisor, I honestly think we spend way too much time trying to figure out how to get around the system, and all the rules that go with it, than we actually do working in the system," he added.

"We have to follow the rules!" Jim exclaimed in a raised voice.

"OK!" said Joe. "Before we go down that path, let's first establish what we think our objective, or goal, needs to be. We need to first set the direction we want to go, and then we'll figure out how to get there and apply the velocity. We've already had some discussion for making money, on-time delivery, and fixing the system. Is there anything else?" Joe asked the group. One of the team leads from Olin Smith's group, Bobby Carson, kept his hand near his side and only raised his hand as high as his head. "Yes?" Joe said pointing to him.

"I think it's all three of those things," he said in a very shy voice.

"What do you mean all three?" Jim asked from across the room.

Bobby stiffened his back and sat up in his chair and said, "All three of them are connected. We can't have one of them without having the other two," he said. "Each one of them is not separated from the other. What I mean is if we have a good system, then the aircraft are more likely to be on time. And if we can deliver them on time and faster, then the business will start making money," he explained.

"That's exactly right!" said Joe. "There is definitely a codependency between them. So, which one should be our objective, or goal?" Joe asked again.

"I think we need to focus on the on-time delivery," Zeke said as Jim shook his head "yes" as did Nathan and some of the other hourlies. "We need a system that allows us to deliver on time, every time," he reiterated.

"Good point," said Joe pointing to Zeke. "Right now, the system is not generating the results that you want it to. So, we need to look at the system and figure out which parts to change to get the results that you want. Not everything needs to be changed or fixed at the same time, so we'll focus our efforts on finding the best leverage points to get the most from the system. Management owns the system and they have the responsibility, and authority, to change the system," Joe said.

"What part do we change?" Jim asked.

"Jim, you've asked the very first question we all want to answer. There are basically three questions we want to ask, and answer, as we go through this exercise. The first question is: 'What do we change?' The second question is: 'What do we change to?' And, the third question is: 'How do we cause the change to happen?'" Joe explained.

"So, you're talking about the entire scheduled maintenance system?" Brad asked.

"For now, yes I am," Joe replied. "I believe there are things we will learn during this project that will also apply to the unscheduled maintenance hangar. But for now, we need to be focused on the scheduled maintenance side. Your system, like most systems, is made up of several subsystems, including procurement, parts inventory, suppliers and vendors for out-of-house repairs, scheduling, policies and procedures, and a host of other subsystems," Joe explained in more detail.

Zeke jumped in, "Policies and procedures?" he asked with a puzzled look on his face.

"Yes!" Joe said. "The policies and procedures are the established rules for how the system should work. We often refer to them as the rules, training, and measures of the system or just R-T-M's. It's the combination of rules, training, and measures for all of the subsystems that allow the overall system to function properly, or not function properly," said Joe.

"And you think we might have bad policies and procedures?" Brad asked.

"Think about the policy for checking tools in and out," Joe said.

Brad nodded his head and conceded, "Enough said."

"I think it will be a combination of several things," Joe replied. "Somewhere in your system you have a constraint, most likely one of the subsystems. It's because of the constraint that the overall system can only produce at a level that is equal to, or less than, what the constraint will allow. That's exactly why we want to include the shop floor folks on our team to help expose what the constraint really is," he explained.

"And what happens when we find this constraint?" Jim asked.

"We fix it!" Joe answered.

Sam was the only one smiling, thinking back to when he had first heard a similar story at Barton and thinking to himself, "This is nuts!" Everyone else in the room was pondering what they were hearing.

"What happens when we fix this constraint?" Brad asked. "It seems like it will just move to another location and become a problem again."

"Exactly!" Joe exclaimed. "The term we use is the constraint has 'rolled' to a new location. When it does roll, it means something else in the system is now slowing it down. Just like the pipe size in the diagram. When the new location is identified, then we fix that one!" said Joe.

Brad smiled and said, "I think I'm beginning to understand what you are trying to accomplish here. It's not something I've thought about in the past, but I can definitely see some merit to what you're talking about," and then he smiled even more.

"That's good!" said Joe.

"So, what do we do next?" Brad asked.

"We still need to define the objective," Joe said.

"I thought we already had," Brad answered.

"OK, what do we want it to be?" Joe asked.

Jim jumped in, "I thought we were going to make a better system for on-time delivery."

Joe walked to the whiteboard and wrote: "Better on-time delivery of SM aircraft."

"Wait a minute," said Zeke. "Let's say 98% on-time delivery of SM aircraft instead. That way, we have an actual number to measure our efforts against and see if we get better or not," he added.

Joe scanned the group for any objections or additional ideas. There were none. In fact, most of the group was nodding their heads signaling "Yes." Joe erased what he had on the whiteboard and wrote: "98% on-time delivery of SM aircraft." He turned and faced the group and asked, "Is everyone in agreement?" Everyone nodded and said "Yes." "OK," Joe said, "then 98% it is."

Nathan spoke up with a statement aimed at informing the group. "Just so everyone understands, there will need to be some major effort and changes to achieve a number anywhere close to that." Joe thought about Nathan's comment and surmised he was setting up an escape clause. He didn't want management to say, "OK, 98% is the new number—go do it!"

"Nathan is right," Joe said. "This will be a collaborative effort from everyone in this room, as well as some other players as well," Joe added to reinforce the point.

"I think we are all committed to make this work," said Zeke as he looked to Brad for reassurance of his statement.

Brad was nodding his head and said, "We need to make this work and we'll do whatever is needed to make sure that it happens." Nathan was satisfied with Brad's response.

Joe jumped back in to direct the group to the next task. "OK, with the objective defined, now we want to spend some time doing an Interference

Diagram and find those obstacles that stand in the way of being able to achieve 98%."

Nathan spoke up again. "Mr. Pecci, before we start that activity, you need to know that everyone from the floor needs to get back out on the floor right now."

"Why?" Zeke asked.

"Well, because it's almost 2:30 PM and everyone needs to get their tools inventoried and accounted for, so they can turn them in to supply before the end of shift. In fact, Agnes and Bette need to be back in the supply room right now to start receiving the toolboxes and getting ready to issue them to second shift," he added emphatically.

"How come it takes an hour to get this done?" Zeke asked.

"Because we have a minimum of 36 toolboxes to sign in, and 36 tool-boxes to sign out," Nathan said. "It takes that much time to stay within the mandates of the Tool Transfer policy," he explained as he looked Zeke squarely in the eyes.

Zeke looked at Jim and said, "OK, then go get it done."

The hourlies started to get up from their chairs when Joe spoke. "Make sure you are back in the conference room at 7:00 AM tomorrow. We'll start earlier tomorrow, and remember, none of you need to sign out a toolbox tomorrow, just be here at 7:00 AM," said Joe.

The hourlies left the room and Joe and Sam were sitting with the management team. Brad let out a sigh and said, "I think we just found our first obstacle."

"I think we did too," said Joe. "And, tomorrow we'll see how many more we can find." Everyone else was quiet. One by one they left the room, except for Zeke and Jim.

Sam and Joe gathered up their stuff and walked out to the front desk with Zeke and Jim. Zeke looked to Joe and Sam and said, "I know we were doing sign in and sign out for tool accountability and I thought it was working. What I didn't know was how long it actually takes every day to get it done." Jim reminded Zeke that it actually happens three times a day at each shift change. Zeke rubbed his forehead with both hands and let out an audible sigh.

Joe and Sam signed out and drove back to the hotel.

"It was an interesting day," Sam said.

"It was indeed," answered Joe. He was feeling tired after a long day in front of the group.

"Do we want to call Connor and give him an update?" Sam asked.

"Yes, I was planning on giving him a call when I got back to the hotel," Joe answered.

When they reached the hotel, they went in and walked toward the elevators. Sam said, "I'll just meet you in the lobby at about 6:15."

"I'll be there," said Joe.

10

MRO Strategy—Day 2: Morning

Sam was in the lobby at 6:10 AM. Joe wasn't there yet. As Sam stood there, he was watching the elevator doors. A couple of minutes later, Joe walked out and headed toward him. When he got closer, Sam asked, "Did you talk to Connor last night?"

"I did," said Joe. "I gave him the *Reader's Digest* version of what happened yesterday."

"And what did he say?" Sam asked.

"Connor just listened and asked a few questions," Joe replied.

"Did he mention anything about Becky?" Sam asked.

"He did," said Joe. "He said they were home now and Becky seemed to be doing quite well."

They walked through the front door of the hotel and started to walk toward the car. Sam said, "When I talked with my wife last night, she said she thought Becky was home from the hospital, and she would call, or go over later today, and see how things were going."

When they got to the car, Joe slid into the driver's seat and they made the 35-minute drive to Aviation Dynamics. At the gate, the guard recognized them and just waved them through. They parked and went into the lobby. This time, Jim was waiting for them in the lobby. "Good morning," Jim said, standing by the reception counter.

"Good morning," they both said almost in unison.

"Just sign in and we'll be ready to go," Jim said.

They both signed in and got their badges out of their bags. Jim navigated them back to the conference room. It was 6:55 AM and when they entered the conference room, everyone else was already there.

"Wow!" Sam thought to himself, "We're early and we're also the last ones here."

Everyone was engaged in small group talk. Brad raised his hand and waved to Joe and Sam, not to interrupt the group he was in. Sam and Joe walked over and got some coffee. When they had their coffee, Joe walked up to the computer at the front of the room and inserted his flash drive, pushed a few buttons, and took a deep breath. He was ready to go.

He walked away from the computer and asked everyone to take their seats and then he addressed everyone in the room. "Good morning to all of you. I'm glad everyone is here and ready to go. We have a lot to do today, so we should get started." Joe recapped yesterday's events and where they had ended up. "So, today we want to start by seeing if we can define what the obstacles are that are keeping us from achieving our goal of '98% on-time delivery for scheduled maintenance (SM).'"

Joe walked to the long whiteboard at the side of the room and drew a circle. Inside of the circle he wrote: "98% on-time delivery of SM aircraft."

Interference diagram goal

"This was the goal we all decided on yesterday," he said pointing with his laser to the circle. "Does everyone still agree this is what we want to do?" Joe asked. Everyone was nodding their heads "Yes."

"OK, the purpose of this next exercise is to see if we can define the obstacles that stand in the way of achieving this goal, or those reasons *why* we can't achieve this goal right now. What we are looking for are those things that steal time away from being able to do this," Joe said.

Zeke immediately raised his hand and said, "One of the reasons is our Tool Transfer policy. After everyone left yesterday, Jim and I went to the supply room to watch what was going on. Sure enough, there were two lines. One line trying to turn in tools and the other line trying to sign them out," he said. "Honestly, I couldn't believe what I was seeing. I guess we'd never taken the time before to look and see what was really going on," he said looking at Jim. "Jim and I talked to a few of the mechanics and asked how much time they were spending in line. Some were hesitant to answer until we told them no one was going to get in trouble, we just wanted to know how much time it took. When we had gathered some information, Jim and I went back to my office and ran some numbers," Zeke said.

"What did you find out from your numbers analysis?" Joe asked.

"Frankly, I was shocked," Zeke said. "Just looking at the informal data we collected was a huge wake-up call for me. Jim pointed out to me that this was happening at both ends of each shift. A new shift coming on was waiting approximately 30 to 45 minutes to get a toolbox. When the same shift was ready to leave, it took another 60 to 70 minutes to inventory and turn in all of the toolboxes. The worst-case scenario would equal approximately 2 hours to handle the toolboxes every 8-hour shift. That's 25% of the total time wasted!" Zeke exclaimed. "Plus, it made me think that there might be other policies that are slowing us down as well," Zeke added. "When I got thinking about it, I realized that the negative effects from the policy were all self-inflicted. We were doing this to ourselves and thinking it was a good idea!" Zeke exclaimed.

Joe was thinking to himself that this was great investigative work that Zeke and Jim had done. Joe walked up to the whiteboard and added a column next to the circle. He also added a square box with an arrow pointing from the circle out to the box.

Interference #1

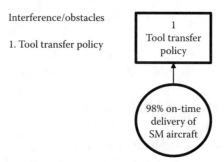

Joe turned from the whiteboard and asked the group, "What else can you think of?"

Hector Gomez raised his hand and said, "Well, there are a lot of times when we are missing parts to finish a job. We order them, but sometimes we have to wait a long time to get them," he added.

Marsha, from procurement, quickly jumped in. "Remember," she said, "we had a mandate from corporate to cut our inventory cost, which we did. Because of the new budgets we were given, we don't always have enough money in each month to buy the necessary parts," she reminded everyone in her defense.

"I understand that," said Hector. "I'm just saying it slows us down when we don't have the parts."

Nathan jumped in and said, "We also have a policy that states that the Unscheduled Maintenance hangar gets the parts first. Sometimes, when we check inventory, it might say a part is there, but before we can go and get it, Unscheduled Maintenance already has it. It just means we have to wait for the next batch of parts to come in and hope we get one," Nathan added.

"And that is an internal policy," Marsha said looking at Zeke and Jim.

Joe quickly jumped in before an argument ensued between Marsha, Zeke, and Jim. "So, parts availability seems to be an issue," he said as he walked toward the whiteboard to write it down.

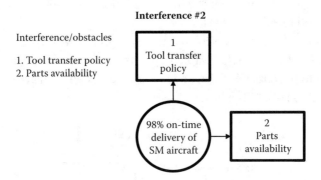

"What else can you think of?" Joe asked.

Brad was looking at the whiteboard and thinking to himself, "Holy cow! It's another policy issue."

Nathan raised his hand and started to speak, "Scheduling can be a problem."

"How is scheduling a problem?" Joe asked.

"Well, sometimes, the work bay schedules overlap each other and we can be waiting for the same resources at the same time," Nathan said. "What I mean is, the resources that aren't actually part of the work bay crew, like avionics and hydraulics, and some of the other outside functions. It can also happen with the special equipment. It happens frequently that each work bay schedule is bumping heads with another schedule. The schedules aren't synchronized; they are totally independent of each other. What we don't seem to have is a master schedule that takes into consideration all of the work being done. It ends up that each work crew has to fight to maintain their own schedule and stay on time, at least the best they can," Nathan added.

"That's true," added Bobby Carson. "Sometimes, it feels like were going in six different directions at once. When that happens, we have to get the team leads and supervisors together to figure which crew gets the resource first. It really does take a lot of time to figure it out," he added.

"And even when we think we have it figured out, it can change quickly," added Hector.

"OK," said Joe, "what I'm hearing is 'No master scheduling mechanism,' is that right?" Joe asked.

"That's as good as any other way to say it," said Nathan.

Joe walked back to the whiteboard and wrote it down.

Interference #3

Interference/obstacles

1. Tool transfer policy
2. Parts availability
3. No master scheduling mechanism

```
                    ┌─────────────┐
                    │      1      │
                    │ Tool transfer│
                    │   policy    │
                    └─────────────┘
                           ▲
                    ╭──────────────╮          ┌─────────────┐
                    │  98% on-time │          │      2      │
                    │  delivery of │ ───────► │    Parts    │
                    │  SM aircraft │          │ availability│
                    ╰──────────────╯          └─────────────┘
                           │
                           ▼
                    ┌─────────────┐
                    │      3      │
                    │  No master  │
                    │  scheduling │
                    │  mechanism  │
                    └─────────────┘
```

"OK, what else can you think of that might be stealing the time from on-time delivery?" Joe asked.

Zeke was thinking, "Good grief, isn't that enough?" He was trying to imagine in his mind all of the time wasted doing non–value-added tasks. Why hadn't he seen all of this before now? he wondered.

Fred Smith raised his hand and Joe pointed to him. "I was thinking about work task inspections," Fred said.

"In what way?" Joe asked.

"Well, sometimes, when we finish a work package on the schedule and we've removed or repaired or replaced a part, and we put it back together, it needs to be inspected by a TI before we can move on," Fred explained.

"What is a TI?" Joe asked.

"That's a Technical Inspector," Fred said. "They have to inspect and approve, and sign off the finished work before we can move on to the next task. It's part of maintaining the aircraft repair logbook and is required by the Federal Aviation Administration," he said.

"So, what happens with the TIs?" Joe asked.

"Sometimes, we can finish a task and it's near, or at the end of a shift, but the TI isn't always available to inspect and sign off what we just finished before the shift is over. The TIs can be in another work bay looking at something else. If the TI doesn't make it back before the end of shift, then the mechanic that did the work might not be there anymore. The team lead is aware of what's happening and they pass the information to the incoming crew. Sometimes, the TIs for the incoming crew won't accept the work because the incoming crew didn't do the work, or the TI didn't see them do it, so he won't sign off. Actually, the TI has a valid point because it's his job on the line, if something goes wrong. Anyway, most times, we have to tear it down and do it again, so the TI will sign it off. It just amounts to a lot of rework, which costs us time on our schedule," Fred said.

Joe noticed some of the others around the room nodding their heads in agreement.

"I mean it's not a big thing, but it does happen, and the rework can cost us a lot of time," Fred reiterated.

Joe walked back to the whiteboard and updated the Interference Diagram.

Interference #4

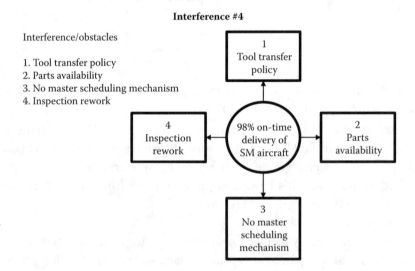

Interference/obstacles

1. Tool transfer policy
2. Parts availability
3. No master scheduling mechanism
4. Inspection rework

Joe faced the group. "We're finding some good things here. What else can you think of?" he asked.

Hector raised his hand again and Joe pointed to him. "Sometimes, we have problems with the paperwork," said Hector.

"How so?" Joe asked.

"Well, paperwork is a very important part of what we do. We have to keep signed documents," Hector said. "Sometimes, we have to go search for the paperwork so we can get it all in one place, which is usually the logbook," he added.

"Why is it hard to find?" Joe asked.

"It's not that it's hard to find, it's just that it's in the wrong place and it's time consuming to go find it. The papers we need are usually someplace else, like in avionics, or hydraulics, or some other place. Sometimes, it's even in flight test where they go through the checklist and find things, or if it passes flight test, we need a record of that," Hector said.

"So, how much time in a day might you spend looking for the paper-work?" Joe asked.

"It can take as much as an hour and a half, by the time you walk to all of the locations and look for it," Hector pointed out. "We can't continue working until the paperwork is complete. All the paperwork has to be there to complete the job," he explained.

Joe walked to the whiteboard and added the paperwork issues.

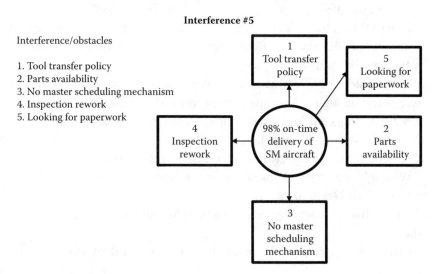

Interference #5

Interference/obstacles

1. Tool transfer policy
2. Parts availability
3. No master scheduling mechanism
4. Inspection rework
5. Looking for paperwork

Joe thought it was odd, but Sam had raised his hand. At first, he thought Sam was reminding him that it was close to lunchtime. Joe quickly looked at his watch—it wasn't. He pointed to Sam.

"What about lunchtime and breaks?" Sam asked.

"Whoa…. Wait a minute," Nathan was quick to reply. "Our collective bargaining agreement allows everyone to get a 30-minute lunch break and two 15-minute breaks. One break in the morning and one break in the afternoon," Nathan added.

"I realize that," said Sam. "But, I don't think your collective bargaining agreement requires everyone to take lunch, or go on break at exactly the same time, does it?" Sam asked directing his question to Nathan.

"No, it doesn't," Nathan replied. "What are you getting at?" Nathan asked.

"What I'm getting at," said Sam, "is that between lunch and breaks, that equals an hour a day, and that's an hour that repair work stops if everyone goes at the same time," Sam explained.

"That's true!" Nathan said.

"I think everyone deserves all of their breaks," Sam said. "And, I'm not suggesting you give them up. What I am asking is does everyone need to take their lunch and breaks at the same time?"

Nathan thought for a moment and then responded. "So, you're suggesting some kind of staggered schedule for lunch and breaks?"

"Exactly!" said Sam. "Perhaps half the work crew goes at one time and the other half goes at a later time. That way there is always work going on for the repairs," Sam added.

"That could work," Nathan said. "We've always had complaints that there aren't enough microwaves in the break room for everyone to use anyway. A staggered lunch could help solve that problem, as well. I see what you're saying," he added.

"So, would that be something to consider?" asked Sam.

"We might have to work out some details, but yes, I think we could consider that," said Nathan.

"So, is this an obstacle, or do we have it worked out already?" Joe asked.

"I think you better put it on the list until it's worked out," Nathan said.

Joe walked over to the whiteboard and added lunch and breaks to the Interference Diagram.

Interference #6

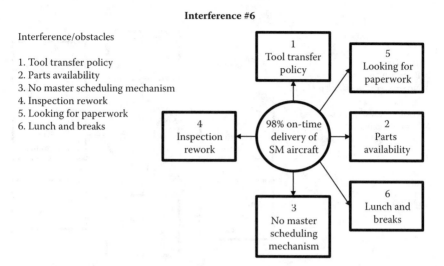

Interference/obstacles

1. Tool transfer policy
2. Parts availability
3. No master scheduling mechanism
4. Inspection rework
5. Looking for paperwork
6. Lunch and breaks

"OK, is there anything else?" Joe asked.

Everyone sat for a moment looking at the Interference Diagram. Finally, Jeff Hunt raised his hand. Joe made a mental note that this was the first time Jeff had raised his hand and quickly pointed to Jeff for his input.

"It's not a big thing, but if we are looking for more time, then this might apply," Jeff said.

"What is it?" asked Sam.

"Well, sometimes, it's the common stock parts or bench stock as some call it. There are common parts such as nut, bolts, screws and washers, and some other things that we sometimes need on every job. We can usually find the parts, but we always have to go back to the supply room, or even over to Hangar 2 to get them, and that takes time," Jeff said.

Again, Marsha was quick to jump in. "That's because of the policy for accountability and foreign object debris (FOD) that we have in place. We want to be able to track all of the issued parts to help control the costs and reduce the FOD," Marsha said.

"I know that," Jeff said, "it just takes time to walk back and forth to the supply room every time we need a screw, or a bolt, or a washer. If we just had the bench stock available on the floor or even in the work bays, it could save some time. If we can't do that, it's probably OK, but if we can do it, there is time to be gained," Jeff finished.

"OK, does everyone agree we should look into this issue?" Joe asked. A majority seemed to nod their heads "yes," so Joe walked over and added it to the Interference Diagram.

Interference #7

Interference/obstacles

1. Tool transfer policy
2. Parts availability
3. No master scheduling mechanism
4. Inspection rework
5. Looking for paperwork
6. Lunch and breaks
7. Bench stock/common stock

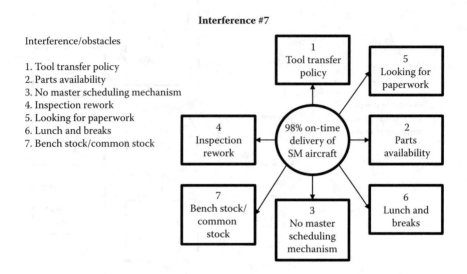

When Joe had finished updating the information, he turned to the group. He noticed Sam had his hand up and was mouthing "10 minutes to lunchtime." Joe looked at his watch, and sure enough it was 10 minutes to 11. It seemed they had worked right through the morning break time and no one had said a thing.

"OK, we've got approximately 10 minutes before lunch, so let's do a quick review on where we are. We've spent the morning discovering things that steal time away from our goal," said Joe. "As you can see," he said, pointing with his laser, "we have a good list of items so far. It also appears that many of these issues are located in different subsystems. For example, bench stock and parts availability are from the procurement system. No master scheduling and inspection rework are associated with the operations scheduling system. The Tool Transfer policy and lunch breaks come from the policies currently in place," Joe added. "I think we have a good mix from several subsystems," Joe continued, "so right after lunch, I'd like to take this list and start building the Intermediate Objectives map, or IO map as we call it. If you remember yesterday's discussion, I told you that, when doing a good systems analysis, it would be very possible to find more than one constraint. What we are finding here are some issues in the subsystems that are having a negative effect on the whole system. Here they are," he said pointing with his laser. "What we are trying to do is first look at the overall system and then isolate the interferences. Each of these interferences is not equal in the amount of time to correct it, or the impact it will have if we do correct it. And they seem to reside in several subsystems of the overall system. But, this list is certainly a good place to start. If you look at the list, we have identified seven interferences. My question to you is, if we want to make real system improvement, which interference do we start with?" Joe asked.

Everyone was looking at the Interference Diagram, but no one said anything. After a minute, Joe answered the question for the group. "Exactly! Just looking at the list now, we have no idea where to begin! So, right after lunch, we'll start aligning the intermediate objectives in the intrinsic order they need to be accomplished," he explained.

"See you after lunch and please be back on time. We still have a lot to accomplish before day's end," Joe said.

Everyone started to shuffle out of the conference room, everyone except Brad that is. He was still sitting at the table with his note pad in front of him writing some things down.

"You know," Brad said, "most of the interferences we have discussed so far are self-inflicted. We thought we were doing the right thing. However, most of these things were only for short-term gains, and the short-term benefit has long since passed," Brad added.

Neither Joe or Sam said anything. They just let Brad continue to ponder his thoughts.

"We dug a hole and we just kept digging it deeper. We just drank all the water from the bottle, as your friend Connor pointed out the last time he was here. I am a little embarrassed that I didn't see what was happening before now," Brad added.

Joe finally spoke. "There is nothing to be embarrassed about. In fact, if it makes you feel any better, the actions you took are what most people would do. It seems to be the most common actions that most organizations revert to when trying to solve a problem. These actions are all aimed at trying to save money. None of them are focused on making money!" Joe exclaimed.

"Look at this," Brad said sliding his note pad around so they could both see what he had been writing. "I've been adding up the numbers from some of the informal data we've been talking about today. The tool policy, inspection and rework, scheduling lag time, and some others, I'm guessing the total impact is approximately 60% of 8 hours spent doing non–value-added exercises and tasks. Things we thought were important, but really have no relevance at all, are actually slowing us down," he said.

"I'm just hoping you guys can help us fill in this hole and get us out of trouble," Brad said. "Prime the pump as Connor would say," he added.

"When you get out of this hole, it won't be because of anything Sam or I did, it will be because of you and your people," Joe said. "You have good people on your team, including the hourlies. All of these people just want to do the right thing, and previously the list they had to choose from was limited. If Sam and I do anything at all, it will be to get you focused on the issues that provide the most leverage," Joe added.

Brad just nodded his head and said, "I need to go check phone messages and e-mails." He walked out of the room.

11

MRO Strategy—Day 2: Afternoon

Everyone returned from lunch on time and Joe was at the front of the room. He welcomed everyone back and then said, "This afternoon we want to revisit the list of the interferences that we came up with this morning. What we want to do is see if we can convert the interferences into intermediate objectives, or IOs as we call them. The IO becomes the action that we want to have in place in order to overcome the negative effects of the interference that currently exists," he said.

Joe walked over to the whiteboard. He had already listed the interferences on a new section and pointed with his laser. "This is the list we want to review," Joe said.

Interferences

Interference/obstacles	Intermediate objectives/injections
1. Tool transfer policy	
2. Parts availability	
3. No master scheduling mechanism	
4. Inspection rework	
5. Looking for paperwork	
6. Lunch and breaks	
7. Bench stock/common stock	

Joe turned and faced the group. "We've had a good discussion already about the interference of some policies, especially the tool policy. Now, we want to find an IO that would eliminate or reduce the negative effects of the tool policy and find a different way to do it," Joe explained to the group.

Both Zeke and Jim raised their hands, so Joe pointed to Jim for his response.

"We need to review that policy and see how we can change it to accomplish what we need and take much less time," Jim said.

Joe was nodding his head in agreement.

Zeke jumped in and said, "Yes, we need to meet our requirements for foreign object debris (FOD) and accountability, but do it in a different way."

"I agree," said Joe. "So, let's summarize what both of you have said. What if we say, 'Tool policy reviewed and updated'?" Joe asked. He added, "We don't need all of the detail just yet, only the overall IO statement."

Everyone agreed and Joe updated the whiteboard.

Injection #1

Interference/obstacles	Intermediate objectives/injections
1. Tool transfer policy	1. Tool policy reviewed and updated
2. Parts availability	
3. No master scheduling mechanism	
4. Inspection rework	
5. Looking for paperwork	
6. Lunch and breaks	
7. Bench stock/common stock	

"OK, the next one is parts availability," Joe said. "This one might be a bit trickier to nail down," he added.

Nathan raised his hand and said, "Ideally, we need to have all the parts available for each maintenance, repair, and overhaul (MRO) in a work bay."

"All of the parts?" Joe asked.

"Well, not all of them, but we do need the parts for whatever task we are working and the part has to be available to complete that task," Nathan added.

Jim raised his hand and said, "We probably need to review the policy on this one as well. We've created a big problem with how we do it now."

Marsha was nodding her head that she agreed. "We might have a tough time changing that policy. After all, it did come from corporate," she said.

Brad spoke up, "Leave the corporate stuff to Hal and me. We'll work that end of it."

Hal looked at Brad with a surprised look on his face. "How are we going to do that?" Hal asked.

"We'll figure it out," said Brad.

"OK," Joe said. "I think this IO should read 'Fully kitted parts for each work task.' Does anyone disagree?" he asked and no one disagreed so he walked to the whiteboard and added it.

Injection #2

Interference/obstacles	Intermediate objectives/injections
1. Tool transfer policy	1. Review/update tool policy
2. Parts availability	2. Fully kitted parts for each work task
3. No master scheduling mechanism	
4. Inspection rework	
5. Looking for paperwork	
6. Lunch and breaks	
7. Bench stock/common stock	

"Number three," said Joe. "No master scheduling mechanism."

Nathan was first again. "We need to integrate the work bay schedules into a master schedule, especially where some of the outside resources are concerned."

"What do you mean by outside resources?" Joe asked.

"You know, things like the avionics and hydraulics groups, and possibly the Return To Vendor (RTV) parts. It's all of those activities that are outside of the work crew area. We need a way to schedule those groups and know when the RTV parts might be returned," he added.

"The RTV parts might be a problem," Marsha said. "They can vary a lot from one week to the next, whenever we send an order in," she added.

Without wanting to get too far into the details just yet, Joe quickly added, "OK, what I'm hearing is we need an integrated scheduling system. Is that right?" he asked. Everyone nodded "Yes," so Joe updated the whiteboard.

Injection #3

Interference/obstacles	Intermediate objectives/injections
1. Tool transfer policy	1. Review/update tool policy
2. Parts availability	2. Fully kitted parts for each work task
3. No master scheduling mechanism	3. Robust scheduling system
4. Inspection rework	
5. Looking for paperwork	
6. Lunch and breaks	
7. Bench stock/common stock	

Joe pointed to the whiteboard and said, "Inspection rework."

Hector spoke. "That might be a double-edged sword. It might be scheduling and it might be just better coordination at shift change," he explained.

"I think it's just better coordination at shift change," said Bobby.

"A process for shift change inspections?" asked Joe.

"That could work," said Hector.

Joe updated the whiteboard again with the latest inputs.

Injection #4

Interference/obstacles	Intermediate objectives/injections
1. Tool transfer policy	1. Review/update tool policy
2. Parts availability	2. Fully kitted parts for each work task
3. No master scheduling mechanism	3. Robust scheduling system
4. Inspection rework	4. A process for shift change inspections
5. Looking for paperwork	
6. Lunch and breaks	
7. Bench stock/common stock	

"Number five, looking for paperwork," Joe said, pointing to the list with his laser.

"I think it's just a procedural issue," said Hector. "We just don't have a good defined procedure for how the paperwork should keep up with the job, so we spend a lot of time looking for it," he added.

"That's true," added Nathan. "Sometimes, the missing paperwork can slow a completed job by 2 or 3 days just trying to round up all of the documents for the logs. We need everything to be in one place to be able to close it out and call it done," he added.

"So, what must be in place for the paperwork not to be a problem anymore?" asked Joe.

Hector and Nathan both looked at each other and semi-shrugged their shoulders. Finally, Nathan said, "I guess some way for the paperwork to keep up with the completed tasks. It's really just a matter of keeping the logbook and documents with the job and keep them updated," he added.

"How about keeping the logbook updated, current, and with the job?" Hector said.

"You guys are the experts," Joe said. "Does anyone disagree?" Joe asked. No one disagreed, so Joe updated the whiteboard.

Injection #5

Interference/obstacles	Intermediate objectives/injections
1. Tool transfer policy	1. Review/update tool policy
2. Parts availability	2. Fully kitted parts for each work task
3. No master scheduling mechanism	3. Robust scheduling system
4. Inspection rework	4. A process for shift change inspections
5. Looking for paperwork	5. Log book updated and current
6. Lunch and breaks	
7. Bench stock/common stock	

"Next is the lunch and breaks," Joe said. "We already had a short discussion on this one, but you wanted to look at it further. Have you done that?" Joe asked.

"This is probably just a matter of developing a new process and procedure," said Nathan. "Figuring out how to divide the crews and setting up the new schedule and posting them, so that everyone knows how it works," he added.

"OK!" said Joe, turning back to the whiteboard.

Injection #6

Interference/obstacles	Intermediate objectives/injections
1. Tool transfer policy	1. Review/update tool policy
2. Parts availability	2. Fully kitted parts for each work task
3. No master scheduling mechanism	3. Robust scheduling system
4. Inspection rework	4. A process for shift change inspections
5. Looking for paperwork	5. Log book updated and current
6. Lunch and breaks	6. Updated lunch and breaks procedure
7. Bench stock/common stock	

"And, finally number seven, Bench Stock/Common Stock," Joe said.

Bobby raised his hand and spoke, "We just need to move the bench stock out to the shop floor. It just needs to be more accessible for use, without having to walk back and forth to the supply room or to the other hangar to get it," Bobby said.

Agnes, from the supply room, jumped in the conversation. "We might not be able to move it all out to the floor, but I think we can move most of the items. We have some extra bins in supply that might work just fine for that," she added.

Joe turned to the whiteboard and updated the list

Injection #7

Interference/obstacles	Intermediate objectives/injections
1. Tool transfer policy	1. Review/update tool policy
2. Parts availability	2. Fully kitted parts for each work task
3. No master scheduling mechanism	3. Robust scheduling system
4. Inspection rework	4. A process for shift change inspections
5. Looking for paperwork	5. Log book updated and current
6. Lunch and breaks	6. Updated lunch and breaks procedure
7. Bench stock/common stock	7. Move bench/common stock to the floor

Joe backed away from the whiteboard and looked at it. "OK, it looks like we have a starting point for the IO map," Joe said. "What we'll do now is start building the IO map. To do that, we'll start with our already defined objective. In other words, the defined objective is the end result of our action that we want to end up with when everything has been completed. If you look at the IOs list right now, the question may be going through your head, 'Where do we start?'" Joe said. "Answering that question is the purpose of the IO map. When we build the IO map, we will be using necessity-based logic, to logically connect the IOs together and determine the intrinsic order to complete these tasks to achieve the desired objective," Joe added. He was scanning the group for those who might have a question. He didn't see any hands or confused looks, so he continued. "Even with the list of IOs that we have, it's also very possible we don't have all of them yet. As we work to build the IO map, it is possible we might surface more IOs, but this list is certainly a good place to start." Joe moved to a clean section of the whiteboard and took a few minutes to draw the structure of the IO map.

Interferences IO map

	100 98% on-time delivery of SM aircraft
Objective	

In order to have ...

I must have ...

**Critical
success
factors**

In order to have ...

I must have ...

**Necessary
conditions**

When Joe finished the drawing, he turned and addressed the group again. "Now, we have to determine what the critical success factors are to make certain we achieve the objective. Look at the objective and ask yourself, 'What must happen just before we achieve the objective?' Or, another way to ask the question is, 'In order to have 98% on-time delivery, I must have ... what?'" Joe asked, encouraging the group to look at the IO list.

"We need all of those things to happen!" Hector exclaimed.

"You're right Hector," Joe said. "But, we don't need all of them at the same time. To achieve 98% on-time delivery, which IO might be most critical to achieve that?" said Joe, encouraging them to look at the IO list again.

The group was silent until finally Nathan spoke. "Well, I think if we are going to have any chance at all for hitting 98% on-time delivery, we'd have to have a robust scheduling system."

"I think so too," said Joe. "Let's plug it in and read it." Joe walked to the whiteboard and plugged in "Robust Scheduling System."

"In order to have 98% on-time delivery of scheduled maintenance (SM) aircraft, I must have a Robust Scheduling System. Does that make sense?" Joe asked. Most of the group were partially smiling and nodding their heads in agreement.

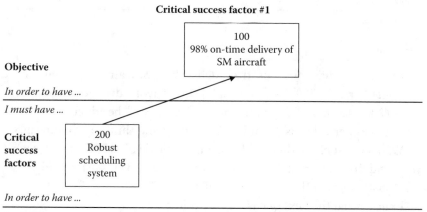

"The number of critical success factors will probably be three or maybe four," Joe said. "If you think there is a critical success factor that is not listed, please feel free to mention it," Joe added.

"Mr. Pecci, I have noticed you keep numbering the boxes. What does the number mean?" Bobby asked.

"Good question Bobby. It's just an address for each box that makes it easier to refer to a box if you have a question about it," Joe replied and Bobby nodded his head to signal "OK."

"Are there any other critical success factors from our list?" Joe asked.

"Well, we kind of have it listed already, but parts availability will be a big factor in getting to 98% on-time delivery," Hector said.

"So, what you're saying is another critical success factor is, Absolute Parts Availability?" Joe asked.

"Yes!" Hector said.

"Let's add it and see how it reads," Joe said, adding it to the IO map.

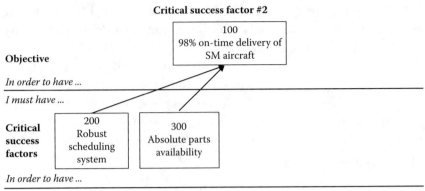

Critical success factor #2

"In order to have 98% on-time delivery of SM aircraft, I must have Absolute Parts Availability," Joe read. "Does anyone disagree?" Joe asked.

"No!" Hector said. "It actually makes good sense," he added.

"It makes perfect sense!" said Brad, smiling and thinking to himself.

"Wait a minute!" Nathan said in a loud excited voice. "I think I see what you are doing here, and it does make sense," he said enthusiastically.

Joe just looked at the group and smiled.

"I know what the next one is!" said Nathan.

"What is it?" Joe asked.

"We need to have all of the tools and equipment available and ready," said Nathan.

"Let's plug it in and read it," said Joe. He walked to the whiteboard and wrote it down.

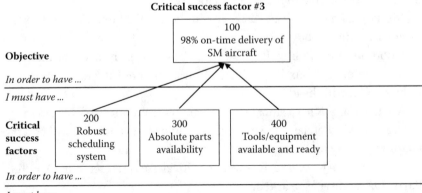

Critical success factor #3

Joe read the new critical success factor out loud. "In order to have 98% on-time delivery of the SM aircraft, I must have tools and equipment available and ready. Does anyone disagree?" he asked.

"I added equipment to this one because I was also thinking of the lifting slings and jigs, and some of the other special equipment we always need," Nathan said. "All of that stuff still comes from the supply room and we have to go get it each time we need it," he added.

"Do we have all the critical success factors, or are there more?" asked Joe.

"I don't know," said Jim. "I'm thinking about some way to do measurements and get the metrics. We need a way to figure out if we're really doing better or not," Jim added.

"That's a good point Jim!" said Joe.

"We do need a way to get some metrics to measure what we are doing. I say that because I think the type of metrics we've been using in the past won't necessarily be relevant in the future," Jim added.

"So, we need effective measures and metrics?" Joe asked, as a statement and a question to the group.

No one disagreed, and most were nodding their heads in agreement, so Joe updated the whiteboard.

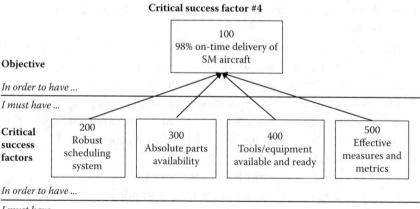

Joe read the statement to the group, "In order to have 98% on-time delivery of SM aircraft, I must have effective measures and metrics. Does everyone agree?" Joe asked and everyone agreed.

Joe backed away from the whiteboard to look at it, and then addressed the group, "We now have our objective and the critical success factors listed in the IO map, at least to start with. Now, we need to determine what the necessary conditions are that support the critical success factors," he said. "In other words, what IO must exist just before we achieve each of the critical success factors? Let's start with the IO 200 and work down from there," Joe added, as he turned and faced the group saying, "If we are going to achieve a robust scheduling system, what must exist just before that?"

Everyone was looking at the whiteboard. Finally, Jim slowly raised his hand and said, "I think we need a way to integrate all of the project schedules into a single master schedule," he said.

"I think that's true," said Nathan. "Right now, we consider each aircraft to be a different project and we develop each of those project schedules in isolation of all the other work going on. When we first get together to do the schedule, and we put it together, it always looks like it will work, and then things start to happen that cause delays, and before long, everything is a mess," Nathan added.

"It happens all the time," said Hector. "When a schedule starts to get behind, then the supervisors and team leads start to fight for resources, or parts, or overtime, or whatever they think is needed to try and regain back some schedule time. Everything ends up being late no matter what we try to do," he added.

"There just doesn't seem to be any flow or synchronization to the work," said Bobby. "It's kind of like every work crew for themselves and damn the other crews!" Bobby added. "Even if a single crew wins, that means someone else had to lose, which means the company as a whole loses! The way I see it, we are all on the same team and one work crew losing shouldn't be an option. We all have to win in order for this to work," Bobby said.

"So, what I'm hearing," said Joe, "Is we have to have integrated project schedules, is that right?" he asked. Everyone nodded their heads so Joe walked over and updated the whiteboard.

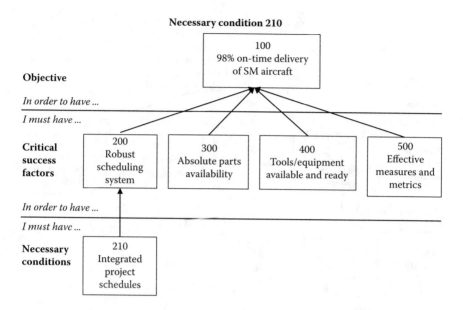

Necessary condition 210

Joe read it to the group, "In order to have a robust scheduling system, we must have integrated project schedules. Does everyone agree?" Joe asked and again, no one disagreed.

"What do we need to have just before we can have integrated project schedules?" Joe asked the group. Everyone was looking at the whiteboard.

"You know," said Nathan, "I'm looking at this and I think before we even think about integrating all of the project schedules together, we need to look at integration of the work crew," he said. "It would still be integration, but at a lower level," he added.

"What do you mean?" asked Joe.

"Well, what I mean is integration between one shift and the next shift, much like the IOs we already have for shift change inspections, and keeping the logbook current," Nathan said pointing to the list.

"I see your point," said Joe. He walked over and updated the whiteboard. "Is this what you mean?" Joe asked.

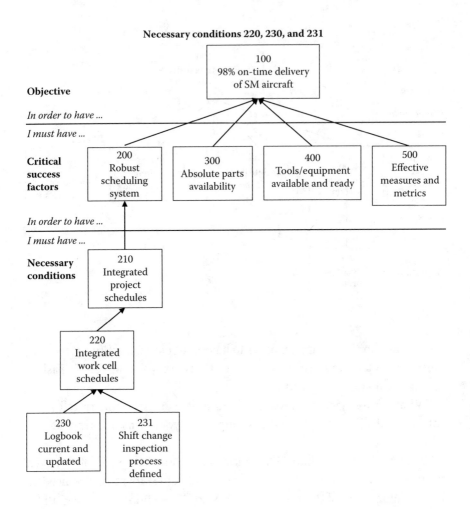

"That's exactly what I was thinking," said Nathan. Nathan looked at the group and asked, "Does everyone see what I'm talking about?" he asked. Heads were nodding to signal "Yes!"

"Let's move to IO 300," Joe said. "What must we have before we can have absolute parts availability?" he asked the group.

"That one is fairly easy," Bobby answered. "We need the bench stock moved out to the floor, and we need fully kitted parts for each task," he said.

"You mean something like this?" Joe said, as he updated the whiteboard.

Necessary conditions 311 and 310

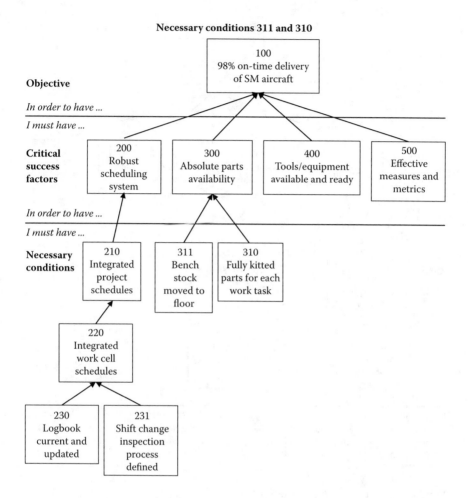

"That looks right to me," Hector said. "Moving the bench stock is pretty straightforward; we just need to make it happen. But, I think the fully kitted parts need some additional IOs," he said.

"Like what?" Joe asked.

"Like having the right inventory in supply to do what we need to do," Hector said. "And, we need to change the parts distribution policy and update the budget amounts for inventory," he added.

Joe went to the whiteboard and updated the IO map. "You mean something like this?" Joe asked.

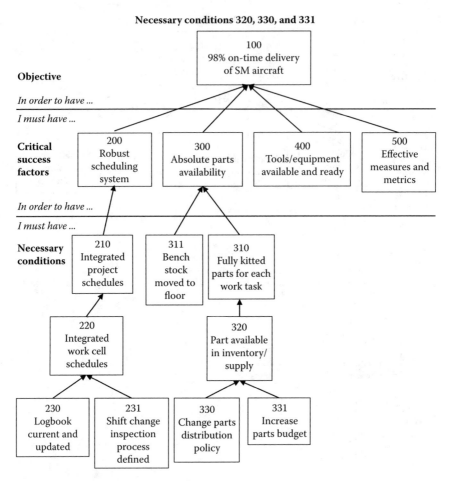

Necessary conditions 320, 330, and 331

"Yes, just like that," Hector said.

"That's exactly what it needs to be!" Nathan added.

"Wait a minute!" Hal said. "Corporate is never going to allow us more money for more parts, they just won't do it!" he exclaimed. "We've worked hard to save money on our parts purchases, and I just don't think corporate will want to give it back," Hal added.

"We need to share with corporate what we are learning here," said Brad. "We have saved money on our parts purchases and look where we are now. We can't save more money and we can't do anymore work. We're just plain stuck, if we keep doing it the same way!" exclaimed Brad. "We just need to convince corporate that this is the right thing to do," he added.

"That is going to be difficult," Hal said. His face was beet red. He wasn't happy with what he was hearing. As of now, all of his cost savings ideas just seemed to be floating away and he couldn't stop them.

"This is what our friend Connor was talking about when he said 'We need to prime the pump,'" Brad said.

Nathan looked puzzled by Brad's last comment and asked, "Prime the pump?"

"It's an interesting story and I'll fill you in later," said Jim looking at Nathan.

Joe looked at his watch. It was now 2:30 PM. They needed to get finished before 3:30 PM, or shortly thereafter, if he and Sam had any chance of getting to the airport on time. Joe quickly steered the conversation back to the IO map.

"OK, let's move to IO 400 and talk about that one," Joe said. "We need to have the tools and equipment available and ready. What do we need before that can happen?" Joe asked.

"I think the answer to that is pretty obvious," Jim said pointing to the interference/obstacle list on the board. "It's the number one obstacle on our list, the one we talked about first, about reviewing and updating the Tool Transfer policy," Jim added.

"You're right," said Joe. "That one is pretty straightforward, so what about IO 500? What must we have in place to accomplish that critical success factor?" Joe asked.

Again, Jim was the first to respond. "I think we need to define what the new measures are. I don't think it will be efficiency anymore, or how much money we are saving on inventory, but something like how fast are we finishing the projects and are we finishing them on time," Jim said.

"We could also measure how many times we don't have the right parts," Hector said.

Joe realized this could escalate quickly into talking about each and every report, so he jumped in and offered, "How about if we just say, 'we need to have the new measures and metrics defined'?" He looked at the group and no one was opposing his idea. He turned around to the whiteboard and added the additional necessary conditions to the IO map.

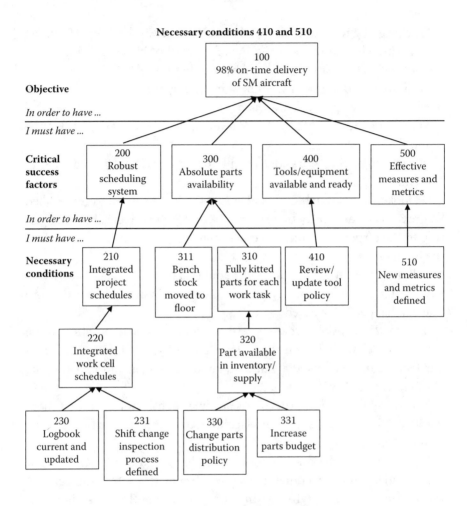

"OK," said Joe, "I think we have a sufficient start point for what we want to do. However, we do have one obstacle left on our list and that is the lunch and breaks procedure. Does anyone have any thoughts where that one might fit in?" Joe asked.

Nathan answered. "I don't think it fits with what we have here, but I do think it will help us. I think we should just keep that one separate and let me work with it from the union side," he said.

"Are there any objections to doing that?" Joe asked. No one said anything, so Joe responded, "OK, Nathan, that one is assigned to you to work offline from the rest of these."

Joe walked back to the front of the room from the whiteboard and said, "Let me congratulate you on what I think was an excellent session for building a simplified strategy and defining what we need to do to reach our objective."

Hal was thinking otherwise. "There are no cost-saving ideas whatsoever in what they had talked about. This will never work!" he thought to himself.

Joe walked to his computer and pushed a button and the following slide appeared on the screen.

Simplified strategy

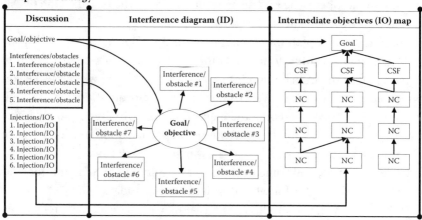

Joe continued. "What we've done through this 2-day exercise is define the objective we wanted to achieve. Then, we defined and discussed the obstacles or interferences that might currently stand in the way of achieving that objective. And finally, we discussed what the IOs might be that are sufficient to overcome the obstacles or interferences. When we placed our IOs in the correct order, using necessity-based logic, the intrinsic order of completion started to expose itself. Now, we have a preliminary plan to go forward with and all of the current IOs are lined up in the order they need to be completed," Joe explained. He scanned the group to make sure everyone understood what he was saying. He took a quick look at this watch. It was 3:15 PM.

"We have our preliminary plan to move forward. If we can't achieve all of the necessary conditions, then it is unlikely we will achieve the critical success factor it is linked to. If we can't achieve the critical success factors, then it is highly unlikely we will achieve the objective," Joe said. "So, our plan moving forward is to achieve all of the necessary conditions and move right up to the objective. Some will be easier than others, but all of them need to be completed," he added.

"Your assignment, moving forward, is to start with the necessary conditions at the bottom of the IO map and start working your way up through them. Divide this team into subteams and assign people to work the different tasks. Get any other resources you might need to help accomplish the tasks. You might encounter some issues along the way, but I have no doubt you'll be able to find the right answer if you just stop and think about it," Joe stated. "However, if you might need some help, here are my and Sam's cell phone numbers," he said as he wrote them on the board. "Don't hesitate to call if you get stuck," he added.

"Sam and I will plan on coming back in 2 weeks or so, to check your progress and accomplishments. Don't worry, Sam has been diligently copying all of the information into a PowerPoint file, so we can leave you with an electronic copy of everything. Are there any questions?" Joe asked. No one raised their hand or asked a question. "You are free to go now, and thank you very much for your attention and participation in what we were doing," Joe finished and looked at his watch. It was 3:25 PM. Perfect.

Hector, Nathan, and some of the others walked up to Sam and Joe and expressed their thanks for what they had learned today.

"I think this will work well," Nathan said. "We have a lot to do to get this turned around," he added.

Everyone else had cleared out except for Brad and Hal. They were standing by the door having a discussion. Hal was still beet red and using his arms to point at imaginary things. Brad seemed to be handling it well. When their discussion ended, Hal left the room and Brad walked over to Joe and Sam and said, "It was an insightful day for all of us, except maybe Hal," he said looking over his shoulder.

"Is everything OK with Hal?" Joe asked.

"It will be," said Brad. "He was just upset that none of the ideas we talked about today included any cost cutting or cost savings," Brad said with a smile. "He's trying to convince me that this new plan won't work."

Now, Joe and Sam were smiling.

"It's all starting to make a lot of sense to me now," Brad said. "What you guys have been talking about is mostly just common sense. I realize now that what we were trying to do before was really just nonsense!" Brad added.

Joe and Sam finished gathering up their stuff, and when they were ready, Brad walked out to the lobby with them. When they had finished signing out and turning in their badges, all three walked outside. As they stood there, Brad said, "I wish I would have called Ron Parsons 6 months ago. He has been telling me about what you guys did at his plant. I didn't believe Ron then, but I certainly do now," said Brad with a smile. "Thanks for coming and we'll see you in a couple of weeks."

"Our pleasure," said Joe. Joe and Sam shook Brad's hand and turned to walk toward the car. While they walked, Joe looked at Sam. Sam was smiling a big smile.

They got back to the Business Air terminal in plenty of time. They turned in the rental car and only had to wait a relatively short time before it was time to takeoff. On the flight home, both of them were mostly silent with their heads back in the seats and their eyes closed.

"Boy, I love flying on a private jet," Sam was thinking to himself.

12

The Hospital—Preliminary Strategy

Becky's health was quickly returning to normal, and she was feeling stronger and stronger every day. But even though Becky was recovering, Connor was still worried about her and was acting more like a mother hen protecting her chicks, than he was a husband. He didn't want to leave Becky alone even for a minute, but his guarding nature was beginning to take its toll on Becky. She loved Connor very much, but she decided it was time for him to back away.

"Connor, as much as I know you care, I can't take your constant hovering over me," Becky said.

"Becky, you're the most important thing in my life and I have to protect you," Connor replied. "I don't want another episode like the one we just went through, and I realize I'm being overprotective, but honey, I can't help it," he added.

"I do appreciate your concern Connor, but it's starting to wear on me," she said. "I know you'll be there when I need you, but I want you to back off a bit," she added.

"OK Becky, I'll back off a bit, but not totally," Connor replied.

"When are you going to start your hospital project?" asked Becky.

"I'm still waiting for Terry Mansfield to call me and set up a meeting," Connor answered.

"Maybe you should call him," Becky suggested.

"I don't have his number, he was going to call me when he was ready," Connor said.

"Maybe you could call Dr. Price and see if he knows anything. Hopefully, he and Terry have been able to talk by now," Becky said.

Connor looked for and found Dr. Price's phone number and dialed it. The phone rang several times until Dr. Price answered. "Hello, this is Dr. Price."

"Hi Jules, this is Connor Jackson."

"Hi Connor, how is my favorite patient doing?" Dr. Price asked.

"She's doing fine, thanks to you. I was wondering if Terry Mansfield and you have talked about when you might want to come by *Jonah's* so we can talk," asked Connor.

"Actually, Terry did talk to me, Connor. He is just waiting for me to get back with him with a day and time. In fact, your phone call is a good reminder that I need to give Terry a call. We need to get this project going and the sooner the better," Dr. Price said.

"OK, just let me know when you are ready," Connor replied.

"Is there anyone else who should be there?" asked Dr. Price.

"I think for our first meeting, it should be just you and Terry. This first meeting will be just laying out the general strategy and information," Connor added.

"Do we need to bring any data or anything?" asked Dr. Price.

"One thing I'd really like to see are some of the performance metrics from your Lean and Six Sigma efforts that you currently use," Connor said. "Just have Terry bring any graphs and charts that you have, but not the actual data," he added.

"I'll get with Terry and see what his schedule looks like and get back to you as to which day is best," replied Dr. Price. "Does it matter what time of the day we get together? I mean, would it be OK if we met in the evening if we had to?" he asked.

"We can meet any day and any time that works for you two," said Connor. "We've had many evening sessions at *Jonah's*, and in some respects, evenings might even be better," he added.

"OK, let me check with Terry," he said. "I have to tell you that I'm very excited to get this project going. We've been doggy paddling with our improvement efforts and it's time we started swimming like Olympians," Dr. Price explained. "Thanks Connor, and I'll call you back and let you know the day and time," he said and disconnected.

"I called and talked with Dr. Price," Connor told Becky.

"Great … when are you meeting with him?" asked Becky.

"He's going to check with Terry and let me know," replied Connor.

"So, what do you have in mind for these guys?" Becky asked.

"I asked them to bring their graphs and charts on the performance metrics that they are currently using," said Connor. "I think just by reviewing that information, I'll discover quite a bit about the current state of the hospital and what things they think are important to them," he added.

"What do you think you'll see Connor?" Becky asked.

"First of all, I expect I'll see several different metrics being tracked to satisfy the requirements of the new healthcare law," said Connor. "The actions required to move many of those metrics will do nothing in terms of patient flow, but it will tell me where they are spending much of their time," he explained.

"So what will you tell Dr. Price and Terry to do?" asked Becky. "I mean they can't just ignore those metrics," she added.

"I know that, but what I want to demonstrate is what metrics they will need in order to determine if they are moving in the right direction. Some of those metrics will most likely be indirectly involved with patient wait times and it's those metrics they need to isolate and create solutions that will move them in a positive direction," Connor explained.

As Connor and Becky were talking, Connor's phone rang. "Hello, this is Connor Jackson," he said as he stepped into the dining room for privacy.

"Hi Connor, this is Jules Price. I talked with Terry about when we could meet at *Jonah's*," he said.

"Great! And when do you want to get together?" asked Connor.

"If it works for you Connor, we'd like to come by tomorrow in the early afternoon," he said.

"That works; let's say tomorrow afternoon around 1:00 PM. My lunch crowd will be starting to thin out around that time," Connor added.

"OK, I'll let Terry know, so we'll see you then. By the way, both of us are very excited to get this project going," said Dr. Price.

"OK, I'll be looking for you then. Good-bye," Connor said and disconnected.

As he walked back into the kitchen, Connor immediately began envisioning how this session would roll out. He thought to himself, "I've already given Dr. Price a brief description of the Theory of Constraints (TOC) and the concept of what a constraint is, and I already know they are using Lean and Six Sigma, but I'll review the TOC information for Terry, so that we're all on the same page."

"Who was on the phone honey?" Becky asked.

"It was Dr. Price. He and Terry are coming by *Jonah's* tomorrow afternoon to start our preliminary planning session," said Connor. "Can you call either Joe or Sam's wife to come over tomorrow afternoon to sit with you?" Connor asked.

"Connor, I really don't think that's necessary; I'm feeling much better now," she said.

"Please Becky, do it for me, so I don't have to worry about you. You said you would do this when we talked about it earlier," he said.

"OK, I'll take care of that right now," she said. Becky called Sam's wife, explained Connor's concern and told her she was welcome to bring her youngest child with her, if necessary. Sam's wife agreed, so it was all set. But even though it was all set, Becky didn't like it.

The next afternoon, right on schedule, Dr. Price and Terry entered *Jonah's*. When they walked in, they spotted Connor at his favorite table in the corner. Connor had a flip chart set up and his laptop was on the table and ready to go. They all shook hands and sat down at the table. Connor asked them if they wanted something to drink and both of them said, "No thank you." Terry said, "Technically we're still at work."

Immediately, Dr. Price had a question for Connor. "How would you like to start today?" he asked. "We brought all of our charts and graphs for our key performance metrics, so if you would like to start with those, we can," Dr. Price said.

Connor smiled and said, "What I would like to start with is similar to what I showed you at the hospital regarding the TOC and the five focusing steps. I already know that Terry is very familiar with Lean and Six Sigma, but I think it's important that he sees why using Lean and Six Sigma, without a focusing mechanism, will not yield the desired optimum results. Is that OK with you guys?" asked Connor.

"Absolutely, I was going to suggest that as a starting point anyway," said Dr. Price. "Terry and I have talked briefly about what you and I talked about, but I wanted him to hear it the way you explained it to me. It had such an impact on me," he added.

"I think it's a great idea for me to see and hear about the TOC and how you integrate it with Lean and Six Sigma. I think it may answer some questions for me about why we aren't getting the significant improvements in our processes that we had hoped for, or thought we were getting," he stated. "Or maybe a better way to say it is, we seem to be removing lots of waste, but our patients aren't flowing much faster," he added.

Connor opened his PowerPoint presentation with the water piping diagram that he had used many times before in these situations. He had actually cut down the number of slides for this meeting, but he also felt it was sufficient to get the point across very quickly. He began by showing Terry the same piping diagram he had shown Dr. Price.

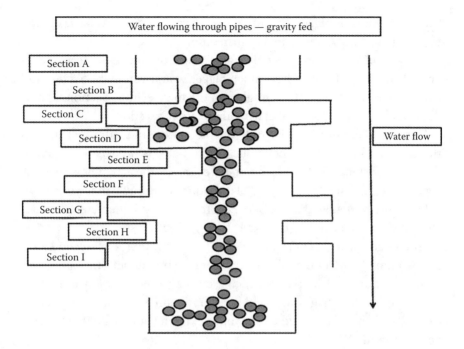

Connor started by describing the drawing, "Terry, what you see here is a cross section of a simple piping system with water entering into Section A, then flowing into Section B, progressing through the remainder of the pipes until it collects in the receptacle at the bottom. This, in essence, is the flow of a system from start to finish. There has been a request to improve the system and someone has told you that the amount of water flowing through this system is not enough to meet the water demand requirements," said Connor. "So, if you were in charge of getting more water to flow through this piping system, what would you do and why would you do it?" Connor asked.

Like Dr. Price, when Terry saw the piping diagram, he was a bit surprised and reacted like so many others had, wanting to know why Connor was showing him, of all things, a piping diagram? Connor asked him to be patient and just answer the question because it would all make sense to him shortly. Dr. Price encouraged Terry to focus on answering Connor's question.

After careful observation, Terry responded. "I suppose that the only way to make more water flow through this system would be to open up

Section E, make it bigger, because it's where all the water is backing up," he said, looking at Connor for confirmation.

"Very good Terry, you're exactly right," said Connor. "Now Terry, here's another question for you, how much bigger would you make Section E?" Connor asked. "What criteria might you use to determine Section E's new diameter?" Connor added to clarify his original question.

Terry looked closely at the slide on the laptop and calmly said, "I'm thinking it all depends on how much more water is needed at the end of the piping system. By that I mean, if, for example, the actual flow rate was 1 gallon per minute and you needed 2 gallons per minute, then you would at least have to double the size of the current Section E diameter," he said. "Is that the right answer?" he asked.

"You've got the concept right and that's what's important, so good job," said Connor. "OK, let me ask you another question about this piping system," said Connor. "Suppose we increased the diameter of any other section of pipe in this diagram, would it result in more water flowing through this system?" he asked. "And I want you to explain your answer to Dr. Price and I," he added.

Terry didn't waste any time at all and said, "No, absolutely not! The only section that would affect the water flow rate through this system is Section E because it's the bottleneck," he added proudly.

"Perfect!" said Connor. "The concept of the bottleneck is important to understand and remember. OK, here's another drawing I want you to look at. It's the same piping system, but we took your advice and opened up Section E's diameter. I want you to look at it and tell me what you see," Connor explained. "What other significant physical changes happened within this system as a result of enlarging Section E's diameter?" he asked.

Terry studied the drawing and said, "I see a couple things that I think are noteworthy. First, I see an increase in the amount of water flowing through the system," he said.

"Good, what else do you see?" asked Connor.

"Probably the most important change is how the bottleneck has moved from Section E to Section B," he said.

"So what does that tell you?" asked Connor. "Why is that an important observation for you?" he added.

"It's important to me because, if I need even more water to flow through this piping system, I know exactly where to go to make it happen," Terry said proudly.

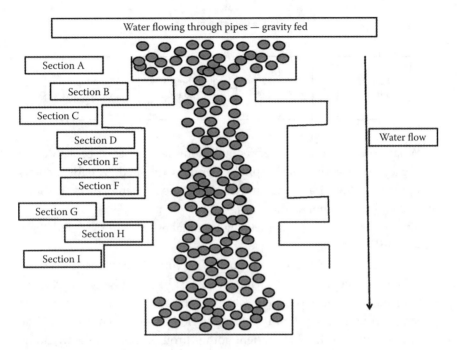

"Excellent!" said Connor. "You have fully embraced the concept of identifying where the constraint is located, and where you must focus your efforts in order to increase the flow of water through it," said Connor. "There are three key takeaways in this little exercise. First is that once you've identified the constraint and improved its capacity enough, the constraint will move to a new location," Connor said. "The second important concept that you've captured is, focusing on any other part of this system and increasing the diameter of that section will not result in more water flowing through this system," Connor added. "And finally, the third important concept that I hope you have observed is that the output of any process, or system, is controlled by a single limiting factor. In the case of a physical process, this limiting factor is the constraint within the system," Connor explained. "We refer to this limiting factor as the *system constraint*," Connor added. "Does that make sense to you?" asked Connor.

"Yes, I understand that," Terry said. "But I'm still confused about why we spent so much time on a piping system?" said Terry in more of a questioning tone.

"As I asked you before, please have patience; I'm sure you will see the overall relevance shortly," Connor said. "OK, let's move on," said Connor, as he loaded the next drawing onto his screen.

Simple four-step process

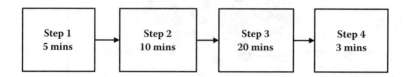

"What you see here is a very simple four-step process, probably not unlike a process within the hospital," Connor explained. "A patient enters this process at Step 1 and then moves on to Step 2, then likewise through Steps 3 and 4," Connor said.

"Finally, we're getting to something that makes sense to me," said Terry with a smile on his face.

Connor smiled back and continued, "As you can see, the processing time for each step is listed in each box. So, just like the piping diagram we just looked at, suppose you were asked to increase the number of patients passing through this system in a given period," Connor continued. "The amount of time for the first patient going through this process would be the sum of the individual processing times, or 5 + 10 + 20 + 3 minutes or a total of 38 minutes, assuming there were no interruptions," Connor explained. "But once the process was full, meaning that as soon as the first patient left Step 1, the next patient begins," said Connor. "Likewise, when patient 1 left Step 2 and patient 2 left Step 1, patient 3 enters Step 1," he explained. "Finally, patient 4 enters this process, after patient 1 completes Step 3 and so on," Connor said. "Do you see how this process is working?" asked Connor.

"Yes, it's just like patients getting something like a magnetic resonance imaging or some other service in the hospital," Terry replied.

"Good! So, once the process is 'full,' what is the fastest a patient can move through this entire process?" asked Connor.

Terry looked at the drawing and said, "We just decided it was 38 minutes."

"Terry, that's only the correct answer for the first patient entering and passing through this process, look again," Connor said.

"I'm not sure I understand what you're asking me to see," replied Terry.

"Let me ask you a different question," Connor said. "If you were asked to increase the number of patients passing through this process, what must you do?" asked Connor. "Before you answer this question, I want you to think back to the piping diagram," he added.

Terry studied Connor's drawing and then he hit his forehead with the palm of his hand and said, "Crap, this is so simple to understand! Because Step 3 is the constraint, as you call it, in order to increase the rate of flow of patients through this process, I would have to focus on Step 3 and reduce the amount of time it takes!" Terry exclaimed. "Now I see the relevance of the piping diagram," he added.

"Good Terry, now just like the piping diagram, would it make any sense at all to reduce the times at Steps 1, 2, or 4?" Connor asked.

"Absolutely not, at least not right away!" exclaimed Terry. "Step 3 is the only step that matters when you're considering increasing the number of patients passing through this system, and reducing the time it takes," he replied. "This is so simple and basic, and it helps me understand right away why we haven't seen emergency room patient wait times decrease!" he exclaimed.

"What did you mean by your statement about the emergency room wait times?" asked Connor.

"Well, it seems to me that we just started at the front end of the process when the patient checks in, when in reality the check-in process was not the constraint," he explained. "If you look at patient wait times, we haven't really affected them at all," he continued. "What we should have done was to first map the process and measure the time it takes to complete each step, just like this drawing shows us," Terry continued.

"And then what should you do?" Connor asked almost tongue in cheek.

"Once you know the average times for each step, then you can identify where to focus your waste and variation reduction efforts. Of course, that initial focus would be on the system constraint!" he said passionately. "We've been doing this all wrong!" he exclaimed. "We were trying to fix all of the processes and then adding together the sum total of those improvements and then saying the wait times had been reduced. I can see clearly now why some of the improvement projects showed good results, but the system as a whole did not improve! We tried to fix everything instead of just the constraint!" he exclaimed.

"Terry, what you've been doing is the way you were taught to do it, so don't beat yourself up too much. There is another way to locate the systems constraint. Can you tell me what that might be?" asked Connor.

Terry looked at Connor and then said, "I'm thinking that you might be able to walk the process and see where the patients are stacked up. It might not be the best way, but it would be another way to do it, I think," he added.

"Terry, you're absolutely right in your conclusion. If you do the *Gemba walk*, you can locate the point in the system where your patients spend a good amount of time waiting, that location could very well be your constraint," said Connor. "Before we move on, I want to highlight another important characteristic. Do you measure and report *efficiencies* in the hospital?" Connor asked.

Both Jules and Terry responded with a forceful, "Yes!"

Once again, Connor loaded a new image on his screen. "OK, so tell me, what is the basis for your efficiency metric?" he asked. "I mean how do you calculate it, and what does it mean to you?" he added for clarity.

Terry was the first to speak, "Efficiency is really a ratio and is intended to demonstrate how well your workers are performing."

Connor replied, "Explain what you mean by ratio."

"By ratio, I mean you have a standard time that a job should take and you essentially compare it to how long it actually takes to complete," he explained. "For example, suppose a chest x-ray is supposed to take 15 minutes, from start to finish based on a standard time, but it's actually taking the technician, on average, 25 minutes," he said. "His efficiency would be, 15 minutes divided by 25 minutes or 60%. In other words, we would say that this technician is 60% efficient," Terry explained.

"And what would you conclude from this percentage?" asked Connor.

"There are actually two very different conclusions that can be drawn," Terry replied. "The first conclusion is that the standard time for the job is incorrect and that it actually takes longer than the standard time calls for. The second conclusion is that the technician is inept and isn't doing his job very well," he explained.

"And do you encourage and measure everyone to achieve higher and higher efficiencies at the hospital?" Connor asked.

"Well yes, of course we do," Terry answered. "Why do you ask that question?" he asked.

"Remember the simple four-step process we just looked at?" asked Connor. Both Jules and Terry nodded their heads, "Yes."

"Let's say this is a process, maybe the x-ray process you just mentioned," said Connor. "My question to you is this, what would happen within this process, if every step ran as fast as it could to its full capacity?" he asked looking at both of them.

"Efficiencies would rise and everyone would be happy, especially our Finance group," said Terry with a smile.

"That is true, the data would suggest that efficiencies are way up, but only some of the efficiencies would rise. Those process steps after the constraint could never achieve a higher efficiency. So, some of the internal data and numbers all point to higher efficiency in some locations, but physically, what would happen inside of the system to the patients?" asked Connor. When neither one answered, Connor put up his next slide.

Simple four-step process

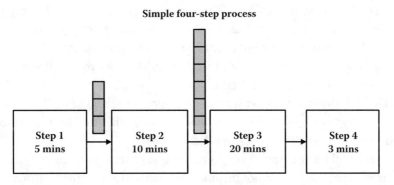

"Do you see that by running each step as fast as you can, there would be a stack-up of patients in front of the slower process steps?" asked Connor. "Because Step 1 is twice as fast as Step 2, a patient stack-up occurs here," pointing to the locations just in front of Step 2. "Step 1 is four times as fast as Step 3, and Step 2 is twice as fast as Step 3, so another stack-up occurs," he said and pointed just in front of Step 3. "The employee in Step 4 is always waiting for Step 3 to send something their way. If we looked at just the data and efficiency numbers, it would appear that Step 4 is the problem—Step 4 has very low efficiency! All of the other processes are working at 100% efficiency, even Step 3. Step 3 completes one unit of work every 20 minutes of time," Connor said, pointing to the chart. "If we analyze just efficiency, then Step 1 is not the problem, nor is Step 2 or 3. Step 4 is the problem! So, what do you think will be happening within this process?" Connor asked.

Jules looked at Connor, smiled and said, "It makes no sense to run every step as fast as it can go, because all we'll get is a buildup of patients within the system," he said confidently.

"I think that, like your example here, if Step 3 is the constraint, then each step in the process should slow down and go no faster than Step 3?" Terry responded more as a question than an answer.

"That is absolutely right Terry," replied Connor.

Terry continued, "At least until the processing time of Step 3 can be reduced. If the time in Step 3 is reduced, all of the other steps have the protective capacity to go faster, if necessary."

Connor smiled and said, "So how do you reduce the processing time of the constraint?"

Terry excitedly replied, "By *focusing* our Lean and Six Sigma efforts on it!"

"Exactly!" Connor replied. "The entire system can, and will, only produce at a rate equal to, or less than, what the constraint produces. In this case, that equals one patient every 20 minutes," Connor said.

Terry looked at Dr. Price and smiled widely. "Do you realize what we just learned here today Dr. Price?"

Dr. Price looked back with an even bigger smile and said, "Yes, it's like unlocking the secret code! We've been missing this tool to help us focus our improvement efforts," he replied.

Terry looked at Connor and asked in a very serious manner, "Connor, why is it that the TOC is not included in Lean and Six Sigma training? This is such a significant part of what everyone needs to know!" he exclaimed.

Connor replied, "Don't underestimate the power of the Lean and Six Sigma tool set. TOC by itself will not take you to the promised land in terms of improvement, but combine it with Lean and Six Sigma and it's a very powerful methodology," Connor explained.

"I see your point," said Dr. Price.

"I do too," said Terry. "I just know that I need to get all of my Green Belts and Black Belts together for a session like we just had today," he added. "This unified improvement method just makes so much sense to me and I am surprised that I haven't seen or heard about this method long before today," he added.

"OK," said Connor. "Now, I'd like to see some of your performance charts and graphs, before we wrap up today. Specifically, I'd like to see any of them that deal with patient flow, or wait times if you have some," Connor asked.

Terry looked at Connor and said, "Frankly, I'm a little embarrassed to show you these charts now. The way we put most of these together has nothing to do with what I just learned."

Terry opened up his backpack and pulled out a file folder. Since Connor wanted to see flow-related metrics, he sorted through the papers and pulled out the first one he found. "Here's one that we use called Door to Balloon Time or D2B Time for short. As you can see, our results have been relatively flat. Our average through time for the D2B Time is right around 90 minutes, which isn't bad when compared to the National Standard," he explained. "But we believe that this standard is going to be changed to around 60 minutes, and if it does, we're in big trouble," he added. "Do you think you can help us with this one?" asked Terry.

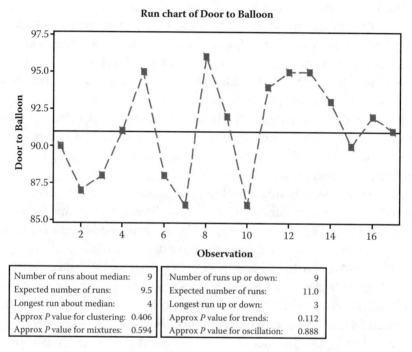

Run chart of Door to Balloon

Number of runs about median:	9	Number of runs up or down:	9
Expected number of runs:	9.5	Expected number of runs:	11.0
Longest run about median:	4	Longest run up or down:	3
Approx *P* value for clustering:	0.406	Approx *P* value for trends:	0.112
Approx *P* value for mixtures:	0.594	Approx *P* value for oscillation:	0.888

"Can you explain to me exactly what D2B Time is, so I have a better understanding of what this is telling me?" asked Connor.

"D2B Time is defined as either emergency room registration or first documentation by a nurse to the time of artery opening for those patients classified as an ST Elevation MI or, a STEMI, as we call it," Dr. Price explained.

"Pretend I'm not a doctor, and explain it to me in language I can understand," Connor replied jokingly.

"Sorry Connor. D2B Time is typically defined as the interval of time from when the patient first arrives in the emergency room until the balloon inflation in a patient's artery in a Catheterization Lab," explained Dr. Price.

"Why is this metric important to track, if you don't mind me asking?" said Connor.

"That's easy. For every 30-minute increase in D2B Time, it results in a 1-year mortality increase of 7.5%. You see, for each minute until the balloon is inflated inside the patient's artery to remove the blockage, heart muscle continues to be damaged, so if you can reduce the amount of time before the balloon is inflated, the patient's chances of surviving increases dramatically," Dr. Price explained.

Connor studied the chart for a moment longer and said, "OK, got it … so this is a very important metric to track, at least from the patient's perspective," Connor said. Connor studied the chart for a few minutes longer and was talking to himself, "This was not a project I had considered in my upfront promise to help Dr. Price with lead times. I was thinking mostly of the emergency room. However, reducing the lead times on D2B would certainly have a profound effect with helping patients." He decided the D2B project would be a good project to work on. Connor looked at Terry and finally answered, "And, in answer to your question about helping improve this one, the answer is yes," Connor added.

The three of them continued looking at the package of metrics Terry had brought with him, until finally Connor said, "We've been at this for quite a while now, and I think I'd like to get back home and see how Becky is doing. So, if you don't mind, can we call it a day?" Connor asked.

"Of course we can, but when can we get together again?" asked Terry.

"As long as Becky is doing well, we can meet whenever it is convenient for both of you," replied Connor. "Only next time, I'd like to meet at the hospital. I'd like to be able to tour some of the key areas like the emergency room and maybe some other areas where patient flow is very important," said Connor.

"Let me get it set up and I'll call you tomorrow," said Terry.

"That would be great!" Connor replied.

Terry and Dr. Price started to collect everything they had out on the table. Terry also extended his appreciation to Connor for taking the time to meet with them, and how beneficial this new information was going to be. When they were ready to leave, Connor walked them both to the door and said, "I'll talk with you tomorrow."

13

Hospital Improvement Team

After Dr. Price and Terry left, Connor jumped into his black Hummer to drive home and check on Becky. As he drove, he was thinking about the run chart on Door to Balloon Time he had just reviewed with Dr. Price and Terry. He thought to himself, "Now here is a very meaningful project that could benefit from reduced wait time." For a moment, Connor imagined the impact on the general population's mortality rate if the wait time could be reduced for the time it takes to get the balloon inserted and inflated.

Connor continued thinking about the simple run chart as he drove home. When he arrived home, he pulled his Hummer into the garage next to Becky's Mercedes. Seeing Becky's Mercedes immediately turned his thoughts to her.

Connor walked into the house from the garage and called Becky's name, but didn't get an immediate response. He called her name again as he walked to the office; she wasn't there and still no response. He walked down the hallway toward the bedroom and noticed the curtains were closed. He walked in and flipped on the light. As the light came on, Becky immediately sat up in bed and shielded her eyes. "Hi Connor, how did your session go?" she asked without hesitation.

"I was worried about you when you didn't answer," he replied. "And, today's meetings went very well, I think," he added.

"I would have called you if something was wrong," Becky said. "Besides, Sam's wife was here up until approximately 15 minutes ago. I told her I was tired and wanted to rest. She said OK and left," Becky added.

"One of the things we talked about today was something called Door to Balloon Time, or D2B as they refer to it," Connor said.

"Whatever are you talking about?" she asked.

"In simple terms, D2B is a metric used at the hospital to measure how long it takes to insert and inflate a balloon inside the artery of a heart attack patient when there's a blockage problem," he explained.

"Why is this so important?" Becky questioned.

"Because for every minute of time this can be reduced, there is less damage to the heart, and more patients have a better chance for a full recovery," he explained. "It wasn't my first choice of projects, but I told Dr. Price and Terry it should be the first one we work on."

"It sounds like a great place to start," Becky replied.

Connor was hoping that improvements in the D2B time would stimulate a higher interest in the TLS (Theory of Constraints, Lean, and Six Sigma) methodology and concepts throughout the hospital.

It was going on 9:00 PM and Connor was getting tired. He was tired from all of the worrying about Becky over the last couple of weeks and all of the other things happening. Becky was already in bed and he was making his way through the house turning off lights. He made his way back to the bedroom to get into bed, and just as he lay down beside Becky, his cell phone rang. He picked it up from the nightstand and answered, "Hello, this is Connor." There was a long pause as he listened to the person on the other end. Finally, he said, "Tomorrow morning? Sure, that will be fine. Around 10:00 AM? Where at? OK, I'll see you then," he said and disconnected.

"Who was that?" asked Becky lying on her side with her eyes still closed.

"That was Terry, at the hospital, and they want to start the improvement effort tomorrow morning at 10:00," Connor replied.

"Wow, you must have impressed them," Becky said.

"Terry sounded excited on the phone and told me he and Dr. Price went back to the hospital and talked briefly with some of the executive staff. Most were interested in hearing more information, so he wants me to briefly talk with the members of the hospital's leadership team. He was able to get them all together at 10:00, but only for approximately 30 minutes. He wants me to give the presentation for the water piping chart to lay out the framework of the improvement effort," Connor explained. "Then we'll meet with the D2B team."

"Sounds like a busy day," Becky said. "Connor, you're not planning on charging them for this are you?" asked Becky with obvious concern in her voice.

"Not this one Becky," he said. "The deal I made with Dr. Price was, if he got you healthy again, I would help the hospital reduce wait times." Connor kissed Becky good night, turned off the light, cuddled, and fell asleep.

At 5:30 AM, Connor woke up, went to the kitchen and made coffee as he did every morning. His thoughts immediately turned to the actions of the day. This would be his first meeting with the hospital's leadership team. He thought about how he might address them as a group and what he might say that would pique their interest and involvement. He thought that it might be a good idea to start with the concept of his unified TLS methodology. He also wondered what the leadership team might be thinking about the results of their current improvement effort. He hoped that by showing them a new way, it might get their attention.

In his customary style, Connor arrived at the hospital early, around 9:30 AM. Connor pulled into the parking lot, found a place, and parked. He followed behind several people entering the hospital. He guessed from the conversations he heard that most were probably friends or family members coming to visit someone. The main entrance was warm and inviting with soft color tones painted on the walls. The last time he was at the hospital, he had come in through the emergency room (ER). Even though he had come to visit Becky, he hadn't really noticed the lobby before now. There was even a door greeter to welcome the people and help them find their way. Connor stopped and asked the door greeter for directions to the main conference room. The woman responded with a very kind and comforting voice. She wore a name tag on her coat that said, "Maria— Volunteer." She knew exactly how to get to the conference room and gave Connor the directions he needed.

Connor walked down the main hallway and found the conference room. The door was partially open so he entered the room. The light came on automatically, which startled him just a little. He immediately noticed on one wall of the room that there was a corkboard with several graphs and charts, which he assumed were the metrics for everything they were measuring. As he scanned the board, he realized that many of the charts were the same ones he had seen yesterday. There were some financial metrics, including his "old friend" efficiency, which automatically told him what he might be up against in terms of cost world thinking. He also noticed metrics that were related to flow, including ER average wait times. The average was plotted on a weekly basis. As he looked closer, Connor recognized the chart as the same one he had discussed with Dr. Price when Becky had been admitted. Connor noticed one other familiar metric with the D2B time. It looked like the same chart from the meeting yesterday. The improvement trend was flat.

Another section of the board was labeled "Active Improvement Projects." Connor looked at the sheet. There were 25, or more, open projects listed on it. There were no specific results posted for any of the projects, just the name of the project and who the assigned lead person was. The lack of any posted results made Connor think that maybe the leadership team wasn't as involved as they should be. All of what he was seeing on the metrics board helped him cultivate his thoughts on how he might address the group. As he continued looking at the wall, he heard a familiar voice behind him. "Good morning Connor, so good to see you this morning," said Terry.

"Good morning, Terry," replied Connor as they shook hands. "I was just admiring your metrics board."

As Terry and Connor continued to talk one on one, each person from the leadership team started entering the room. Terry tried to introduce Connor to as many as he could when they entered, but a few got past him. Connor was looking around the room and noticed Dr. Price had just entered. He walked over and shook his hand.

Dr. Price took the lead and welcomed everyone. He then proceeded to introduce Connor. Dr. Price's hands were clasped in front of his chest and it reminded Connor of a surgeon awaiting gloves. "Good morning everyone. I want to introduce you to Connor Jackson. I met Connor a couple of weeks ago while treating his wife after a visit to the ER," he said and paused. "There were some negative things that happened during that visit, and because of those issues, I have since received a valuable education about some of our improvement efforts, and more importantly how to do it correctly. Terry Mansfield and I," Dr. Price said pointing to Terry, "have decided that it would be advantageous for Connor to meet with the leadership team and explain some of his ideas to help us reduce wait times." There were noticeable smiles on some faces, indicating to Connor that they didn't believe any real wait time reductions were possible.

From this initial reaction, Connor sensed that he had his work cut out for him. "So, with that, I want to turn the time over to Connor Jackson," Dr. Price said, gesturing with his hands for Connor to come up to the front of the room.

Connor started by thanking them for the opportunity to be there. Connor continued by asking the group a simple question: "How many of you, or a family member, have been treated in your ER?" he asked. He scanned the room, but not a single hand went up. He continued. "It's a pity that none of you have had to experience the ER like my wife did recently. Our wait time to be admitted was a little more than 5 hours!" he said.

"I have another question for you. How many of you have gone through at least some training in Lean, Six Sigma, or both?" Connor asked. Almost everyone's hands went up, indicating that they had some training or exposure to these two methods. "OK, how many of you have actually been a part of an improvement team working on improving something in the hospital?" Connor asked. Connor was not surprised to see only Terry and Dr. Price raise their hands. Connor looked at one gentleman who was seated up front. Terry had introduced him as Jeffrey Osborne, the Chief Financial Officer. Connor pointed and asked, "So Jeffrey, exactly why haven't you been on a team yet?" Connor asked.

"That's not my job," said Jeffrey. "That's what the Continuous Improvement group is for," he said somewhat sarcastically.

"So let me get this straight," Connor paused, looking directly at Jeffrey, "You don't see continuous improvement as your responsibility?"

"Well, yes, of course I do, but I don't have time to be on any improvement teams," Jeffrey snapped back.

"Is that the same way the rest of you feel?" Connor asked looking at the group. When nobody acknowledged his question, Connor asked, "If none of you are involved, and none of you think that being on a team is important, then stop and think about what kind of message you are sending to the workers at this hospital! Realistically, will anyone, on any of the teams, think that what they are doing is important, if you don't demonstrate that it is?"

Most of the leadership team nodded their heads in agreement, but no one said a word, except for Jeffrey. He was the one that did not agree. Connor was not at all surprised by this lack of buy-in. Besides, Jeffrey already said, "it wasn't his job!" Connor knew, then and there, that if he was to gain Jeffrey's support, he would have to demonstrate that there is a better way and the importance of leadership involvement. It wouldn't be easy, but it would clearly be necessary.

Connor turned and walked toward his computer to start the water piping presentation just like he had presented to Dr. Price and Terry. Connor presented the water piping diagram, the four-step process, and the five focusing steps to demonstrate the concept of a constraint and why it was so important to understand where the constraint is and what the constraint does to the system. Connor sensed that everyone understood what he was talking about, but no one had any comments by the time he finished.

"Having looked at some of your metrics information," Connor said pointing to the wall of charts. "I might guess that some of you might not be happy with the results you're seeing?" he asked directly. Some people were nodding in agreement. "Whatever you do, do not blame Lean or Six

Sigma or the people working on the Continuous Improvement projects! I'm here to tell you that it is not their fault. It is a *systems failure*, not an *individual failure*," Connor said.

"Because of the promise I made to Dr. Price, I am committed to helping this hospital reduce wait times. As Dr. Price will attest, my wife and I had a very bad experience here.

"After some discussions with Dr. Price and Terry, the first project we want to analyze is the D2B time and show the team how they can take meaningful time out of this process," said Connor. "I've seen the most current results and it appears as if your efforts are suspended right around 90 minutes on average," Connor said, pointing to the D2B chart on the wall. "I believe that it's possible to reduce that number to around 50 minutes or less, in very short order," he explained. The level of interest in the room seemed to perk up immediately when Connor mentioned this. "I plan to use this project as a springboard to demonstrate how the combined methodology of TLS works and then have your Continuous Improvement group apply it to other ongoing projects."

Connor noticed Terry at the back of the room. He had his left arm up in front of him pointing to the face of his watch with his right index finger, indicating to Connor that the allotted time was almost up. Connor acknowledged Terry's gesture with a head nod. Connor looked at the group and said, "Unless there are any other questions from this group, you are free to go."

There was one hand that went up. Jeffrey raised his hand and asked, "Just exactly how much are your services going to cost us? I mean, we've already spent lots of money on Lean Six Sigma training and I don't think we have seen an acceptable return on that investment," he added.

"Not to worry Jeffrey, I don't have any plans to charge you anything," Connor replied. "I made a deal with Dr. Price, so I plan for this to be my payback and pay it forward," he explained. "It's my pro bono to Saint Luke's Hospital. Is that price low enough for you?" Connor added and everyone laughed. Jeffrey was a bit taken back by Connor's generosity and said that he thought Connor's offer was acceptable and again everyone laughed. Connor thanked everyone and asked them to consider what they thought the overall goal for the hospital was. As the executive team was leaving, they went on a quick break. Terry had the D2B project team waiting in the hallway.

When the break was over, Dr. Price welcomed everyone from the D2B team and asked Terry to say a few words about why they were all here.

"Good morning everyone, I'm so happy you could all be here on such short notice," said Terry. "First, I want to thank everyone for their hard work so far, but I also want to tell you that I have discovered why we haven't made much progress on some of our projects." Terry continued, "Less than 24 hours ago, I had an opportunity to meet with Connor and I learned something that you will be learning in the next hour or so. What you will learn will change your entire approach to your improvement projects. With that said, I want to introduce you to Connor Jackson and turn the time over to him. Connor?"

Connor walked back to the front of the room and said, "Good morning everyone, I'm very happy to have the opportunity to be here with you today. A couple of weeks ago, my wife was having severe abdominal pain. We came to the ER and, after 5 hours of waiting, she was finally admitted to the hospital," he explained. "It was after my wife was admitted that I met Dr. Price, who was my wife's primary care physician at the hospital. During our time in the ER, we had some issues with wait time, so that's why I'm here," he added. "I've had a meeting with Terry and Dr. Price already. We were reviewing some of your projects and metrics. One project that we talked about extensively was the D2B. I have to tell you that I don't have much experience in hospitals. However, I will also say that I am an expert with systems analysis, and hospitals use systems just like any other business does." Connor scanned the group and asked, "Are there any questions before I get started?" No one asked any questions.

Connor walked to his laptop and projected his piping diagram presentation up on the screen. He went through all of his normal questions and most of the team members grasped the concept of the constraint very quickly. He then repeated the same exercise with the four-step process and the five focusing steps. Once again, the team seemed to grasp the concept of the constraint and the five focusing steps.

A petite woman, sitting near the back of the table, raised her hand with a question. Connor pointed to her and asked, "Yes?"

"My name is Sally Lu and I was wondering why something so obvious isn't a standard part of Continuous Improvement training, like Lean and Six Sigma?" she asked. "It all makes sense to me," she added.

Connor was about to answer, when Terry jumped in and said, "Sally, you have made an excellent observation and I promise you going forward that this new TLS training will be part of every new training session we do. I'm also planning on attending the next American Society for Quality (ASQ) meeting and recommend that the TLS methods be included in their curriculum," he added.

"Thank you Terry," Sally said. "Where can I learn more about Theory of Constraints?" she asked.

Terry looked at Connor for an answer and Connor replied, "Sally, I have a few books that I can lend you. Get with me at the first break and we'll talk about it."

Sally said, "Thanks," as she made some notes.

"Now, the first thing I'd like to do is something you are all familiar with," said Connor. "I'd like for all of us to go on a *Gemba* walk and you define for me the pathway for D2B process. The first step I always take is to walk the process to better understand it," he said. "When we come back, I'd like to start the *Current State* process map, so please everyone take good notes," he added. "We'll also perform a Value Stream Analysis (VSA), which I'm sure you're all very familiar with. Because of your Lean training, you all know that a process step is categorized in one of three categories. First, *value-added*. Second, *non–value-added but necessary*. And third, *non–value-added*. Once we have the map in place, we'll color code each step as green for value-added, yellow for non–value-added but necessary, or red for non–value-added. We'll then create a *Future State* map," he finished.

Terry noted that it was close to lunchtime and that everyone should take a lunch break and when they returned they would start the *Gemba* walk.

When they returned from lunch, the group left the conference room and followed Dr. Price and Terry to the ER to see firsthand the process involved in the D2B process.

The team slowly walked through the process that a heart attack patient follows for D2B. They asked lots of questions to the people in the ER and took excellent notes. There were many side conversations with the employees that support ER activities, such as x-ray and lab techs. After approximately 90 minutes, Connor signaled for everyone to return to the conference room to review their findings. Connor listened intently and was working on his laptop. Connor asked Terry to lead the effort to create the Current State process map.

When the discussions ended, Connor said, "First of all, great job! I can see that you are all actively participating and that is very important if this team is going to make good things happen. After hearing what you have said, and based on conversations of my own in the ER, I've been working on something that I want to share with you," he said as he flashed a new image onto the screen.

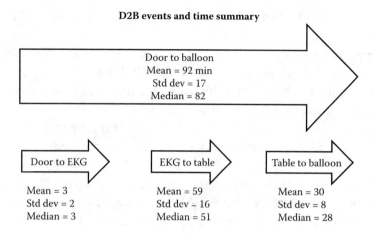

D2B events and time summary

Door to balloon
Mean = 92 min
Std dev = 17
Median = 82

Door to EKG

Mean = 3
Std dev = 2
Median = 3

EKG to table

Mean = 59
Std dev – 16
Median = 51

Table to balloon

Mean = 30
Std dev = 8
Median = 28

"As you can see, I've broken down the D2B process into three major events," Connor explained. He pointed to the slide on the screen and said, "The way I see it, there are three major events associated with the D2B process. The first event is the Door to electrocardiogram (EKG). The second event is the EKG to Table, and the third event is the Table to Balloon.

"As you can also see, on the basis of the preliminary data, I've made some rough calculations that are listed directly under each event," Connor said. "Clearly, the EKG to Table is the constraint within this process, so I'd like you to first focus your improvement efforts there. Find and eliminate as much waste as you can," Connor instructed. "Right now, with a total mean value of 92 minutes, the EKG to Table is consuming roughly 59 minutes," he noted. "Number two on the list is Table to Balloon at 30 minutes, but we won't worry about that one unless the EKG to Table drops below the 30 minutes estimate. I want you to spend the rest of your time today working through your VSA and color code the steps as green, yellow, or red," he explained. "And please, go back to the *Gemba*, if you need more information, or if you have any questions about the process," he added.

The teams spent the rest of the day working the VSA with Terry and Dr. Price actively involved as facilitators for the exercise.

It was now approaching 3:30 PM and many of the team members were at the end of their shift and ready to leave. Dr. Price and Terry had arranged for this team to have the conference room all week, so they were instructed to leave all of their work in place and come back tomorrow at 7:00 AM. After the team had departed, Dr. Price and Terry approached Connor to chat. "Well, what do you think? How did the team do today?" asked Dr. Price.

"I think they did extremely well for their first day. What do you think?" asked Connor.

"Terry and I were just talking and neither one of us can remember as much enthusiasm as we've seen today," said Dr. Price.

Terry said, "I've been doing this for a long time and I have never seen excitement and enthusiasm like I've seen today."

"So, realistically Connor, how much do you think we can reduce our D2B time and how quickly do you see it being reduced?" asked Dr. Price.

"Realistically, with the mean at 92 minutes, you should be able to reduce it to around 60 minutes with no problem and maybe lower," said Connor. "I also think you can get there in 1 to 2 weeks, if not sooner," Connor added.

"Wow!" Dr. Price exclaimed. "You really think it could happen that quickly?" he asked.

"Yes, but of course it all depends on how much cooperation the team gets from the people on the floor and from the leadership team," Connor explained. "People get stuck in their old ways and sometimes have difficulty changing from their current comfort zones," Connor replied.

"What do you plan on doing with the team tomorrow?" asked Terry.

"Tomorrow, we'll review the analysis for the value stream map, and I'm going to teach them about a lesser used thinking tool called an Interference Diagram (ID)," said Connor.

"What is an ID?" asked Terry. "I've never heard of, or used an ID before," he added.

"Hold that question until tomorrow Terry and it will all become very clear to you," Connor said. "I have used the ID many times before in several different industries and it has never failed me," he said.

"Connor, I'm going to say something and I don't want you to get angry with me," said Dr. Price.

"Go ahead, I seldom, if ever, get angry over something anyone says to me," Connor said.

"OK, and please take it in the spirit it is intended," said Dr. Price. "I am so very happy your wife had to come to the ER," he said. "If she hadn't gotten sick, we would never have had the opportunity to meet you and learn these new methods of process improvement," Dr. Price said.

Connor laughed and said, "I'll tell Becky she has a physician that likes her being sick. I'll see you guys tomorrow," Connor said, as he left to go home.

As Connor was driving home, he was thinking about his first day and smiled. He thought to himself, "This is going to be fun and it should help the hospital improve their image within the community."

Connor's thoughts quickly turned to Becky, so he decided to call her.

The phone rang three times before Becky answered it. "Hello Connor! How did your day go?" asked Becky.

"It went fine. Look Becky, you've been cooped up in the hospital and at home for long enough; how about let's go out to dinner tonight?" he asked.

"Oh Connor … Are you asking me out on a date?" she said with a laugh.

"Yes babe, will you go out with me tonight?" he asked.

"Let me check my social calendar and see if I'm free," she replied humorously. "You're in luck," she said. "I think I have an opening. Just let me get cleaned up and I should be ready by the time you get home."

When Connor arrived home, Becky met him at the door and all he could do was smile and say, "Wow! You look great!"

"Thank you Connor! I know this is your favorite outfit," she said.

Connor took her hand, led her to the Hummer and they drove to their favorite restaurant. Becky and Connor talked about a variety of different things including Connor's day at the hospital. Connor told Becky what Dr. Price had said about him being happy that she had gotten sick and they both laughed about it. Becky also asked about Joe and Sam and how they were doing at Aviation Dynamics. Connor said he thought everything was going well and that Joe and Sam were doing a great job so far. They had been able to complete the ID and the preliminary Intermediate Objectives map and the internal team was now working the issues. Connor also mentioned that Joe and Sam were scheduled to go back in about a week or so, to get an update of the progress.

Becky asked, "Will you be going back with them?"

"I'm not sure, but I think I might," Connor replied. "I need to make sure you're doing OK before I go anywhere," he added.

"In a week, I might be ready to go back with you," Becky said.

Connor wasn't so sure about Becky going with them and told her not to rush it. She just smiled and said that he worried too much about her. After an hour or so of great conversation, and their customary bottle of Chianti, they went home and went to bed. They both slept well for the first time in a couple of weeks.

The next morning, Connor was up early and prepared for another day at the hospital. His strategy was to review the VSA map and introduce them to the IDs. He arrived at the hospital early and set up two separate flip charts.

Everyone arrived on time and they were all seated in the conference room by 7:00 AM. Connor welcomed all of them back and then reviewed the work on the VSA. They discussed the VSA for several minutes and everyone seemed happy with their efforts so far.

Connor told the group he wanted to introduce them to a new thinking tool, which he referred to as the ID. Connor had his laptop ready and projected the ID slide onto the screen.

Interference Diagram Structure

Connor explained that the purpose of the ID was to surface all of the obstacles that might be interfering with their ability to achieve the stated goal or objective. He emphasized the need for the team to agree on a common objective for the ID. The team discussed the wording of the objective and finally agreed on "Complete EKG to Table Time in Less than 35 minutes." Connor agreed and instructed the team to list all of the interferences/obstacles that might block their ability to achieve their objective. Connor also asked them to estimate the current times for each interference listed.

The team left the conference room and went back to the ER to conduct some additional interviews and collect their estimates of the time for each of the interferences. When the team felt they had enough information about the estimated times, they returned to the conference room to start the ID effort.

Terry and Connor facilitated the effort to construct the ID, and after a short while, they had a preliminary ID ready to go.

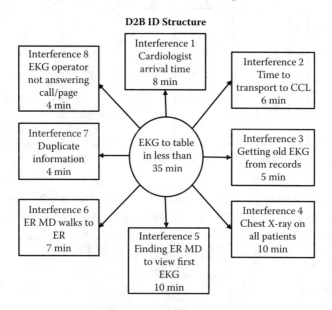

D2B ID Structure

"The next step would be to ask the question, 'are there any of these interferences we can stop doing immediately to reduce the time?'" Connor asked the group. After a lengthy discussion, everyone agreed that all of the interferences were required, but they just took too much time.

"So, what do we do now?" Terry asked.

"If there are none that can be immediately removed, then we prioritize them," Connor said.

Sally Lu raised her hand and asked, "Do you have a good way to do that?"

"Great question Sally," said Connor. "I'm going to introduce you to another tool I use for an analysis just like this," Connor said. He was searching his laptop for the slide he wanted and finally found it and put it on the screen.

Prioritization Matrix for improvement actions

	1	2	3	4	5
5					1, 2, 5
4					
3			3	4	
2		7			
1	8				

Improvement payback (vertical axis) — Ease of implementation (horizontal axis)

"What you see on the screen is called a Prioritization Matrix and it's used to analyze the actions that you have developed to reduce the time. When you look at the actions, you would look for those actions that are both high payback and easy to implement," Connor explained. "As you can see, going up and down the matrix, there are boxes numbered 1 to 5 under the heading 'Improvement Payback.' Likewise, moving left to right, there are boxes numbered 1 to 5 representing 'Ease of Implementation,'" Connor explained. "For example, suppose you have an action item that will give you very high payback in reducing time and it's relatively easy to implement," said Connor. "You would rate that action as a 5 for payback and a 5 for ease of implementation," Connor explained as he pointed to the chart. "You would then place the number of the action item from the ID directly inside the box 5 and 5. Likewise, you would rate each action item and place its number inside the appropriate box of the Prioritization Matrix. When you've placed all of your action items inside the matrix, you work on the highest-payback and easiest-to-implement actions first. Like in this example on the screen, you would focus on actions 1, 2, and 5 from your ID to get the maximum leverage first, and then start 3 and 4, then 7, and finally 8," Connor explained.

"That makes our jobs much easier, so thank you very much for sharing this method with us," said Sally. "Are all of your methods so easy Mr. Jackson?" asked Sally.

Connor smiled and replied, "I'm a simple kind of guy … what can I say."

They worked diligently for the rest of the day developing solutions to their interferences and the action plans to implement them. It was now nearing the end of the day.

Once again, Sally had a question for Connor. "Yes Sally?" Connor said.

"It seems to me that since we already have our plan ready to go, we could start implementing right away. Is this your plan for us tomorrow? Or, should we develop our Future State maps?" Sally asked.

"The answer is yes," replied Connor, meaning that the team needed to develop the Future State map and then start implementation. "You'll develop your Future State map with any waste removed and your actions to reduce the time. You'll also perform a VSA on your Future State map," Connor explained. "Does this sound like a plan to all of you?" he asked.

As a group, they all concurred. The team was also very surprised that they had been able to develop an action plan so quickly. By simply identifying the constraint and then focusing their efforts on the constraint, they were able to pinpoint what their improvement effort should be, to gain the maximum leverage. This approach was something very different to them.

Time went by fast, and before long, it was 3:30 PM and time to adjourn for the day and Connor was ready to excuse the team. Before everyone started to leave, Sally said, "I don't know about anyone else, but I want to stay and complete our Future State map so that tomorrow we can begin implementing our action items." The rest of the team agreed. They all decided to stay some extra time and complete the Future State map.

While the team kept working, Connor talked with Terry and Dr. Price. He told them he thought the team was heading in the right direction and doing some excellent work. Connor decided he would leave for the day and check the status of the Future State map in the morning. He would be back at 7:00 AM.

When he arrived home, he noticed Becky was outside working on her flowers and shrubs. Becky smiled and waved when she saw Connor's Hummer pull into the driveway and Connor smiled and waved back. Seeing her outside was a clear sign that she was feeling better. He thought to himself, "Becky is gorgeous. I still can't believe she married someone as plain as I am." Connor walked over to Becky, took her into his arms, told her he loved her, and kissed her.

"Connor, what if the neighbors see you?" she asked in a flirting manner.

The next morning, Connor arrived at the hospital around 6:00 AM. He wanted to check out activity in the ER. He walked to the ER and it appeared as though everyone was busy. He also noticed what he thought was a rather full waiting room. He decided to sit down and talk with a few people about their experience. What he heard were negative comments about how they had checked in and then just sat and waited for someone to come and check on them. On the basis of the comments he was hearing, about half of the people had been in the waiting room for 45 minutes to an hour, or more, without any contact with the nurses or doctors. Connor made a note to himself that just by acknowledging contact with the patients after they arrive would have a positive influence on their experience.

Connor moved from his chair to watch the flow of the ER and noticed things like centralized printers that resulted in employees having to walk quite a distance just to retrieve a copy of something. Connor thought, "It might be that delays resulting from having to walk to printers are costing the hospital much more than the cost of a couple of small printers." He noticed the same thing with computer locations, meaning that there were only a few computers available, and when more than two people needed to use one, they had to wait. It seemed to Connor that maybe having something like tablets available for the employees would clearly reduce this waiting time. Connor watched the flow for a while longer before heading to the conference room.

When everyone was seated, Connor asked to see the color-coded Future State map. Terry was on his laptop and quickly put it on the screen. Connor asked a few questions, which were answered and they quickly moved on.

Connor asked the team to present their finalized Prioritization Matrices and the action plans. This activity generated much discussion between about how to divide up the work and how much more detail might be required. So far, Connor was happy with the effort and the outcome.

Dr. Price and Terry huddled the team before they started. Dr. Price said he had talked with the head nurse in the ER the previous afternoon. She had relayed to him that the ER personnel were ready to get started. They had received instructions from their management that this was coming and they should be prepared to follow it through.

Terry reminded the team that this was going to be a two-phase approach. The first phase was the action items from the ID and to see if, and where, any time could be reduced. The second phase was to make any necessary changes to the policies and procedures. Dr. Price reminded them that any policy changes or procedural changes needed to be approved by the internal policy board, which was chaired by the Chief Medical Officer. Dr. Price was also a member of this board. Any changes would need to be fully documented and approved before they could take effect.

The team was ready to go. They had their plan and knew where to focus and what actions to take to gain the most leverage. Because of the actions the team had surfaced with the ID, they understood how important it would be to get the solutions from the true subject matter experts, the employees working in the ER, and those who supported the ER. Doing it this way would help achieve ownership for the changes being made. Only time would tell how effective the new process might actually be.

The team had to come up with a way to make sure everyone understood the new process. One of the team members had suggested that they have "mock drills" whereby one of the team members would be designated as someone having a heart attack and they could move through the new process. This seemed like an acceptable idea to document, and discover, any pinch points with the new process. The team wanted everyone ready when a real heart attack patient enters the ER. The team left for the ER.

Terry and Dr. Price were still in the conference room and asked Connor if every team he works with operates this fast. Connor smiled and said, "Many teams generally operate quickly, but this team seems to be much more motivated than most. I suppose it's because we're dealing with life-saving actions rather than moving products through a manufacturing process," he added. Connor packed his things and was getting ready to head home. He was feeling very good about what this team had accomplished.

"When will you be back?" asked Dr. Price.

"I guess that depends on you guys," Connor answered.

"We will need some time to walk through the process a few times and check the procedures against the new process, and then make changes as required. Then we'll need to get everything documented, updated, and approved. That could take a couple of weeks or more," Dr. Price cautioned.

"I might suggest that when the team finishes, they make a presentation to the executive staff and walk them through what they did and why they did it, and any policy and procedural changes they think are necessary," Connor said. "Perhaps, when that happens would be a good time for me to come back. If they still have an interest in all of this, then we could schedule a 1-day event and introduce the executives to the Intermediate Objectives map and help plan some strategy going forward."

"We'll be in touch," said Terry. They both left to walk to the ER and be with the rest of the team. Connor finished gathering his things and headed home.

With a couple of weeks to go before his next meeting at the hospital, Connor decided it might be a good time to go visit Aviation Dynamics again with Joe and Sam. He called them both when he got home and set up a meeting to discuss a return visit.

14

Aviation Dynamics—The Return Visit

When Connor called Joe and Sam, he had arranged for the meeting to take place the next day at *Jonah's*. Joe and Sam arrived on time to find Connor sitting at his regular table in the corner. They both walked over and sat down.

Connor smiled and asked, "How's it going guys?"

Both said, "Fine," and immediately asked about Becky.

"She's doing great," Connor said. "She's getting back to her old self and feeling stronger every day."

"How is the project at the hospital going?" asked Joe.

"It's going well," said Connor. "In fact, we've made some very good progress already with the Door to Balloon Time."

"What's Door to Balloon Time?" Sam asked.

"We'll talk about that later. Right now, I want you guys to get me caught up on Aviation Dynamics. I know it's been a while since we last talked, but have you heard anything from them?" Connor asked.

"Actually, no we haven't," Joe said. "They have been awfully silent about what is going on there. I thought about giving Brad a call, but decided against it. We'll just give them some time to work the issues and let them call us if they think they have a problem," Joe added.

"When are you planning on going back?" asked Connor.

"We haven't made any definitive plans yet," said Joe. "We've actually been waiting to hear from them to see if we needed to go back sooner than we originally thought."

"OK, when you do make those travel plans, include me in the planning. I'm confident Becky is doing better and me being gone for a couple of days will probably be alright," Connor said. "Besides, I think Becky would like me gone for a couple of days," he added with a smile. They all smiled and laughed out loud.

Connor opened a folder on the table and pulled out the Intermediate Objectives (IO) map from Aviation Dynamics that Sam had previously sent him and said, "Let's review this and see where we're at."

Connor laid it on the table in front of them and spun it around so it was facing both of them.

"Are there any particular areas that caused any concerns for you guys? Perhaps something that came up in conversation that might be a big problem?" Connor asked.

"Not really," said Joe. "We actually had great participation from both management and the hourlies. The only real concern was Hal. He was upset that none of these new ideas had anything to do with saving money," Joe said. "When we talked about inventory and parts issues, it was clear that Brad understood the situation they were in and how they'd gotten there. Brad took the action that he and Hal would call, or go visit with, the corporate office to talk about it."

"I'm glad Brad is going to follow through with that action," Connor said. "It's an issue that will need to come from his level to be effective and I think he can control Hal as well," he added.

"Are there any others items that caused you any concern?" Connor asked.

"None that I can think of," answered Joe. "But, I do think they will have some problems with the scheduling segment," Joe added.

"I agree," Connor said, "The current way they do it won't allow for good integration of all the individual schedules they have. Their system still assumes each project as separate entities and that will be a problem for them. Did you by chance discuss Critical Chain Project Management?" Connor asked.

"Not yet," Sam said. "We were hoping that their research might take them in that direction, but we need to wait and see."

"OK!" Connor said. "Is there anything else that you guys needed to do before we go back?"

"We haven't heard anything from them yet, so as of right now I don't think there is anything," Joe said.

"Joe, why don't you give Brad or Zeke, or maybe even Jim, a call and see how things are going? See if you can work out when we might be going back and finalize with them. I've got approximately 2 weeks before I meet with the executive staff of the hospital to develop their IO map," Connor said with a smile.

"I'll do that," Joe said. "And, I'll let you know what they decide."

"Great!" Connor said. "Let's get ready to knock this one out of the park," he added.

They talked about a few more items before Joe and Sam headed back to Barton. When they got back, they went into Sam's office to call Brad. Sam found Brad's business card and dialed his office number. The phone rang twice and Helen, his administrative assistant, answered. "Good afternoon, Mr. Carter's office," she said.

"Hello, this is Sam Henderson and Joe Pecci calling, is Brad in?" Sam asked.

"Hello, Sam! Brad is not here right now. He and Hal are at Corporate Headquarters attending some meetings. May I take a message for him?" she asked.

"Do you know when he might be back?" asked Sam.

"He is scheduled to return this Friday afternoon," she replied. "I'm not sure if he will come to the plant or just go home," she added.

"OK, thanks," Sam said. "By chance can you transfer this call to Zeke Evans or Jim Barnes?" Sam asked.

"Let me try Mr. Evans, I believe he is in his office right now," Helen said.

There was a click on the phone while the connection was being made. A few seconds later Zeke answered his phone, "Hello, this is Zeke."

"Hello, Zeke, this is Sam Henderson and Joe Pecci calling," Sam said. Sam switched the phone to speaker so Joe could hear and talk, as well.

"Hi guys, what's going on?" Zeke asked.

"We were calling to ask you the same thing," Joe said. "We were curious about how the project is going so far?" Joe added.

"We've been as busy as a beehive. Brad and Hal are at corporate with some meetings, and the other team members are busy as well," Zeke said.

"That's good to hear," Sam said.

"We wanted to call in to see if you guys have a particular day in mind for us to return?" Joe asked.

"You know, we were just talking about that this morning in our morning meeting. We usually have a 15- or 20-minute meeting every morning to get status and make sure nothing is blocking what we need to do. Anyway, someone asked when you guys were coming back and Jim said he didn't know for sure yet. Honestly, I think if you came back the middle of next week that would be good. Brad and Hal will be back the end of this week, and we can update you on what's been going on," Zeke said.

"That sounds fine," Joe said. "So, we'll plan on being there Wednesday and Thursday of next week if that works for you?" Joe asked.

"That works fine. I'll tell everyone during tomorrow morning's meeting when you're coming in," Zeke stated.

"By the way, Connor will be coming with us," Joe added.

"That's great! We'll all be happy to see him again. I'll get everything set up on this end," Zeke said.

"OK then, we'll see you next Wednesday at 7:00 AM," Joe said.

"See you then. Good-bye," Zeke said and disconnected.

"Now we need to call Liz at the travel agency and get everything set up," Sam said. "Should we do the private jet again?" Sam asked.

"It will certainly be the easiest thing to do," Joe said. "Let's just go ahead and set it up."

Sam made the call to Liz and set up the travel arrangements for all three of them. Liz called them back approximately 20 minutes later with all of the information. Sam made the call to Connor to let him know what the plans were. Connor told them thanks and that he would see them next Tuesday evening at the Business Air terminal.

The following Tuesday, they all met at the Business Air terminal around 5:00 PM. As usual, the flight to Houston was uneventful, except for the smile on Sam's face. He still looked like a 10-year-old boy riding a carnival ride.

When they arrived, the rental car was waiting at the terminal, so they loaded their bags in the trunk, drove to the hotel, parked, and checked in. Everyone decided just to go to their room and skip dinner. They would meet in the morning at 6:10 AM in the lobby.

The next morning, Connor was the first one in the lobby. He didn't have to wait long for Joe and Sam to show up. They all walked out to the car and loaded their bags in the trunk, and Joe slid into the driver's seat. Sam was in the front seat and Connor got in the back as they made the drive to Aviation Dynamics. When they arrived, they talked with the gate guard for just a minute or two before he waived them through. They parked in their usual visitor parking slot, got out, and retrieved their bags and headed for the front door. When they entered the building, Connor noticed the same woman at the reception desk and her eyebrows immediately went up expressing a bit of panic when she saw Connor. He just smiled and said, "Good morning, how are you today?" She replied, "Fine," looking almost fearful he might start asking her more questions again. She hurried and picked up the phone to make the call and notify someone that they were there. They all signed in and got their badges while the receptionist finished her call. A few minutes later, Jim entered the lobby and said, "Good morning," to everyone.

"Connor, how nice to see you again," Jim said. "How is your wife doing?" he asked.

"She's doing well!" Connor exclaimed. "Thank you for asking," he added.

They followed Jim back to the conference room, and when they entered, everyone was already there. This time, there was a much bigger crowd with the full team in place than what Connor remembered from before. Brad immediately walked over and asked Connor about Becky. "She's fine," Connor said. "She just scared us for a week or so until we got everything straightened out."

Without wasting any time for small talk, Joe moved to the front of the room, plugged in his flash drive, and started pushing buttons and moving the mouse around until he found what he wanted. Then, he faced the group and took a moment to introduce Connor to the new members of the team. Nathan waved at Connor from his seat at the table and Connor waved back and smiled. Joe hit another button and the full IO map they had completed the last time they were there appeared on the screen.

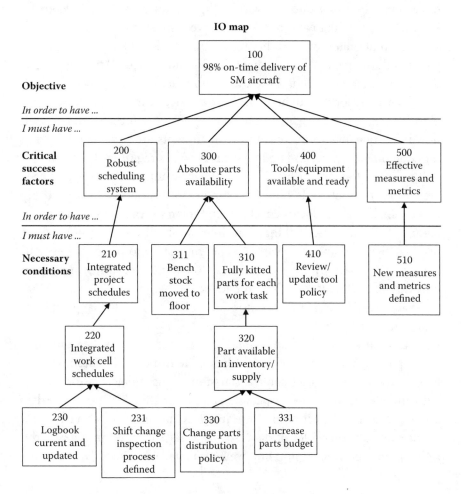

Joe wasted no time in getting the conversation going. "We talked with Zeke last week and he told us that today would be a good day to come back and get some progress and status reports on some of your activities," Joe said.

Joe turned and faced the screen. "Here is the IO map that we finished the last time we were here," Joe said pointing with his laser. "What we want to do today is figure out how much has been completed, if anything, and how much progress you have made," he said. Joe reminded them of the instructions they had been left with, which were to start at the bottom of the IO map and work up through the arrows toward the top. With his laser, he pointed to the screen and asked, "What about necessary condition 230?"

Hector was first to raise his hand and Joe pointed to him. "230 was part of the team I was assigned to work with," Hector said. "We developed a Future State flow map and decided how we wanted it to work. We didn't do a Current State flow map because it only had one box that read, 'Go pick up all the papers!'" Everyone laughed and smiled. "Anyway, we put together a flow describing how the documents for the logbook should move with the job throughout the entire process, making sure we have all of the signed documents in one place. We decided the team lead will now be responsible to make sure the documents are signed and entered into document control and update the logbook as required. The team lead will keep the logbook at his desk. We haven't quite finished yet, but we are thinking about some kind of a simple notification system, probably using e-mail to send documents back and forth for those areas outside of Hangar 1. We are also looking at an internal mail routing system where original signed documents can be sent from place to place, as needed," Hector said. "Actually, we are very close to having everything in place to take care of the documents," Hector added.

"That's great!" Joe said. "Let's move on to NC 231, 'Shift change inspection process defined.'"

Nathan raised his hand and said, "That would be me. When our subgroup got together, we talked about 'why' the inspection issues might be happening. Anyway, after some discussion of the problem, we came up with the idea to have the inspectors start their shift 30 minutes earlier and overlap the inspectors that are just leaving shift. We haven't had a chance yet to gather a lot of data, so we're not sure if 30 minutes is the right amount of time, or not. But, we haven't had any issues with the shift change inspection since we started doing this. We'll continue to watch it and see if any issues arise," Nathan explained. "We'll probably wait a while longer before we create the policy about how it works. We just need to cycle through the process a few more times and look for glitches before we document the process," Nathan added.

"Excellent work, Nathan," Joe said. "Just keep an eye on it and make sure we get it documented when you understand how you want it to work," Joe added.

"OK, let's move on to NC 330, 'Change parts distribution policy.' Who worked on that one?" Joe asked. Zeke, Jim, Marsha, Agnes, and Bette all raised their hands. Joe asked, "Who wants to be the spokesperson?" Joe asked.

"I will," said Jim. "When we got together, we first reviewed the policy and what it was intended to do. I think we all understood what the policy was originally intended to do, but that isn't what happened. When we looked deeper, we discovered that parts for the scheduled maintenance are known in advance. We basically know which parts and how many we need, and when we need them. What we didn't know for sure was how many parts the unscheduled maintenance hangar might need. It was a total unknown because we simply don't know in advance what's wrong with the helicopters in unscheduled maintenance. We discovered that the scheduled maintenance was the hangar ordering the parts, but Hangar 2 was most likely using them. Hangar 1 was constantly ordering but sometimes had to wait for extended periods before they got the parts they needed," Jim added.

"That's true," Marsha said. "Hangar 1 was ordering on the basis of their repair schedule and when the part would be needed. However, the policy allowed Hangar 2 to take and use the parts if they needed them first to get a helicopter flying again. Sometimes, it was a vicious cycle of parts and no parts. If parts weren't available, then the work stopped in scheduled maintenance and the pressure was on procurement to get more. Sometimes, the needed parts could have extended lead times, and that was a major problem," Marsha added.

Zeke jumped in the conversation, "When we really stopped and looked at what we were doing, we realized the error of our ways. We thought that if unscheduled maintenance had the parts first, we could still make money. We didn't realize how much that action was slowing down the on-time delivery and revenue from the scheduled maintenance side, but now we do," Zeke added.

"When we analyzed the real parts availability," Jim said, "we realized that scheduled maintenance had a much higher level of certainty about which parts they needed and what day they might need them. The unscheduled maintenance side was total uncertainty. We didn't know from day to day which parts or how many," Jim said. "It was the uncertainty of the needed parts that was driving most, if not all, of our problems."

"We asked Marsha to collect some data from the procurement history and see if she could determine which parts were most often used by both hangars," Zeke said. "Then, we organized the data by part number and part type into a Pareto chart to analyze the results. It was very revealing what was happening," Zeke added. "We looked at total demand for each part and how many went to Hangar 1 and Hangar 2 and what the current inventory was. It was obvious that we were getting enough parts to support all of the work in Hangar 1, but sometimes Hangar 2 was taking a very large percentage of those parts," he explained.

Marsha jumped back in. "What the team decided, on the basis of the Pareto analysis, was that we needed some extra inventory of the most common parts to help us overcome the effects of the uncertainty from unscheduled maintenance. For the most commonly used parts, we needed a 'parts buffer' to help us better control and manage the uncertainty. We used the Pareto analysis to help determine which parts those should be," Marsha added.

Zeke said, "In order to move forward with this parts buffer concept and create the necessary inventory, we needed some additional dollars to do that. Marsha put together some cost numbers to see what the total dollars might be and then we compared the cost estimate to how much additional revenue we might gain by being able to complete the projects on time. It was a huge number!" Zeke exclaimed. "By being able to spend some money and create the parts buffer, the actual revenue increase was exponential. We gave our parts analysis and cost estimates to Brad when he and Hal went to corporate," Zeke added.

"Well done!" Joe exclaimed. "Your analysis was comprehensive and detailed and provided some very necessary and important information," said Joe. Joe continued to look at Zeke and finally asked him, "Were you surprised at what the analysis revealed?"

"Honestly, I was very surprised," Zeke said. "I honestly thought we were doing the right thing with the policies we had in place. I didn't truly understand the real consequences of the cost cutting and policies until last week, when we reviewed the results." Joe nodded his head and smiled.

"Let's shift our attention to NC 331, 'Move bench stock to the shop floor,' who has that one?" Joe asked.

Both Agnes and Bette raised their hands. Joe pointed to Agnes and asked, "What's the progress?"

"Well, Bette and I have been looking at the number of usable bins we still have in the supply room. When we previously started the inventory reduction actions, there were some bins left over. On the basis of what we have right now, we can get started, but we might need some more bins later on. When we first talked about how we might want to do this, we were thinking that each work cell would need its own bench stock location, but we have since changed our minds. That would require an awful lot of bins and a significant expense. Anyway, we decided we could set up a central common stock location on each side of the hangar, one for each supervisor, but we haven't decided for sure yet. Anyway, when the bins are moved and set up, Bette will start by checking those bins three times a week and see which ones need more parts. It won't be an actual minimum/maximum system because we won't need to count the parts. Bette will just do a visual from the inventory she sees in the bin. This process might require some additional part requisitions to order more often, but the folks in procurement say that's OK!" Agnes said. "We're moving forward to pick the best location that will be best for everyone. We won't move all of the parts, but we have a good idea of the most used, and those are the ones we'll move first," Agnes said. "It's just a matter of finding the time to get it done!" Agnes added.

There had already been significant conversation back and forth between the team about the necessary conditions discussed so far. So far, everyone had agreed that the plans presented were probably a good place to start and they could make any other changes, as required, and if necessary.

Sam signaled to Joe that it was almost lunchtime. Joe looked at his watch, it was 10:45 AM, so Joe did a quick summary and then released everyone for lunch with the promise they would all be back in their seats at 11:30 AM. The conference room emptied quickly, except for Brad and Zeke, and they both walked over to Joe and Sam.

Joe looked at Brad and said, "Looks like you're up, right after lunch."

"I guess I am," Brad said. "This has been very interesting to me so far. When we finally turned the people loose, to help solve the problems, they did some excellent work. What surprised me the most was that the people understood the problems better than we did! As a management team, we were trying to implement solutions without really understanding the problem. We thought we had an answer, but we really didn't understand the problem. We were ignoring the subject matter experts! The lesson learned for me is to not make that same mistake again. I'm very pleased to see the level of thinking they are using on their projects," he added.

Connor smiled and replied, "You guys had the answers all along. You just didn't know it."

Brad smiled back and said, "That's very true! What I'm most intrigued with is how we missed it from the start. What I realized was we were looking in all the wrong places and then trying to correct all of our problems with just cost cutting. We spent a lot of time trying to fix things that didn't necessarily need fixing," Brad explained.

"Most people and organizations do miss it," Connor said. "Instead of doing a good system analysis to find the problem, they tend to take actions based on symptoms, or those negative things that seem to keep happening. What companies most often fail to understand is the real core problem for 'why' something happened and 'why' it keeps happening. They see the systems effects, but they don't understand the causality for why the effect happened. Symptom solutions tend to generate short-term, if any, results. Until the core problem is removed, the symptoms will resurface. Sometimes, what looks like a really good idea can generate significant negative effects through time. Unless you identify and remove, or change, the core problem, you keep getting the same results," Connor added.

"I see your point," Brad said. "What we are doing now does make a lot of sense. In fact, I used a lot of what the teams had presented internally when I went to corporate to explain the situation," Brad added.

"Hopefully you had good results at corporate?" Joe asked.

"I think we did. If nothing else, I caught the attention of several key players who had an interest in what I was talking about," Brad said.

"We'll be interested to hear your results right after lunch," Joe said.

Brad and Zeke left the conference room, probably to go check for phone messages and e-mails.

Joe, Sam, and Connor sat down at the table. Connor spoke first, "They are doing some good stuff here."

"Yes they are!" Joe said.

Sam was nodding his head in agreement. "It's actually more than I expected. I wasn't sure what to expect, knowing the tension that we thought existed between management and the union. I was prepared for a lot more disagreement than we're seeing," Joe added. "They seem to be working together just fine to analyze and solve the problems," Joe said.

"Having good results starts with having good information," Connor said. "I'm interested to see how the rest of this goes." Joe and Sam nodded in agreement. They sat and chatted about Becky and some other subjects until lunch was over. When everyone started to reassemble in the conference room, Joe prepared himself for the second half of the day.

When everyone was finally seated, Joe walked back to the front of the room and said, "Welcome back. Let's get started because we still have a lot to cover before the end of the day. Let's move on to NC 331, 'Increased parts budget,'" Joe said, pointing with his laser to the box on the screen. "Who had that one?" he asked. Brad raised his hand and smiled. Hal raised his hand also, but he wasn't smiling.

Brad spoke, "As most of you know, Hal and I made a trip to corporate last week to make a presentation and talk about the situation we are in. For the most part, I think it went very well. There was some resistance to our message, but there was also some acceptance. We discussed the efficiency measure and some of the negative outcomes from that. We also talked about the need for an increased parts budget. This was a subject that generated the most attention," Brad said. "As best as I could, I explained how cutting the parts budget was actually slowing down the work and hurting the revenues. We explained the huge increase in workloads and trying to do the work with the same parts budget. Everyone seemed to understand that issue and agreed that more dollars would be necessary to complete the work on time. In fact, they wanted to know why we hadn't brought up the issue before then," Brad said as he looked at Hal. "With the procurement analysis from Zeke, Jim, and Marsha and the rest of the procurement group, they could see how spending some more on parts could exponentially influence the revenue by having parts available. I related to them the story about priming the pump," Brad said looking directly at Connor. Connor just smiled and nodded his head. "The end result was corporate understood the need for some investment in order to get where we need to be," Brad said. "We still have some work to do on our parts list to continue the analysis and estimate what kind of costs we are looking at, but for the most part, they agreed with us."

"That's great news!" Joe said. "You must have made a great presentation about defining the needs," Joe added in the form of a compliment.

"Most of what I put in my presentation was things I've learned during our discussions here and the teams working the issues," Brad said. "We still don't know how much money will be available, or when it will be available, but we have the commitment that it has to be something," Brad added.

"That's all good news Brad, and thanks for the update," Joe said. "Let's move on to NC 410, 'Review/update tool policy,' who worked on that one?" Joe asked.

Zeke, Jim, Hector, and Nathan all raised their hands. There were also a couple of other people who raised their hands as well. Joe pointed to Nathan because he could tell that Nathan really wanted to talk about this one.

"We reviewed the tool policy with the group, knowing that the tool accountability and foreign object debris (FOD) requirements wouldn't change," Nathan said. "We just had to find a way to meet those requirements and reduce the amount of time it takes. We created a small process flow map and looked for the non–value-added things that we were doing. Once we laid it out, it became very obvious where the problem was," Nathan said.

"And what did you discover as the problem?" Joe asked.

"Well, our policy was making the assumption that every mechanic had to have accountability for the tools, even though the same tools were being used on all three shifts. So, we decided that the responsibility was set too low and moved it back to the work crew team leader," Nathan said.

"By the way, that was Nathan's idea," Zeke said.

Nathan blushed and continued. "Anyway, by doing that, we could keep the tools in the work areas and not have to turn them in and check them out after each shift. From now on, the crew team leader will do the inventory, which allows for the tool accountability and FOD check. The transfer will now only occur between the team leaders during shift change. It will save us an enormous amount of time," Nathan said proudly.

"How much time do you think it will save?" Sam asked.

"We think with the new process we can now do it in 15, or 20 minutes, or less," said Jim. "We've been working through some trial runs to see if we forgot anything, but it should work reasonably well and still allow us to maintain accountability and control FOD," Jim added.

"Also," said Hector, "We've included any special equipment, jigs, slings, and everything else not in the toolbox. What will happen now is the team leader will make sure any special equipment is already checked out and available in the work cell when it's needed," said Hector. "We will make it the responsibility of the team leader to make sure everything is signed out, and instead of waiting until we get to a task that requires special equipment, the team leader will be looking ahead to determine when the equipment will be needed and go to the supply room and check it out. It's kind of like a kitting process, except it's just for special equipment. When the work crew has finished with it, the team lead will return it to the supply room for the next crew," Hector added.

"When the team talked about this, we could see an advantage for having things ready to go before it was needed, rather than needing it now and having to go get it," Jim said. "It will certainly reduce our time if the special equipment is already in the work cell and ready to go," Jim added.

"When they get the process finalized, I will rewrite the policy and procedure to match the new process," Zeke said.

"That's excellent!" Joe exclaimed. He looked at Connor and Sam, who were both smiling. "Let's move on to NC 510, 'New measures and metrics defined,' who had that one?" Joe asked.

"I did," said Jim. "We talked at length about this one as a group, but decided we weren't ready to define what the measures and metrics are until we get everything else in place and see where we're at, and what we are doing. That will help us to better define what the real metrics need to be under the new way of doing business," Jim said.

"That's fair enough," Joe said.

"Let's go back and update our IO map and see where we're at. Let's take a 15-minute break, while I do some updating," Joe said. Everyone went on break and Joe walked up to his laptop and started making the updates to the IO map by color coding the progress. When everyone returned from break, he put the slide back on the screen.

Updated IO map

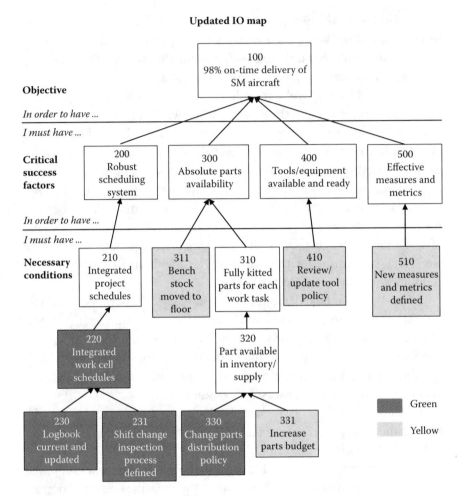

"OK, here is the updated IO map. Those boxes colored green indicate they are done. Those colored in yellow are started, but not done yet, and those with no color haven't been started yet. Does that make sense to everyone?" Joe asked facing the group. Everyone seemed to be nodding acceptance to what Joe had just said.

"So, if we have NC 230 and NC 231 complete, then we can achieve NC 220, correct?" Joe asked. Everyone nodded in agreement. "If we have 220 then, we can have 210. Correct?" Joe asked the group.

"Mr. Pecci, you just hit on a problem that we found about a week ago," Nathan said. "When we got together with the scheduler, they agreed that the schedules could be integrated at the work cell level, but what we'd end up with is six different master schedules. We'd only have one schedule for each work cell and not a total integrated master schedule. We couldn't figure out how to get a master schedule from all of the work cells using the system we currently have," Nathan added.

"He's right," said Hector. "We'd just be back to having six separate schedules again and that won't work. We'd still have the same problem scheduling resources and be back to having all of the meetings, trying to figure out who goes where and when," Hector added.

"So, there is something missing?" Joe asked.

"Yes, there is," Nathan said.

"What is it?" Joe asked.

"Well, overall, what we decided was we didn't have a way to combine all the schedules into a master schedule, especially for some of the resources," Nathan said.

"So, is this what is missing?" Joe asked, as he walked back to the computer and added NC 221.

Added IO 221 integrated schedules

"That could work," Nathan said. "We need the work cell schedules and we need a way to integrate all of the schedules and look for any resource conflicts," he added.

Joe pondered the implications of getting into the scheduling discussion at this point in time. He looked at his watch and realized it was already 2:15 PM. The scheduling discussion was important and necessary, but time was working against them and running short. He decided to try and divert this discussion until tomorrow when they would have a full day to talk about it.

Sam was thinking to himself and smiling, "Wow! Both Connor and Joe predicted this scheduling issue would happen. I'm glad they are both on my team."

Joe looked at the screen and then turned and faced the group and said, "The scheduling discussion is important and necessary to do. You have discovered another necessary condition that must be in place in order to achieve the integrated master schedule. However, time is growing short today, and I know this scheduling discussion will take some time to resolve. So, I'd like to propose that the scheduling issue be the first item on the agenda for tomorrow morning. I'd like to continue with the remaining IOs. Are there any objections to that?" Joe asked.

No one objected to Joe's offer, so he continued with the discussion. "OK, that's good," Joe said. "Let's continue looking at the other necessary conditions," Joe said. He pointed his laser to NC 320 and said, "Parts available in inventory and supply. We know that NC 320 can't be completed yet because NC 331 is still yellow! As Brad explained earlier, you still owe corporate some estimated numbers for parts and getting approval for some additional dollars," Joe explained. "Until all of that comes together, this box will remain yellow," Joe explained.

Joe turned and faced the group. You could tell by his facial expression Joe was pondering a thought. He asked the group, "Are those the only two necessary conditions we need for all the parts to be available in inventory and supply?" Everyone, except Sam and Connor, had a puzzled look on their face. Joe waited for a response.

Finally, Marsha spoke. "Those are both necessary conditions to help manage and control available parts. I'm not sure I understand what you mean when you ask are those the only two?" Marsha questioned.

"Are those the only two things necessary to have ALL the parts available in inventory and supply?" Joe asked again.

"Wait a minute!" Nathan said. "I don't think we've fully considered the impact of the Return to Vendor (RTV) parts that we always seem to be waiting for. Is that what you mean?" Nathan asked.

"That's exactly what I mean," Joe said.

Marsha was quick to jump back in and said, "We send the parts out to be refurbished or repaired, as quickly as we get them. We just have to wait for them to come back, and sometimes that takes a while," she added.

"What if you didn't have to wait?" Joe asked.

"What do you mean?" Marsha said. "We always have to wait!"

"What if you had a replacement part already to go and didn't have to wait for it to be returned?" Joe asked.

"Oh man, that would help our schedules a bunch," Nathan said. "If we could turn one in and get a refurbished part the same day, that would be wonderful. Something like that could save a huge chunk of time on the schedule," Nathan added.

"But, we don't have one," Marsha said. "We have to wait for it to come back!" she exclaimed.

"You're right Marsha, you do have to wait. But, what if you had a part here and ready for use? What if you had an inventory buffer of the most common RTV parts that require refurbishment or repair, at least for those parts that take the longest time to refurbish?" Joe asked.

"Oh, that would be awfully expensive to have that many parts," Marsha said.

Hal jumped in. "No way can we buy that many parts. If we did, we'd be right back where we started with high inventories, and that wouldn't be good. It's just too expensive!" Hal exclaimed.

"Maybe not," Joe said. "We just need enough to have a small inventory, something big enough to meet demand. Think about it," he said. "We only need enough parts to start the cycle, to prime the pump if you will, to get all that we need. Once the parts start cycling, you won't need to buy more," Joe stated.

"What do you mean by that?" Hal asked.

"When a part comes back from the RTV, it is just put back in the aircraft it came from, which usually results in much longer wait times. What if the incoming part was just put back into inventory and used during the next demand cycle?" Joe asked.

There was silence in the room, finally Marsha spoke, "Wait a minute, what you're saying is the part turned in for refurbishment doesn't necessarily have to be the same part put back in. In other words, if we already have a refurbished part in the inventory, we could use that one, while the part that just came out is being refurbished?" Marsha asked.

"That is exactly right!" Joe exclaimed. "Would that somehow be a problem?"

"Not at all!" exclaimed Nathan. "As long as it's a certified refurbished part, it would work."

Connor and Sam were smiling. Connor thought to himself, "Joe is doing a great job with this discussion. Helping them connect the actions to solve the problem." Brad was smiling as well. It was ALL starting to make sense to him.

"I think Joe's comments and ideas require some consideration," Brad said. "Marsha, I need you to consider some numbers for the RTV items in our cost estimates. I need to know the impact for doing something like what Joe is suggesting," Brad added.

Joe walked back to the computer to make the IO map updates. He added NC 321 and put it on the screen.

Added IO 321 RTV parts

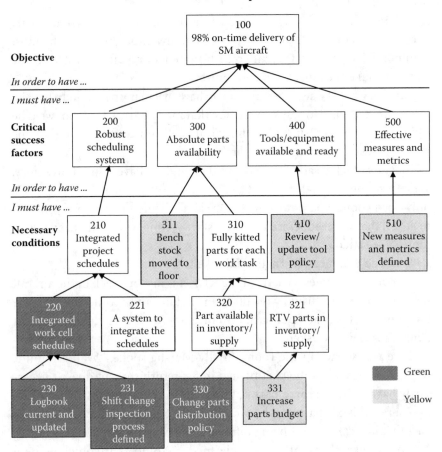

Joe pointed to the screen and said, "I've added NC 321 to the IO map. As you can see, it is also connected to NC 331, because some parts budget will be required to make this happen. Are there any questions?" Joe asked. No one raised their hand. Joe looked at his watch and it was 3:20 PM. He decided to release the group until tomorrow morning.

"OK, this is probably a good stopping point," Joe said. "When we come back in the morning we'll start the discussion on the scheduling issue. Make sure you are back in here at 7:00 AM tomorrow and ready to go. Thanks everyone, it was a good discussion today," Joe finished.

Everyone was filing out of the conference room. Brad stayed behind to walk them to the reception area and sign them out for the day. Connor, Joe, and Sam were picking up their stuff and putting it in their shoulder bags. Brad was standing close by and finally spoke. "You know, these ideas you are proposing are simply amazing. Your idea to focus on the system and find the best leverage points is just simply phenomenal! We've just never taken the time to do that. In fact, I'd never even considered it before," Brad said.

"Most of these ideas your team is coming up with will cost you nothing, except changing the way you think about getting things done," said Joe.

Brad was nodding in agreement and said, "Even the money we do spend will go a long way to increasing our output from the system. I now just consider the money as a necessary condition to get the upgrade we need."

They all walked back to the lobby, signed out, and drove back to the hotel. During the drive, Connor said, "Let's do dinner at six and enjoy some Chianti." Both Joe and Sam agreed.

15

MRO—Scheduling Discussion

At dinner that evening, they talked about the day's events and what had taken place. Connor was very complimentary to Joe for conducting the session. Connor said he had thoroughly enjoyed himself with the questions, answers, and debate. They all raised their glasses and toasted Joe's efforts.

"You know, tomorrow we will be talking about the scheduling stuff," Sam said. "And, I'm thinking we need to introduce them to Critical Chain Project Management (CCPM)."

"You are correct," said Connor. "The only way they can achieve the level of schedule integration they need is from the pipelining feature of CCPM. Right now, the best they can do is manage a single project and schedule and continue to fight for resources and parts. Without a way to manage multiple projects at the same time, the resources and parts will remain a problem for them," Connor said.

"They have made some impressive gains with their projects," Joe said.

"Yes they have!" Sam said. "They really seem to be working together to solve the issues."

When dinner was finished, Connor said, "Gentlemen, what do you say we call it a night? I'd like to get back to my room and give Becky a call and see how she's doing."

"Let's meet at 6:00 AM in the lobby," Joe said. "I'd like to be the first one there tomorrow morning." Connor and Sam smiled at Joe. They paid their bill and walked toward the elevators to return to their rooms.

The next morning, Joe was the first one in the lobby. He already had three coffees in travel containers and was just waiting for the other two. Connor and Sam arrived approximately 5 minutes later and he gave each of them a coffee. They walked to the car, got in, and started the drive. When they were finally moving in traffic, Joe asked Connor how Becky was. Connor answered, "She's fine. She spent most of the day yesterday working in her flower beds. She said it was a great day to be outside," he added.

When they got to Aviation Dynamics, they pulled up to the gate. The guard came out and said, "You guys are extra early today. There's nobody in the lobby yet to sign you in," he added. Joe was driving and both Connor and Sam looked at Joe and raised their eyebrows. "So much for being early," Sam said.

"Marisa should be here in a few minutes. You can just park and wait for her," the guard said. "Or, if you'd rather, I can try to find someone to come sign you in?"

"That's fine, we'll just wait," said Connor. Joe pulled ahead and parked the car. They didn't have to wait long before Marisa showed up and opened the door. They all got out, opened the trunk to retrieve their bags and walked in. Joe opened, and held the door for Connor and Sam. Marisa was still putting her things away when they walked up to the desk. She slid the logbook their direction and they all signed in. She made the call for someone to come and get them. Jim showed up a couple of minutes later and walked them to the conference room. They entered a half-empty room and Joe walked to the computer and slid in his flash drive. Brad walked in and said, "Good morning," to everyone. He seemed cheerful and had a smile on his face and was shaking hands with those who were there.

By 7:00 AM, everyone was in their seats and Joe started the day. "Good morning, everyone," Joe said. There were some mumbled "good mornings" back to him. "Yesterday, I promised you we would start the day with a discussion about scheduling," Joe said. He pulled up the updated Intermediate Objectives (IO) map from the day before and showed it on the screen and pointed specifically to NC 221.

"You decided yesterday that you were missing a necessary condition to be able to integrate your work cell schedules into a master schedule," Joe said. "And today, we want to talk about how you make that IO a reality. You also indicated yesterday that your current scheduling system will only allow you to control and monitor activities at the work cell level, but not at an integrated level," he explained as everyone nodded their heads in agreement.

"Today, I want to introduce you to a concept known as Critical Chain Project Management, or CCPM as we call it," Joe said. "It's a scheduling concept that is used for Project Management, and in your case, multiple project management. There are several advantages to using CCPM that can help you overcome most of the issues you are now faced with," Joe added. "It's a concept that is not much different from the piping diagram you've already seen, in that the limited resource needs to be managed," Joe said.

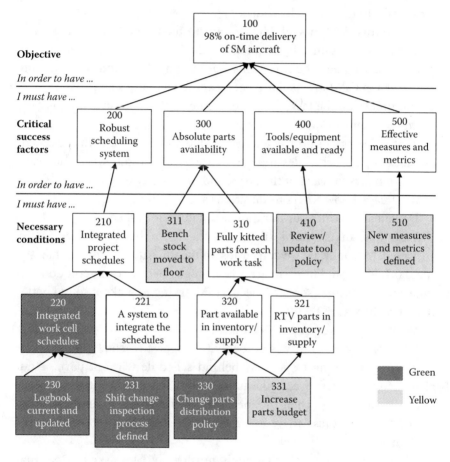

"Most project planning software uses a concept known as the Critical Path Method, or CPM. The way CPM works is to find the longest duration of tasks in a project and link them together to determine the critical path," Joe explained. "It's a scheduling concept that has been around since the early 1950s and hasn't changed much for 65 years. However, it also doesn't work very well in a multiproject environment, especially when there are common resources required to complete those projects. It's the primary reason you are having the problems you are having," Joe added.

"So, how is CCPM different?" Jim asked.

"Most notably, CPM is focused on finishing the tasks on time, and CCPM focuses on finishing the project on time," Joe answered.

"But, we have to finish the tasks before we can complete the project," Nathan said.

"That's exactly right!" Joe said, "And, we want to focus on completing those tasks in less time," he added.

"I'm confused," Jim said. "If we want to finish the tasks in less time, shouldn't we focus on task completions like CPM does?" Jim asked.

Joe smiled because he knew this was coming. "Yes and no," Joe said. "The tasks in CPM are date driven, meaning you have a start date, a time of duration to do the task, and an end date. Is that correct?" Joe basically asked the group.

"That is correct!" said Hector. "We spend a lot of time with the scheduler to set up the schedules and make sure they are right. We already have standard hours for each of the tasks, and they pretty much stay the same, so we already know what our durations are," Hector added.

"Do you always hit your duration estimates?" Joe asked.

There was an extended silence in the room before Hector finally answered. "Actually, no we don't. Most of the time, it takes longer than the standard duration, but there are a few times when we can get it done on time, and sometimes sooner," Hector said, trying to make it sound better than it really was.

"Why does it take longer?" Joe asked.

"Well, parts availability is probably the biggest reason," said Nathan. "It doesn't take long to get way behind schedule without parts. And, also the internal resources, like avionics and hydraulics. Plus, if another schedule catches up, then the meetings start so we can get everything untangled … I guess there are a lot of reasons why it takes longer," Nathan said.

"What about those tasks that might finish early?" Joe asked. "Does that mean you can start the next task early as well?"

"No!" said Bobby. "Sometimes, starting too early can create as much trouble as starting too late. If a scheduled task stops, we review the schedule for a different task we can start, just to have something to charge our time to," he explained.

"He's right," said Hector. "If we get too far ahead of ourselves, then it's almost certain the parts won't be available, and we end up having to wait anyway. So, there is really no point in starting earlier than the schedule says we should, because parts aren't scheduled to be there yet. Sometimes, we start a task that we know can't finish, but we do it anyway trying to maintain efficiency. Eventually, we have to go back and finish all of the tasks started early when a part does show up, or something else becomes available to finish the task. At times, it seems like the schedule can be all over the place. The schedule says we are doing fine because we started a task, but then it takes a long time to finish that task. A lot of tasks started, but not many finished," he added.

"So, what I'm hearing," Joe said, "is if you do finish a task early, the system doesn't allow you to take advantage of any time you gained. Is that correct?" Joe asked.

"That is very correct," Nathan said. "We always quickly lose any time gained because the start date or the next task is out in the future, but the system is always ready to punish us for being late," Nathan said.

"In essence, you have six different schedules, each schedule working in isolation of the other five, and all needing similar parts and resources, at the same time; is that correct?" Joe asked.

"I think that pretty much sums it up," Jim said. "Now you know why it's so important for us to be able to integrate ALL of the schedules," Jim added.

Joe was nodding his head in agreement. Connor and Sam were smiling and waiting for Joe to continue. "Before we move on," Joe said, "I need to ask one more question, and that is, Do you always start a job as soon as you get it?"

"We certainly do!" Jim exclaimed. Everyone else was nodding in agreement. "It's the only possible way we can hope to get the job done on time. We start everything as soon as we can," Jim added.

Joe walked up to the computer and fiddled with the mouse and finally a slide appeared on the screen.

Project 1	T-1 5 d	T-2 4 d	T-3 4 d	T-4 3 d
	Res-A	Res-B	Res-C	Res-D
Project 2	T-1 5 d	T-2 4 d	T-3 4 d	T-4 3 d
	Res-A	Res-B	Res-C	Res-D
Project 3	T-1 5 d	T-2 4 d	T-3 4 d	T-4 3 d
	Res-A	Res-B	Res-C	Res-D

"Suppose we have three different projects, all scheduled to begin at roughly the same time," Joe said pointing to the slide with his laser pointer. "As you can see, Task 1 requires 5 days and uses Resource A to do the work. Task 2 takes 4 days and uses Resource B. Task 3 also requires 4 days and uses Resource C. Task 4 takes 3 days and uses Resource D. If we add up all of the days, each project should take 16 days to complete. Does everyone see how I got that number?" Joe asked. Everyone was nodding they understood. "Let's say Nathan is the lead for Project 1, Hector is the lead for Project 2, and Jim, let's say you are the lead for Project 3. My question is, Which one of you gets to start your project first?" Joe asked.

"I do!" Jim said.

"Why is that?" Joe asked.

"Because I'm the boss," Jim said with a smile. Everyone laughed and smiled, including Joe.

"If all three projects need the same Resource A to start, who gets access to Resource A first?" Joe asked.

"I guess this is the point in time where all of us would need to get together and have a meeting to determine project priority," Nathan said.

"But, wait a minute," Joe said. "Isn't the purpose of a schedule to determine priority and task sequence?" Joe asked.

"Mr. Pecci, what you are describing here is what happens all of the time," Hector said. "Only it's usually six schedules and not just three. It doesn't always happen at the start. It can also happen at any point in the schedule. Some schedules might be a little ahead, but most are behind," Hector added.

"That is exactly it!" Joe exclaimed. "The point I want to make here is 'why' your schedules are always behind," Joe added. "Let's assume, for the sake of discussion, we let Project 1 use Resource A first. If Project 1 uses all 5 days, then Project 2 starts 5 days late. By the time we get to Project 3, it's now 10 days late starting. Remember, each project was only planned for 16 days!" Joe added. "Let's also suppose during the planning meeting, that Hector mentioned earlier, the three of you realize what will happen to the schedule. All of the projects need to show some progress toward completion, so you decide to divide the efforts of Resource A among all three projects. In other words, Resource A will multitask between each of your projects. You decide to let Resource A work on Project 1 for 1 day and then move to Project 2 for 1 day, and then to Project 3 for 1 day, and then back to Project 1. You continue this cycle until Resource A has completed all 5 days worth of work on all three projects. This is what happens," Joe said and walked to the computer to show the next slide.

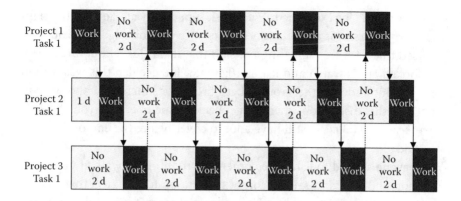

"Project 1, Task 1 takes 13 days to complete," Joe said, pointing to the slide with his laser. "Project 2, Task 1 takes 14 days and Project 3, Task 1 takes 15 days, and that's just to do Task 1!" Joe exclaimed.

"Good grief!" Zeke was thinking to himself, "We do that a lot and we thought it was the right thing to do ..."

"Resource A is very busy working on *ALL* of the projects, moving from one project to the next one," Joe added.

"Well, maybe we just need to hire more Resource A people," Jim said. "That would solve the problem and help us get the work done faster," he added.

"What about when the work moves to Resource B, and C, and D?" Joe asked.

The discussion continued back and forth on the merits of hiring more people. Finally, Nathan said, "Maybe if we had more people at all of the resource locations, the problem would go away and we could do the work as it was scheduled."

"So, the solution required to solve the problem is that we need to hire two or three times as many people for each resource; is that what I'm hearing?" Joe asked.

"NO!" Hal exclaimed. "We can't do that! It would cost way too much money and our expenses would skyrocket. Why would you even suggest such a thing?" Hal asked.

"I didn't suggest it," Joe calmly said. "Your team did!"

Hal looked at Jim and scowled as if to suggest, "Be quiet!"

"There just has to be another way to do this," Hal said. "I think the shop floor people just need to work harder and do the work within the standard hours," Hal said. Now, it was Jim scowling at Hal and suggesting, "Be quiet!"

"They can't!" Joe exclaimed. "Each task supposedly already has the right standard hours in it and that doesn't seem to be working," Joe said, and noticed that Sam was signaling the sign that it was just about lunchtime. He looked at his watch and it was 10:40 AM. Joe decided this was a good break point and told the group, "Let's break for lunch now and we will continue this discussion when we get back. Remember, everyone back in their seats at 11:30. We still have a lot to cover before the end of the day," Joe said.

Everyone started to leave the conference room. Brad walked up to Joe, Connor, and Sam and said, "I forgot to mention to you guys that I had a phone call from Ron Parsons. He apologized for not being able to make it to any of our discussions, but he did ask how it was going," Brad said. "I told Ron that, so far, it had been a real learning experience and I was beginning to understand better why we are in the situation we are in," Brad said. "Ron told me to keep an open mind and do whatever you guys told me to do." Everyone laughed. "I need to go check my e-mails and phone messages," Brad said. He left the room and headed back to his office.

Connor looked at Joe and said, "You are doing a great job so far. I've been scanning the group while you were talking and I think it's starting to sink in," Connor added.

"Thanks Connor," Joe said. "But, I also want you guys to feel free to jump in the conversation at any time," he added.

"I will," said Connor. "But, so far there hasn't been a need to do that. You're doing exactly what I would do."

The afternoon session started and Joe welcomed everyone back. "Just before we broke for lunch, we were talking about the standard hours and multitasking of projects. Right now, I want to discuss Project Planning and how you do it," Joe said. Joe walked to the whiteboard and picked up a marker. "There are basically three things that control project planning, project progress, and project completion," Joe said. He turned and started to write the following:

1. Multitasking
2. Student syndrome
3. Parkinson's law

"We've already discussed the negative effects that come from multitasking. Even though it seems like a good and necessary thing to do, it can quickly generate many negative consequences that you have to deal with," Joe said.

"The student syndrome is directly related to the start and end date you put in your schedule. It basically says you start the work as late as possible and then ask for more time to complete it. In your case, the late start is not always a choice but sometimes forced on you because of the system. When you get the late start, for whatever reason caused it, you always want more time to complete the task," Joe said. "It's similar to what happens with your procurement system. Using the minimum/maximum system, you wait until the minimum number is reached before you order parts. When you do order parts, the lead time to get the parts can exceed the scheduled need date, so procurement asks for more time to get the parts," Joe added.

"Parkinson's law states that 'work expands to fill the available time.' This too is related to the start and end dates in the schedule. I'm going to guess that you try and maximize the number of days you are given for a task. In other words, if a task has 10 days, but you could really do it in 5 days, the work is slowed down to make sure you consume all 10 days," Joe said. Joe noticed that some in the group were nodding their heads in agreement to what he was saying. "The cumulative consequences from all of these factors, either working in tandem, or in isolation on a single schedule, usually means you'll miss your scheduled due date," Joe said. "The purpose of these actions is trying to finish the project tasks on time by adhering to the start and end dates. It's the fundamental basis behind CPM, which is to follow and finish the critical path tasks on time," Joe said. "That's a primary difference with CCPM in that the focus is on completing the project on time, not the tasks," Joe added.

"I'm not sure I understand the difference," Jim said. "Aren't both of these methods trying to complete the project on time?" Jim asked.

"Yes, basically you are correct," Joe said. "But, the difference is the way they do it. With CCPM, you build and use a project buffer by taking time from the task durations, sometimes as much as 50%. It also employs a feeding buffer concept, which in your case would be parts and Return To Vendor (RTV) parts, and possibly internal resources," Joe said.

"I still don't get it," Jim said.

"Me either," Nathan and Hector said, almost in unison.

Joe walked back to the computer and pulled up another slide to explain the concept.

Original project schedule with "slack time" added in each task.

T-1 5 d	T-2 4 d	T-3 4 d	T-4 3 d
Res-A	Res-B	Res-C	Res-D

Scheduled with CCPM and "slack" removed

T-1 2.5 d Res-A	T-2 2 d Res-B	T-3 2 d Res-C	T-4 1.5 d Res-D	Project buffer 4 d

Feeding buffer	

"This shows the original project schedule we used in our previous example," Joe said pointing to the screen. "If you look at Task 1, it originally had 5 days duration, which was probably based on some kind of historical average for standard hours. The standard hours are based on how long it *should* take, and the actual hours are based on how long it *did* take. In time, it is possible that the standard hours will go up based on the actual hours. Because it is an average, it means that sometimes you used fewer standard hours and sometimes you used more," Joe said. "It might even happen that a scheduler, or supervisor, might even add extra time because they know that Task 1 rarely goes as planned," Joe said. "That's what accounts for the slack time added to the tasks. It's time used to help protect against all the bad things that can, and do, happen to make sure the task finishes on time. It's insurance time for the task and the same is true for the other three tasks associated with this project using traditional scheduling methods," Joe added.

"Now, look at the CCPM scheduled durations," Joe said pointing at the slide. "What this schedule shows is that the original duration was reduced from 5 days to 2.5 days and we move 2.5 days to the project buffer. The same thing happens with the other three tasks as well, meaning that the task durations are cut in half and all of the detached task time is moved to the project buffer. Once you have accumulated all of the time in the project buffer, you cut that number in half as well," Joe said.

"Good grief!" Jim said. "How in the world can you expect us to do the task in half the time, when we can't even get it done in the time we have now?" Jim asked.

"Simply, by using focus and leverage," Joe said. "Focus on the task that needs to be done, and only that task. Work on that task until it is complete, and leverage the rest of the system to support completing that task.

No multitasking, no student syndrome, and certainly no Parkinson's law!" Joe exclaimed. "CCPM does not use any start dates or end dates. What it does is start the task and continue working the task until it is complete. If extra time is required, then time is *withdrawn* from the project buffer to cover the time overrun. If the task happens to underrun and finish early, that time is *deposited* back into the project buffer for another task to use. You provide task status by updating how much time you need to finish the task being worked, versus an actual end date. In most cases, you'll finish the task early if this is the only task you are working. When that task is complete, you start the next task. There is no need to wait for a start date, you begin the work on the next task when the previous one is complete," Joe added.

Nathan was studying the slide and listening to Joe and said, "This kind of system appears to let us take advantage of completing work early, if there are no start dates and end dates."

"It actually does more than that," Joe said. "Besides taking advantage of any time gained, it also protects the project against tasks that might take even longer."

"How is that possible?" Jim asked. Nathan was thinking the same thing.

"Look at the project buffer," Joe said. "When time is gained, that time is deposited to the buffer. If a task takes longer, then time is withdrawn to cover the additional task time," Joe added.

"I don't understand," Jim said. "If a task overruns the time, then it over-runs the time. How do we make up that time?" Jim asked.

"You don't necessarily make it up, but you do buffer against the variation of extended task times," Joe said pointing to the screen. "Suppose that, for example, Task 2 takes 3 days to complete rather than 2 days. By accumu-lating time in the project buffer, every task is allowed to make a deposit of time if they finish early, or make a withdrawal if they need extra time. The end date of the project is not affected," Joe said. "Instead of trying to con-trol the variation at the task level, with slack time, you can now control the variation at the project level with the project buffer. In traditional sched-uling, a task that takes longer will move the entire schedule to the right, equal to the number of days the task is late. It's like train cars that are all linked together; when one moves, they all move. Without a project buffer, the end date moves with each overrun, and the only way to recover from the overrun is that downstream tasks need to be completed in less time, and that doesn't happen very often," Joe added. "In our example of Task 2 taking 3 days instead of 2 days, the additional time is withdrawn from the project buffer. By adding or using time from the buffer, the project is better managed to stay on schedule," Joe said.

"I think I'm beginning to understand what you are talking about Mr. Pecci, and I like it!" Nathan said.

"I like it too!" Hector said.

Joe pointed to the screen again and pointed to the feeding buffer and said, "Another important factor is the feeding buffer. This buffer is established to make sure all of the parts, internal resources, and RTV parts are available and ready when they are needed. The small block at the end suggests that all of the parts, special equipment, RTV parts, or whatever is assembled and ready to go ahead of the need. It's a segment you have already discussed in building a buffer in procurement, and having tools and special equipment ready to go," Joe added.

"OK, this might work for a single project, but how do we do it for all six projects?" Zeke asked.

"That's a good question," Joe said. "In CCPM, there is a function that allows for what is commonly called pipelining the projects. When multiple projects are involved, and each project requires access to some type of limited resource, it allows the limited resource to be scheduled and used for the maximum effect. In other words, based on the time available for the limited resource, the pipelining tool will alert you and tell you when to start the other projects. It's a way of integrating all of the projects, much the same as the staggered start we just discussed with our three projects," Joe said. "In fact, a better term might be, it allows for the synchronization of the projects," Joe said as he walked back to the computer to pull up another slide. "One of the ways you have used in the past to counter the effects of this problem was multitasking a single resource. I also believe that we showed earlier the fallacy in trying to take that approach and the chaos it will cause to the system and the schedules. It certainly creates many more problems than it solves," Joe said as he pushed some buttons looking for the slide he wanted. He finally found it and put it on the screen.

"Instead of trying to start all of your projects as soon as you get them, the pipelining feature will determine when each project should start, based on limited resource availability," Joe said pointing to the slide. "What this means is, some projects might start later, but will still finish on time," Joe said. "You'll notice, by looking at this slide, that you can now do all three of the projects in almost the same amount of time it would have taken to do a single project," he added.

"That's incredible!" Zeke said.

"It's also very possible," Joe said, scanning the group.

"Those are the same kinds of results that Ron Parsons was talking about at the helicopter production facility," Brad said, speaking to the group. "I didn't necessarily believe Ron, or understand what he was talking about before, but I'm starting to understand now," Brad said with a smile.

"OK, I like what I'm seeing here," Nathan said. "But, I guess we have to watch each schedule and determine if we are ahead or behind from where we need to be?" Nathan asked.

"Not necessarily," Joe responded. "CCPM also has a feature that will give you project status based on how much project buffer has been used, compared to the actual work completed. It will identify which projects have used more project buffer, and in turn might risk being delivered late," Joe added.

"How does that work?" Nathan asked.

"It uses a feature known as a 'fever chart'," Joe said. He walked toward the computer to pull up another slide.

Original project schedule with "slack time"

T-1 5 d	T-2 4 d	T-3 4 d	T-4 3 d
R-A	R-B	R-C	R-D

Scheduled with CCPM using pipelining

T-1 2.5 d R-A	T-2 2 d R-B	T-3 2 d R-C	T-4 1.5 d R-D	Project buffer 4 d

2.5 days delayed start →

| T-1 2.5 d R-A | T-2 2 d R-B | T-3 2 d R-C | T-4 1.5 d R-D | Project buffer 4 d |

5 days delayed start →

| T-1 2.5 d R-A | T-2 2 d R-B | T-3 2 d R-C | T-4 1.5 d R-D | Project buffer 4 d |

"The fever chart provides a dual purpose. First, it will track each project individually to give a status. Second, it can track all of the projects to provide an overall status of the projects in the work bays. The fever chart is displayed using three different zones. The first zone is the red zone. If your project is in the red zone, it means you are consuming the project buffer at a faster rate than you are completing the work. So, you instantly know this project will require some attention to get it back on track. The yellow zone means you are consuming time from the project buffer, but you are also completing work as well. The yellow zone is cautionary, meaning you need to keep this project on your radar and avert going into the red zone," Joe explained. "The green zone means that work is being completed faster than the buffer is being consumed, so everything should be OK for on-time delivery. The chart on the screen is for a single project, but the same rules apply when you look at all of the projects. It will show you a red, yellow, or green status for each project plotted on the basis of the total work completed and the amount of project buffer consumed," Joe explained. Joe moved the mouse and clicked on a slide to show an example of a multiple-project fever chart.

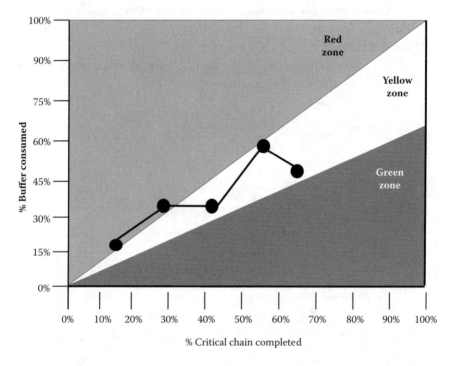

Zeke had been studying the slides and finally asked Joe, "So, what you're saying is, we can see each project individually, or look at all of the projects at once?" Zeke asked.

"That's exactly right," Joe said. "Each day, the supervisor, or maybe even the team lead for each shift, will update the information in the system at the end of each shift. They will enter how much more time they think is necessary to complete the task. It will show you real-time status on the basis of the updated information," Joe said.

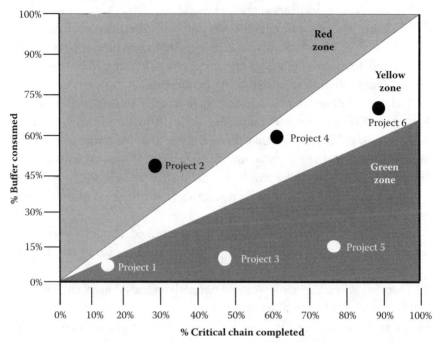

"That means I won't have to leave my office anymore to figure out what's going on with the shop floor," Zeke said with a smile. Everyone laughed.

"Only if you spot a problem with the status then you will need to assemble the necessary folks to identify the problem and get the problem fixed and back on schedule again," Joe said.

"How do we get this CCPM system and get it working here?" Brad asked.

"CCPM is software, of which, there are many out there. The best part of CCPM is that it will integrate and overlay with your current scheduling system. CCPM will just analyze the information differently and show you the critical chain of resources, versus the critical path of the tasks. You don't have to necessarily learn a new scheduling system, but you do have to implement some new rules about scheduling," Joe added. "Basically, all of the things we have been talking about today," he added.

"Where do we find out more about this?" Jim asked.

"There are a number of vendors who sell this software, and some are better than others. I can leave you with a list and you can contact them. Prices will vary and support and training will vary, but you should be able to pick the one that best fits your need," Joe said.

"We want the very cheapest one," Hal said.

"No, I think what we want is the one that works best for us," Brad said.

Joe looked at his watch. It was 2:10 PM. That gave him approximately 1 hour and 20 minutes to get things wrapped up. Joe started his summary in anticipation that there would be more questions.

"Today, we talked about a scheduling alternative to help achieve a necessary condition in your IO map," Joe said. "I think you can see, on the basis of today's discussion, that there is more than one way to schedule tasks in a project. The right way, and the wrong way," Joe said with a smile. "Hopefully, you now understand what the difference is."

"I certainly do," Nathan said. "I think this is just the kind of thing we've been looking for," he added.

"Are there any questions about what we talked about yesterday, or today?" Joe asked. No hands went up, but Joe was sure they had unasked questions and smiled.

"There are still some items we need to finish on the IO map, and I'm sure you will work hard to complete them. For our next visit, or perhaps maybe with just a phone call or two, we will be able to get progress on your IO map," Joe said. "If there are no questions, I think we are done for today," Joe said.

"Wait a minute," Brad said. "Before everyone leaves, I want to tell you all thank you for your time and effort. This is a very important project for all of us and we need to make sure we find sustainable solutions that allow us to keep our current contracts and keep winning new contracts. I'm confident that if we can do all of the things that Joe, Connor, and Sam are telling us, we will be in a much better position," Brad said. "I'd also like to make some additional assignments. When we get the list from Joe, I want Marsha, Jim, Zeke, Nathan, and Hector to be part of the software review process. We need to make this priority number one and get the issues resolved. If there is nothing else, then you are free to go," Brad said. Everyone started moving for the door. Brad, Jim, and Zeke stayed behind. When everyone else had left the room, they huddled at one end of the table with Joe, Connor, and Sam.

"I have a question," Brad said. "I know that what we are going to do will probably work wonders for our scheduled maintenance efforts, but I'm still worried about the unscheduled maintenance side. We haven't talked about it much and I was wondering if you guys have a plan for that as well?" Brad asked.

"We do!" Connor said. "But, before we start that effort, I'd first like to stabilize the scheduled maintenance effort. The solution we will propose for the unscheduled maintenance will be different from this effort," Connor said.

"That's fair," Brad said. "I just wanted to make sure you haven't forgotten about unscheduled maintenance. As you've taught us, when you fix one problem, it just rolls to the next location in the system and I want to be prepared when that happens," Brad said.

"In fact, I'm working another project in a hospital that might very well provide the answer to your unscheduled maintenance," Connor said.

"How can a hospital help us?" Brad asked, with a puzzled look on his face.

"It will make more sense when we roll it out for you," Connor said with a smile.

"I'll be ready," Brad said.

Brad walked with them back to the lobby. When they arrived, they all signed out and turned in their badges. When Connor turned in his badge, he smiled at the receptionist and said, "See you next time." She said nothing, but did offer a smile.

Brad walked outside with all three of them to shake hands and have a final discussion. "You know, not long ago, I didn't think there was much hope for turning this place around. I just couldn't find any more places to try and save money. In fact, I had even considered starting a job search, knowing that I might be let go if things didn't improve. Now I feel a lot more confident since you guys have been helping us. I am surprised at how much of this is really just about systems thinking and common sense. We didn't do much proactive thinking before; we were only reactive with cost cutting. I'm very happy to know there are alternatives to cost cutting," he said.

Everyone shook hands. As they walked back to the car, Joe looked at his watch. It was 3:35 PM. They got in the car and headed for the Business Air terminal. Most of the ride was in silence, but Connor did mention to Joe what an outstanding job he had done with the group. Joe was all smiles when he said, "Thank you!"

In his mind, Connor was now shifting gears back to the hospital. He was wondering what kind of progress they were making with the Door to Balloon Time project. It had been a week since he had heard anything from them.

16

Hospital Executives

Connor was in his home office thinking about all of the things on his calendar, including the Aviation Dynamics turnaround and the hospital project. He recognized the importance for both of them. But, since Joe and Sam appeared to have the Aviation Dynamics project under control, he decided that he would focus on his efforts at the hospital. He was looking at the calendar and realized that it had now been 12 days since he'd heard anything from the hospital. He was debating with himself if he should call them, or wait for them to call him. He remembered that Dr. Price thought it might be 2 weeks, or more, to get everything taken care of, and 2 weeks was almost up. Connor was drumming his fingers on his desk when his cell phone rang. He looked at the caller ID and it was Terry Mansfield. Connor smiled as he reached for his cell phone and thought to himself, "WOW! What a coincidence! I was just getting ready to call him."

Connor picked up his cell phone and answered, "Hello, this is Connor."

"Hi Connor, this is Terry Mansfield," he replied.

"Great to finally hear from you," Connor said. "What's new?"

"I know it has taken us a while to get back with you, but I have great news! We have been very busy working the new Door to Balloon (D2B) process and trying to cut our time down. The team went through several "mock runs" and we were able to narrow down the procedure and define what the new policy should be. Everyone did a good job and we practiced the process several times. We made our presentation to the Internal Policy committee, and with Dr. Price's help, we were able to move it through faster!" Terry exclaimed.

"That is great news," Connor said.

"You haven't heard the best of it yet!" Terry exclaimed. "Around 5:30 last night, there was a flurry of activity in the emergency room (ER) when a patient with chest pains had been rushed to the hospital. Since everyone in the ER had been trained on the new D2B procedure, they used it for the first time on this patient. As was expected, not everything worked exactly as planned, but most of it did. What previously had been averaging roughly 90 minutes before the changes now only took only 53 minutes to complete using the new process. This effort represented a 42% reduction in time!" Terry said, excited to share the news.

"That's even better news," Connor said.

"Dr. Price and I were in the ER this morning getting the information and the results. As soon as we had the information, I updated the D2B chart and we made a visit to some of the executive staff to share with them what had happened. They couldn't believe it, but they were impressed. We talked about getting you back in to help them with a strategy to implement these concepts throughout the hospital. With these kinds of results, they were anxious to get you in and discuss more. They suggested maybe early Friday morning, would that work for you?" Terry asked.

"What time do you want me there?" Connor asked.

"We were hoping for about 7:00 AM in the executive conference room," Terry said.

"That works for me," Connor said. "I'll see you on Friday morning." They disconnected.

Friday was still 3 days away, and it gave Connor some time to put together his own strategy for the executives. Connor realized that he would only have one chance to make a positive impact concerning the operation of the hospital, so he spent quite a bit of time thinking about what might be the best approach.

Connor was deciding in his mind what the rollout should look like; he decided that he had to include, at the very least, things such as the following:

1. Development of a strategic plan, including the executive's role in the continuous improvement effort
2. Performance metrics and their impact on organizational behaviors
3. Overcoming resistance to change
4. A comparison of Cost Accounting and Throughput Accounting, if they had the time

Connor knew, from past experience, that the normal attention span for most senior executives was usually no more than 30 minutes. He needed to do something impactful right up front to draw them into an active discussion. As he thought about it more, Connor realized that items 1, 2, and 3 were the essential points he had to make. His first priority was to walk them through the development of a strategic TLS (Theory of Constraints, Lean, and Six Sigma) plan for moving the whole hospital forward.

On Friday morning, Connor arrived at the hospital early for his daylong event. As he entered the hospital, he walked through the main lobby and down the hall toward the conference room. When he entered the conference room, he was immediately drawn to the graphs prominently displayed on the wall. As he walked over for a closer look, he noticed the updated run chart for D2B time and smiled. There had been three additional data points added to the chart since he had talked with Terry 3 days ago. All of the new entries were less than 60 minutes, which had been the target number for the D2B team. Connor smiled.

Seeing the latest run chart gave Connor an idea. If he could post the original electronic copy of the chart in his presentation and then compare it to the current results, the executive's receptiveness to the TLS ideas might spike even higher. Connors decided he would use the original D2B run chart showing results before teaching the team about TLS. He remembered that back then, the average time was around 92 minutes. He would then follow that with the latest run chart, which was now averaging less than 60 minutes. In doing so, it should lead to an immediate swing in the credibility for the concepts he was proposing, and hopefully, the executive team would be more engaged. Connor was sitting at the table with his laptop searching through his files trying to find the original D2B run time chart. He found it and made a slide in his presentation.

As the start time drew closer, the executive team began filtering into the conference room and the D2B time chart was the primary topic of discussion in the small groups. In fact, some had walked to the metrics board just to get the latest information, which Terry had posted just that morning.

Terry and Dr. Price entered the room at the same time and both walked immediately over to Connor. Connor stood and shook both their hands.

"Did you see the latest D2B run chart as of this morning?" Terry asked with a big smile.

"I did!" Connor exclaimed, returning the smile.

"The D2B process is the talk of the hospital right now," Dr. Price said.

The three of them talked for a minute or two longer and it was decided that Dr. Price would start the meeting.

When everyone was seated, Dr. Price walked to the front of the room and started the meeting. "Good morning everyone, I want to welcome you back to this strategy planning workshop that I think you'll find very interesting and informative. As most of you may, or may not know, Terry posted another update to the D2B time run chart this morning," Dr. Price said pointing to the wall. "We now have four data points below 60 minutes and the improvement continues to trend favorably." Most had already seen the new posting. Dr. Price continued, "Anyway, I'll turn the time over to Connor to begin today's activities."

"Good morning everyone and thank you for coming today," Connor said, as he moved to the front of the room.

Before Connor could continue, William Walters, the COO, raised his hand and began to speak. "Mr. Jackson, I just wanted to tell you 'Thank You' for what you have done with the D2B times."

Connor smiled and replied, "First, call me Connor. Second, I didn't do anything!"

"But, these results would say otherwise!" William exclaimed.

"Not true!" Connor exclaimed. "These results are the product of several hospital employees, not me. I just pointed the way; they did all of the work and achieved the results. I can tell you that everyone involved with this effort has embraced this new approach, and as you can clearly see from the graph, it appears to be working very well," Connor said pointing to the graph on the wall. "Now that you know it is possible to achieve these kinds of results, the next task is to find a way to sustain them and spread it to other departments within the hospital." Connor took this opportunity to bring up the original D2B time run chart. He walked over to his computer and put the slide on the screen.

"As you might remember, this is what the D2B chart looked like just a few weeks ago. As you can see, the average D2B time was around 92 minutes, fluctuating between 85 and 97 minutes. The recognized healthcare standard for this metric should be less than 90 minutes, so the hospital was above what the average should be," Connor explained. "Dr. Price put together a team along with Terry Mansfield and they all worked on this problem for several days trying to figure out a way to reach a target of less than 60 minutes. The improvement methods the team used were a combination of Theory of Constraints, Lean, and Six Sigma, which we refer to as TLS. The combined benefits of the TLS techniques have worked very well in other industries and I was convinced that it could also work very well in the healthcare industry as well.

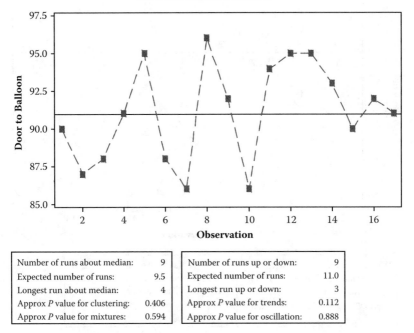

Run chart of Door to Balloon

Number of runs about median:	9	Number of runs up or down:	9
Expected number of runs:	9.5	Expected number of runs:	11.0
Longest run about median:	4	Longest run up or down:	3
Approx P value for clustering:	0.406	Approx P value for trends:	0.112
Approx P value for mixtures:	0.594	Approx P value for oscillation:	0.888

"So, based on where we were," Connor said pointing to the slide on the screen, "to where we are," pointing the graph on the wall, "many of you might be wondering 'What happened' to cause such a dramatic shift?" Connor asked the question they were all thinking. Several heads were nodding ever so slightly in agreement. Connor had their attention.

"Let me ask a question to Dr. Price and Terry," Connor asked, pointing to both of them in the back of the room. "How much new equipment did you have to buy to achieve these results?" Dr. Price and Terry looked at each other with a somewhat puzzled look. Finally, Terry shrugged his shoulders and replied, "None!"

"OK ... then, how many new employees did you have to hire?" Connor asked them. Again, the answer was "None!"

"No new equipment and no new employees; then what changed?" Connor asked. This time, he was the one acting puzzled.

The room was silent. Finally, Connor spoke, "What changed was the way you think about solving the problem. By taking the time to do a good systems analysis, you were able to find the problem and *focus* on it. When you focused on the problem, you were able to *leverage* the maximum improvement!" Connor exclaimed.

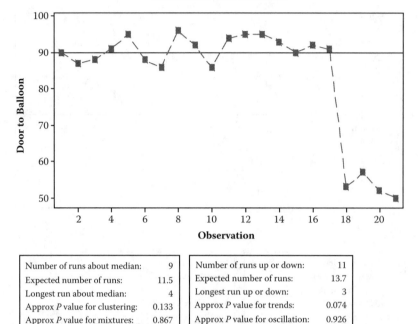

Run chart of Door to Balloon

Number of runs about median:	9
Expected number of runs:	11.5
Longest run about median:	4
Approx *P* value for clustering:	0.133
Approx *P* value for mixtures:	0.867

Number of runs up or down:	11
Expected number of runs:	13.7
Longest run up or down:	3
Approx *P* value for trends:	0.074
Approx *P* value for oscillation:	0.926

The executive team mumbled comments to themselves, and there was clear excitement as they pondered the latest results of the D2B run chart and the team's efforts. Connor said, "As you can see from this updated graph, the average time for the last four data points is 53 minutes or roughly a 39-minute reduction in D2B time."

William raised his hand and asked, "I want to ask you a question regarding sustainment of the improvements you have shared with us. My question is: We've had initial successes just like this before, but after a period, the results seem to erode and we're right back to where we started. So, what are you going to do differently to sustain the gains that we do make?" William asked.

"That's a great question, William," said Connor. "But, it's not what I'm going to do; it's what you are going to do!" Connor exclaimed. When Connor answered the question, there were several people who promptly raised their eyebrows and, in some cases, looked over the top of their glasses directly at Connor.

"What do you mean when you say 'What we are going to do'?"

"Let me quantify that statement; you, the executive team, need to establish what's important for this healthcare facility. And that's exactly what we will be discussing today with the development of a strategy moving forward," Connor said. "On the other hand, if these kinds of improvement aren't important to you, then, please, just continue doing what you've always done and you'll continue to get the same results you've always gotten," Connor said rather forcefully. Connor let that statement sink in for a moment and then continued. "If you look around the country at those healthcare organizations that are doing well, sitting at the top of the list is ThedaCare. Their CEO, Dr. John Toussaint, wrote a book entitled *On the Mend: Revolutionizing Healthcare to Save Lives and Transform the Industry* and was awarded the 2012 Shingo Research and Publication Award. This book has changed the playing field for much of the healthcare industry and I might suggest that you find this book and read it. One of the major points Dr. Toussaint makes in his book is that ALL improvements start with leadership, so until you're ready to lead this effort, we'll just be wasting our time here today," Connor said rather forcefully.

If Connor was looking to get the executives' attention, he had succeeded! William seemed to be a little embarrassed and commented to everyone around the table that perhaps they should all pay attention to what was being said.

Connor walked back to his laptop and was getting ready to start the Intermediate Objectives (IO) map discussion when he looked up and noticed Thomas Vincent, the CEO, had his hand up.

"Yes, Thomas," Connor said, pointing to him.

There was an immediate silence in the room when Thomas finally spoke. "What you talked about before and what you are talking about today is starting to make some sense to me. I'm beginning to realize that we have to change our approach if we're going to make any real improvements to our system and processes. I can assure you that we as an executive team are absolutely ready for such a change and we appreciate you being here today to help us understand what we need to do." Thomas continued, "And, although I think we understand the '*what to change*,' we obviously don't understand '*how to change it*.' Your point about executive involvement rings true and I, for one, will admit that because I didn't really understand continuous improvement efforts, I just passed it off as someone else's job. I can definitely see now the blunder of my thinking."

"Thank you, Thomas," said Connor. "I would be honored to show you the '*how*.' But, having said that, I also want to warn you that what you're about to do is embark on a journey that has no final destination. No matter what you think the end point might be, it's a continuous process of improvement and it will require a series of short-term strategies blended into a long-term strategy. So, if you are ready to embark on this journey, I'm ready to show you the way," Connor said as he scanned the faces in the room. Thomas assured him that everyone was ready to begin.

As an overall discussion point, Connor explained that there would be some successes and maybe some setbacks, but setbacks can also be overcome, and they would succeed.

"I want to start by introducing you to a thinking tool that will help you organize your thoughts and develop your overall strategy for success. This thinking tool is often referred to as an Intermediate Objectives map or simply an IO map as it is often called," Connor explained.

"The IO map is constructed using necessity-based logic, meaning it uses the syntax, 'In order to have entity "A," I must have entity "B".' In other words, in order to have the entity at the tip of the arrow, you must first have the entity at the base of the arrow." Many of the executives were making notes on what Connor was saying. "When you first construct an IO map, you start by defining a Goal statement, or overall objective, that you want to accomplish. The objective will be defined by you, the executive team," he continued. "Supporting that objective will be three to five entities referred to as Critical Success Factors, or CSFs. The CSFs must be achieved, meaning they are active and functioning, in order to achieve your stated organizational goal. Both the Goal and CSFs are written as terminal outcomes. In other words, written as statements that already exist," Connor said.

"I'm not sure I understand what you mean by terminal outcomes?" William asked. "Could you maybe give us an example?"

"Yes, I can. As an example, suppose your objective was to have a fire. What must you have before you can have a fire?" Connor asked.

William answered, "Well, the first thing that popped into my mind was we'd need to have a permit to have a fire." Everyone laughed, including Connor. Connor wasn't surprised by this answer, especially because healthcare was an industry that lived and died by regulations, procedures, and of course permits. Connor seized the opportunity to make an important point and addressed the group. "That's a great answer William, and an answer that may very well be true! Even though William's answer seemed humorous, it is an important point to consider any necessary regulatory compliance when you establish any kind of strategy. There are certain rules and regulations that must be followed, and they must be considered when strategy is developed," Connor stated. "But, in this case, let's assume we have all of the necessary permits to proceed. What must you have in order to have a fire?" Connor asked again.

"I guess there must be something to burn, and a way to start the fire, like some kind of heat source, and there must be oxygen present, because a fire can't burn without having oxygen present," William said.

"And what happens to your ability to make fire if any one of those three things is missing?" Connor asked.

"Quite simply, you will not have a fire if all three are not present when needed," declared William.

"So, in constructing the IO map for having a fire, we can say that without all three CSFs, we simply won't achieve our Goal of a fire, correct?" Connor asked. "The three CSFs are written as terminal outcomes, as though they were already in place," Connor explained. "Does that make sense to everyone?" Connor asked, scanning the group.

"Yes, I totally understand. So, if I were reading the IO map for the Goal of having a fire, I would say something like, 'In order to have a fire, I must have a fuel source, and I must have a heat source, and I must have oxygen,' is that correct?" William asked.

"Yes, that's absolutely correct. If anyone of those is missing, you won't have a fire," Connor replied.

"I have a question for you," Thomas asked raising his hand. "It seems to me that in order to achieve each of the mentioned CSFs, there must also be something in place, kind of like a sub-CSF?" Thomas asked not knowing for sure if he had worded his question correctly.

Connor smiled and said, "Thomas, you are absolutely correct and we call those sub-CSFs Necessary Conditions, or NCs. But, unlike the Goal and CSFs, the NCs are written more as activities, or tasks, rather than terminal outcomes," he added. "Let me show you an example of a completed IO map," said Connor as he pulled up the next slide on his laptop and it appeared on the screen.

"This is an example, but also an actual IO map from a hospital that I helped a friend of mine construct. This particular hospital decided they wanted more patient throughput as their Goal," he explained. "As you can see, the Goal sits at the top, with three CSFs underneath it," he added.

"Is there a minimum, or maximum, number of CSFs you can have?" asked Thomas.

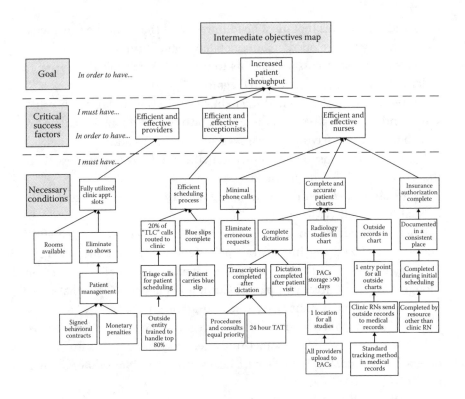

"Another good question," Connor replied. "Generally speaking, you should try to limit the number of CSFs to not less than three and no more than five. However, I have seen IO maps with up to seven CSFs, and for that situation, it did make sense. For practical purposes, I always try to limit the number to no more than five," Connor said. "You will also notice the NCs directly beneath the CSFs," said Connor. "For the NCs, I try to limit the number of layers to three or four, but as you can see in this example, they actually had five NC layers," Connor explained.

"The purpose of the IO map is not to define the detail, but rather set the course and point the way. Details will come later. Remember, the IO map is based on necessity logic and is read from the Goal downward through the NCs," Connor added. Connor took some time to read the IO map to the group and carefully inserted the syntax "In order to have … I must have" between each entity. As he was reading the IO map, Connor noticed many of the people nodding their heads. This was a visual confirmation to Connor that they understood what he was saying.

When he finished, he asked, "Are you ready to get started with your IO map?" everyone was nodding their heads "Yes."

"Remember, we will set the boundaries of this IO map to consider just the continuous improvement efforts at the hospital. However, you can also use this same concept to develop a higher-level strategy, if you so desire." Everyone agreed to the boundaries.

"The first thing you must agree on is what the Goal should be. What is it that you want to achieve at the hospital in relation to continuous improvement?" he asked. There was conversation between people and numerous ideas presented for the Goal. There was also a distinct lack of agreement. At times, the discussions became somewhat heated. Many were proposing ideas focused on cost reduction as a way of improvement, especially Jeffrey, the CFO. It seemed as though the leadership in each department wanted the Goal to be one that satisfied only their organizations' particular needs, rather than the needs of the overall hospital. Finally, a woman in the back of the room raised her hand and asked for everyone's attention. Connor noticed on the name plate that it was Vanessa White, the Chief Medical Officer. "Excuse me everyone, I think Vanessa wants to say something," said Connor as he pointed to her.

"Thank you Connor." She continued, "It seems to me that we want our Goal to be something that is going to benefit the entire hospital and the ideas I've heard during these discussions have been very narrow. For me, I think what would benefit the hospital the most is to develop an effective continuous improvement approach that crosses all organizational boundaries from surgery to maintenance. So, what if we said something along those lines as our Goal?" she asked. "Isn't that the reason Connor is here, to help us develop our continuous improvement program?" she asked, looking at the others around the table.

Connor thought to himself, "Finally, a voice of reason." Connor jumped in to continue with Vanessa's thought and said, "I think Vanessa has made an excellent point. What does everyone else think?" he asked.

Thomas was the first to respond and said, "I totally agree with you Vanessa. We need something that is going to benefit the entire hospital, something that will cut across all departmental lines, and something that will engage everyone in the hospital," he added. "Does everyone agree?" he asked. Everyone in the room seemed to agree.

"OK, so let's create your Goal statement with that thought in mind. Vanessa, since you started this discussion, how do you think the Goal statement should read?" Connor asked.

"What if we just kept it simple, something like 'An Effective and Vigorous Continuous Improvement Program'?" she said.

Thomas said, "I like that Vanessa. It's simple, and yet it crosses all the departments," he added. After a short discussion, everyone agreed that this should be the Goal statement. Connor walked back to his laptop and entered it onto his IO map template that was on the screen.

"OK, in order to have 'An Effective and Vigorous Continuous Improvement Program,' what must you have in order to make that happen?" Connor asked the group. "Remember, we're looking for the CSFs. What are those things that must happen just before you achieve the Goal?" Connor added.

Vanessa spoke again, "I think we'll need some kind of a common improvement methodology, so that everyone, in all organizations, is generally using the same approach." Everyone agreed, so Connor added it as a CSF and connected it with an arrow.

"OK, good start everyone, so what else do we need, in terms of CSFs, to achieve your Goal?" Connor asked.

"As you previously pointed out with your water piping diagram the first time you were here, I think we need to select projects that will benefit the hospital as a whole," said Thomas. "I think one of our problems in the past has been that we just selected a project without giving it much thought; much like increasing the diameter of a pipe that didn't need fixing," he added. "In the past, it was usually the person, or department, who complained the most, and yelled the loudest that was able to get an improvement team assigned. I think all that did was isolate some improvement efforts; that really didn't help improve the overall system," he added.

```
              ┌─────────────────────┐
              │          100        │
              │ An effective and vigorous│
              │      CPI program    │
              └─────────────────────┘
Objective
```

In order to have ...

I must have ...

**Critical
success
factors**

In order to have ...

I must have ...

**Necessary
conditions**

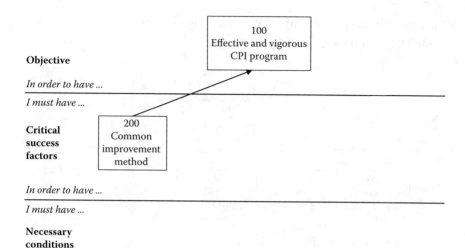

"So what if we stated our next CSF as something like, an 'effective project selection method'?" said Connor. Everyone agreed, Connor added it to the slide.

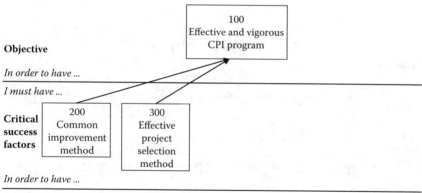

"What else?" Connor asked as he scanned the room for ideas.

"I think we need something along the lines of employee engagement," said Vanessa. "Something like 'full participation of the work force,'" she said.

Connor added it to the IO map and asked again for another CSF.

"Connor, you made it very clear to us, that unless we, the leadership team, are willing to 'lead' this effort, it will be doomed before we start.

So I was thinking something like leadership commitment or maybe full leadership involvement," said Thomas.

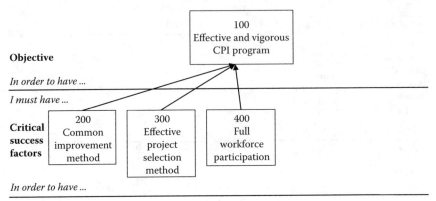

Again, everyone liked that one, so Connor added it to the IO map.

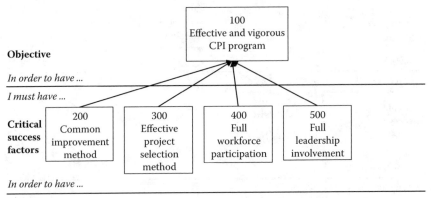

"Are there any other CSFs you think we need?" asked Connor.

"I think another problem we've had in the past is when we form a team, we haven't necessarily freed up the team members for the time required to participate," said Vanessa. "So I was thinking something along the lines of resource availability during events or something similar to that," she added.

"How about the team members freed up for events?" Johnny Creatura, the Director of Maintenance asked. "Or maybe focused team member participation?" he added.

Everyone agreed. Connor added it as the final CSF.

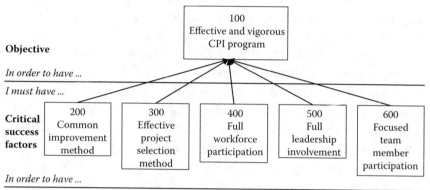

Connor looked at the Goal and CSFs and was generally pleased with what he saw. The team went back and read each CSF to make sure the wording was acceptable. Connor looked at his watch; it was nearly lunchtime, so Connor suggested that they take a break and have lunch.

Thomas quickly responded, "Connor, I took the liberty of having lunch catered today because I wanted to make sure we were able to finish all that we needed to do. I guess we can consider it a working lunch. I think lunch should be arriving shortly," Thomas said, looking at his own watch. Just then, there was a knock at the door. Dr. Price walked to the door and opened it. It was the food service personnel and he let them in to set up the lunch buffet. The group took a small break; everyone got a plate to take back to the table.

Dr. Price walked over to Connor and said, "Connor, it seems to me one of the things the executives need to know about is Throughput Accounting. I noticed during the IO map discussion that there was a lot of focus on cost cutting."

"I noticed that as well," Connor said. "How did you know about Throughput Accounting?" Connor asked with a surprised look on his face.

"Ever since you first introduced me to the Theory of Constraints, I have been researching and reading about it. I came across a couple of articles on

Throughput Accounting and I was blown away with what they said. We, at the hospital, have always been looking for ways to cut costs in order to improve profitability and that's simply the wrong approach in my opinion," he added.

"In many ways you are correct. However, I'm going to hold off on the Throughput Accounting. I think Vanessa has effectively shifted the thinking away from cost cutting," Connor said. "I'm just not sure we will have enough time today. I think finishing the IO map will take all of our remaining time," Connor stated. "However, I think with your new-found knowledge, you can start to plant some seeds about Throughput Accounting, especially with your CFO. I think coming from you it might have more of an impact. Maybe to hear it from one of their own could have a big impact. I can certainly be available, if required, to help you along the way. I've also got some of my materials on Throughput Accounting that I can send you." Dr. Price looked hesitant, but agreed he could start some conversation internally.

When everyone had returned to the table with their lunch, Connor announced, "OK, let's continue working the IO map. Under each of the CSFs, we need to determine what NCs are required to achieve the CSF. Remember, the NCs are written more as activities to be completed," he added. "So let's look at CSF 200, 'Common Improvement Methodology,'" he said. "In order to have this CSF, what must happen just before achieving this CSF?" Connor asked.

"Connor, it seems to me that everyone involved would need your TLS training," Vanessa said. "So maybe we say something like, 'TLS in place and functioning,'" she said.

Connor liked it and asked Vanessa, "Vanessa, what must you have in place just before that NC?" just to keep the conversation going.

Vanessa thought for a moment and said, "Well, I think all of the team members need to understand what this unified TLS methodology is about."

"Great, and in order to have the TLS knowledge, what must be in place just before that?" Connor asked.

"There would need to be TLS methodology training for all employees," she replied. Vanessa was looking at the IO map and said, "It seems to me that by laying out this IO map, we will, in effect, form the basis for our overall improvement plan, am I correct?" Vanessa asked.

"You most certainly are. By the way, that's a very astute observation," Connor said. "Does everyone else understand what Vanessa has just said?" asked Connor.

Everyone seemed to be able to make the logical connections between the Goal, CSFs, and NCs. Connor summarized Vanessa's comments and added them to the IO map.

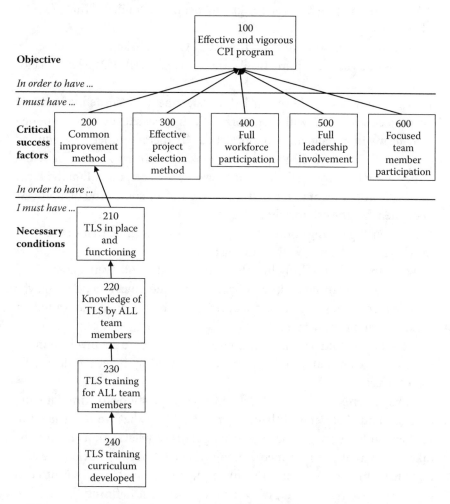

"Now, we need to do the same thing for the other CSFs and find the NCs to support completion of those CSFs," Connor said. "Let's look at CSF 300. What must happen just before we achieve that one?"

Everyone was thinking about it and finally Terry Mansfield spoke. "I think we need to establish some kind of criteria that a project needs to meet in order to be considered as actually improving the system as a whole."

"That's a very good point Terry," Connor said. "I think what you mean is, you need a way to filter the frivolous many projects from the important few projects. What I mean by that is there are many projects we *can* do, but what are those projects we *must* do that will benefit the system, is that correct?" Connor asked looking at Terry.

Terry was nodding his head in agreement and responded, "That's exactly what I mean."

"So, how do you want to word this NC?" Connor asked.

Vanessa was quick to jump in. "We need to have well-defined criteria for what a good project is."

"OK … how about these words for a statement, 'Well-defined criteria for project selection,' will that work?" Connor asked. Everyone nodded their heads in agreement. Connor asked, "Is there another NC required to accomplish NC 310?" Vanessa was looking at Terry to see if he had a response. So far, he was silent. Connor waited for a response. Finally, Terry spoke. "It would seem to me that we need a way or some kind of a process to define what the criteria should be."

"Are you suggesting some kind of a review committee that determines the criteria for the projects?" Vanessa asked.

"I'm thinking something like that," Terry said. "But, even a committee would need something to determine what the guidelines should be, maybe some kind of a master plan or document." Connor listened and waited for the discussion to continue.

"Connor, you told us when building an IO map not to get involved in the details, but keep it at a higher level; are we starting to get too detailed?" Vanessa asked.

"What you're doing is thinking and asking questions to stimulate discussion, and that's not all bad," Connor said. "What we don't need to see here, at least not yet, are the exact details of what actions need to be taken; only that the intermediate objective (IO) needs to exist. We also don't need to know who specifically might be assigned to a committee to create the criteria. I think, for your purposes, just defining the need to have criteria is sufficient for now." Connor added the NC to the IO map.

"Let's move on to CSF 400 and define any NCs to achieve that one," Connor said, as he turned and faced the group.

"You know," said Thomas, "this might be a good place for the executive team to get involved and make sure we get the full workforce participation. If they actually hear this message coming from us, I think it would help overall participation for what we want to do."

"That's a great idea Tom," said William. "And, I think if the message came from you personally, it would have the maximum impact."

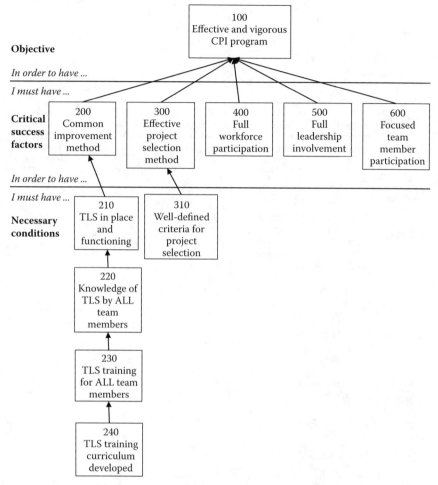

"I like that!" Connor exclaimed. "Coming from the top would certainly convey the message of importance for what you want to do with your continuous improvement program. Does anyone disagree?" Connor asked. No one disagreed, not even Thomas. Connor added it to the IO map.

"Let move on to CSF 500 and determine the NCs," Connor said.

"I've been waiting for you to get to this one," William said. "One way to get the leadership more involved is to have the improvement teams present their projects to us. That way, we could understand the status and progress or get involved if there are any issues we can help them solve."

"That's a great idea, and something that will be a very necessary condition for success," Vanessa said. "We can't just leave it up to the improvement teams to succeed on their own, we need to help them succeed," Vanessa added. Connor added it to the IO map.

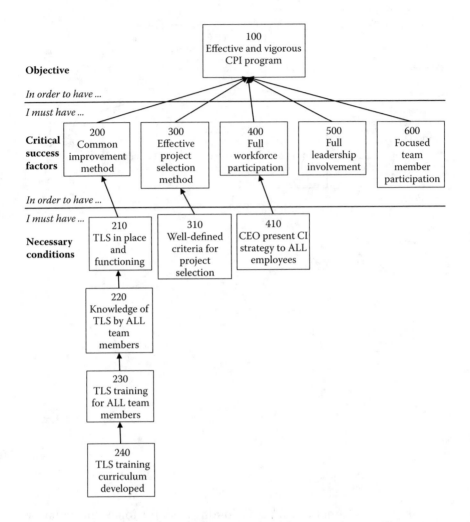

"OK … let's move on to the NC for CSF 600," Connor said. For the first time today, a woman at the center of the table raised her hand. Her name plate said "Connie Taylor, VP of HR." Connor quickly pointed to her for her input.

"Yes, Connie."

"Well, we need be able to free up some time for those employees who might be assigned to a project. I don't know for sure if that means some after-hours time with pay, or being able to overlap some shifts during the day, or what. But, we need to look at that in more detail and figure out a way to make it work."

"So, what I'm hearing is 'Team members freed up for team events,' and you'll figure out the details about how to do that, is that correct?" Connor asked.

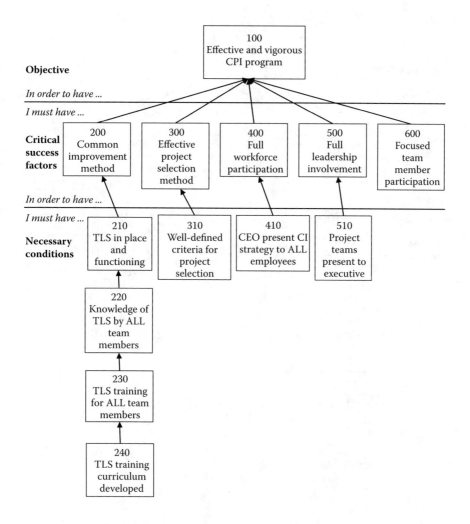

"For now, that's what I'm thinking," Connie said. Connor added it to the IO map.

Connor asked, "Well, what do you think?"

"I think we have our work cut out for us with all of the things we need to do," Thomas said.

"I don't think we're done with the IO map yet," Vanessa said staring at the screen.

William turned in his chair to look at Vanessa and asked, "What do you mean not done?"

"There is still something missing. As we were discussing the last four NCs, it popped into my head that there was an additional NC that was missing and it is necessary to support ALL of those," Vanessa said.

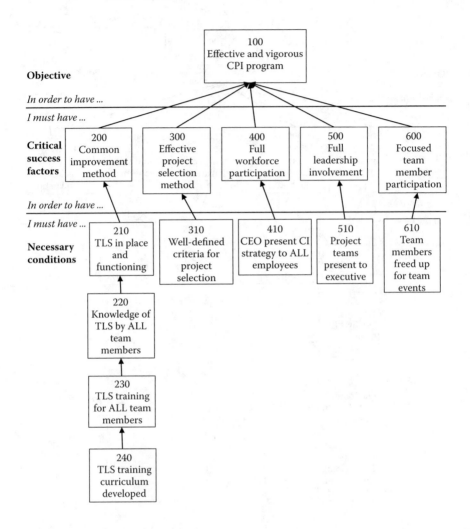

"Which one is that?" asked Thomas.

Vanessa slid her chair back from the table and walked up to the screen pointing with her finger and said, "Look at these last four NCs. I think there is a common denominator, or NC, that is required for all of these. I think I know what it is. Does anybody else see it?" she asked looking at the group.

Everyone was looking at the IO map trying to figure out what it was that Vanessa was talking about. Connor was at his computer ready to input what Vanessa might be suggesting, and smiling.

"It's something we mentioned, and talked about when we discussed NC 310," Vanessa added as a hint.

"You mean some kind of a document to define how we do this?" Terry asked.

Vanessa turned and pointed directly at Terry and said, "Exactly! What I think is missing is a comprehensive continuous improvement strategy plan that defines what the criteria should be, and defines what Tom will present to the employees, and how often presentation should be made for executive review, and of course how we intend to free up time for participation. Does that make sense to you?" she asked.

William was smiling and said, "Yes, that does make sense and I can see how that would be necessary to complete the other four NCs.

"And, I think there is one more connection to consider. Before we can develop a continuous improvement strategy plan, we ALL need the TLS training to make sure we are covering the correct concepts and methods."

Connor was updating the IO map on the screen.

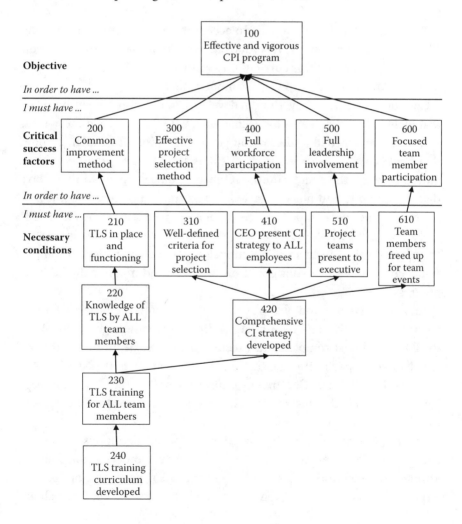

When Connor had finished, Vanessa pointed to the screen, "Does this make more sense now?"

Everyone was nodding in agreement and no one said they disagreed.

"My question is, how do we know where to start?" Thomas asked.

Without hesitation, Vanessa, still standing up front and pointing to the IO map said, "The way I see it is there is already an intrinsic order that links all of these actions together."

Connor waited for her to say more.

"For example, the Training in TLS methods cannot begin until the training curriculum is developed," she said. "Tom, I think the answer to your question is we need to begin with the NC 240, the TLS Training Curriculum. Everything that follows is in one way or another connected to that one."

Terry immediately volunteered to accept the action item and work the TLS Training Curriculum. Terry looked at Connor and asked, "Will you be able to help me put this curriculum together?"

"Yes, I'd be happy to help you," Connor replied.

Connor told them they should develop a more comprehensive plan that included all the details for each action, who was assigned the action, and what they needed to do for completion. Connor also explained how they could color code the IO map for status and monitor progress as they moved through the actions on the IO map. Connor explained that a box that is still white had not yet started. A box that was colored yellow had started, but not yet completed. A box colored green had been completed, and a box colored red was a warning that the activity might be in serious trouble and might need some additional help to be completed. Using the visual color codes, everyone could instantly see and monitor the IO map progress.

Thomas began a round of applause for Vanessa and thanked her for her meaningful insights and her understanding for what was going on. With the IO map almost complete, the executive team was beginning to realize they had developed a strategic action plan that contained the NCs for "An Effective and Vigorous Continuous Improvement Program." Connor realized immediately that internally Vanessa was going to be the fulcrum for the success of the project.

Connor was satisfied with what the group had accomplished today, but he also felt the executive team still needed understanding about Throughput Accounting, especially when it came time to develop the criteria for project selection. Even though he had talked to Dr. Price about starting the conversation, he was feeling more of a need to spend some time with Dr. Price about the concepts. Connor also thought that Terry would want to move rather quickly to get everything started. Fortunately, because the development of the TLS Training Curriculum would probably take a few days, he could also involve Dr. Price and go over the Throughout Accounting when they added it to the TLS training. Then, Dr. Price could present it.

Connor asked the group if they had any more questions. No one raised their hand so he dismissed the group and started to gather his things. Dr. Price and Terry walked over to Connor and thanked him for his time. Connor told Terry he would e-mail an electronic copy of the IO map to him.

Dr. Price noted that he thought the executive staff had remained engaged in the discussions, and he was pleased with that. Dr. Price added, "I know of a lot of other subjects this group has talked about that didn't go nearly as well as this did."

They all left the conference room and entered the hallway. After waving good-bye, Connor continued out the front door to his Hummer. He had a pleasant drive home and was anxious to see Becky again.

17

Follow-Up Meeting—Hospital Executives

Connor was preparing dinner for Becky and himself when his cell phone rang. "Hello, this is Connor."

"Hi Connor, this is Terry Mansfield and I was wondering when we could get together to work on our TLS Training Curriculum?" he asked.

"Hi Terry, great to hear from you," said Connor. "When would you like to get together and where would you like to meet?" he asked.

"I would like to get started as soon as you can find the time. I'd like to do this at the hospital if you don't mind," Terry replied. "I can get us a conference room so we can have some privacy," he added.

"How about tomorrow morning, will that work?" asked Connor.

"That would be great. How about if you come by the hospital around 8:00 AM?" suggested Terry. "What do I need to have ready when you get here?" he asked.

"Eight is fine," Connor said. "As far as what you should have ready, I think you should bring your current Lean Six Sigma training materials and we'll review them. I doubt we'll need to change much, if any, of your material. I'll bring the Theory of Constraints (TOC) training materials I have used before, and then it's just a matter of combining it all together," Connor explained.

"OK Connor, sounds good to me. I'll see you in the morning," said Terry.

After Connor and Becky finished dinner, Connor decided he would review his training materials now and not wait until morning. He wanted to make sure that no company names, or logos, were included in any of his materials. Connor also decided to review his Throughput Accounting (TA) materials and make sure everything was in order.

The next morning, Connor drove to the hospital and left in plenty of time to make sure he was there by 7:30 AM. As he entered the hospital, Connor realized that Terry hadn't mentioned which conference room they would be in. Connor called Terry on his cell and he answered on the first ring. "Hi Terry, you forgot to tell me which room we are meeting in this morning?"

"Sorry Connor, take the elevator to the third floor and when you get off, turn right and walk to the end of the hall; the conference room is the last room on the left," Terry replied.

Connor was able to find the conference room, and when he entered, he saw the familiar face of Dr. Price sitting at the table. "Hi Jules, are you going to join us this morning?" asked Connor.

"Yes, at least for a while," Dr. Price replied.

Connor sat down, opened his shoulder bag, and laid his training materials and laptop on the table. He was almost done when Terry entered the room. Terry shook hands with Dr. Price and Connor and took a seat across from Connor. Terry began, "So Connor, what materials do you think we should review first?"

"I'm not very concerned about your Lean and Six Sigma materials because they're pretty standard," said Connor. "What I really want to discuss is how to integrate the TOC with Lean and Six Sigma," he added.

"I'm excited to learn more about the TOC methods, because in the short time that I've been exposed to the TOC, it has had an impact on my entire approach to improvement," Terry said excitedly.

Connor started, "When I first began using the integrated improvement model, I was asked to write a paper on how it all worked. That paper eventually turned into a book," he added. Connor brought up a drawing on his laptop and showed it to Terry.

"This diagram is what I referred to as the 'TLS Improvement Cycle,'" Connor said. "What you see here is my vision for how to integrate the TOC, Lean, and Six Sigma, which is what I refer to as the 'TLS Improvement Cycle,'" Connor explained. "As you can see, there are three concentric circles, each representing a different element of the TLS improvement methodology. Lean is the outermost circle. The next one is Six Sigma, and the inner circle is the TOC. You'll notice that the steps around the circle are numbered with an alphanumeric character, designating what should happen at each step. For example, in Step 1a, you identify the value stream, the current and next constraint, and the performance metrics that are being used to monitor the system," he said.

"Connor, I have a couple of questions," said Terry. "First, is there a reason why you have TOC as the innermost circle?" he asked.

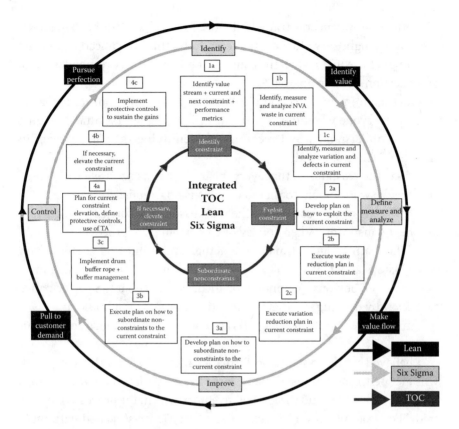

Connor smiled and asked, "If I asked you to guess why I did that, what would you say?"

"Well, you've already told me that TOC provides the necessary focus, and that the focus seems to be missing from many improvement initiatives. So I think you did this because any system improvements should begin by focusing on the constraint," Terry replied. "In other words, by putting TOC in the center, it's kind of like a magnifying glass, so that you emphasize the need for focus and leverage?" he added.

"Terry, your answer is correct!" Connor said with a smile.

"I do have another question," Terry said. "Why do you say to identify both the current and next constraint?"

"That's a very good question," Connor answered. "Why do you think I recommend identifying both the current and next constraint?" asked Connor.

"I'm guessing you're doing that to alert the improvement team that when the current constraint is fixed, then where is the most logical, or probable, place that the system constraint will move to next," said Terry. "I'm guessing that it might serve to alert the team to be thinking ahead as to what they might have to do when the constraint moves?" Terry responded more as a question than an answer.

"Once again, your perception is correct. That point is not immediately clear to everyone when they see this drawing for the first time. I assume you also understand why I recommend identifying the value stream in this step?" Connor asked.

"I'd say the reason is so that everyone understands precisely which process they're working on, so there's no confusion," replied Terry.

"That's part of the reason, but the real reason is to identify the current and next constraint. When you lay out a current state process map, you'll want the team to 'guesstimate' the actual cycle times maybe based on some historical data if you have it, so that the current and next constraint become more obvious," Connor explained. "What about the performance metrics, why do I suggest that you identify those?" Connor asked.

"I'm not sure about that one," Terry replied, looking to Connor for an answer.

"I believe that the system's performance metrics, currently being used, will dictate the system user's behaviors. Those results could affect things like the process flow and the level of inventory within the process," Connor said. "For example, if the current process metric is associated with measuring operator efficiency or equipment utilization time, then you can pretty much be rest assured that at any given point in time there will be excessive inventory in the system. In your case, this inventory would be in the form of patient waiting queues," he added. "Does that make sense?" asked Connor.

"It makes perfect sense," replied Terry.

"If you continue following the steps in the drawing, you'll see that the next two steps, 1b and 1c, focus on identifying, measuring, and analyzing the types of waste that exist, and the amount and type of variation and defects that might be present. This, of course, is intended to be the focus of Step 2 in the TOC cycle, 'Develop a Constraint Exploitation Plan,' or decide how to exploit the system constraint," Connor explained. "As you can see, Step 2b and 2c involves removing any non–value-added waste and reducing the non–value-added steps that might be necessary, but still have waste and variation. So, by having the knowledge of any existing waste and variation, you can now plan the best way to reduce both of them at the current constraint," Connor explained. "At this point, there is one very important concept to remember; most improvement efforts, that I'm familiar with, have a tendency to look for waste and variation throughout the entire system and are not necessarily focused on the single process or process step that is considered the system constraint. I believe that looking at the entire system without the proper focus ends up creating a lot of wasted effort," he explained. "What happens is you end up trying to fix a lot of processes or steps that don't necessarily need fixing, at least not yet. It's my belief that by focusing your efforts only on the current constraint, improvement comes at a much faster rate," he added.

"Connor, your drawing of the TLS Improvement Cycle makes it much easier to see how to unify TOC, Lean, and Six Sigma," said Terry. "My question is, why in the world hasn't this concept been previously taught?" asked Terry. "It seems so logical to me," he added.

"I have been asked that same question many times over the years, and to be quite honest, I truly believe that within each improvement methodology, there are, what I call, *protective zealots* who believe that their method is the only superior application to solve problems and make improvements. There have been attempts for blending two of the methods when Lean and Six Sigma merged, but so far, there are only a limited number of improvement practitioners who push for the unification of TOC, Lean, and Six Sigma," Connor said. "Any more questions before I continue?" asked Connor.

"Not right now, but like I said, I'll ask them as they come up during your explanation," Terry replied.

"How about you Dr. Price, do you have any questions?" asked Connor. "You've been very quiet so far," he added.

"No, I'm good. You and I have talked about some of this in the past, so I do understand what you're talking about," replied Dr. Price.

"OK, then let's continue," said Connor. "You'll notice that Step 3 involves developing your plan on how to subordinate the nonconstraints to the current system constraint," Connor explained. "I might add that this step is probably the step that most organizations have the most trouble with," he added. "Do you have an idea why this might be so difficult for many organizations to comprehend and apply?" Connor asked.

"My guess would be that it's counterintuitive to the performance metrics that the organization currently measures and uses," Terry replied.

"Explain to me why you think that?" Connor asked.

Terry thought for a moment and said, "Well, for example, if an organization is using manpower efficiency or equipment utilization, then they would want every process to operate at full capacity and keep everyone busy. And when they operate this way, all they do is create excessive amounts of work-in-process inventory, which creates a huge backlog of work in the system. It's like in our case, where patients just stack up in front of the constraint and wait to be treated," he added.

"That's exactly right! You hit the legendary nail on the head!" Connor exclaimed. "The subordination concept is probably the most important and least understood. In its most basic form, it implies that nonconstraints should not try and '*outperform*' your constraint. If you do, then like you said, patient wait times increase because more and more patients are pushed into the process," said Connor.

"So what you are telling me is that we need some kind of scheduling mechanism to avoid having so many patients inside the system, is that correct?" asked Terry.

"Yes, that's correct, and if you notice, on Step 3b, I tell you to execute the plan on how to subordinate nonconstraints to the constraint. In box 3c, I recommend implementing Drum–Buffer–Rope (DBR) and Buffer Management (BM)," Connor said. "When you do implement DBR and BM, you end up with a system that is better synchronized with the subordination concept of one-piece flow. In my next slide, I get into the actual tools of TLS and you will see on that slide I have added 'optimize your buffer size.'"

"What do you mean by optimize the buffer?" Terry asked.

"Terry, you've done such a good job of answering the questions already, let me just ask you what you think it means?" Connor asked.

Dr. Price jumped in the conversation and said, "Let me try to answer this one. My guess is that you should start with a certain buffer size, on the basis of your current state process, but as you make any improvements to the constraint, you probably don't need as much buffer as what you started with," he said. "You also said that you should limit the activities of the nonconstraints, to be equal to, or less than, the activities of the constraint, so that is probably the natural outcome of DBR and BM," Dr. Price concluded.

"That's a very good answer! As you continue operating, and monitoring your DBR system, you should keep a record as to why the constraint might be taking longer than you had planned. By doing this, you will identify new ways to reduce any slow time, or downtime, at the constraint, and as you implement solutions, you will automatically improve the uptime of the constraint and be able to process more patients," he explained. "We kind of jumped ahead into the next slide's material, so let me get back to the rest of the cycle on this slide," said Connor.

"In Step 4a, I'm telling you to create a threefold plan. The first part of the plan deals with developing a strategy or plan to elevate the constraint, but only if you need to. The second part of the strategy is to develop protective controls," Connor explained.

"Connor, just so I know what you mean, what do you mean when you say 'to elevate the constraint'?" asked Terry. "I think I know, but I'd like to hear it from you this time," he added.

"Most of the time, because there is so much waste and variation in your process, you will be able to significantly increase the capacity of your constraint by using the first three steps of the five focusing steps," said Connor. "By that, I mean, when you develop and implement your exploitation plan, generally you will always increase the capacity of the constraint to a level that is sufficient to satisfy the current demand being placed on it. But, let's suppose that, even though you have done a good job of improving the flow of patients through whatever process you're improving, you still haven't increased capacity enough to satisfy the current demand. Elevating the constraint simply means that you might have to hire more people, or maybe even purchase additional test equipment, or whatever, to satisfy the demand," Connor added.

"So what you're implying is that during the first three steps, you probably don't have to spend much, if any, money, but if you're forced to elevate the constraint, you probably are going to have to spend some money?" Terry asked.

"Yes, but I want to emphasize that elevation is the fourth step in the process, not the second," Connor replied. "I would estimate that elevation is usually only required 15% to 20% of the time," he added. "The third thing I tell you to do in Step 4a is to begin using TA. Using TA to help in your decision-making will be an absolute must for you, but we'll get to that later in the training package," said Connor.

Dr. Price jumped back into the conversation explaining that he had a meeting he must attend, but that he would come back after the meeting finished. He wanted Connor to hold off on the TA until he returned. Connor said he would wait until he returned to discuss TA. Dr. Price left the room.

Connor continued with Terry, "In Step 4b, I tell you to elevate the constraint if necessary. In the next slide, I go into the need to perform both a capacity analysis and a cost–benefit analysis, because, like most organizations, you're going to have to justify spending any money."

"Trust me Connor, this hospital is no different from any other organization and maybe we are even more focused on cost savings," said Terry.

"I do understand that, and that's why I want to include a section on TA in our training. In the last step, 4c, I tell you to implement protective controls. This step is intended to make sure that all of the gains you've made aren't lost. One of the best ways to do this is through process audits. I also recommend performing an analysis of all policies that are in place that could potentially have a negative impact on your gains. Too many times, I have seen it happen where improvement teams have done a great job of making the flow better, only to have an existing policy get in the way," said Connor. "I'll cover this in much more detail in the next slide on tools."

"Can you give me an example of a policy that might get in the way?" asked Terry.

Connor thought for a minute and answered, "Suppose there is an across-the-board policy mandate that no overtime will be used," he said. "That might work for nonconstraints, but it might not work if the constraint gets behind with its work. Another example, for a hospital, might be that discharges will only happen during a 2- to 3-hour window in the morning," he explained. "Do you understand what I mean?" asked Connor.

"Yes I do and we do have just such a policy on discharges," replied Terry. "So Connor, how do you know which improvement tool to use for each step?" asked Terry. "This is all very helpful, but knowing which tool to use for each step would be very helpful for the improvement teams," Terry said.

Connor had anticipated this question and without hesitation pulled up another drawing on his laptop and showed it to Terry. "Great question Terry," replied Connor. "It just so happens that I have another graphic that combines not only the common tools to use but also the necessary actions to take as you work your way around the TLS Improvement Cycle," said Connor.

"This is exactly what I was hoping for," said Terry. "Not only are the tools listed, but the intrinsic order to use each one is obvious," he added.

"Terry, when you look at this graphic, keep in mind that these tools are not the only tools you can use," said Connor. "What I've tried to do here is list some of the most common tools and the actions that I might typically use when improving a process or system, so you're not limited to just these," Connor explained. "I want to emphasize again that these are not the only tools that you can use, but instead, are the tools that I recommend," he added.

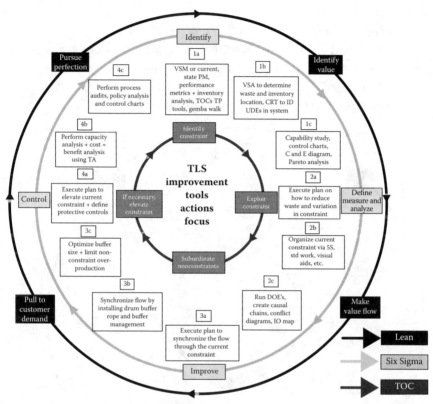

"Wow, Connor, these two drawings make the integration so easy to see and understand," said Terry. "This will be some great information going forward," Terry added.

"One other point I want to make is that I created these drawings back in the 1990s and just recently I updated them to make them more understandable for everyone," Connor explained. "I have made some changes, but for the most part, these concepts are what I've used most of my career. I'm telling you this because I want you to make these two drawings your own and if you think that there could, or should, be different tools to use, then change them as you think necessary," said Connor. "You should always be reinventing and improving what has been developed in the past," he added. "You should never believe that what has already been created is the only way to do anything," he said. "If you don't change them from time to time, they will quickly become out of date," Connor said.

"One other change I have incorporated is to add a third set of circles that I refer to as TLS deliverables," Connor explained as he loaded the next slide onto the screen.

"Why did you add this Connor?" asked Terry.

"What I found, over the years, is that many people just go through the motions without understanding why they are doing what they are doing," Connor explained.

"Can you give me an example of what you mean Connor?" asked Terry.

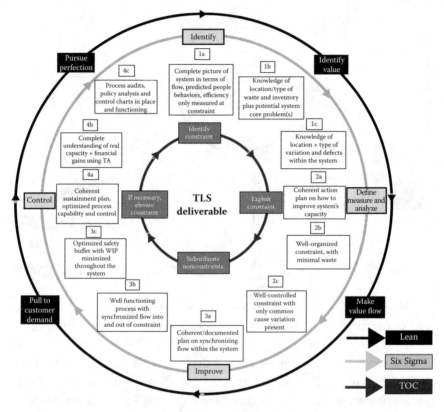

"Let me explain what I mean in a different way," said Connor as he flashed the new slide on his laptop. Let's take box 1a and look at it on all three circles. In the first set of circles, I tell you to 'Identify the Value Stream plus the Current and Next Constraint plus the Performance Metrics that are being used,'" he explained. "In the second set of TLS circles, I tell you to use a value stream map, a current state process map. I also tell you to do an analysis of the performance metrics and the inventory, and I suggest using TOC System's Thinking Tools and a *Gemba* walk. So, in the first two

TLS circle diagrams, I'm telling you 'what to do' and 'how to do it.' Are you following me Terry?" he asked.

"Yes, I understand," he replied.

"The new TLS circle diagram is intended to explain what you should expect to accomplish if you follow the first two diagrams. So, in this example, Step 1a, what you should end up with is a complete picture of the system in terms of existing flow and the predicted behavior of people because of the metrics being used. I also state that efficiency should only be measured at the constraint," he explained. "Does this make sense to you Terry?" he asked.

"Yes, and I can see where this will be very helpful to the hospital TLS teams because they will fully understand what the expected outcome should be," said Terry. "I do have a suggestion for our training Connor. I think it would be very beneficial to walk the teams through the three circle diagrams just like you did with me today. When you did it that way, it was very clear to me," Terry explained.

"I think you might be right about that Terry," Connor said.

"OK, let's move on," said Connor.

"What about changes to the Lean and Six Sigma training materials?" Terry asked.

"Like I said earlier, I think the materials you have will work just fine," said Connor. "I do want to add the piece on TA to the curriculum, so we'll talk about that when Jules returns," he added. "Do you have any questions about what we've talked about so far?" Connor asked.

"No, I think what you've presented so far makes perfect sense to me and I can't wait to present it to my teams," Terry said.

"OK, let's take a short break and walk down to the cafeteria and get some coffee while we give Jules some time to return from his meeting."

They both walked to the cafeteria and talked. Terry was interested to learn more about Connor's background and how he had become involved in all of the continuous improvement methods. When they returned from the cafeteria, they found that Dr. Price had returned from his meeting and was in the conference room. "Welcome back Jules," Connor said.

"I'm actually glad to be back. I didn't want to miss anything, especially about TA."

"You haven't missed anything. In fact, we were just about to begin the discussion on TA, and we were waiting for you, so your timing is perfect," Terry said.

They all sat back down at the table and Connor started. "OK, then let's talk about the concepts of TA. I'm not sure how much you already know about traditional Cost Accounting methods, so please, if I present something you're not familiar with, stop me and I'll explain it to you in more detail," he added. "I know Dr. Price has done some previous research on the Internet, but he also wanted to hear this discussion."

"Most organizations, including hospitals, use an accounting system that was developed decades ago, and at the time, it seemed to work well. However, since then, things have changed dramatically, but unfortunately the accounting system hasn't changed to keep up with the changing times and hasn't kept pace with what's happening now. Even though the business model for most organizations has changed, the accounting systems have remained dormant in terms of updates and change," he added.

"Why hasn't it changed?" asked Terry.

"I'll explain that in a bit, but first let me give you a comparison of the 'old' accounting system, often referred to as 'cost accounting,' and the accounting system I advocate using, referred to as 'throughput accounting,'" Connor said.

"I have a feeling this will change our entire approach for calculating how improvements are affecting the bottom line of the hospital," said Dr. Price. Connor smiled.

"Throughput accounting, often referred to simply as TA, or as some people call it Throughput-Based Decision-Making, made its debut in the early 1980s. It was primarily developed by Dr. Eliyahu Goldratt who, believe it or not, was a physicist and not an accountant.

"Dr. Goldratt developed TA for several important reasons, but the most notable reason was that traditional CA motivated organizational managers to make incorrect decisions by motivating employees to exhibit the wrong behaviors," he explained. "Maybe even more important, TA was able to provide real-time cost information that enabled managers to make real-time decisions, rather than having to wait for weekly, monthly, or even quarterly financial reports. It should come as no surprise that last month's information simply doesn't reflect what is happening today. What managers really needed was access to today's current information," he added.

"That makes sense," said Terry.

Connor continued, "Unlike traditional CA measures, TA's measures are much simpler to learn, are more logical, and require much less data and calculations. In fact, many people have told me that when they learn TA, for the first time in their careers, they finally understand accounting. As I said, TA permits managers to see, in real time, the bottom line impact of their day-to-day decisions."

"Are there formulas that you can show me Connor?" asked Terry.

Connor smiled and replied, "In its most basic form, TA uses three easily understood measurements: Throughput, Investment/Inventory, and Operating Expense. We call it T, I, and OE. Throughput is the rate at which the system generates new money through sales. The key word in this definition is *sales* because product produced, but not purchased by the consumer, is simply inventory waiting to be sold. As such, inventory has no real value until it is sold. Money must be received from the customer before any actual throughput is achieved. So, in the hospital's case, throughput represents patients that have passed through hospital processes and then revenue is received from patients and insurance companies. The formula for Throughput is Selling Price – Totally Variable Costs, or T = SP – TVC," Connor explained.

"What are totally variable costs?" asked Terry.

"Totally variable costs are those costs that stay the same with each sale of a single unit of product, or service, and include things like any raw material costs, sales commissions, shipping costs, and so on. In the hospital's case, that might include things like supplies used in the emergency room or used for surgery or maybe drugs and medicine used to treat a patient," Connor explained. "Some people argue that labor should also be added as a variable cost, but that is simply not true. Labor is no longer considered a variable cost, it's a fixed cost! If you think about it, the hourly labor rates you pay employees when they are on vacation, holidays, and sick leave don't change. You pay them while they are not making anything, or providing any services! In other words, employees cost you exactly the same amount of money whether they are at work or not. Using this example, labor is an operating expense and not a variable cost associated with products or services," Connor said.

"So how does that apply to inventory or investment?" Terry asked.

"Inventory or Investment represents all of the money tied up in the system in things the organization intends to sell. If you were a manufacturing company, then part of this measure is inventory, which includes raw materials, work in process, and finished goods, and part of it includes those things owned by the company that are intended to generate Throughput, such as buildings or equipment," he explained. "In your case, this would include all of the supplies you buy to sell to patients when they are in the hospital. It could also include your radiology and magnetic resonance imaging equipment or other pieces of equipment used to treat patients. Do you understand what I mean?" he asked.

"Yes, that makes sense to me," said Terry. "Me too," said Dr. Price.

"Operating Expense includes all of the money spent by the organization in the conversion of investments and inventory into Throughput. Here is one of the major differences between traditional Cost Accounting and TA. Using TA, OE includes labor expenses and also includes items like supplies or any cost needed to create Throughput for the company," Connor explained. "At this point, you might be tempted to push back and tell me that, since you are a hospital and not in the business of manufacturing consumer products, these measures don't apply. I would tell you that they actually do apply. In the hospital's case, you make money based on the number of patients that pass through your hospital," he said. "I want you to imagine what would happen to the hospital's bottom line if you could reduce the cycle time it takes to treat patients, especially outpatients!" Connor exclaimed.

"So how do you calculate things like profit margins or return on investment using TA?" asked Dr. Price.

"Good question Jules. TA combines T, I, and OE in different ways to provide the fundamental performance measures. For example, Net Profit (NP) is simply Throughput minus Operating Expense or NP = (T − OE). Return on Investment is a measure of the effectiveness of the bottom line to the top line performance measures of the company. The formula for ROI is Net Profit/Investment, or ROI = (T − OE)/I. I want to remind you again that TA is in no way intended to be a replacement for Cost Accounting. But what TA does do is to provide an easy and effective way for the hospital management team to make financial decisions in real time," Connor explained.

"I really like what I've heard so far, and I really think that having our leadership understand this accounting method should really help," said Dr. Price.

"Let me just add a few more things about the differences between these two accounting methods," said Connor. "One of the major problems I have with Cost Accounting is the continuing belief that the key to profitability is based on how much money can be *saved* through cost cutting," he added.

"I'm confused," said Terry. "Why is trying to cut costs or save money such a terrible way to manage a business?" asked Terry. "Isn't that what most companies and organizations do?" he added.

"Yes, that's exactly what most organizations do, but just because most organizations do it doesn't make it the right thing to do," Connor replied. "What TA teaches is that the best way to improve profitability is by changing the focus from *'saving money'* to *'making money,'*" he added.

"What is the difference between the two approaches?" asked Dr. Price.

"There is a significant difference!" Connor exclaimed. "Last week, I was having a discussion with a client of mine and the subject came up about the best way to improve profitability. This person was a staunch advocate of manpower efficiency and by now you know that I am not a fan of this metric at all, except when used correctly. I asked him why he thought manpower efficiency was such a good metric and his answer floored me. He explained that if he could get more product out of a single worker, then his profits would improve since, in his mind, increasing efficiency was a surefire way to know if he was getting more or not. He told me that he treasured this metric," said Connor as he relived what had happened during the conversation. "This is not an unusual response from those people, or organizations, who believe in this metric, but in my opinion, they are simply wrong. It will never produce the results they think they are going to get. When I told him that the key to profitability was not through *saving money*, but rather *making money*, he got such a confused look on his face," said Connor.

"I understand his look of confusion," said Terry.

Connor continued, "In the early 1900s, Cost Accounting was just coming of age and was starting to be widely used. Then, like today, business people understood that, if they wanted to stay in business and make money, then the selling price of their products or services had to be greater than the cost to make the product, or provide the service, like the hospital. This basic premise hasn't changed since then and it's still true today. However, the way you do it has certainly changed."

"How has it changed?" asked Terry.

"Unlike today, where we have a mostly 40-hour workweek, most of the workers back then were paid based on a piece-rate system. A piece-rate system is based on how many "things" you make or how many services delivered. In other words, labor costs were strictly variable in nature. If the worker made something, you paid them. If they didn't make anything, you didn't pay them," Connor explained. "Through time, the pay for workers changed from the truly variable piece-rate system to a total fixed rate. In other words, workers were now being paid an hourly rate, or weekly rate, which, of course, changed the pay method to a fixed cost. But even though the pay methods had changed, the accounting system did not," said Connor.

"So why is that such a problem?" asked Terry.

"When these changes happened, it became very apparent to the business owners that in order to increase their profits, they had to get more products out of their existing workforce. To that end, one of the major outcomes was the birth of the performance metric, manpower efficiency," Connor explained. "The invalid assumption then, as now, was that if you could drive efficiencies higher, then profits would also increase. The end result from this thinking was that the factories began making lots of products that hadn't been ordered yet, so they had to build warehouses to store all of the excess products. They did all of this just to make the efficiency measure and cost-per-part measure look better. In other words, the factories were overproducing to achieve a false reduction in the cost per product. The problem was, and still is, that although labor costs have changed from variable cost to fixed cost, the Cost Accounting rules have not changed—it still assumes a variable cost for labor. This is just one of the problems with the cost saving mentality," Connor explained.

"Gosh, I'm beginning to better understand the problems from using Cost Accounting to run a business," said Terry. "It just seems to me that TA makes more sense, so why isn't TA being used by more organizations?" Terry asked.

"That's a great question," replied Connor. "On the basis of what you've heard so far, why do you think companies are still using traditional Cost Accounting?" asked Connor.

"I'm not sure, but maybe it's just a question of not even knowing about TA," Dr. Price replied. "I'm at a loss Connor," he added.

"That's part of the answer, but that's not the entire answer," said Connor. "Like I've already mentioned, TA is focused on providing accurate and necessary information for decision makers to make much better decisions in real time. If the goal of the organization is to make money, then any decision being considered should move the company closer to that goal. So, with the three simple financial metrics, T, I, and OE, profitability decisions are much easier. Quite simply, any good business decisions will cause Throughput to increase, Inventory/Investment to decrease or remain the same, and Operating Expense to decrease or remain the same," Connor explained.

"That makes perfect sense Connor," said Terry.

"How many times have you heard or read about companies laying off employees in order to reduce costs and become more efficient? These companies are so focused on saving money that they are ignoring, or for-getting, how to make money. Think about it, if the key to profitability is through saving money, then cost reductions through layoffs have a dis-crete lower limit and if you go below that limit, you can actually weaken the organization," Connor explained.

"Why don't they understand this is the wrong approach to profitability? Is it because they've never learned about TA? It just makes so much sense to me," Terry said.

"You have to understand that Cost Accounting has a tight and stran-gling grip on most companies and organizations that they simply don't have any incentive to learn a different or better way."

"I agree with you, but maybe our CEO will see the wisdom of this approach and convince everyone else that this is the way to go," Dr. Price said.

"I hope so," said Connor. "Without his acceptance and concurrence, this will be a tough fight," he added.

"I think we covered pretty much everything we wanted to cover today," said Connor. "Do you have any more questions?" Connor asked.

"I don't have any questions, but I do have a request," said Dr. Price.

"What's that?" Connor asked.

"I think you should be the one to make the TA presentation to the executive staff. You have a much deeper understanding than I do, and I think both Terry and I would appreciate your help in getting these points across," Dr. Price said.

Connor thought for a moment and finally said, "I'll do it if you can set up the meeting for tomorrow."

Dr. Price and Terry both looked at each other. Terry said, "Wait here for a few minutes while we go find out if that is possible." Both left the confer-ence room to go to the executive offices to see if they could set something up. They both returned approximately 30 minutes later with a smile on their face. "OK, we talked with Bradly and he will contact the rest of the staff. He wants to hear what you have to say and he wants to do it early in the morning, at 6:30 to be exact, in the executive conference room. Will that work?" asked Terry.

"I'll be here," Connor replied.

The next morning, Connor arrived at 6:00. He entered the executive conference room and walked directly to the metrics board to see some results. He smiled when he saw that two more Door to Balloon data points had been added to the run chart. The two new data points were in the same range as the previous ones, which told Connor that the team was on an improvement path to sustainment. Connor set up his laptop and then continued reviewing the various charts and graphs; the conference room door opened and in walked Dr. Price.

"Hi Connor, how goes it today?" he asked with a smile on his face.

"Things are going well today, and you?" Connor asked.

"I'm doing well," said Dr. Price.

"I'm anxious to see the group response to what I'm going to present today," Connor said. "I suspect that I'll get a big-time pushback from William Walters, your CFO," Connor said as he looked at Dr. Price.

"Why do you think that Connor?" asked Dr. Price.

"Experience has taught me that, for the most part, Cost Accountants and some finance people have a problem with TA. It is so different from what they were taught," Connor explained. "It's like a threat to them," he added.

One by one, the members of the executive team entered the conference room and took their seats. Everyone was in place at 6:25 AM. Connor recognized Bradley Osher, the CEO, and Vanessa Chambers, the CMO. Connor shook everyone's hand and welcomed them to the session. When everyone was seated, Connor noticed that William Walters wasn't in the room. Connor asked where William was and he was assured by Bradley that he would be coming soon. He had a few things to take care of first. Connor walked to his laptop and loaded his presentation. Just as he finished, William entered the conference room and took a seat. Shortly after that, Terry entered the room and took a seat next to the wall in the back. Connor started his presentation, which was the same material he had presented to Dr. Price and Terry yesterday. At the end of the presentation, Connor asked if there were any questions and as he had expected, William raised his hand.

"Yes, William?" Connor said pointing to him prepared for the worst.

"It's more of a comment than it is a question," said William. "I've been in Accounting and Finance for 25 years and I have never heard of TA before. I have to tell you that during the first 20 minutes I almost got up and left, but the more I listened, the more sense it started to make," William explained. "I've never had anyone present material quite the way you did and although it might come as a surprise to you, I really think that we should review your ideas further and see if we can possibly incorporate some of your accounting method into our day-to-day operations," he added.

Perhaps for the first time in Connor's life, he was somewhat speechless. He had expected a battle from William, but so far, the results were far from it. William might have been the first CFO Connor had ever met who actually took the time to think about and understand TA. Connor knew immediately that his promise to reduce wait times at the hospital might not be as difficult as he might have originally thought. One thing was for certain, Connor knew the road to improvement had just been made easier with William's buy-in to consider the TA approach. The executive team was eager to get going, so Connor thanked everyone for coming and everyone except Dr. Price and Terry left the room.

"Connor, if I hadn't seen it with my own eyes, I wouldn't have believed it. William shocked you, but believe me, he shocked me as well," said Dr. Price.

"William just made our improvement journey much easier," said Connor. "We might encounter some roadblocks, but we'll work through the issues as they happen. My biggest concern now is how soon do you want to start our improvement effort?" Connor asked.

"How about a week, or 10 days from now," Terry said. "We have some internal things we need to do and I'll need to get everything set up and we'll let you know," Terry replied.

"That sounds fine," said Connor. "But, let's make it closer to 10 days, rather than a week. I do have some other projects I need to work on," Connor said. "Have you been thinking about your team for this project?" Connor asked.

"No, but I'll start pulling that together today," Terry said. "And I do remember you telling me about using subject matter experts for the team," he added.

They all agreed that Terry would contact Connor when they had things ready to go. Connor left the hospital and headed home.

Connor had spoken with Joe and Sam the day before and they said Aviation Dynamics had reviewed several vendor proposals and selected the vendor they wanted to implement the Critical Chain Project Management (CCPM) scheduling software. They wanted Connor, Joe, and Sam to return and review the software and the training modules they had selected. They had mentioned that the vendor would probably be on-site at the beginning of next week to start the software training and review the internal IT system, load the software, and get ready to input information. They also wanted Connor, Joe, and Sam to be there when they started to implement, mostly to act as advisors and help them along.

Connor now had a few days before he needed to return to the hospital and this would give him the time he needed to think about, and plan, the hospital implementation. It was also the time he needed to help get Aviation Dynamics well on their way to a successful CCPM implementation. Connor also knew he needed to have a discussion with Joe and Sam about the unscheduled maintenance strategy, but only after they had implemented the wait time's strategy at the hospital. The hospital wait time implementation was the key element to the unscheduled maintenance solution. When he got back home, Connor called Joe and Sam to get the latest update from Aviation Dynamics. They decided to meet in person at *Jonah's* the next morning.

18

MRO Scheduling Rollout

The next morning, Connor, Joe, and Sam got together at *Jonah's* to discuss the latest activities at Aviation Dynamics. When Joe and Sam entered *Jonah's*, they spotted Connor sitting at the usual table in the corner. They both walked over and sat down.

"Hi guys," Connor said.

"Hello," Joe and Sam said almost in unison as they sat down with Connor.

"I want to talk about the latest developments at Aviation Dynamics," Connor said sliding his note pad in front of him with pen in hand.

"We haven't heard from them since the day before yesterday," Joe said. "It was Zeke and Jim that called us on a conference call and as you know they did have some updates. The teams have been busy working the unfinished necessary conditions in the Intermediate Objectives (IO) map. The scheduling review team had researched and made contact with two different critical chain software vendors. Both vendors made presentations to the scheduling evaluation team and they have picked one," Joe continued. "Jim said the presentations were very similar and each vendor seemed to understand the situation very well. The vendor they picked was able to start immediately, and the other vendor had a 2-week wait time," Joe added.

"What Zeke was asking for, when we talked with him, was if we could come back on Monday and just be there while all of this was going on," Sam said. "They've set it up to begin the software training and have their Information Technology (IT) guys review the current IT setup, make sure everything will work, and then figure out where the IT workstations and input locations will be," Sam continued.

"Zeke also said that Brad and Hal had made a return trip to corporate with all of the cost data breakdowns they had pulled together. It must have impressed the corporate folks because Brad was able to secure some money," Joe added. "He said they didn't get all of the money they asked for, but they did get enough to get things going. Zeke said Brad was a little worried when he and Hal got back. Apparently, the Chief Finance Officer had given them 60 days to show some significant improvement in the revenue and profit category or he was going to cut off the money and go back to the way things used to be. Brad is feeling some pressure to perform," Joe said.

Connor was nodding his head and said, "I understand the pressure and 60 days should be more than enough time to make the pressure go away and start showing some very good results."

"I think we can show results much faster than that," Joe said. "In fact, I think they can already show some results in what they have accomplished so far," he added.

Connor and Sam were nodding their heads in agreement.

"Did Zeke tell you who the software vendor is?" Connor asked.

"He did," Joe said. "It's a company called Software Scheduling Solutions and I think they are located right in Houston."

"I know that company!" Connor exclaimed. "I've worked with them a couple of times before and they'll do a good job. They understand this stuff very well, so that was a good choice Aviation Dynamics made," Connor added.

"That's great!" Joe exclaimed. "That might make our job and their job a lot easier."

"OK, now we need to plan a trip back to Aviation Dynamics. Why don't you guys take the lead on the travel arrangements and get everything set up," Connor said looking at both of them.

"We can do that," Joe answered. "In fact, we'll go back to Barton right now and get everything ready to go," he added. There was a pause and finally Joe asked, "Will Becky be going back with us?"

Connor thought for a moment and said, "I think she probably will, but I want her efforts to be low key. I don't want her getting stressed out," he added.

"OK, we'll make arrangements for all four of us," Sam said. "It will be nice to get her back in the game again. We'll make the arrangements to be there for 2 days, Monday and Tuesday. I think that should be plenty of time to get things going and heading down the right path," Sam noted. "Before we call the travel agent, we'll call Zeke and Jim and let them know the preliminary plan and make sure we have the right days," Sam added.

"When you get it all set up, give me a call and send an e-mail with the itinerary and I'll let Becky know. She's going to think this is great!" Connor exclaimed with a big smile.

Joe and Sam headed back to Barton to call Zeke and Jim and make sure nothing had changed. When they got the "OK," they made the travel arrangements. When they got everything in order, they sent Connor the e-mail and gave him a call. They were set to leave Sunday evening from the Business Air terminal for the short flight to Houston.

On Monday morning, they arrived at Aviation Dynamics at 6:55 AM. They had learned their lesson about getting there too early. They chatted with the gate guard, parked, and went into the lobby. Both Zeke and Jim were waiting for them. When they saw Becky, they spent a few minutes getting caught up on what had happened and how she was feeling. When everyone finished signing in and getting badges, they went through the double doors and walked to the conference room. When they entered the conference room, Brad immediately noticed Becky and walked over to talk with her and welcome her back. They spent a minute or two talking about what had happened. Brad made Becky promise that she wouldn't scare them like that again.

Becky smiled and said, "I promise!"

The rest of the team was filtering into the room. Joe had stepped to the front of the room, set up his laptop, and inserted his flash drive. They had decided, on the plane, that the first thing they wanted to do was get a status on the remaining necessary conditions that weren't finished yet. At 7:05 AM, Joe started the meeting. He welcomed everyone back and said he heard from Zeke and Jim that they had been very busy working the issues. Everyone was nodding.

"The first thing we want to do is go back and get a status of the necessary conditions that were either not started, or started and not completed yet," Joe said. "By updating the IO map, we'll know exactly what is complete and what is remaining to complete," he added.

"We have a copy of the one you guys left us last time you were here," Jim said. "If you want, we can use that one?" he asked.

"Thanks for the offer, but I think we'll just update this one and create a new master IO map if that's OK with you?" Joe asked. Jim agreed.

Joe found his file and pulled up the IO map they had used during the last session.

"Let's look first at necessary condition 221. It's the one we talked about extensively on our last visit and it was left white because nothing had started yet. Does anyone want to offer an update for 221?" asked Joe.

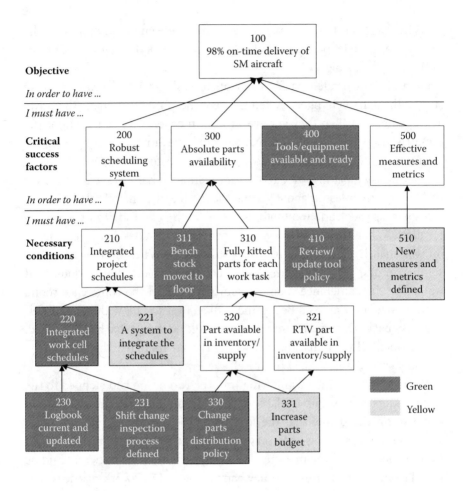

Most of those who were on that team raised their hands. Joe decided to call on Jim for his response, so he pointed to Jim and he responded, "Well, we got together as a team and did an Internet search for Critical Chain Project Management (CCPM) vendors. We found several and we read the profiles about the companies. We finally narrowed it down to three and made some phone calls. One of the vendors couldn't come and talk to us for at least 3 weeks. We eliminated them, knowing we wanted to get it done much faster than that," Jim explained. "The other two vendors both came and made their presentation. We met with each of them for a half-day, but one of the vendors couldn't start on our project for at least 2 weeks, so we eliminated them. The vendor we picked actually has their main office right here in Houston, so we considered that as a plus," Jim continued. "Anyway, we selected Software Scheduling Solutions and made arrangements to get going. In fact, their IT guys are here this morning working with our IT guys to do some kind of IT systems analysis," Jim added. "After the IT guys finish their work and determine the system compatibility, then we'll plan the first training sessions. They think we should be up and running in about a week or 10 days, depending on how things go," Jim said.

"Thanks for the update," Joe said. "So, we'll color the box yellow, which means it has started, but not yet complete, does everyone agree with that?" Joe asked. They all nodded in agreement.

"Next, let's go back to necessary condition 311, bench stock moved to the floor. Last time we talked, you were working this one, but not yet finished. Who has a status on that one?" Joe asked. Both Agnes and Bette raised their hands and Joe pointed to Agnes, the supply room supervisor.

"Well, we used all of the bins in supply to set up a bench stock location. We finally decided to set up a location on each side of the hangar. Because of that, we did need to order a few more bins to make it work, but it wasn't that expensive. We can't get all of the bench stock out there just yet, but we can get the most used parts out there and make it work. Bette, said Agnes, pointing to Bette on her left, "will check the bins every 3 days to start and order when the current inventory seems low. We'll need to collect some data for usage and that will help us determine a more accurate resupply timeline. We'll keep our eyes on this for a while and see if there are any changes to be made, but as of right now, I think we're ready to go. I'd give it a green status," Agnes said.

"OK, a green status it is," said Joe. He walked back to the computer and updated the IO map.

"Let's move on to necessary condition 331, Increase Parts budget. Brad, I believe you and Hal had this one?" Joe said.

"We did," Brad said. "When we got all of our internal data together and determined what our cost estimates might be, Hal and I made a trip back to corporate with the information. We had a meeting with the decision makers, and frankly I think it went very well. The corporate people actually thought our numbers were going to be much higher than we presented, so in that regard, I think they were pleased," Brad explained. "They didn't give us all of the money we wanted, but they gave us approximately 90% of the total and I think if we are smart in our spending, it should be enough to get us going and sustain us for a while," Brad added. "By the way," Brad said looking and speaking to the group, "just so you know, they gave me 60 days to show some very significant improvements. If we don't get the improvements, then the money will be cut off and some heads will roll—most likely my head!" Brad added. Hal was thinking if they failed, his head would roll as well.

"OK, so you've gotten some additional budget to buy parts," Joe said.

"Well, we got some additional budget, but what we spend it on is up to us," Brad said.

"Fair enough," Joe said. "Is it fair to say we can color necessary condition 331 green?"

"Yes, we have money to start," said Brad. Joe walked back to the computer to update the IO map.

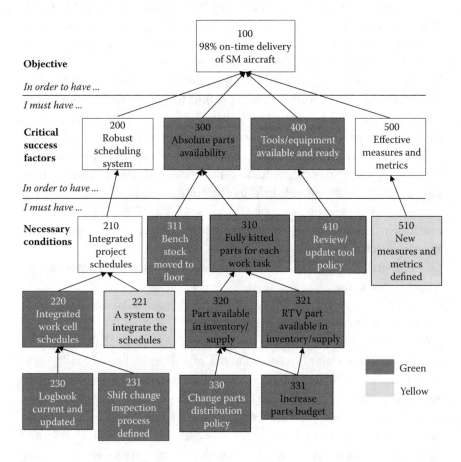

Joe pointed to the screen and said, "Look at the impact of completing necessary condition 331 has had on the IO map. Now, we can make 320, 321, 310, and 300 all green. Now, we only have two more necessary conditions, and two more critical success factors, to complete before being able to achieve our objective," Joe added.

"Your efforts so far have been impressive," Joe said as he faced the group. "Now, you can see the impact of your hard work on being able to achieve your objective. You are currently working necessary condition 221—A system to integrate the schedule. When you finish, you'll have a much better idea what you want to measure for 510," Joe added.

Marsha raised her hand and said, "With regard to necessary condition 321, we are still collecting the data to figure out which parts will benefit the most from having an in-house buffer, but now that we have some budget, we can finish that process in no time. Having some budget was all we were waiting for," she added.

Nathan raised his hand and said, "I'd also like to add that we have finished our new tool policy and procedure, and frankly, it's working very well. The time savings so far have been huge. We are still working out some issues with the special equipment and special tools, but I think we're almost there for making it work," said Nathan.

Just then, the conference room door opened and Helen, Brad's administrative assistant, stuck her head in and signaled for Brad to come to the door. Brad slid his chair back, got up, and walked to the door and stepped out to talk with Helen. A few seconds later, he reappeared with a smile and said to the group, "Good news! The IT people have completed their assessment and they say we are good to go! No new equipment is required to get this project rolling. The project manager from Software Scheduling Solutions should be here within the next 20 minutes and wants to meet with everyone. He's put together an implementation agenda and schedule and wants to present it to the group," Brad said. "So, unless Joe has anything further, let's just take a break in place and wait for him to get here," Brad added.

Fifteen minutes later, everyone was engaged in small talk and little group conversations. The door to the conference room opened and Helen walked in followed by another gentleman. She quickly signaled for Brad to come their direction. Brad got up and headed for the door. When he got there, Helen said, "Brad, this is Mr. Collin Anderson from Software Scheduling Solutions."

"Nice to meet you Mr. Anderson," Brad said and thrust his hand out for a handshake.

"Nice to meet you, as well," Collin said, shaking his hand. "I've been assigned as the project manager for this effort. I got your company name and address from the sales and marketing people and wanted to meet with you first thing this morning. When I called earlier, Helen told me to come right over. I hope I'm not interrupting a meeting?" Collin said apologetically.

"Not at all," said Brad. "In fact, everyone in this room is waiting to hear what you have to say," Brad said.

As they were talking, Collin heard a voice behind him. "Collin Anderson, it's been a while since I've seen you." Collin turned somewhat startled and came face to face with Connor. "Good grief, Connor Jackson, how are you doing?" Collin asked.

Brad looked at Connor and then to Collin and asked, "Do you two know each other?"

"Yes, we do," Connor said extending his hand. "Collin and I have worked together on a couple of projects in the past," he added.

"Successful projects I might add," Collin said. Brad was smiling and thinking to himself, "This might turn out better than I ever imagined. What a coincidence this is," thought Brad.

"I thought you retired?" Collin asked Connor.

"It's a long story," Connor said. "Perhaps you can join us for dinner at our hotel this evening and we can get caught up?" he asked.

"I just might have time to do that, especially since you are involved with this project," Collin said.

"First things, first," Brad said. "We need you to address this group and tell us all what you have planned for us," said Brad.

Brad left the group and walked back to the front of the room to call the group back to order and make the introduction for Collin. Collin was looking at the screen and noticed the IO map and asked Connor, "What's that?"

"It's the second part of a nifty tool we have in our arsenal now and it is proving its worth with this project," Connor said. "It's called an Intermediate Objectives map or IO map as we call it, and you have a starring role to complete one of the necessary conditions," Connor said with a smile.

"I do?" Collin questioned with a surprised look.

"You do, but first you just need to explain to the group what your implementation plan is," Connor said.

Just then, Collin heard his name and looked up to see Brad pointing his direction so Collin started to walk to the front of the room. Brad introduced Collin, saying where he was from, and what his role on the project would be. Everyone in the room clapped. It was obvious that Collin was a little embarrassed by the attention.

Everyone was now seated, so Collin began. "Hello, my name is Collin Anderson. First, I want to tell you what a pleasure it is for me to be here and I'm really looking forward to this project. I work for Software Scheduling Solutions and I'm a Senior Implementation Project Manager. I've been assigned to help you implement your project using our software," Collin said. "Typically, we have three phases during an implementation. The first phase is for the IT people to verify that a system is ready and capable of handling our software. I'm happy to report that I received a text message from our IT guy saying your system had been verified. The second phase is to conduct the necessary training for the system users and make sure everyone understands what they need to do and when they need to do it. The third phase is implementing the actual software. This phase usually takes the most time for everyone involved. During this phase, we'll need to dissect one of your projects and lay it out task by task with a specific analysis of your estimated duration times, and the locations of the feeding buffers, for each project. If I understand correctly from the sales and marketing folks, you have several different aircraft you might work on. We'll need to build a template for each of those aircraft as they come due for overhaul," Collin said. "Are there any questions so far?" Collin asked. Nathan raised his hand and Collin pointed to him and said, "Yes sir."

"Well, it's not really a question, but more like a comment. I think Mr. Pecci, Mr. Henderson, and Mr. Jackson have already explained a lot about how CCPM works, so I think most of us have a good understanding about that," said Nathan.

Collin looked directly at Connor and said, "I'm not at all surprised.

"If it's OK with you Mr. Carter," Collin said looking at Brad, "I can have a training team here first thing in the morning to begin the training."

Brad nodded and said, "The sooner, the better."

"OK, good! Now, we'll need to identify those individuals who will be in the first round of training," Collin said looking around the room.

Zeke raised his hand and asked, "What are your recommendations for those who need the training? I don't think everyone has to attend, do they?"

"No, not everyone needs the training. What we'll want, up front, are those individuals who will be designated with the primary responsibility of updating the scheduled work," Collin said.

Nathan raised his hand and said, "We currently have an assigned scheduler for each supervisor's area and each supervisor is assigned three work bays. Right now, the team leads update the supervisor on progress and the supervisor passes the information to the scheduler to update the schedules.

I think we need the schedulers, the supervisors, and a team lead from each area as an alternate," said Nathan.

"I think that's pretty close to what we are looking for," said Collin.

"How long will this training last?" Jim asked.

"Right around 4 hours," Collin replied.

"Why don't you start your training at seven in the morning? If it's 4 hours long, then that will take us right up to lunchtime," Jim pointed out.

"That works for me," Collin said. He looked at his watch and realized it was almost 11 now. "Do we need to stop for lunch right now?" he asked. Everyone in the room seemed to look at their watches at the same time.

"It's probably a good point to break it off and then get together again after lunch," Jim said. Everyone else agreed and started getting out of their seats and moving toward the door.

"I want everyone back in their seats at 11:30 sharp," Jim said.

When the room had emptied, Collin walked over to Connor who was still sitting at the table with Joe, Sam, and Becky. As he got closer, Connor stood and shook his hand again and made the introduction to the group. "Collin, I'd like you to meet some friends of mine. This is Joe Pecci and Sam Henderson," Connor said as he pointed to each. "And, this is my wife Becky."

"This is your wife?" Collin asked, reaching out to shake Becky's hand.

"Like I said, it's a long story," said Connor.

"It's a pleasure to meet you," Becky said.

"Actually, the pleasure belongs to me," Collin said as he smiled and shook Becky's hand.

They all sat down at the table and Becky asked, "So, you two know each other?"

"I've had the pleasure of working with Connor before. If I remember correctly, I think there were at least three times we teamed on projects and every one of them was a big success!" Collin said. "I'm looking forward to the same thing with this project." Collin shifted his gaze and conversation to Connor. "So, how did you end up here, doing this?" Collin asked.

"We'll talk about that over dinner this evening, if you are still able to make it," Connor said.

"I wouldn't miss it for the world," Collin said with a huge smile. "So, give me your assessment of where we are right now," Collin asked as he looked at everyone at the table.

"It's a classic story of a company that was trying to improve themselves by saving money. They got caught up in the saving money concept to the point they had dug a deep hole. They had saved themselves to the point that they couldn't function anymore," Connor said. "Actually, Joe has pretty much been the lead on this one, so I'll let him fill you in," Connor added.

Collin looked at Joe and Joe said, "Their scheduled maintenance is taking, on average, 65 to 70 days, and they realize they need to do better. They have a backlog of work that seems to just keep getting bigger. They have some contracts coming up for rebid, and they are unsure about winning them because of the extended overhaul times and some late deliveries. Between their data analysis and our analysis, we estimated that only 40% of the time was actually being spent working on the aircraft. They were spending a lot of time on non–value-added activities. They also have the typical parts and limited resource problems, and the flow for the project is chaotically out of synchronization. We also discovered some policies and procedures that were having some very negative effects, but I think we've gotten those turned around now. The last piece of the puzzle we are missing is the scheduling segment, and that's where you come in," Joe said looking at Collin.

"It sounds like you've done your homework, and they seem to understand what they need to do to move forward," Collin said. "That should make my job much easier," he added.

"I hope so," Joe answered.

Collin looked up at the screen where the IO map was still displayed, pointed to the screen, and asked, "What is that?" Joe provided an explanation of the IO map and how they were using it.

Collin had a smile and said, "I like it!"

People were slowly starting to filter back into the room. Becky looked at her watch and announced to everyone that it was 11:25. When everyone was back in their seats, Collin walked back to the front of the room. "OK, I think we have identified those people for the first round of training, and we'll begin that first thing in the morning. Now, we need to identify those people who will be involved with looking at the tasks and durations. I'm hoping to start that activity tomorrow afternoon," Collin said. There was a pause before Collin continued, "I'm going to insist that the people doing the evaluation of task and durations are the subject matter experts. In other words, those people who actually perform the work," Collin added. "We'll use their expertise of the process and go through each task as it is currently listed."

"Why do you want just those people?" Jim asked.

"Truly, they have the most knowledge and can provide the best information about task durations and issues," Collin answered. "They also understand the best points for feeding buffers," he added.

Jim looked puzzled, as did Zeke, but both accepted the answer.

"We can use this same conference room for the training. What do we need to have ready for you?" Jim asked.

"The training will be in two parts. First, we'll have some classroom presentation materials, and second, we'll do some hands-on training with the software and start learning your way around the different commands and screen setups," Collin said. "Those people attending the training need to bring a laptop. Also, we'd need adequate extension cords to plug them all in," Collin said.

Zeke looked at Jim and asked, "Will that be a problem?"

"I don't think so. We should be able to cover all of that," Jim said.

Nathan raised his hand and spoke. "It seems to me that the people involved in the training will be the same people involved with reviewing the tasks and durations, and we might want to include some of the other team leads from the work areas," he added. "That might end up being about 8 to 10 people, is that alright?" Nathan asked.

"That's fine, as long as we have the best subject matter experts," Collin responded.

"I need to get out to the shop floor and talk with Olin Smith and let him know what's going on," Nathan said. "He'll need to talk with the team leads in his area and make sure he's got everything covered so they can attend the scheduled review training."

"I have nothing further for today. In fact, I need to go make some phone calls and get the training team ready," Collin said.

"If you can get us the names of the training people who are coming, we can have everything ready to go with the gate guard and the receptionist when they arrive," Jim responded.

"I'll do that! I should have the names in approximately 30 minutes," Collin said. "OK, if there are no more questions, then I'll be back in the morning at seven," he added.

Becky looked at her watch, it was 1:15. Everyone was collecting their stuff and leaving the room. Jim had stayed behind to walk them out. Collin walked up to Connor and asked, "So, about dinner. What hotel are you staying at?" Connor told him the name of the hotel and they agreed that they would meet around five for dinner. When they had all finished collecting their stuff, they walked to the lobby with Jim. They all signed out and walked outside. Collin said he was heading back to his office to take care of the training. They all shook hands and departed for their separate locations.

At 5:00, Collin was at the hotel. They all met in the lobby and walked to the restaurant and sat down for dinner. The same waitress that had waited on them many times before was on duty and when she walked up to the table, Connor put up five fingers and said, "Chianti." Connor already knew that Collin liked Chianti.

For the next $2\frac{1}{2}$ hours, they enjoyed dinner, while Connor, Joe, Sam, and Becky related the stories about Barton, SIMCO, Fabrics-R-Us, Connor getting married, and finally the connections about how they ended up at Aviation Dynamics. Toward the end of dinner, Collin said, "It's a small world we live in." They finally finished and everyone said their good-byes until morning.

"We'll see you in the morning," Collin said as they all stood in the lobby.

"We'll be there," Connor said.

19

MRO Review and Training

The next morning, everyone met in the lobby and drove to Aviation Dynamics. When they got there, Collin had just arrived and was just finishing signing in. He was accompanied by two other gentlemen that everyone assumed were the trainers. Moments later, Jim arrived and waited for Joe, Sam, Connor, and Becky to sign in. All seven of them walked with Jim to the conference room. The two guys with Collin immediately began to set up their laptops and get the handouts from their bags and set them on the table. Jim left for a few minutes and returned with some extension cords. The Aviation Dynamics team members were filtering into the room and each had a laptop with them. They seated themselves around the table and got their laptops powered up and ready to go. Within a few minutes, everyone was ready to begin. Joe, Sam, Connor, Becky, and Jim took a seat next to the wall.

Collin walked to the front of the room and welcomed everyone to the training session. He went over a brief agenda for the day and touched briefly on each topic. He introduced his two associates, Larry and Brent, and explained they would be doing most of the upfront training. When he finished, he walked over and took a seat next to Connor.

"I'm looking forward to this," Connor whispered to Collin.

"These are my two best guys, and they do an excellent presentation," Collin whispered back.

Brent walked to the front of the room. His laptop was already set up and he was ready to go.

"Good morning to everyone and I want to say what a pleasure it is to be here with you today. The first thing I want to do is a comparison between the Critical Path Method (CPM) and Critical Chain Project Management, or CCPM as we call it. I want you to have a good understanding about what you're moving away from and what you're getting into. There are some very subtle differences between these two scheduling methods and you all need to be aware of what they are," Brent said. "I don't necessarily want to cover all of the differences right now, but I do want to highlight some of the major differences we will be working on this afternoon when we start building your scheduling template." He walked back to his computer and pushed a button and a slide appeared on the screen.

CPM and CCPM comparison #1

CPM	CCPM	CCPM Benefits
• Focused on completing the tasks.	• Focused on completing the project.	• Allows for project monitoring rather than task monitoring.

"CPM is focused on completing tasks on time, especially those tasks on the critical path. CCPM is focused on the project completing on the due date. With CCPM, you monitor the project and not just the tasks. This is a major difference in the way you have done it in the past, and for some of you, it might be hard to make the switch. Just remember: it's not as important to complete the task on time, but it is very important to complete the project on time," Brent said. The next slide appeared.

CPM and CCPM comparison #2

CPM	CCPM	CCPM Benefits
• Focused on completing the tasks.	• Focused on completing the project.	• Allows for project monitoring rather than task monitoring.
• Tasks have "start" and "end" dates.	• Task starts as soon as it is ready and necessary.	• Project managed based on "completion events," not "scheduled events."

"Another major difference is that start and end dates for tasks are not required. The benefit is the project is managed based on the *completion of events* and not *scheduled events*. Tasks will be updated and monitored based on the number of days remaining to complete the work," Brent said. Brent moved to the next slide.

"CPM uses slack time, or safety time, to protect a task from the uncertainty that seems to exist in all projects. The slack time is used as a way to protect against all those things that can go wrong, and usually do. CCPM uses the concept of 'buffers,' and there are three types. The first is a project buffer. The second is a feeding buffer, and the third is a resource buffer. Project buffers are created from the safety time (slack time) that is removed from the task. Usually, the total task duration is cut in half, with half the time remaining in the task, and the other half is moved to the project buffer. Feeding buffers are specific buffers located at strategic locations when two tasks need to come together to start a third task. An example would be to ensure parts availability in order to continue an assembly," Brent explained. "The third buffer is the resource buffer, and as the name implies, it is focused on the scheduling of the critical resources in the project. This requires that the available resources be level loaded in the system," and Brent moved to the next slide.

CPM and CCPM comparison #3

CPM	CCPM	CCPM Benefits
• Focused on completing the tasks.	• Focused on completing the project.	• Allows for project monitoring rather than task monitoring.
• Tasks have "start" and "end" dates.	• Task starts as soon as it is ready and necessary.	• Project managed based on "completion events," not "scheduled events."
• Tasks have additional "slack time" or "safety time" to protect the task.	• The project is protected using "project buffers" and "feeding buffers."	• Buffers are used to protect ALL tasks throughout the project.

CPM and CCPM comparison #4

CPM	CCPM	CCPM Benefits
• Focused on completing the tasks.	• Focused on completing the project.	• Allows for project monitoring rather than task monitoring.
• Tasks have "start" and "end" dates.	• Task starts as soon as it is ready and necessary.	• Project managed based on "completion events," not "scheduled events."
• Tasks have additional "slack time" or "safety time" to protect the task.	• The project is protected using "project buffers" and "feeding buffers."	• Buffers are used to protect ALL tasks throughout the project.
• Resource contention is prevalent and "normal."	• Resource issues are completely managed.	• Resources are level loaded and resource "bottlenecks" identified.

272 • *Focus and Leverage*

"Probably the number one major difference is that CPM assumes infinite capacity of resources, which turns out to be a big problem for project management. Most resources are somewhat limited and some resources are very limited. The limited resources are the resources that will move a project into the 'trouble zone' quickly," Brent said. "However, if the resources are level loaded, CCPM can identify which resource is the bottleneck and for what length of time. It allows project managers to focus on the critical resources and focus on preventing project issues because of them. It's no longer a mystery! You know who they are and how long they will be the problem," Brent said.

"Those are the major differences. There are others, but I'm sure you are reaching a saturation point of information!" Brent said with a smile. "It's not that you don't need to know what they are, you just don't need to know right now. As the situations arise during the task discussions, we will talk about them then," Brent added. "Are there any questions?" Brent asked the group. No one raised their hand.

"OK then, I'll turn it over to Larry and let him continue," Brent said. Larry walked to the front of the room and clicked his first slide.

"Good morning," Larry said. "I have a few things I want to cover. In this first segment, we will review some of the obstacles we want to overcome with CCPM. The first phenomenon is multitasking," Larry said. "Multitasking has always been considered a necessary characteristic for managing projects not only for employees but also for project managers. The truth is multitasking can cause more harm than it provides benefit. Multitasking has a way of making employees look busy, but it does very little toward completing a project, especially if you spend your time jumping back and forth between tasks, or moving from project to project. In the end, tasks and projects will take longer and due dates will be missed. With CCPM, the goal is to reduce the negative effects of multitasking by providing the necessary focus on a single task at a time. Multitasking can be a very hard habit to break, because it's what you always do, and it's what you know how to do. Even with CCPM, you will be tempted to multitask, but you need to avoid the temptation. CCPM will slow the project to work only the tasks that need to be worked. It is possible that, by going slower, you can actually go faster and complete the work on time," Larry explained.

"The second phenomenon is the student syndrome. The student syndrome supports the learned behavior of procrastination and is directly related to the start and finish dates assigned to tasks. Honestly, we've all done it. Think back to when you were in school. Suppose it was Thursday or Friday night and you had a homework assignment due on Monday morning. When do you start doing the work?" Larry asked scanning the group with a smile. No one said anything. It seemed as if no one wanted to admit when they really started the work, even though they knew the answer. Finally, Larry answered his own question and said, "You probably wouldn't start until at least Sunday night, and then you find you can't get it done and you want more time to finish it," Larry said. Heads were nodding in agreement. "With CCPM, you need to start the task as soon as it is available, do the best work you can, and then pass it on. By not waiting for the start date to begin, or the end date to finish, but rather doing the work when it is available, you can gain time for the entire project," Larry explained.

"The third phenomenon is Parkinson's law, which states that, 'Work expands to fill the available time.' The translation is, if you are given 3 days on a schedule to complete a task, then you use all 3 days. The rationale is, 'If you don't use the time, someone will take it away the next time,'" Larry said. There were some nodding heads. "What CCPM aims to do is remove any expansion time because of start and end date. If there is not an actual start and end date, then start the work, do a very good job, and pass the work on no matter what the date is," Larry explained.

"By controlling and eliminating these three from your daily activities and planning, your projects will finish faster and that's the overall goal we want to achieve. Are there any questions so far?" Larry asked. No one raised their hand.

Larry had everyone open their laptops and pull up the scheduling software. Brent was walking around the room helping people get the correct information on their screen. They spent the next little while going through some of the key points and key strokes on the software. This was the software familiarization they needed for the afternoon session when they started the task evaluations.

Toward the end of the presentation, the trainers cited some examples from previous projects they had been involved with. Most of the results appeared to reveal data in the range of 40%–50% reduction in repair cycle times, meaning those organizations could now do twice as much work in the same amount of time, with the same number of people. Jim was listening intently and looking at the results almost in disbelief. Finally, he raised his hand and asked, "These results are very impressive, almost to the point of being unbelievable. I have noticed in your discussions that you never mentioned how many more employees you had to hire in order to do the work twice as fast. How many more employees were necessary to do this?" Jim asked.

"None!" said Collin as he jumped to his feet to address the group. "The reality is all of this work was completed with the same number of employees," he explained. "I'll admit, it seems to be a common assumption that if a company wants to do twice as much work, then they need to hire twice as many employees and buy more equipment, and get bigger buildings, and all of the other perceived needs that go with expansion, and that's one way to do it! It's not the best way, but it is one way!" Collin added. "All of these organizations Larry and Brent are talking about achieved these results, not because they hired twice as many people, but rather because they completed the work twice as fast," Collin said with a sincere emphasis. "What this system allows you to do is remove the obstacles and wait time, or queue time, and focus on the project and not just the task. By taking all of the slack times and wait times and turning it into productive time, it's certainly not unreasonable to think a project could be completed twice as fast," he added.

Connor was thinking to himself, "This is the Collin I remember!"

"There is no doubt there will be some new rules, and some new ways of thinking for how you plan and schedule your projects, but the results speak for themselves," Collin explained. "By spending the time necessary to synchronize the flow and to establish correct feeding chains and feeding buffers, the negative effects of multitasking—the student syndrome and Parkinson's law—can be greatly reduced or eliminated," he added.

Jim jumped back in the conversation and said, "I'm still stuck in my mind about what I've heard from Joe, Connor, and Sam and now these guys," he said, pointing to the trainers. "It just doesn't make sense to me that we can somehow reduce the task work time by half and still get the work done on time, or even get it done at ALL!"

"You're right!" Collin said. "This whole thought process seems totally counterintuitive from what you think the right answer should be. I'm not sure, but have you completed any time studies to find out how much wait time or down time there is?" Collin asked looking mostly at Connor.

"We have," Jim said, almost embarrassed.

"What did those time studies tell you?" Collin asked.

"Well, it wasn't pretty," Jim said. "What we found was that only 40% of the time available was actually being spent repairing the helicopters. The other 60% was involved in non–value-added tasks, or waiting for parts, or actually looking for other work to do," he explained.

Collin smiled and asked, "What if you could utilize that 60% and turn it into productive time?" Collin asked to the group and not just Jim.

Nathan spoke up and said, "Well, we have done some things that will allow us to regain some of that time, but not all of it."

"So, whatever time might remain, if you were able to utilize that time for repairs, how many more helicopters could you repair?" Collin asked.

Jim let out an audible sigh and said, "Probably twice as many." Everyone else was slowly nodding their heads.

Collin looked at his watch. It was now 10:50 AM. He looked at Jim and asked, "Is this a good time to break for lunch?"

Jim looked at his watch and said, "It probably is."

Collin dismissed the group for lunch and reminded them to be back in their seats at 11:30. He explained that during the afternoon session, they would start to familiarize everyone with the software and do a scheduling exercise to review tasks and task time. Everyone filed out of the room.

Collin walked back over and sat next to Connor. Connor looked at him with a smile and said, "Great job Mr. Anderson!"

"Thanks!" Collin said. "I haven't forgotten everything that you taught me from the times we have spent working other projects," he added with a smile.

Joe and Sam got up from their seats and walked closer to Connor and Collin. "Good job Collin," Joe said. Collin just nodded his head.

"It will be interesting to see how they engage with the task times," Sam said.

"I think they'll do just fine," Becky said. "It seems to me they are ready to go and want to get this started," she added.

The two trainers walked over to Collin and he introduced them to Joe, Sam, Connor, and Becky. Collin and Connor spent a few minutes reminiscing back to their previous projects and telling stories about those engagements. Everyone was smiling, and at times laughing out loud.

When the afternoon session began, Collin was back in the front of the room. He was making the introduction for the afternoon topic.

"This afternoon, we want to spend some time getting familiar with the software and building a template for a project. If you could all please open your laptops and get them turned on, we would appreciate that," Collin said. The two assistants were going around the room making sure everyone had the right screen visible. When all of the laptops were ready, Collin walked over to one of the whiteboards on the side wall and then faced the group.

"What we want to do is walk through the tasks for planning a project and then set up a project template based on one of your repair schedules. My two great associates, Larry and Brent, will be walking around the room to give you some individual help, if you need it," Collin said. "Now, if you would please open the manual in front of you to section one, we will begin," he explained.

"What I want to do is build a template for the most common type of helicopter that you do repair work on. I realize there are several, but I want to focus on the most common, the one you work on the most," Collin said. "By the way, do we have any master schedulers in the room?" Collin asked. Two hands went up. "Is it possible you can find, and display, on your laptop a copy of a current schedule that matches one of the aircraft we are talking about and that you currently have in repair?" Collin asked.

"I'll do that," said Scott, one of the master schedulers.

"Thank you," Collin said. Scott immediately logged into the internal system to pull up a schedule.

Collin moved back to the front of the room and said, "OK, the first thing we want to do is identify the tasks involved for completing the effort. I'm going to assume that, because each project is essentially the same, the tasks remain pretty much the same. Is that correct?" he asked the group. Everyone was nodding in agreement.

"It does depend on the type of aircraft, but yes, the task list remains pretty much unchanged from one to another," Nathan said. "The only difference might be an engineering change order, but that doesn't usually happen that often," he added.

"So, if we know the task sequence and it stays fairly static from one project to the next, then the next thing to look at is the task durations," Collin said.

"The task durations are pretty much the same as well," Hector said. "We have standard hours that we apply to each task and we've developed those standard hours based on a fairly extensive historical database," he added.

"So, your database tells you how long you 'should' take and not necessarily how long it 'could' take, is that correct?" Collin asked.

"What do you mean?" asked Nathan. "The database tells us historically how long it should take. It's the same amount of hours that we base our project cost estimates on," said Nathan.

"Exactly," Collin said, turning to point at Nathan. "Does it ever happen with a project task that you actually finish the task early?" Collin posed the question to the group.

"It could happen, and it sometimes does, but we don't necessarily like to report early finishes," Scott, the master scheduler said.

"Why not?" asked Collin.

"Because if we start posting early finishes, then the standard hours will start to go down, and that's not what we want to happen," said Hector.

"This is a classic example of Parkinson's law and it's one of the reasons why your standard hours are inflated and stay high," Collin said. "It's a form of 'safety time' in the task, and even though you do better, you don't report it. The reason you don't report it is because you don't want to have the time taken away from you, correct?" Collin asked. There was silence in the room.

"We're always looking for more time," Jim said, breaking the silence and admitting nothing.

"What if I told you that you could do the task in half the time with a very high on-time delivery rate?" Collin exclaimed.

"I'd have to see it, to believe it," Jim said. Jim was still very skeptical about the concept of doing it in half the time, and making money.

"Then let's make you a believer!" Collin said. "Let's look at how we can make that happen. I want you to consider three things for each task we evaluate. First, consider the task duration and the risk involved with that task. As a rule, the more you know about a task, the less risk there is. And, inversely, the less you know, then the more risk there is. Every task will carry a certain level of statistical variation for completion. It's just normal fluctuations in the process. However, variation and uncertainty are two different things and must be evaluated differently. Not every task we evaluate will have the same variation or uncertainty. The less you know about a task, and by that I mean finding unexpected things that also need repair, or replacement, then the higher the uncertainty. Let's consider the first task of the project and look at your standard hour's duration," Collin said.

Scott pulled up the project schedule that he had retrieved from the internal IT system and plugged the projector into his computer so the information would show on the screen. Collin looked at it and faced the group. "As we go through this, there are some things I want you to remember and think about. First, and foremost, is this group will probably be together working the template for at least the next few days and possibly longer," Collin said. "As we go through each task, there will be a series of points we need to discuss for each one," he added.

Collin continued, "The first consideration is the task duration. It's the time you use for the planning phase. If you consider that every task has two different durations, it might make it easier to think about. The first duration is the actual *hands-on* time to do the work. The second duration is the *wait time*. Every task has some kind of wait time associated with it. You've already demonstrated you have wait time because of not wanting to give up any of your standard hours. What you are actually doing is extending the project time for fear of losing project time. It can also happen because of parts, inspections, approvals, paperwork, certifications, resources, and so on. Any one of those can cause a task to wait, and wait time increases the overall project schedule duration. If you really want to shorten the schedule time, we have to attack and remove the majority of the wait times. For most projects, it is probably a fair guess to estimate that 30% to 40% of the total project time is wait time," Collin added, looking for the effect. "In fact, your own data suggested something around 60%!" Everyone was silent and listening.

Collin continued, "We can start to eliminate wait time by implementing a feeding chain with a feeding buffer located at the right location for things like parts, or special equipment, or whatever it might be. If all the parts are in the right place at the right time, then wait time can be reduced, or eliminated. We can also reduce wait time by assigning the correct resources to be in the right place at the right time. Resources like the mechanics or inspection, avionics and hydraulics, or whatever other limited resource you might find, or need.

"So, when you think about task duration, think in terms of the actual 'touch time' and don't include the 'wait time.' Assume that most, if not all, of the wait time will be eliminated. If everything was in the right place, at the right time, then how fast could you actually complete the work for the task?" Collin asked in a rhetorical fashion.

Nathan raised his hand and Collin pointed to him. "You know, along this same concept of wait time, we've been having some conversations on the shop floor. We've talked about how we can reduce the overall time and one of the things we've been talking about was being able to do an aircraft inspection the very first thing." Collin noticed others in the room shaking their heads.

"Why do you want to do an aircraft inspection the very first thing?" Collin asked.

"Well, we've learned from past experience that sometimes we run into some parts or systems that need to be fixed or replaced and it's not necessarily a task on the schedule. Sometimes, these items are not on our standard checklist of things to look at, and we only find them after the fact.

MRO Review and Training • 279

Sometimes, not having these parts can slow us down the most, because they are unexpected," Nathan said. "If we could do a full inspection first, and find these issues, if they exist, then we could order those additional parts early enough to be available when we need them. Something like that could compress the schedule even more," Nathan added.

"So, this is something that could help you determine what you need in one of your feeding buffers at some point later in the project?" Collin asked.

"Exactly, if something is needed, we want to know it as quickly as we can and get that part on order," Hector said. "It could also help us reduce the 'uncertainty' that you spoke about earlier, and make sure it doesn't become the reason for a late project," Hector added.

"Knowing that we're in the process of looking at the project tasks, we were wondering if that could be the first task," Nathan asked.

"How long might the inspect task take?" Collin asked.

"Right now, we think about a day and a half," Nathan answered. "But, it won't be a day and a half of just inspection before anything else can start. What I mean is, we were thinking we could inspect the front of the aircraft first, and then work our way back to the tail section. Once the front inspection is complete, then the overhaul tasks can begin. Once inspection has begun, it can work in tandem with the upfront tasks. The work tasks begin at the front of the aircraft anyway," he added.

"I think it is an excellent idea!" Collin said. No one else seemed to disagree.

Scott, the master scheduler, was making notes on his laptop and added "Incoming Inspection" as the first task.

"That brings us to another point of consideration, which is 'variation' versus 'uncertainty,'" Collin said. "With variation, you always hope that any tasks that take longer will be offset by those tasks that take a shorter time. The hope is that, by the end of the project, everything has evened out and equals an on-time delivery. However, that rarely, if ever, happens and most often the cumulative variation will be skewed to the right, which means the project takes longer and is late. With 'uncertainty,' you are dealing with the unknown. As an example, until you tear down the helicopter, there is uncertainty as to the physical or mechanical condition of the parts. Some parts may need to be replaced, some may be repaired, and others will need to be refurbished. You just don't know the impact until you tear it down and look. Also, you don't know what else might be lurking and hidden from view," Collin said. "This is precisely the reason I like your concept of the inspection task you just mentioned. If you can find, and surface, any of the hidden issues, then you can reduce the uncertainty, and that's a big plus!" Collin exclaimed.

"Another consideration is the location and size for the feeding buffer. This would be in reference to parts or perhaps special equipment and special tooling that might be necessary to complete a specific task. By using a feeding chain, and having everything ready to go before it is needed, wait time is reduced. Reduced wait time becomes a big 'plus' for the overall project," he explained.

"Another consideration is the task duration. As a general guideline, whatever your current standard hours are for durations, my team will challenge you to cut those times in half! However, you need to remember this is a guideline and not necessarily a mandatory rule. There can be exceptions for some tasks that can't be cut in half, but it won't be many," he added.

"You know, this is the part that has bothered me since the first time I heard it," Jim said. "I just can't imagine we can do all of this work in half the time and just give up the remaining time," he said.

"You aren't necessarily giving it up. You're just moving it from one location to another. Any time removed from the tasks will be allocated to the project buffer, at least for a period of time. This time can now be used to support the entire project and not just the task it came from," Collin said. Collin knew this concept was still bothering Jim because they had talked about it earlier. He thought for a moment and said to Jim, "Think for a moment that you have four quarters in your left hand and those four quarters equal the current total task time. Now, take two of those quarters and place them in your right hand, which is equivalent to the project buffer. You still have the same amount of quarters, or time, but it is split between two different locations. Does that make sense to you?" Collin asked.

"Yes it does," Jim replied with a smile. "Now I understand what you're talking about. As we talk about each task, any extra quarters will be put in my right hand. When the mechanics are working on task, and they can finish faster, then they might have an extra quarter, or two. If they do, they put them in my right hand. Then, any of the tasks that take more time and are running late can get an extra quarter, or two, and put it back in the left hand to finish their work!"

"You got it!" Collin said. "One other point, when all of the extra time has been placed in the project buffer, you will also cut that number in half as well.

But, don't worry too much about that right now because it is highly probable there will still be plenty of quarters in Jim's right hand," he explained.

"Another point to remember is that each task does not need an exact start date or an end date; we just need the total estimated task duration. Start dates and end dates will not matter so much anymore. What will matter is when the system is set up and running, you will be required to provide status on whatever tasks you are working on, and the status will be in the form of 'How many days do you need to complete the current task?'" Collin said. "It won't be percentages, such as 25% complete or 50% complete, but rather how many days are needed before you are complete. If your task is going to overrun the estimated duration, don't worry about it—Jim has a hand full of quarters," Collin said with a smile and everyone laughed.

"There is one more consideration I want you to think about, and that is the configuration type for how you do the repairs," said Collin.

Everyone looked puzzled and finally Nathan asked, "What do you mean by configuration type? You mean the way our work cells are set up?" he asked.

"No, that's not what I mean," Collin said walking over to the whiteboard. "Let me explain. In the Theory of Constraints body of knowledge, there are references and definitions for different plant configurations, or process configurations. There are basically four types of configurations that explain the way things are done. Sometimes, the configurations are stand-alone, and sometimes several configurations can be linked in a single system. These four types of configurations are 'A,' 'V,' 'I,' and 'T,'" Collin said as he wrote them on the board. The puzzled looks were even more prominent now and everyone was thinking "What is he talking about?"

"When we talk about an 'A' plant configuration, it is strictly a symbol for the type of configuration used. As an example, an 'A' configuration represents the activities from the base of the 'A' to the apex, or top. In essence, it's an assembly plant where several different raw materials or parts come together to make a final single product at the apex," Collin explained while holding his hand in the shape of a big "A." "A laptop computer would be an example. All of the separate components are assembled and the finished product is a laptop.

"The 'V' shape is symbolic of where you start with a single raw material and make many different products. An example of a 'V' configuration would be a saw mill. At the base of the 'V,' you start with a single log, but make many different products at the top of the 'V.' In your case, the 'V' plant would resemble the disassembly of the helicopter into the component sections.

"The 'I' configuration is just a linear flow from start to finish. What you start with is what you end with. The 'T' configuration is an 'I' line that separates, or splits, at the end to form many different versions of the same thing, perhaps different color choices," Collin explained. "The reason I bring this up is because your scheduled maintenance system is a combination of a 'V,' 'I,' and 'A.' It's important to understand this because each of these configurations have different attributes and consequences associated with them, and as you move through a single project, you will move through these three different configurations," Collin explained. Collin turned and faced the whiteboard and drew a picture.

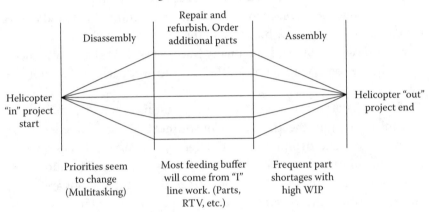

"If we start with the 'V' plant and turn it on its side, this drawing will make sense. In this phase, the helicopter is disassembled down to the necessary level and divided into its component parts. The parts are moved to the 'I' line for repair, replacement, or refurbishment. The 'I' line will provide the majority of the feeding buffers to make sure everything is ready and back in place for reassembly at the base of the 'A.' The 'A' configuration is where everything is reassembled and a finished product is produced," Collin said as he explained his diagram.

"For the 'V' configuration, the most common problem is the constantly changing priorities, which eventually leads to multitasking. The new CCPM system will eliminate multitasking. The focus will now be working on one task until it is complete. However, you still need to watch for it. Don't let your emotions dictate that multitasking is a good thing and therefore try to do it. Just follow the plan and work one task until it is complete and move on," Collin explained.

"The 'I' line will become the location where many of the feeding chains are located and you'll need to carefully consider the feeding chain buffer sizes and locations. This would represent your repaired, refurbished, or replaced parts before reassembly. Through time, you'll learn whether you need to increase or decrease the buffer size," Collin added.

"The most common problem with an 'A' configuration is part shortages and that's why the feeding buffers are so important. If you don't have the parts you need to continue the assembly, it stops! If the feeding chains have been set up correctly and are placed in the proper locations, then part shortages will be greatly reduced or eliminated entirely," Collin said. He scanned the group looking for facial response to what he was saying. Everyone seemed to be on board with his comments. Finally, he asked, "Are there any questions?" No hands went up.

"OK then, that about wraps up what you need to think about with each task. All of this information is contained in the first 15 pages of the manual in front of you. You can use it as your guide when the task discussions begin," Collin said. He looked at his watch; it was now 2:15. He announced to the group to take a 10-minute break before they started the task evaluations.

Collin walked back over to where Connor and everyone else were sitting. Connor stood and extended his hand and told Collin, "Excellent presentation! I've never seen it done quite that way before, but I liked it!"

"You've seen it done this way before, I learned it from you!" Collin said.

Becky looked at Collin and said, "It was a great presentation. I learned a lot listening to what you had to say. You brought up some very good points that I hadn't thought about before," she added.

Brad walked through the door into the room. He spotted Connor and the group and walked over to them and asked, "How's it going?"

"It's going very well," Joe replied. "Collin just gave an excellent presentation and the team is getting ready to start the task evaluations," he added.

"Great, I'm glad to hear that," Brad said. Brad looked at Collin and asked, "Do you have everything you need? Are there any issues, or something I can help with?"

"No, I think we've got everything ready to go. Now, the real work begins when we evaluate the tasks and create a project scheduling template," Collin said. Brad smiled.

Brad looked at Connor and said, "Connor, I want to make sure we haven't forgotten about the unscheduled maintenance side of the operation."

"We haven't forgotten. We are still evaluating the solution and we want to make sure the scheduled maintenance side is stable and operational before we tackle the unscheduled maintenance issues," said Connor.

Brad looked at Collin and asked, "So what happens next?"

"This team is going to evaluate the project tasks, using the new CCPM rules. This effort might take a few days or so, depending on how many actual tasks there are, and what kinds of issues we might run into. I think it will go fairly fast. This group seems well prepared for what's coming up, thanks to Connor and his gang," Collin said.

"I had very little to do with their preparation," Connor said. "It was actually Joe and Sam that have prepared them to this point," said Connor.

"Well, good job to both of you guys," Collin said looking at Joe and Sam.

Collin turned back to Brad and said, "In addition to what's going on here with this team, we'll also have the IT guys involved with getting everything set up on their end. When we finally get the template, we should be ready to go with the entire system," he added.

"If you need anything or run into any problems, just let me know," Brad replied. "My office is right outside of the door. If I'm not there, then just talk with Helen and she can find me."

"Thanks," Collin replied. Brad left the room and walked back to his office. Collin looked at his watch. Break time was over and it was time to get going again. Before Collin walked off, Connor said, "I think we'll be heading out now. This next phase is all your area of expertise. If you need anything, please let us know," Connor said, handing Collin a business card.

Joe, Sam, and Becky all handed Collin a card as well and then they all headed for the door.

Joe asked, "Do we need somebody to escort us out?"

"I think we know the way," Connor replied with a smile.

In the lobby, they signed out and headed out toward the car. They drove back to the airport, turned in the car and waited in the Business Air terminal for their plane. Connor was thinking mostly about his upcoming challenges at the hospital and his desire to make sure they came away with a good and sustainable solution.

20

Hospital Wait Times

Connor was anxious to begin his wait time reduction initiative at the hospital and woke up extra early on the morning they were to begin. Connor tried to imagine how this first day would go and couldn't wait to meet the team that Dr. Price and Terry had assembled. He decided to dress casually for this first day and wore dress slacks and a button-down shirt, but no tie. The team meeting was scheduled to begin at 8:00 AM, but as usual, he arrived early. He walked into the conference room and immediately walked over to the performance metrics charts for a review.

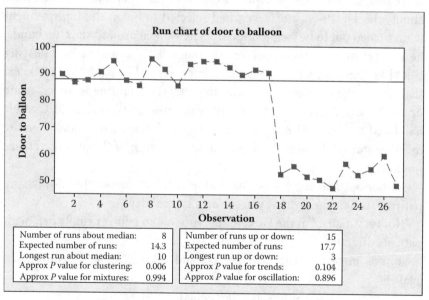

Number of runs about median:	8	Number of runs up or down:	15
Expected number of runs:	14.3	Expected number of runs:	17.7
Longest run about median:	10	Longest run up or down:	3
Approx P value for clustering:	0.006	Approx P value for trends:	0.104
Approx P value for mixtures:	0.994	Approx P value for oscillation:	0.896

As he looked at the updated Door to Balloon (D2B) time run chart, he noticed that there were three new data points that had been added and he smiled broadly because the new posting meant that they had maintained their new, low level of D2B times, which made Connor very happy. The mean value before the team attacked D2B time had been 91.1 minutes with a standard deviation of 3.30 minutes. The new mean value was now 52.9 minutes with a standard deviation of 3.0 minutes. Connor thought to himself, "That's almost a 60% reduction in time."

Connor's thoughts were interrupted by the conference room door opening. The person entering was not anyone Connor had met before.

"Hi, my name is Samantha Ridgeway," she said as she walked over and shook hands with Connor.

"Nice to meet you Samantha, my name is Connor Jackson. Are you here for the improvement team kickoff?" asked Connor.

"Yes I am, and I've heard so many good things about you from the D2B team, so I'm very excited to be here," said Samantha.

"What do you do?" Connor asked.

"I'm the Director of Nursing," replied Samantha.

Connor thought to himself, "Hmm, seems like a very high level employee, but maybe she's here to show her support and not a member of the improvement team." Within minutes, the room began filling up with more people and Connor went around meeting everyone. Connor's fears about who Dr. Price, and Terry, had selected to be on the improvement team turned out to be well founded. As he walked around shaking hands, he asked them what their position was in the hospital and he kept hearing titles like Director, VP, and Manager, but no frontline staff. Connor knew that unless the true subject matter experts, the frontline workers, made up the bulk of the team, then very little progress would be made. Connor had faced a similar dilemma in the past, so he knew what to do. When the meeting started, he asked a single question to each of the proposed team members.

Connor approached Samantha and asked, "So, Samantha, how many patients would you say that you see on a typical day?"

"Not very many, I'm the Director of Nursing, so I don't usually deal with patients directly."

Connor moved to the next person and asked, "What is your name again?"

"My name is Joyce Simpson," she replied.

"What is your role at the hospital and how many patients do you see on a typical day?" asked Connor.

"Well, I don't see any, unless there is some kind of problem with billing. I'm the Finance Director," she replied.

Connor continued this line of questioning until he had asked everyone in the room the same question and received a similar response from each. When he was finished, he turned to Dr. Price and Terry asked, "Do you see a problem here?"

"What problem are you referring to?" asked Dr. Price.

"The team you have selected does not have any true subject matter experts. While these people all have excellent credentials, they have no daily involvement working with any patients. While I'm certain every person in this room is very intelligent, they couldn't possibly understand the issues that the front-line employees face every single day. I do believe that each person you have selected is quite capable of recommending someone from their area that could, or maybe should, be a contributing member to this team," Connor explained. "Please understand that I'm not downplaying the competence level of anyone you've selected, but rather I'm saying that if you truly want your wait times to be reduced, then the people involved in the process must be able to define and own the solutions. And the only way they will have ownership is if they are permitted to develop their own solutions. I can tell you, from personal experience, that successful teams are the ones who own the solutions," Connor explained. "I might add, as an example, that the D2B team has been very successful and it happened because the team was made up of the frontline nurses, nurse's aides, technicians, interns, and so on, and they were able to develop their own solution, mostly because they understood the problem the best."

"I do understand what you are saying Connor," said Vanessa. "I would like to start by naming one of my interns to be on this team. Her name is Tracy Templeton and I think she will do quite well," she added.

One by one, each of the original team members nominated someone from their areas to be part of the team. Terry was writing down the names. When they had finished with their selections, Connor addressed the group, "One thing that I want to make very clear is that these team members can't be just part-time members. This effort will require their total commitment, and this will be their only activity for the week, and you need to send a clear signal as to just how important this effort really is," he added rather sternly.

"Connor, if we are able to get this team in place within the next hour, can we begin the improvement effort today?" asked Dr. Price. "I really don't want to delay it any longer," he added.

"Yes, today is primarily training and a *Gemba* walk, so we will still have time. But, you need to put this group together right away," Connor replied. "I want to tell you one more thing; as long as any potential solutions don't violate any healthcare policies, hospital policies, or safety requirements for the employee or patients, you must permit the team to implement their solutions. Can everyone agree to that?" Connor asked. "Because if you can't agree, then we're wasting our time here today," he added.

"But what if we don't agree with the solution?" asked one of the directors in attendance.

"Let me answer that question," said Dr. Price. "Mr. Jackson has been working with organizations for a long time and if he believes this is a necessary component of any improvement initiative, then we need to abide by the request. I think everyone would agree that previous attempts to improve quality and timely delivery of healthcare have been dreadful, so we must try a new direction and a new methodology," he explained as everyone nodded their heads in agreement.

Dr. Price instructed his original team members to go talk with the newly selected team members and have them return within the hour. He also wanted them to come back with the new team members to verbally commit to Connor's requests as an indication of their commitment to this initiative. Everyone left the room to go find their new team member selections. Within 45 minutes, everyone was back in the conference room. Dr. Price addressed the group.

"I want to welcome everyone here today and apologize for the last-minute confusion about team members," said Dr. Price. "We are about to embark on a new initiative that will hopefully take us to a new level in terms of patient satisfaction," he continued. "For everyone on the team, I need to express to you how very important this effort is. The highest organizational levels of the hospital have all committed to this effort. For the next week, your sole activity will be to participate on this team and help develop solutions to a problem that has plagued us for quite some time, which is excessive patient wait times," he explained.

As Dr. Price was about to continue, a hand went up in the back of the room and Dr. Price acknowledged it, "Yes?" he asked, pointing to the person.

"I'm Philip Main and I am a nurse in the surgical unit. We have started initiatives like this in the past and it seems like each time we do, we put together a team; they study the process and then make recommendations for improvement. But, what usually happens is that management either does nothing or rejects the recommendation outright. Why is this team going to be any different?" he asked.

Connor spoke up immediately and said, "I can't speak to your past, but I can tell you that, going forward, things will be different. I can assure you that no matter what your solution is, it will be evaluated and reviewed for implementation as long as it doesn't violate hospital policy, healthcare regulations, or your and your patient's safety," explained Connor. "Is that not what we agreed on earlier?" asked Connor looking directly at Dr. Price.

"Yes, Connor, that is exactly what we agreed on and you have my word on that. In fact, if you run into any problem along these lines, I want you to come see me personally!" he replied in an exclamatory manner.

"Now, if you don't mind, we need everyone, except the assigned team members, to leave so that we can get started," said Connor. "We need everyone in a supervisory role to come back at 4:00 PM, so we can give you a report-out on our progress," said Connor.

"I want to make sure you understand; being on this team, at least for the upcoming week, will be your only activity," explained Dr. Price before everyone exited the conference room.

Connor walked to the front of the room and addressed the group. "Hello, my name is Connor Jackson, and for most of my life, I've been a consultant who specializes in fixing broken companies. I want to tell you up front that I'm not an expert in healthcare, but I don't need to be because *you* are the subject matter experts and my job is to teach you a new way of looking at your processes and systems and solving problems. So today, I want to start by providing some basic training using improvement tools and techniques. By a show of hands, how many of you have already been through Terry's Lean Six Sigma training?" asked Connor.

"I have," said one of the team members. "I learned about the type of wastes that exist within every process," he added.

One by one, all eight of the team members related that they had all received some form of Lean/Six Sigma training, with three of the team members having achieved Green Belt status. Terry confirmed that the group, as a whole, had in fact received different levels of training, which made Connor feel much more at ease. Connor said, "I'm going to ask Terry to give you a rapid refresher on the types of waste and then I want to give you some training on something called the Theory of Constraints, or TOC for short," he explained as he turned the meeting over to Terry.

Terry did an excellent job delivering his training materials and even spoke about the success that the D2B team had achieved in applying Connor's integrated TOC, Lean, and Six Sigma (TLS) methodology. Terry also presented the project charter with the Goal defined as reducing patient wait times. He also related Connor and Becky's experience in the ER to explain why Connor was here leading this team. When he was finished, it was time for the first break and Terry instructed them to be back in 15 minutes.

When the team was back in place, Connor began by addressing the group. "If I were to ask you why this hospital has excessive patient wait times, what would you tell me?" he asked as he scanned the team members. One of the team members raised her hand and Connor said, "Yes and what's your name and position here?"

"My name is Jennifer Hudley and I'm a nurse in the ER. I can tell you from my experience that one reason is because patients needing to be admitted have to wait for a room to become available," she explained. "Another reason is because, when we order blood work or other diagnostic tests, for example, it seems like the delay to get results is unreasonable," she added.

Tim Branch, a laboratory technician, seemed to take offense with that statement and said, "Wait a minute Jennifer, we are just following our laboratory's policy that states that we have to wait until we have two sets of draw orders before we draw blood and then test it."

Connor listened intently to the seemingly endless supply of excuses on why patient delays occur and then said, "I think we can all agree that there are many reasons why these delays happen. One of the first things I want to talk about are three important concepts. The first is skewed distributions. The second one is statistical fluctuations. And the third is dependent events," said Connor as he projected his first image on the screen.

Dependent steps

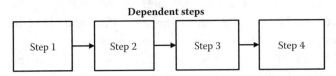

"First, let's look at dependent events. In this graphic, it should be apparent that Step 2 can't begin until Step 1 has been completed and that Steps 3 and 4 can't be completed until Steps 2 and 3, respectively, have been completed," Connor explained as everyone was nodding their heads in agreement. "So, if any single step is delayed, then every step after it is also delayed. In other words, any delay will be passed on through the remaining steps," he said. "For example, your discharge process may have several different action items that must be completed before a patient can be discharged from the hospital," explained Connor as he inserted a new image on the screen. "Dependent events are a feature of all processes and they are not necessarily a bad thing, but when they are combined with the time variation it takes to complete a task, the impact on the rate of patients through the process can be slowed.

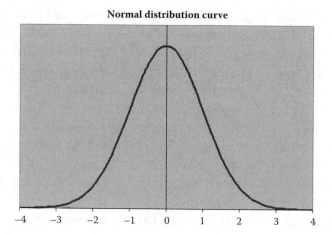

Normal distribution curve

"Statistical fluctuations, or variation in the time it takes to complete a task, can often result in an upstream resource taking longer to complete a task than the historical average time.

"What you see here is a normal distribution curve," Connor explained. "If hospital processes were always normally distributed, things would be so much easier, but unfortunately, they aren't. In fact, these processes are usually skewed to the right, sometimes severely," Connor explained as he inserted a new image on the screen. "The fact is, through time, many process steps do take much longer to complete than we expect them to, so they are said to be skewed to the right as in this graphic," he explained.

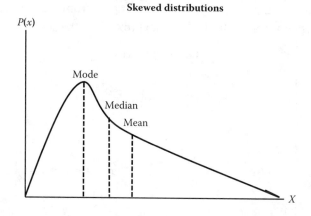

Skewed distributions

Connor continued, "I always like to use the example of driving to work. You typically take the same route, and most of the time, your trip takes the average time, plus or minus a few minutes. Sometimes, you can actually make the trip much faster than the average, but some days it takes much longer than the average. The key point that I want you to understand is that, the faster times are much closer to the average time than the days when you are delayed. The distributions for completing a task are typically skewed to the right. In fact, many times the completion times may be even two, three, or even more times the average completion time. The significant impact of this phenomenon is that it makes it virtually impossible to complete the process on time when any one task in a process takes longer to complete than expected. The chances of the remaining process steps being completed on time become very remote. I think most of you have experienced this before," Connor said as most of the team members nodded their heads in agreement.

"So, what this ultimately means is that any delays are passed on to the next step. In addition, when you combine these dependent events and the statistical fluctuations, these two phenomena acting together can cause significant delays to the timely discharge of patients," Connor summarized.

"There's one additional phenomenon that probably exists, and it is the impact of the convergent points within a process. One simple example of a convergent point in your hospital might be surgery. The surgical process requires inputs from many different resources, such as the patient, the surgeon, medical records, sterile goods, the laboratory, blood, and sometimes even specialized equipment. If even one of these inputs is missing, then it's possible that the surgery might be delayed or even canceled. But a more relevant example might be the patient discharge process itself. Discharging a patient is not a simple task and it requires inputs from multiple resources," Connor explained as he flashed his next image on the screen.

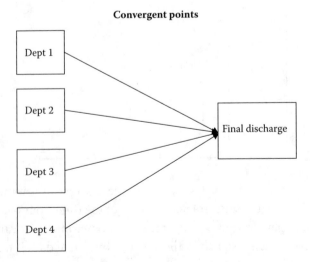

Convergent points

"As you can see in this slide, the final discharge requires the synchronized input of four different departments. For example, it would require the physician to make a decision to discharge the patient and maybe the pharmacy to prepare any medication that will be sent home. The discharge might also need an occupational therapist to complete any relevant assessments that the patient might need and maybe even a nurse or nurse's aide to transport and assist with the physical discharge, and maybe even a family member to assist with the patient's discharge," Connor continued as the team members again nodded their heads in agreement.

"The point I'm making here is that discharges can be delayed for a variety of reasons. In fact, the probability of all of the resources completing their discharge requirements on time is actually much lower than you might think," said Connor. "For example, let's say that a patient being discharged requires some form of input from five different departments, all of which are very reliable. Let's say that over a period, for every patient discharged, each resource completes their input on time, 9 out of 10 times," said Connor. "That seems pretty good, right?" Connor asked in a rhetorical manner as everyone nodded their heads in agreement. "Remember, your discharge process is a convergent point, and as such, it requires that all five departments must complete their work before the patient can be discharged. Would anyone care to calculate the probability of a single patient being discharged on time?" he asked the group.

When none of the team members volunteered to answer, Terry said, "I'd like to take a shot at calculating it. If I remember correctly, when you have five different departments each having a 90% probability of completing their work on time, the total chance of all five completing at the same time is the multiple of the individual probabilities or $0.9 \times 0.9 \times 0.9 \times 0.9 \times 0.9$, which equals roughly 59%," he said somewhat in disbelief as he looked at the number on his calculator.

"Terry, that is absolutely the correct way to calculate the overall probability," said Connor. "Now, imagine what would happen if one of these departments has a rating of 60% instead of 90%?" he asked. "That calculation would be $0.9 \times 0.9 \times 0.9 \times 0.9 \times 0.6$ or roughly 35.4%," he said answering his own question as the team murmured their own surprise.

Connor looked at his watch and could see that it was almost time for lunch, so he told the group that he wanted to summarize what they had discussed so far. "So let's review the important points we discussed this morning. All processes have dependent events where one process step must finish before another one begins. We talked about the impact

294 • *Focus and Leverage*

with statistical fluctuations that cause a typical process to be skewed to the right, meaning things take longer than they should. We also talked about convergent points and how even one department being late can significantly delay things like a discharge process. We also discussed how these convergent points combine to significantly decrease the probability that all departments will finish on time. When you come back from lunch, we're going to talk about something called the Theory of Constraints (TOC). See you in approximately an hour. It's now approximately 11:30 AM, so make sure you are back at 12:30 PM," said Connor as he dismissed the team for lunch.

Everyone left the room except Terry. He approached Connor to chat and said, "Connor, the way in which you addressed this team using common examples from healthcare really impressed me. I had never considered calculating probabilities as a result of dependent events and statistical fluctuations. Have you done work for other hospitals and used this material before?" he asked.

"Yes and no. Yes, I have done some work for other hospitals, but I don't consider myself an expert in healthcare matters, but no, I've never used what I presented today," he replied. "I actually came up with this last evening and thought it might be relevant today," he added. "In fact, the closest thing to healthcare that I have done previously is for a contractor who supplies maintenance services on helicopters," he said.

"How in the world would that relate to healthcare?" asked Terry with a very bewildered look.

"We'll answer that question later on today or later this week," replied Connor.

Even though Connor had instructed the team to be back by 12:30, everyone was seated and ready to begin again by 12:15, indicating to Connor that they were probably anxious to get started with their improvement efforts. Connor began the afternoon session with his water piping diagram so that the team would see the relevance of why it was so important to identify the constraint and determine the flow of patients. He then walked them through his simple four-step process and presented the five focusing steps. Connor also presented the concept of policy constraints and their potential devastating effects. When he felt sure that the team understood why it was so important to find both the physical constraint and potential policy constraints, he suggested that they go on their 2-hour *Gemba* walk, just like the D2B team had done. Before they left, Connor instructed them to not get too far into the weeds with their analysis, but rather to identify the most notable steps in the process. He also defined the start point to be either patient arrival by ambulance or the patient walks in by themselves and the end point to be one of three choices: the patient is treated and discharged to go home; the patient is admitted to the hospital; or the patient is transferred to another hospital.

The team left with a new level of enthusiasm and ready to go. They stayed in the emergency room (ER) for the entire 2 hours, and when they returned, they had actually created a simple process flow map of what they had observed. One of the team members downloaded the image onto Connor's laptop for viewing on the screen by everyone. The team was very proud of what they had accomplished and were smiling at each other.

Connor addressed the team and asked, "So, have you identified the constraint within this process?"

"We haven't timed it, but I think we all know where it is," said one of the team members. "We're pretty sure it's the emergency room physicians since we only have three of them," she added.

"So, you're telling me that if you can reduce the time waiting for an ER physician, then you will reduce the wait times?" Connor asked pointing to the slide on the screen.

Patient flow through the ER

The group all nodded affirmative, but Connor kept pushing the subject. "I can tell you this, when my wife and I visited the ER not so long ago, I saw many patients waiting on gurneys and all of the ER patient rooms were full. In fact, we actually were able to see a physician relatively quickly.

"If that's true, then why do you think the constraint is the ER physicians?" asked Connor.

A hand went up in the back of the room and Connor acknowledged it. "Mr. Jackson, the reason so many people in the ER are on gurneys is because sometimes they're waiting for a room to be ready in the hospital," he explained. "We also have to wait for test results so that we can get the right diagnosis for treatment," he added.

"So, is it possible that the primary reason, or the constraint for the ER, actually lies outside of the ER completely?" asked Connor. "In the ER, you just see the effect, but the cause is someplace else? Can anyone tell me why the patients have to wait so long for a room?" asked Connor.

"One reason is that the hospital has a policy that all discharges must be completed before noon or the patient stays until the following day," said Terry.

"So what I'm hearing you say is that we might be up against a policy constraint?" Connor asked. "What would happen to bed availability if this policy didn't exist?" asked Connor.

Tim Branch immediately stood up and said, "Holy crap ... the number of patients waiting for a room would decrease considerably! Are you suggesting that our ER wait times could be controlled by hospital discharge policy?" he asked.

"I don't want to jump to any conclusions just yet, but yes, it might be entirely possible. I know my wife had to wait 5 hours to get admitted, so maybe one of the reasons was that they had to wait for a bed to become available," said Connor. "I think this team needs to go check out the hospital's discharge process and see what you can find," he added. "Be back no later than 3:45 PM because we have a report-out at 4:00 PM," Connor instructed.

The team left the conference room, divided into teams so they could review multiple nursing units and then went to each unit to determine both the steps required to discharge a patient and to determine if there were any policies in place that would have a negative impact on the time it took to discharge patients. As scheduled, the team was back in place by 3:45 PM, waiting for the supervisory team to come back for the report-out. The teams were anxious to talk about what they had found, but Connor told them that they needed to talk to the supervisory team and that they could wait until the morning to discuss their findings. He also told them not to share their findings of the discharge process at the report-out so that the team could discuss what they had found.

The supervisors were all in place by 4:00 and were anxious to hear from the improvement team. Connor led the discussion and asked for someone from the team to speak about what they had learned during their first day.

Tim Branch was the first to speak and said, "The most important thing I learned today is that if you want to speed up a process, you must first find the constraint, but the constraint is not always something physical."

Ann Secrest, a registered nurse on the team, was the next to speak and said, "Tim's right, but the other important thing I learned is that the constraint might not always be in the immediate process you're trying to improve."

The remaining team members each had something to say about their day, and at 4:30, Connor thanked them for all of their hard work and told them to be back in the morning at 7:00. Several of the team members wanted to give their findings to Connor, but he told them that he didn't want them to rush through their results, so they should save everything until the morning. Everyone packed up their materials and left for the day. When everyone else was gone, Terry approached Connor.

"Connor that was the single best session I have ever been associated with in my life!" said Terry. "I've been facilitating team events for more than 2 years and I have never seen a team so engaged," he added. "The questions you ask are right on the money and they stimulate thought for the entire team," said Terry. "What I really like is that you don't provide answers to questions ... you let the team come up with their own answers. And if the answer isn't quite right, you have a way of asking another question until they do get it right," he said.

"Thanks Terry, but improvement is all about using basic common sense, logic, and discovery. It was clear to me that the wait time problems were not all associated with what's going on in the ER," said Connor. "I think what we'll hear tomorrow will be very enlightening to say the least," he added. "I need to leave now because I've got a conference call with two of my colleagues, so I'll see you in the morning Terry," said Connor.

"OK Connor, I'll see you in the morning and thanks for a very enjoyable day. I learned so much today about how to effectively lead a team," said Terry.

On the way home, Connor thought about what had happened with the team and what he thought they might present to him in the morning.

He thought, "If I can just get them to think holistically, from a system's perspective, they can solve their patient wait times in the ER." When he arrived home, he was met with a kiss from Becky, eager to hear what he had found at the hospital. Connor deferred his conversation until after his conference call with Sam and Joe about Aviation Dynamics. The phone call was short with Joe and Sam. When Connor got Joe and Sam on the phone, they indicated no problems had been reported yet and things seemed to be going smoothly. They ended the call and Connor went back to talk with Becky.

"So, how did it go today honey?" asked Becky.

"It went very well, once we were able to get the right team in place," said Connor. "It never ceases to amaze me how the leadership of most organizations fails to recognize who the true subject matter experts really are," he continued. "If leadership would only realize that the frontline employees, who live and breathe every day in the system, are the people who know best how to solve the problems, it would be so much easier. If they would only seek input and truly listen to what they have to say and then turn them loose to solve the problems, things would be so much better and easier. And Becky, it doesn't matter what industry it is or how intelligent leadership is, they all miss this important point," Connor said.

The next morning, Connor arrived at the hospital around 6:30 and headed to the conference room to prepare for the day. To his surprise, several members of the team were already seated and seemed to be anxious to start the day's activities. By 6:45 AM, all of the team members were seated.

Connor began the day's session by asking for volunteers to review their findings from yesterday. "So, who wants to tell me what they found yesterday?" asked Connor. Five team members raised their hands, but Connor decided to pick a team member who had been virtually silent the day before. "Why don't we start with you," said Connor pointing to one of the five who had raised their hands.

"Good morning Connor, my name is Jeff Simpson and I'm an ER technician. I want to first say that I don't normally say much when I'm on a team, but today will be different. What I learned yesterday forced me to think differently, and for the first time ever, I am convinced that we can solve the problem of extended wait times in the ER. We all went to the various nursing units around the hospital and we even created a basic process map of the discharge process, which I might add, is full of waste. But the most significant thing we found was the hospital's policy of only completing discharges before noon," he explained.

"And why was that so significant Jeff?" asked Connor.

"Because for the afternoon and early evening, no beds can be freed up for new patients!" he said emotionally. "A typical day in our hospital, in terms of when patients actually need an inpatient bed, start to occurs in the early afternoon because the morning's surgical cases are finishing up; the ER is starting to heat up; and our various clinics are feeding us patients that might need to be admitted. In all of these cases, everybody needs a bed in an in-house unit," he explained.

"So, what are you recommending to fix this problem Jeff?" asked Connor already knowing the answer.

"We need to radically change our discharge policy and then work to remove the waste that exists within it," he replied.

"So, if you were king for a day, what might this new policy look like?" asked Connor.

"For starters, I would eliminate using a set block of hours that the units have to complete discharges," he said. "I asked everyone on the various nursing units why they are limited to discharging patients by noon and everyone told me the same thing, 'it's hospital policy,'" he added.

"So Jeff, why do you think the hospital has this policy?" asked Connor.

"Because we're stupid!" came a voice from the back of the room and everyone chuckled.

Smiling, Connor said, "I don't think it's stupidity; it's more the lack of systems thinking. By that I mean, if whoever came up with this policy had been using systems thinking, then they would have realized that it was not a patient-centered policy," he added. "OK, let's assume for a minute that this discharge time policy did not exist, where would the constraint be then?" asked Connor and again several hands went up. "Yes?" said Connor pointing to a woman at the end of the table.

"My name is Crystal Hodges and I'm an ER nurse. I think we don't have enough information to say for sure where the constraint would be," she said. "I think we would need to do extended time studies to determine how long each step in the process takes," she added.

"Crystal, doing time studies will take a considerable amount of time, so can you think of a different way we might be able to find the constraint?" Connor asked.

Crystal replied immediately and said, "I'm thinking we could become a patient ourselves and actually walk through the process. I don't mean we would actually be a patient, but we could each attach ourselves to a patient and see where they get hung up," she added.

"Crystal, I think that is a great idea," said Connor as everyone else nodded their heads in agreement. "So, why doesn't everyone follow Crystal's direction, pick an ER patient, and glue yourself to them," said Connor. "I don't mean that you should be intrusive, just follow their progress," Connor explained. "But before we do that, what did anyone else find yesterday?" asked Connor.

"I too found that the hospital's policy of limiting the time for discharge has a negative effect on bed availability, but I think we have to be careful not to discharge some patients, especially elderly ones, too late in the day," said Jeff. "I say this because some patients might have other problems, such as their nighttime vision being impaired or maybe, if it was in the middle of the night, there may not be buses running and cabs are expensive," he added.

Connor was impressed with the level of sensitivity that Jeff had expressed, related to patients, and he liked that. Jeff was truly embracing the philosophy of patient-centered care and that was a good thing in Connor's mind. The remaining members of the team presented their findings and then Connor dismissed them to go become "a patient" as Crystal had suggested.

The team left the room and headed for the ER to learn firsthand why the patient wait times were so long. Connor thought more about Crystal's recommendation and smiled. "She's a very logical person and seems to have the patient's well-being at the forefront," he thought. The team was gone for approximately 2 hours and a few members started trickling back into the conference room. When they were all seated, Connor asked them what they had discovered.

As expected, Crystal was the first to respond. "Mr. Jackson, I followed two patients and both of them were supposed to be admitted to the hospital, but because there were no rooms available, they had to wait on gurneys in the ER," she explained. "I left both of my patients and went to the unit they were expected to be admitted to, to see if I could find the reason there were no beds available," she continued. "In one case, the admittance order had been written, but they were waiting for housekeeping to clean the room before the patient could be officially admitted," she added.

"How long had this patient been waiting and why was it taking so long to get the room cleaned?" asked Connor.

"This patient was an elderly woman who had been waiting for 3 hours. I was told that the hospital needed to cut costs, so they had recently laid off some of the housekeeping staff. It seems that the remaining housekeeping staff is now supposed to focus on cleaning the surgical areas and the ER first and then patient rooms," she added. "And when housekeeping does come to clean the room, it's only one person doing it. It seems to me that if they had two people doing the cleaning, they could cut the time in half, maybe more. As far as the other patient goes, he was an elderly man who had been waiting for $2\frac{1}{2}$ hours. The other reason the unit gave me was that the discharge paperwork for several patients didn't arrive until after the noon deadline, so the patients had to stay one additional day," she explained.

As Crystal explained what she had found, some of the others were nodding their heads in agreement indicating that they had found similar things. Connor was not surprised at what they had found and thought it might be a good time to introduce the team to a different type of constraint. "What Crystal found, regarding the layoff of the housekeeping staff, is a classic example of something I refer to as a 'dummy constraint,'" said Connor. "Think about just how much one of the housekeepers would cost the hospital and compare that to the financial impact of the lost revenue," he explained. "What you're witnessing is the negative impact of Cost Accounting, whereby the key to profitability is thought to be achieved through cost cutting," he continued.

Crystal raised her hand and said, "Mr. Jackson, I think I understand what you are saying. If we hadn't cut the housekeeping staff like we did, and if we didn't have the current discharge policy, then we could process, discharge, and admit more patients at a faster rate. And if we could process more patients, then we could have more cash entering the hospital," she continued. "So I think that what you're saying is that the cost savings of these so-called dummy constraints pale in comparison to the potential gain in new revenue. Is that right Mr. Jackson?" she asked. "And, the discharge policy change shouldn't cost anything," she added.

"Yes, Crystal, that is exactly what I am saying. In fact, by adding back some of the laid-off housekeeping staff, then setting up the team approach to cleaning the rooms, which you described, and by changing the discharge policy, where do you think the constraint would be located?" asked Connor.

At the far end of the conference room table, Jeff raised his hand and said, "I'm pretty certain that, if we were to remove the current constraint, then the next constraint would be the physicians in the ER."

Terry interrupted and said, "I get now why in your training you recommend identifying the current and next constraint ... it makes perfect sense!"

Crystal said, "So how do we go about addressing these two problems so that we can make more beds available?"

"Great question Crystal," said Connor. "My suggestion is simple. What if we were able to collect some data on how many patients were affected by the extended wait times as a result of the housekeeping and discharge policy? We could then compare the number and frequency of available beds and the financial impact this might have. We can present the analysis at our 4:00 report-out?" said Connor.

Terry was the first to speak and said, "I'm not sure we can do all of that by 4:00. What if we just presented the concept to them? After all, you did present Throughput Accounting to them and from what I saw, it was received very well," he added.

"Maybe Terry's right, let's go collect the data and hold the calculations until tomorrow," Connor replied. "Go see what kind of data are available and be back here by 3:30 so we can put together some talking points," he added. The team split up, with part of them going to the ER to record patient wait times and the other half going to the nursing units to see how many patient discharges were delayed because of the discharge policy.

At 3:30, the entire team returned and they were obviously anxious to report their findings. Once again, Connor asked who wanted to give their report, and once again, Crystal was the first to speak.

"My team visited all of the hospital nursing units and found that 13 patients couldn't be discharged because of the discharge policy," said Crystal. "In addition, there were 3 patients that were discharged in violation of the policy," she added.

"Thank you Crystal. How about the team that went to the ER, what did your team find out?" asked Connor.

Jeff spoke up and explained, "We found four patients that had been in the ER for more than 4 hours, three patients that had been there for between 3 and 4 hours, and two patients that had been there between 2 and 3 hours. And, I might add, this was not a super busy day in the ER," he added.

Connor listened intently to what the teams had to say and then asked, "But how many people in the ER experienced delayed admittance because they were waiting for a bed?"

Jeff replied, "On the basis of the information we gathered, we found that three of the 4-hour patients and two of the 3-hour patients were told by the ER nurses that they would be admitted when an in-house bed became available."

Just as they finished their team reports, members of the supervisory team began entering the conference room for the 4:00 team report-out.

When they were all seated, Connor asked for a volunteer to summarize what they had learned today.

Jeff jumped up and began relating the team's experience saying, "Today was such an eye-opener for us as a team. We collected some very interesting and important data relating to patient wait times and discovered that one of the biggest causes of extended wait times in the ER was actually our discharge policy. It seems as though the policy states that all discharges in the nursing units must be completed before noon, each day. If it's not done, the patient must remain for another day and occupy the bed. Not meeting this time requirement is causing extended wait times for ER patients," he added.

Dr. Price was very interested in this comment and wanted to hear more about the data they had collected. The team presented the minimal data they had collected earlier, and after much discussion, Dr. Price said, "So what you are telling us is that, if we change our discharge policy, then our ER patient wait times should decrease?"

"That's exactly what we're telling you Dr. Price," Jeff replied. "We only have one day's worth of data, but we're confident that by extending, or removing, the discharge time to later in the afternoon, we should be able to reduce the wait time," he added. "I've been thinking about this and I think it will also positively affect our metric, Patient Left without Being Seen," he said.

Crystal stood up and said, "There's something else we discovered yesterday and today and that is, on many occasions, one of the reasons why patient rooms are delayed from being ready is that housekeeping takes too long cleaning the rooms. Because of the recent layoffs, there simply are not enough housekeeping employees to clean the necessary rooms, quickly," she added.

"Are you suggesting that we rehire these employees?" asked Dr. Price. "Remember, Crystal, these people cost us money. By being able to decrease the operating expense, we hoped to improve our profitability," he added.

"Yes, we know why you took this cost-cutting action, but if you consider the impact on the system in terms of having rooms available to admit patients and reduce ER wait times, we think it's a decision that should be reconsidered," said Crystal. "As we've learned, the better way to improve profitability is to increase the amount of new revenue entering the system," she added.

"Does anyone else have something they'd like to add?" asked Connor. When nobody else raised their hands, Connor said, "How about the executives ... any comments?" he asked.

Dr. Price stood up and said, "I think we have a lot of new things to consider and we did promise to consider all recommendations as long as they didn't violate our policies or safety. I do think that at our next executive staff meeting, this Friday, we need to discuss both of these recommendations and the potential positive impact they could have on revenue. I feel confident that both of them can be implemented," he added, which brought a smile to the team members' faces.

"Dr. Price, did you say you would consider all recommendations from this team?" asked Connor with a piercing look on his face.

"My apologies, we'll do more than just consider them; we'll implement them if they don't violate safety or any other healthcare regulations," said Dr. Price.

Connor smiled, thanked everyone for their efforts, and told the team to be back at 7:00 in the morning to begin looking at the new constraint in the ER. He excused everyone for the day, and everyone except Terry left.

"Connor, I truly do think that the executive team will implement what the team has recommended. My question for you is, what do you see us doing in the ER to improve the flow of patients?" he asked.

"Tomorrow, we're going to talk about a new ER scheduling system called Drum–Buffer–Rope and I have a new idea about how that might roll out," said Connor.

"What's Drum–Buffer–Rope and what's your new idea?" Terry asked.

"You'll hear all about it tomorrow, so be here bright and early tomorrow morning," said Connor. "Tomorrow could be a very interesting day," he added.

21

Emergency Room—Wait Time Reduction

As usual, Connor arrived at the hospital early to begin preparing for the improvement team's new focus: wait times. Connor knew that the solution he had in mind for the hospital would also be a possible solution for unscheduled maintenance at Aviation Dynamics. When Connor entered the conference room, he immediately walked over to the performance metrics board and noticed two more data points had been added to the Door to Balloon Time run chart. The two new data points were in the same population as the most recent entries, which meant that, so far, the improvements were being sustained. Connor smiled.

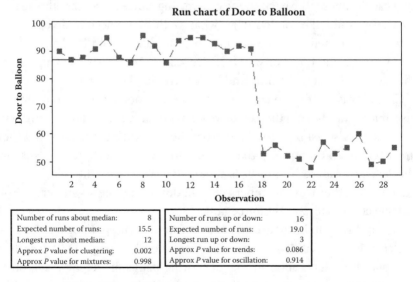

Run chart of Door to Balloon

Number of runs about median:	8	Number of runs up or down:	16
Expected number of runs:	15.5	Expected number of runs:	19.0
Longest run about median:	12	Longest run up or down:	3
Approx *P* value for clustering:	0.002	Approx *P* value for trends:	0.086
Approx *P* value for mixtures:	0.998	Approx *P* value for oscillation:	0.914

As he was scanning the other performance metrics, he heard the conference room door open as several members of the team had arrived early.

Connor walked over, shook everyone's hand and welcomed them. By 7:00, the team was assembled and ready to begin. Just before Connor was ready to begin, there was a knock on the door and Dr. Price walked in. From the back of the room, he asked, "Connor, do you mind if I say a few words before you begin?" Dr. Price asked.

"No, by all means, take as much time as you need," Connor replied.

"Good morning everyone, I wanted to let you know that yesterday the executive team had a meeting to discuss your proposed recommendations. I'm pleased to inform you that the executive team has decided to implement both of your recommendations. They have decided to rework and update the discharge policy and will notify to contact the previous housekeeping employees to see if they are interested in returning. If they aren't available, or they decline, HR will post the jobs and find new candidates," Dr. Price said. There were some claps and cheers in the room.

"When the executive team met, we talked about why the current discharge policy was written the way it was and no one could make a strong case for keeping it the way it is. We also considered what Crystal had recommended about doubling up on cleaning rooms and it made good sense. I just want to say thank you, to all of you, for all your hard work and the executive team is looking forward to hearing, and reviewing, any new recommendations you might come up with." Everyone was smiling and patting each other on the back. "One other thing, since these were this team's ideas, we would like you to review what we think we need to do before we actually implement any new policies or procedures," said Dr. Price.

"Are there any questions?" Dr. Price asked. No hands went up, so he thanked Connor for the time and left the room.

Crystal was the first to comment and said, "I don't know about anyone else, but for me, having the executive team not only accept our recommendations but also asking us to bless what they put together means that they are listening and accepting what we have to say as important. The fact that they even considered our ideas is a marked change from the past," Crystal added. The other team members were nodding their heads in agreement. No one else spoke, so Connor began.

"Today, I want to introduce you to a scheduling concept known as Drum–Buffer–Rope, or DBR for short," Connor said. "Although DBR was first introduced for application in manufacturing plants, in recent years, other industries have begun incorporating it as well. The basic premise behind DBR is really quite simple, but mostly just logical. And although thinking logically is nothing new, it is simply not the way most people think. The fundamental concept of DBR is to focus on the system as a whole, rather than only a single segment of the system—at least until you have clearly identified the constraint," Connor said. "And, from what you believe so far, you think the new constraint is the ER physicians?" he stated, scanning the team for concurrence.

Connor continued, "When viewing a system through the eyes of DBR, it becomes quickly apparent that improving every process in the system is not required, nor will the sum total of all of those discrete process improvements equal an improved overall system. When conducting a systems analysis, with the intent of implementing DBR, an important consideration is to know and understand the location of the *system constraint,* or the slowest operation. In Goldratt's five focusing steps, this is Step 1—Find the constraint! Once you know where the constraint resides, you now have the information necessary to know where to focus your improvement attention," he explained. "In essence, when you look at a system, the entire system can only produce at a rate that is equal to, or less than, the output of the constraint," he added.

"What if we're not right about the physicians being the constraint?" asked Jeff.

"I promise you Jeff, if you haven't identified the correct constraint, it will rear its ugly head and let you know where it really is," Connor said.

"So, with the constraint process properly identified, you have effectively isolated the 'drumbeat' of the system, and knowing the location of that drumbeat is the first step for implementing DBR. Knowing this location is mandatory!" Connor added with emphasis.

"The second consideration is you must make sure the constraint is busy all the time, not just part of the time," Connor explained.

"Mr. Jackson, why is it so important to have the constraint busy all of the time?" asked Crystal.

"Why don't you try to answer that question before I give you my answer Crystal," said Connor.

Crystal thought for a moment and then said, "On the basis of what you've taught us about Theory of Constraints, I would say that any time lost at the constraint is time lost forever; you can't make up that time. If the constraint stops or slows down, then the entire system will stop or slow down," Crystal answered.

"That is exactly right Crystal!" said Connor emphatically. "It's the single point in the system where efficiency really matters."

Crystal raised her hand again. "So I guess that the best way to accomplish this is to make sure work is always waiting in front of the constraint?" Crystal asked.

"Yes!" Connor answered.

"In other words, we should create something like a buffer of patients in front of our constraint," she said.

Connor smiled and said, "Crystal, you are correct about the buffer of patients in front of the constraint, but only if you have the right constraint. I say this because the total system output is not the sum output from each process, but rather only the output from the constraint. In fact, the system constraint not only determines the amount of throughput you can achieve, but it also determines the correct number of patients that can be in the system at any single point in time. The correct number of patients will be reached when patient output is equal to patient input and system subordination is actively pursued and implemented," Connor explained.

"You have explained the drum and the buffer, but what the heck is this rope that you mentioned earlier?" asked Jeff.

"The *rope* is actually a communication mechanism that controls two different functions," Connor replied. "Can anyone tell me what those two functions might be?" he asked.

Jeff raised his hand and said, "First, I would think one of the functions is that the rope determines how many and when to release patients into the system?" Jeff responded in the form of a question.

Connor explained. "In the ER, the most common practice is to tie an artificial 'rope' from the ER physician back to the entry point for patients. When the constraint completes treatment of a patient, the patient is passed on to the next operation, which is either the patient is released to go home or the patient is admitted to the hospital, or perhaps admitted to another hospital. When one of those three things happens, the signal from the rope is to release another patient into the constraint buffer," Connor explained. "What we're trying to achieve is synchronized patient flow and a smooth transition of patients through the system," Connor explained.

"What's the second function of the rope?" asked Jeff.

"The second function of the rope is to make sure that subordination happens at all of the other steps in the process," said Connor. "With active subordination, the nonconstraints can only work on what has been released into the system," Connor added.

"So, even if the nonconstraints can do more work, they are restricted from doing more by the act of subordination and only allowed to work on the patients required to keep the constraint busy?" Jeff asked.

"Yes, no more and no less," said Connor.

"Mr. Jackson, I have a question," Crystal said. "How do we know how large the patient buffers should be?" she asked.

"Good question, Crystal. In the case of the hospital, it depends. It depends on how many patients are waiting. The loads on the systems are never quite the same from day to day. Some days there will be a lot of people and other days not so many. On the slow days, a buffer won't make any difference. On the busy days, a buffer with synchronization will make all the difference in the world. If the loads are constant and heavy, then as a general rule, the buffers should equal about one and a half times the number of patients. It will also depend on how many physicians are available in the ER. For example, if an ER doctor can treat one patient every 15 minutes, then the buffer should be approximately 45 minutes, or roughly three patients. You may decide in time, that the buffer is too large or too small, so you can adjust it either up or down depending on what you've learned from the system and your need," Connor explained.

"Mr. Jackson, I have another question about our situation here in the ER," said Crystal. "Since we have more than one doctor in the ER, does that mean we have more than one constraint?" she asked. "I mean if the ER physicians are the next constraint, does that mean we will have more than one drum?" Crystal added as a question.

"Yes you do Crystal and another great observation! You have a situation of multiple drums!" Connor exclaimed. "What Crystal has just described is something that I have been thinking about since my wife Becky was admitted to the hospital and we had so many issues in the ER. This concept is relatively new and I refer to it as Multiple Drum–Buffer–Rope, or M-DBR," he explained. "This is a point of separation between traditional DBR and M-DBR. Traditional DBR is based on the fact that the output from a constraint is very predictable. As an example, in a typical manufacturing environment, the constraint usually has a cadence or rhythm that is very predictable and steady, for instance, a constraint machine that is able to produce a part every 7 minutes, or whatever the time may be. Knowing the constraint time allows you to be relatively accurate in establishing a buffer. In other words, there is a constant, but predictable normal variation at the constraint. However, in your situation at the hospital, the constraint time can vary significantly. Each time a patient enters your constraint, there can be a lot of uncertainty for when the patient will finish, depending on what needs to be done. You don't know what patient is coming in with what problem and the ER physician's time can vary greatly form one patient to the next," Connor explained. "Under those kinds of circumstances, it's very difficult, if not impossible, to establish any kind of an accurate buffer.

"Back to Crystal's question about having more than one drum," Connor continued. "If the ER physicians are truly the constraint, then how do we manage to keep them fully occupied to reduce wait times?" Connor asked rhetorically.

"It seems to me that we would need to know the real-time status of each constraint," said Diane, an ER nurse. "What I mean by that is, if we knew how much longer each physician believed they had with their current patient, then we could check and see which patient is next and get them ready," she added.

"That's a good possible answer," Connor said. "And, if we already have a buffer in place, then we should know which patient is next. But let's go back and think for a moment about how you establish the buffer. Remember, M-DBR will be different from traditional DBR, mostly because of the uncertainty involved," Connor explained. "Typically, when a patient comes into the ER, you perform a triage to determine severity, or urgency of the situation, is that correct?" Connor asked.

"As best we can, that is what we do," Diane said.

"What happens during the triage activity?" Connor asked.

"Well, we evaluate the patient and determine a level of urgency. Something like a broken leg would take precedence over a stomach ache," Diane said. "And that by itself can cause some problems for people already in the waiting room. For example, a less severe patient, who has already been through triage, might end up waiting even longer if two or three more patients show up with a higher priority. For those people, the wait time can be very frustrating! Some people don't seem to mind if it happens once, but when it gets up to two or three times, it starts to wear on their nerves a bit," Diane explained. "It can happen that a patient, who has already been waiting for a long time, might keep getting pushed back because a more urgent case comes in," she explained.

Connor thought for a moment and asked Diane, "What if we had a system that would allow the lower-priority patents to get through faster?"

"I'm not sure how you might do that because everyone is waiting to see a doctor and they have to wait their turn," Diane said.

"Remember," Connor said addressing the group, "if you reduce wait time, you can also increase the hospital revenue."

Diane looked confused and said, "Honestly, I could care less about hospital revenue. I care much more about good patient care."

"I couldn't agree more," Connor said. "But what if there was a way to do both?" he asked.

"I still can't see how you're going to do that," Diane said. "Everyone still has to see a doctor," she added.

"Exactly, and everyone will see a doctor," Connor said with a smile looking directly at Diane.

"Well, I guess you're right; everyone will see a doctor if they wait long enough," Diane said. "But, waiting a long time to see the doctor is the opposite effect that we want," said Diane. "How do you plan on making it faster?" she asked.

"Again, you are correct, at least if you keep doing the same things you are doing now," Connor said.

"What do you mean?" Diane asked.

"Right now, you have everyone on the same priority list, based on a triage ranking, and essentially everyone is in the same buffer location, the waiting room," Connor said.

"Yes, that's how we do it, but I still don't understand," Diane said.

"Let me narrate a story to you," Connor said. "Suppose you are in a supermarket and you go in for only a few items. Let's say five different items. You find your five items and move to the front of the store for checkout. You notice there are only four lines open and each line has three or four people already in it. You scan the lines and determine that each person has a fairly full shopping cart with many more items than you have. Through a random selection process you pick a line and get in it. Now you are forced to wait for those in front of you to finish, and they could take a long time. They do have a sizeable number of items in their cart. Here's what happens; the effects of the system's codependency has now been passed on to you! What do you do?" Connor asked.

Diane put her head in her hands to cover her face. There was a huge smile on her face with an almost audible laugh. She answered, "I'd go get in the express line!"

Connor smiled and said, "I would too! And, any others who were in the other checkout lines, and met the criteria for the express line, could also move that direction. It's possible they could be finished and gone before it would even have been their turn in the other line," Connor added.

Terry was the first to break the silence that followed and said, "But we don't have an express line in the ER!"

Connor spun on his heels and pointed to Terry and said, "Why not?"

"Well, I'm not sure, but it sounds like maybe we should," Terry said. "Now, it makes sense to me what you said earlier about everyone sees a doctor, wait times can be reduced, and the hospital can bring in more revenue," Terry added.

"It makes sense to me," said Crystal. "We could change how we use our ER capacity to meet the needs of the patient loads. Sometimes, there can be a huge variation between those who can get in and out fast and those who might need a longer time with the doctor. We could decide how many express lines to have, depending on the patient loads and triage classifications," Crystal added.

"You know," said Terry, "I can now see how we might have been unknowingly punishing some of our patients by forcing them to use the system we have in place. In a lot of ways, the system worked for us, but it didn't work for them, at least not to a high level of satisfaction. We made our patients victims of a poorly organized process and system," Terry said with a much lowered voice almost as if he was talking to himself and he didn't want anyone else to hear.

Connor spoke up. "Remember, this is only one possible idea for the front end of the process. We still need to consider the back end of this process for getting new patients admitted, other patients discharged, and rooms cleaned and ready to a usable condition. Why don't we take a break," Connor said looking at his watch. "Be back in approximately 10 minutes."

Most of the group didn't leave the room, but rather assembled into smaller groups with lots of discussion going on.

When the time was up, everyone sat down again and Connor spoke. "If we change the current system, there are some things that will happen," Connor started. "Basically, we will shift the system from an 'I' configuration to a 'V' configuration."

"Change it from what to a what?" Crystal asked.

"It's not something we have talked about before, at least with this group," Connor said. "But, it will be important to understand. With an 'I' configuration, you basically start with one product, or service, and end with the same product or service," he explained.

"That's kind of what we do now isn't it?" Crystal asked.

"Yes, it is," Connor said. "All of your patients are in the same 'I' line, but if we added an express line, then it will shift to a mini 'V' line. What I mean is, after the triage is complete, a decision will be made if the patient continues in the system down the express side, or do they continue down the regular side. I use the term *regular side* because I don't currently have a more precise term," he added. Everyone nodded. "Even with the patients who continue down the regular side, there is another decision gate when you decide if they are admitted or released. If you turn the 'V' on its side and consider the bottom to be the start point for the flow of patients through the 'V,' you can now visualize three different paths and each will have its own drumbeat, if you will. Each path will, in essence, move forward based on a different drum or cadence," Connor added. "When you consider a 'V,' there are characteristics and consequences to be aware of. If not managed correctly, this type of improvement can cause a multitude of additional issues.

"The characteristics of a 'V' are," Connor walked to the whiteboard to write, "Number one, the number of end items can be many. In your case, the end items are three. Number two, all items are produced essentially the same way. In your case it's the flow through the ER system. And, number three, equipment to produce the end items can be capital intensive. In your case, the x-ray machine, magnetic resonance imaging (MRI) machines, laboratory work and personnel to do the testing, and so on," Connor said.

"It's also important to understand the consequences of the 'V' configuration. They are as follows," he continued to write on the board, "Number one, misallocation of materials. In other words, you commit material too soon. Number two, poor customer service. In other words, it can be easy to get 'stuck' in a 'V' configuration. Number three, priorities seem to change constantly. In other words, you and your system get hung up in the cyclical nature of *multitasking*. You start jumping from one patient to another trying to get something done. It's not the situation you want to be in," Connor added. "And, number four is the constant complaint that you are being unresponsive to the patient's needs. In the current situation, the patient is continually asking themselves, 'What about me?'" Connor explained.

"If we take a moment and look at the system now, you can see the real goal is not necessarily to create or maintain an appropriate buffer, but rather to have the buffer, or triage priority list be as close to zero as possible. Does that make sense to you?" Connor asked. He scanned the group and heads were slowly starting to nod in agreement.

"This is how an M-DBR system would work. There are different paths, and each path has a different drum. The beat of the drum determines how fast the next patient can be moved forward. If the system loads are present, in your case people waiting in the waiting room, then they need to be assigned a path to get to the finish line," Connor stressed, looking for understanding on the faces of the group. So far, he thought he was seeing it. "So overall, the goal in M-DBR is not to create, or maintain a buffer, but rather to assign the buffer down the different paths and reduce it as quickly as you can. In this case, a zero buffer is the best," he explained.

"Now, let's work our way down the regular path to the next decision gate. At some point in the system, it will be decided if the patient can be released, or in fact, needs to be admitted, or transferred. This decision is very likely supported by various test results and information gathered from x-ray, or MRI, or whatever. If it is determined that the patient can be released, then they proceed to the finish line and exit the system. However, if it is decided that the patient should be admitted, then a new set of problems arise, specifically bed availability. You need somewhere to put the patient, in order to admit the patient," Connor said.

"When my wife Becky and I came to the ER, getting in and seeing the doctor was not the real problem. We did have some wait time that seemed extreme to me, but I also understand now that I was in a panic mode. I wanted answers!" he said, with a semi-smile. "When we arrived at the ER, it was early afternoon, and according to your then current policy, no more patients were being discharged. What we were waiting for was a room to be cleaned and finished, so my wife could be admitted and put in the room," Connor said. "The entire time we waited for the hospital room, Becky was in an ER exam room, which meant that because we couldn't move forward, the next patient behind us couldn't move forward either. The system flow had stopped because Becky had nowhere to go," Connor explained. "We ended up having to wait until 6:00 PM before we finally got her into a room. Once she was in her room, she was considered to be admitted. Before the room becoming available, we were just Work-in-Process inventory that was polluting the ER system. We couldn't get out and no one else could get in. In fact, I can remember seeing some gurneys with patients on them, just sitting in the hallway waiting to be moved somewhere," Connor reminisced.

"So, in order to complete the flow through the system, it is imperative that we spend some time looking at the discharge policy and housekeeping staffing," Connor said.

"According to Dr. Price, the executive team already approved those recommendations," said Terry.

"They did approve the recommendations, and the recommendations were to change the discharge policy and approval to rehire, or hire, more housekeeping staff," Connor said. "And they did say they want you to look at the new discharge policy before they implement it. My question for this group is, what are you going to change the policy to, and how much more housekeeping staff will be needed?" Connor asked.

"I see your point Mr. Jackson," Crystal said. "We have permission to change it, but we don't know for sure what we should change it to!" Connor smiled. "So, we need to discuss what a good policy looks like, and how better to improve housekeeping," Crystal said.

"That sounds like an excellent place to start. Does anyone have a comment for that?" Connor asked.

"I do," Terry said. "I'm not a medical professional, but I think it should be based on when the patient is ready, and not what time of day it is," he added.

"I agree," said Crystal. "Part of the housekeeping problem right now is many patients are released between 11:30 AM and noon. That keeps the release within the policy, but it also creates a situation where many rooms become available for cleaning all at once before a new patient can be admitted. Housekeeping goes from waiting for rooms to clean, to having too many rooms to clean all within the span of approximately 30 minutes. Sometimes, housekeeping can just get overwhelmed," said Crystal.

"It's probably true that more rooms would become available in the morning hours, but if you miss the noon deadline, because of some unforeseen issue, then you have to wait until the next day. So, we have a room being occupied by someone who might not have to be there, and there is someone else waiting for a room they can't get into yet. It's just crazy when you stop and think about," Diane said.

"So, what I'm hearing is, remove the deadline and release patients based on good medical protocol, and the patient's comfort and needs, no matter what time it is. Is that correct?" asked Connor.

"I think that pretty much sums it up," Diane said. "There will be some details to work out, but overall I think it's a good approach," she added.

"So, if we remove the deadline from the policy, does that mean that patient releases will be more evenly distributed?" Terry asked.

"It's possible," said Crystal. "But, I still think the morning will be the favored time for release, and that means that a lot of rooms will need to be cleaned at the same time," she added.

"What stops them from cleaning the rooms faster right now?" Connor asked.

"Honestly, I think they do try and clean the rooms as fast as they can right now," Crystal said. "There are several things that must be taken care of before a room is ready for a new patient and it does take some time to do that. And, we did have the layoff. I don't know for sure how many that might have been, but it did have an impact," Crystal added.

"How long do you think it takes to clean a room right now?" Connor asked.

"I guess that depends, but to do a really good job might take 45 minutes to 1 hour," Crystal said. "There is a lot to do. New sheets, new towels, cleaning the bathroom including toilet and shower, or tub, and wiping everything down and sanitizing the room, including the floors," she explained.

"Let me relate a story to you," Connor said. "Suppose it's Saturday morning and you want to have four new tires put on your car. You also want to fill the car with gas and you might even want a Slurpee. How long does it take to get all of that done?" Connor asked the group. Everyone was contemplating the question and formulating an answer.

Finally, Diane raised her hand and said, "I'd guess approximately 2 or 3 hours."

"Anyone else have a guess?" Connor asked.

"Well, I know a guy at the tire shop, so I think I could get it done in less than 2 hours," said Crystal. "Hey, it pays to know people in the right places," she added. Everyone laughed.

"I think 2 hours might be about right and I don't even know anyone at the tire shop," Terry said.

"I agree with Diane, I'm thinking more like 3 hours," said Bill, who had been quiet for most of the discussion.

"So, the best time so far is 2 hours," said Connor scanning the group. "Any other guesses?" No one said anything. "What if I told you I know where you can get all of them done in 16 seconds," Connor said.

"No way," someone said.

"Yes way," Connor replied. "Think about a pit crew at a race track. They can change all four tires, fill the tank with gas, and give the driver a drink, all within 16 seconds," Connor said.

The faces around the room showed a look of surprise. Many broke out with a smile.

"He's right!" someone in the room said.

"The previous best guess had been 2 hours, but now you know a better way. So, in terms of housekeeping, and the assumption that it takes a long time, ask yourself, 'How can we convert housekeeping into a well-organized pit crew? What is the pit crew doing that housekeeping isn't?'" Connor asked. He could see, if not hear, the wheels turning. Connor smiled.

"I think having more housekeeping people will help a lot," said Crystal.

"How many more do you need?" Connor asked.

"I don't know for sure, but if we want to do it that fast, then we might need three times as many people," Crystal said.

"Wow!" Connor said. "I don't think the executive team will go for that amount of an increase."

"Why not, they promised to follow our recommendations," Crystal said.

"Yes they did, but within reason," Connor pointed out. "Let's step back and look at the problem again," he said. "Sometimes, organizations think that the only way they can do more work is hire more people. In some situations, that might be true, but most of the time, it's not. The real trick is to understand how to better use what you have, and not necessarily piling more people into an already bad system," Connor explained.

"Yes, but a pit crew has a lot more people than we do," Crystal said. "We only send one housekeeper to do a room, not six or seven."

Connor smiled and asked, "What would happen to the effectiveness of the pit crew if it was only one person doing all of those tasks?"

"Well, it would take a lot longer and you would probably lose the race," Crystal said.

"No doubt," Connor said. "What if you considered that when a room was ready for cleaning it was equal to a car being in the pit?" Connor asked.

"We'd still need more people. The current housekeeping staff is scattered all over the hospital on different floors. They assign housekeeping based on areas. Each housekeeper gets assigned so many rooms and hallways and public bathrooms and common areas that they need to maintain," Crystal explained. "When we had the layoff, the work increased even more. So, when a room needs cleaning, and it's in your area, you are the one that does it," she added.

"Does that mean that at any point in time, some housekeepers could be very busy and some not so much?" Connor questioned.

"Wait a minute," Terry said, "I think I see where you are going with this. If I understand correctly, we probably have the right amount of staff; we just have them in the wrong locations! That could be especially true in the mornings when there could be a surge of rooms that need cleaning," Terry said. "When we first made our recommendation to increase the housekeeping staff, and we talked about having two people on a cleaning team, I was actually seeing the need to double the staff," Terry said with a certain amount of doubt in his voice.

318 • *Focus and Leverage*

"I think you might need more housekeeping, but certainly not three times more," Connor said.

Crystal looked at Terry and said, "If a room that needs cleaning is like a car in the pit, then that makes sense. We can't use the room in its current condition and somebody might be waiting for it. The sooner it's cleaned, the sooner we can get somebody admitted, which is just like getting the car back in the race!" Crystal exclaimed.

Diane jumped back in and said, "What we need are room pit crews, but maybe just during peak loads, like in the morning. We could pull other staff from other locations until the rooms are cleaned and ready. Then, the other staff could go back to their assigned locations!" Diane exclaimed.

"That makes a lot of sense to me," Jeff said. "Housekeeping can still have assigned location, but if the need is there, we can move housekeeping where they are most needed. I like it!" Jeff said.

"How many people should be on a room pit crew?" Diane asked as a question to the group.

"As many as we need," said Terry.

"I agree," said Diane. "But, how many is that?"

"Again, think about the pit crew," Connor said. "Each person on the crew is assigned a specific part of the race car. There is someone on the left front tire, on the left rear tire, and the same for the right side. There is also someone putting gas in, and someone assigned to jack the car up and down. Now, think about the housekeeping crew. What are the critical areas that need someone assigned?" Connor asked.

"Maybe we should talk with the housekeeping supervisor and get the information we need," Jeff said.

"I agree," said Crystal looking at Jeff. "Let's you and I go do that right now." Both Crystal and Jeff left the room. Connor put everyone else on break until they got back.

They both returned approximately 15 minutes later and sat in their chairs.

"Well, I think we've got what we need," Crystal said. "We talked with Nancy, the housekeeping supervisor, and told her what we were thinking about. She seemed a bit surprised that anyone would take any interest in housekeeping. We told her how important this was and we needed the information," Crystal said. "When she talked about the critical areas, she mentioned all of the linens, including bed sheet and towels, cleaning the bathroom including sinks, toilets, and shower stalls, and making sure the garbage cans are emptied and cleaned with new plastic liners inserted. Also a top priority is making sure everything is wiped down on all of the flat surfaces. The last critical step is cleaning the floor as you leave the room," Crystal said.

"From what I'm hearing, I think we might need three people on a team. We want them to be able to do their work without constantly running into each other," Terry said. "I think we need to get with Nancy and describe in more detail what we're thinking about. We need to put a practice team together and watch them go through the steps. We can apply Lean and Six Sigma and better define how the process would work and the correct order for doing the steps. We can document our findings and create a preliminary process and work from there," Terry added.

"That's a good idea," Crystal said. "Mr. Jackson, would you mind if we all went back to housekeeping to talk with Nancy?" Crystal asked.

"Not at all," Connor said. "It's the next step for what we need to do. Besides, it's almost lunchtime, so we'll meet back here at 2:30 to review your findings. Does that give you enough time?" Connor asked.

"I think it might," Crystal said. "Even if it's not enough time, it will give us a good start," she added.

The team gathered up their things and headed out of the room toward housekeeping. Connor stayed in the room. He was thinking about how this same concept would apply to unscheduled maintenance at Aviation Dynamics and he needed a whiteboard to do some thinking.

At about 2:20, the team started to assemble back in the conference room. There seemed to be a lot of chatter and excitement with the group. When everyone was seated, Terry was the first to speak. "We talked with Nancy. She seemed OK with the idea, but the first thing she said was, 'We'll need more people to do that.' We explained to her about what we had talked about earlier, that we might have enough people, we just had them in the wrong location. Anyway, she started to warm up to our idea," Terry added.

"Because it was the noon hour, there were a lot of rooms to pick from. We looked at her list of rooms and picked one on the second floor. Nancy looked at the list as well and determined that the fourth floor had only one room to clean. She called the housekeeping lead on four and asked her to send two people to the second floor. According to the list, the second floor had the most rooms to clean," Crystal said.

"When everyone was assembled, we explained to the housekeeping personnel what we wanted to do. We went over the list of critical tasks, and they all agreed," Terry said. "We divided the tasks among the three, with one person assigned to change the bed sheets and gather towels. We assigned the second person to the bathroom to clean everything, and the third person was assigned to do the wipe down. The third person would also do the floors when everything else was done, while the other two moved on to the next room," Terry added.

"When they started, I had a stopwatch on my phone, so I timed them," Jeff said. "They completed the room in 13 minutes. That's almost five rooms an hour!" Jeff said.

"We also had Nancy inspect the room when they were finished to see if we had forgotten anything," Crystal said. "Nancy said they did a good job and the room was ready!"

"The other two had moved to the next room and the third person was close behind them," Terry said.

"I went with the first two and started the stopwatch again when they started," Jeff said. "When they finished the second room it took only 12 minutes," Jeff said. "At that rate, it is five rooms per hour! That's a big improvement over one room every 45 minutes to 1 hour when just one person was assigned," Jeff added.

"Nancy inspected the second room and said it was also ready," Crystal said. "She was totally amazed at how fast they could do it, and how well it was done," she added.

"We did a third room and it was also approximately 12 minutes," Jeff said.

"I think if we look at this process a bit closer and apply some Lean and Six Sigma, we can reduce the time even more," Terry said. "Honestly, I was so amazed to see how fast it could be done," Terry added.

"I think we might be on to something here," Crystal said. "I think we need to fine-tune the process for figuring out which rooms need cleaning, where to assemble the room pit crew staff from, and then notify Admitting which rooms are ready to go," she added.

"Excellent!" Connor said, as he walked toward the whiteboard. "Now we have our three injections to help reduce the wait time." He wrote the following on the board:

1. Express lane
2. Update and change the discharge policy
3. Implement room pit crews

"Now, as a team, you just need to fine-tune these ideas and get ready to make them happen," Connor said. "Unless you have more comments or questions, I think you should get back to working these new ideas,"

Connor added. No one raised their hand. As they started to exit the room, most seemed excited to get back to what they were doing. Terry stayed behind to talk with Connor for a few minutes.

"Thank you Connor, this has been an exceptional day, at least for me. I've come to realize over the past couple of weeks the importance of doing a good system's analysis and applying good systems thinking. I would never have considered any of the things we found without the systems thinking to understand how it was all linked together. I understand much more clearly now how important it is to *focus* on the real problem and not get caught up in trying to fix everything. There is a lot of *leverage* in making the system better," Terry said.

"Thanks Terry, but let me add that you and your group have been exceptional students!" Connor said. "I think you are well on your way to making Saint Luke's a world class hospital," Connor added with a smile.

"I can hardly wait until our next regional hospital conference so I can present some of these results and what we've learned from you and your TLS (Theory of Constraints, Lean and Six Sigma) methodology. Everyone will want to come to our hospital and see what we are doing," Terry said with a smile.

Connor just nodded his head in agreement, smiled, and said, "Keep in touch Terry. If you run into any problems, let me know."

"Thanks Connor, I'll do that and I'll be sure to let Dr. Price know what has happened and what we're doing."

22

MRO—Unscheduled Maintenance Strategy

Sam had called the day before and talked with Zeke to set up a time for a conference call. Sam, Joe, and Connor were hoping to get an update about the Critical Chain Project Management (CCPM) implementation. The next day, Joe and Connor were in Sam's office at the designated time and they made the call to Zeke. He answered on the second ring. Jim and Collin were in Zeke's office and the conversation started with Connor asking, "How's it going down there?" There was a short silence and finally Zeke answered, "Actually, it's going very well. Collin and the group have finished the repair template and have started on a second one. Everyone thinks the second template is going much faster, based on what they learned from the first one."

"That's good news," Joe piped in.

"In fact," Jim said, "we had a new aircraft come into the hangar yesterday morning and the timing was perfect. We'll apply our new CCPM template model and see what happens."

"Are you expecting problems?" Connor asked.

"Not at all," Collin said. "This has been a very smooth transition so far, and any issues that have come up have been quickly resolved. Probably the biggest issue so far is getting the feeding buffers set up with the correct materials and parts. We know what we want and when we want it. Procurement has issued the purchase orders, so we are still looking at the estimated times and buffer sizes. The good thing is everyone is aware of it and we will watch it closely," he added.

"Actually, the crew began the aircraft inspection process yesterday morning on the new aircraft. We're still working our way through that to see if any issues arise, but so far nothing has jumped out as a real problem.

We've also developed a procurement fast-track notification system. If we identify the need for any additional parts from the inspection, we can get those parts on order right away," Collin said. "We also have everything set up from the information technology side and have been able to complete all of the necessary testing."

"Sounds like everything is moving right along," Joe said.

"When are you guys coming back?" asked Zeke.

"I guess we can be there anytime, if you need us," Joe said.

Zeke answered, "Brad talked to us yesterday and he's still worried about the unscheduled maintenance side. He thinks we should get together and have a discussion about the plan moving forward," he added.

Connor was not surprised by this request, and he did understand Brad's desire to get going on the unscheduled maintenance. He also felt a much higher confidence level for Multiple Drum–Buffer–Rope (M-DBR) based on the work he had just finished at the hospital. "We can be there Thursday morning and give you our preliminary strategy for unscheduled maintenance," Connor said.

There was some mumbling and discussion on the other end of the phone. Finally, Zeke responded, "That will work. We'll expect to see you on Thursday morning."

"We'll be there," Connor said. "Is there anything else for today?"

"Not right now," Zeke said. They all said good-bye and disconnected.

Joe, Sam, and Connor stayed in Sam's office and called Liz at the travel agency to get things set up. Liz took all of the information and said she would make the phone calls and get everything ready and call them back when it was done. When they disconnected from Liz, there was a pause in the conversation until Joe finally spoke, "It all seems to be moving along quite well, and very fast."

"Indeed it does," Connor said. "The last couple of weeks at the hospital have proven beneficial to help with unscheduled maintenance. Our earlier thoughts that M-DBR could play a significant role for unscheduled maintenance are proving worthwhile," he explained.

"How so?" asked Sam.

"There is an uncanny resemblance between a hospital emergency room and unscheduled maintenance. Each of these systems is dealing with an unknown problem that needs to be identified and taken care of as quickly as possible," Connor said.

"If an aircraft has a suspected issue or a possible reason why it can't fly, it needs to be evaluated by a mechanic to determine the severity of the problem. It's similar to doing a patient assessment and triage in an ER. Once a possible problem is identified, then the next steps can be determined. It might even be possible for a mechanic to diagnose and repair the problem right on the flight line, or like an ER physician to simply treat and release. Depending on what is discovered during the assessment, it might require the aircraft to be towed back to the hangar for additional testing and repair, similar to getting admitted to the hospital. Depending on the magnitude of the problem, it could require a longer-term stay in the hangar," Connor explained.

"I see what you mean," Joe said.

Connor smiled and continued, "Each unscheduled work bay is like an ER exam room and it can be difficult to schedule because the duration of time is not known. It's a drum without a predictable cadence. In fact, scheduling is probably the wrong term to use. It's really just a resource available when they need it. You just have to stay focused on the problem until it's corrected, however long that might take," he added.

Sam's office phone rang and he could see on the display that it was Liz calling. He answered the phone with the speaker button so that Joe and Connor could hear. Liz explained that everything was ready to go for the trip on Wednesday evening. The plane from Business Air was scheduled; the room reservations were made and a rental car would be waiting. She would send the itinerary to Sam. They all thanked her and disconnected.

"OK … looks like we are ready to go again," Sam said.

"Yes we are," Joe said.

"I need some time to collect my thoughts for the group to explain the strategy for the unscheduled maintenance. I think you guys have a pretty good idea what I'm thinking right now, so I think I'll just go back home and finish this," Connor said.

"Do you need any help with the presentation?" asked Joe.

"I think I'll be fine. What I want you guys to think about is the CCPM implementation and focus on that aspect. I'll work the unscheduled maintenance. I'll see you guys at the airport tomorrow evening, if that's all right?" Connor asked.

"It's fine with me," Joe said.

"Me too," Sam said.

Wednesday evening, they all met at the Business Air terminal for the flight to Houston. The flight was uneventful, and when they arrived, the rental car was waiting. They drove to the hotel and checked in. Since it was late, all of them agreed to meet in the lobby at 6:15 AM.

The next morning, they made the drive to Aviation Dynamics, cleared the gate guard and were in the lobby at 6:55 AM. Marisa was behind the desk with the sign-in logbook ready and Zeke and Jim were in the lobby waiting for them to arrive. They signed in and got their badges and all of them made the walk to the conference room. When they got there, the room was empty. Jim turned on the lights and walked over to the overhead projector and turned it on. A few minutes later, Brad and Collin walked in. Greetings were exchanged and hands were shook. At the side table Jim was busy making a pot of coffee. A few minutes before they started, Hal and Marsha also walked in. They all took a seat around the table. Zeke was first to speak and explained that the rest of the team was busy on the shop floor. With the first aircraft in the new CCPM system, there was plenty of excitement and plenty to do.

"That's fine, it's the best place for them to be right now," Connor said. "Have you encountered any issues since the last time we talked on Tuesday?" asked Connor.

"None," Zeke said. "At least none that I know about," he added looking at Jim and Collin.

"So far, nothing has surfaced that is causing any concern, but we are only a few days into our first one," Jim said.

"The upfront inspection went well and they didn't find anything that caused any concerns, at least as far as parts go. The inspection actually took less time then everyone thought it would, so we're already ahead of schedule," Zeke said.

"The software is on the server, and the input stations have been identified. We have completed three more training classes and everyone seems ready to go. We are getting status from the system and everyone is anxious to start seeing results," Collin said.

"Speaking of results," Jim said, "we had some fever charts made that are three foot square. We mounted them behind some Plexiglas and placed them in each work bay so they are visible when you walk down the center aisle. We can use an erasable marker to make updates and track the day-to-day progress of the work completed compared to the buffer used. The schedulers have been assigned to update their respective charts each morning. It's a great visual that everyone can see," he added.

"What about parts and procurement?" asked Joe. Everyone seemed to look at Marsha for the answer.

"When the team finished, we sat down with everyone and went through the tasks defined in the template. We determined which parts would be needed and when they would be needed on the basis of the feeding chains and buffers. The buyers have placed the necessary orders, on the basis of the historical turnaround time for those parts. Again, it's our first time and we are learning as we go, but so far it looks good," Marsha explained. "The biggest worry now is what impact this will have on parts availability for unscheduled maintenance since we changed the rules and unscheduled maintenance does not have first preference for the parts. We are still evaluating data to create a Pareto chart for the most commonly used parts in unscheduled maintenance, especially those parts with the longest lead times. We are almost finished researching the data, and once we have that information, we'll have a better idea what good looks like. Then, we can use some of our extra budget to establish a more accurate parts buffer for both scheduled and unscheduled and RTV parts," Marsha said.

"That's very impressive!" Joe said. Connor and Sam were both nodding their heads in agreement.

There was a silence in the room as everyone on the Aviation Dynamics team took a moment to pat each other on the back for the work that had been accomplished. Confidence was at a high level. Connor broke the silence and said, "There are some things that will happen in the future and you need to be aware of them. In terms of cause and effect, as more and more aircraft are brought into the system and you continue to reduce the overall time for scheduled maintenance, you might start to expose excess capacity. This probably won't be quite as evident up front as you work through your backlog, but it will happen. When it does happen, you will be tempted to lay people off and reduce your operating expense. My suggestion to you is not to succumb to that temptation," he added.

"Why not?" asked Hal. "If it's another way for us to save money, why wouldn't we do that?" Connor was thinking to himself that Hal had still not made the transition from "saving money" to "making money."

"When we first started this project, you had two objectives you were concerned about. One was being able to keep your current contracts and the second was being able to get new contracts. In your old system of doing business, achieving either one of those objectives was almost impossible," Connor said.

Brad was nodding his head and thinking, "He's right!"

"When the excess capacity is exposed, you need to use it to your competitive and marketing advantage. Your competitive advantage will be being able to keep your current contracts by delivering on time, or even ahead of schedule. Your customer satisfaction will go up and your customers will be happy. Your marketing advantage will be selling your excess capacity. At some point in time, the work you're currently doing will only take about half the time it does now. Without that excess capacity, you have nothing to sell. That's when you have the marketing advantage to take on more work," Connor said. "The constraint for your company will move from being an internal constraint to being an external market constraint. You'll need the new business to utilize your capacity," Connor explained.

Brad asked, "So, as we continue to improve, we should have a pretty good idea, based on the reduced times, how much more work we can handle; is that correct?"

"Exactly, but I would also caution not to oversell your capacity. Don't dig another hole that you can't get out of. Having some internal excess capacity is not a bad thing and it gives you some wiggle room to make any necessary adjustments or overcome the 'Murphy' effect ("anything that can go wrong will go wrong"; also often referred to as "Murphy's Law")," Connor said. "With the CCPM system in place, the common denominator between scheduled and unscheduled maintenance becomes your procurement system and the ability to maintain the necessary buffers."

Brad looked at Connor and said, "Speaking of unscheduled maintenance, do you guys have a plan about how we are going to improve it? Last time we spoke about it, you mentioned something about a hospital, and I'm curious about how all of this fits together?" he asked.

"Yes, I think we do have a plan we can talk about," Connor answered. "As you might remember, my wife Becky and I had an unplanned event to visit the ER when she suffered from a partial bowel obstruction. It was our experience in the ER that later led to a project in the hospital. During the time of the ER visit, I was totally perplexed by the amount of time it was taking to move from the ER and get Becky admitted into the hospital. No doubt I was an emotional wreck, but the scientist in me couldn't help but notice the hospital system. It just seemed broken and nonsupportive of good patient care and patient satisfaction," he explained.

"Excuse me Connor, but if you are going to talk about unscheduled maintenance, should we invite the hangar manager to be in this meeting?" Brad asked.

"That's probably not a bad idea. It would make sense to get the hangar manager involved now," Connor said.

Brad looked at Jim and said, "Could you please walk out to Helen's desk and ask her to give Andy a call?"

"I'll do that," Jim answered. He got up from his chair and left the room. He was back in a few minutes and reported that Andy was on his way over.

Jim looked at Connor and said, "Andy Peterson is the hangar manager for the unscheduled maintenance. Andy and I have been talking during staff meeting the last few weeks and he has been curious about what is going on. I told him not to worry because it would soon be his turn in the hot seat," everyone laughed. Jim continued to talk about Andy while they waited for him to arrive. "Andy has worked here for several years and has been in his current position for approximately 5 years. Andy is good at troubleshooting and he has done an excellent job in Hangar 2 with unscheduled maintenance. I've been telling him about CCPM and all of the changes we have been making. Of course, some of those changes have affected Hangar 2, especially with the procurement changes, so he is interested to get on board and learn whatever he can. He wants to do CCPM with unscheduled maintenance and see if that will make the difference we are all looking for," he added.

"Well, just so you know, we won't be doing CCPM with unscheduled maintenance," Connor said.

"Why not?" asked Jim. "It seems like it will work very well with scheduled maintenance and Andy wants to use it for unscheduled maintenance."

"We'll talk about that when Andy gets here," Connor said.

A few minutes later, Andy arrived and Jim made the introductions. Andy was tall and slender and his hair was grayish and cut short, which, to Connor, suggested a military background. He had a pleasant smile and scanned the room to make eye contact with everyone there. Andy took a seat next to Jim. Brad took a few minutes to bring Andy up to speed about what was going on and turned it back over to Connor.

Connor started again, "Anyway, because of my wife's visit to the ER, I got involved with a project at the hospital to reduce their ER wait times. At one point during Becky's stay, it hit me that the hospital ER and unscheduled maintenance had many things in common, and I knew if we could help solve the hospital's problem, we could help unscheduled maintenance perform their work faster."

"I'm not sure I understand what you're talking about," Jim said.

"Let me explain it a little deeper. Both systems are involved with high levels of uncertainty. With unscheduled maintenance, you never know what kind of problems you might have with an aircraft, or when it might happen. It's the same scenario in a hospital ER. If an aircraft has a problem, then mechanics are usually dispatched to the flight line to diagnose the problem. It might be something that can be fixed on the spot, or it might require towing the aircraft back to the hangar for a more in-depth repair. The mechanics, in essence, are doing a triage to determine the extent of the problem and what needs to be done. It's the same thing in an ER. Patients arrive at the ER and are evaluated by a physician, and then a decision must be made. Some patients can be treated and released, some will require more extensive testing, and some might even be admitted to the hospital," Connor explained.

"When we solved this problem at the hospital, we didn't use CCPM. Instead, we used a concept we have developed that we refer to as Multiple Drum–Buffer–Rope or M-DBR as we call it. The reason CCPM won't work with unscheduled maintenance is that, for the most part, the repair task durations are very short. It would be possible to fix an aircraft and have it flying again before you could even get the information loaded into the CCPM software," Connor explained.

"With M-DBR, we can consider each work bay as having its own drum-beat. If I'm not mistaken, Hangar 2 has six work bays, is that correct?" asked Connor.

"That's correct," Andy said.

"And, each one of those work bays can do essentially the same type of work and repairs, is that correct?" asked Connor.

"That's true. However, there is one work bay that is more specialized than the others and we use it when necessary, for working on a particular type of aircraft, but that rarely happens," Andy said.

"How do you schedule the aircraft into the work bays?" asked Connor.

Andy thought for a moment and responded. "Well, that depends. Normally the pilots show up at the hangar and change clothes in the pilots' dressing room. When they are ready, we have some golf carts we use to give them a ride to the flight line. The cart is usually driven by a mechanic. When they arrive at the aircraft, the pilots do their preflight checklist. If there are issues, the mechanic will try and diagnose the problem and get it fixed. If the problem can be fixed, it gets fixed and then the pilots take off and do whatever they need to do. And the mechanic goes back to the hangar," he added.

"What if the problem can't be fixed on the flight line?" asked Connor.

"If the mechanic's evaluation determines a more serious problem, or something that might require more testing, then he calls for a tug to tow the aircraft back to the hangar and get it checked," Andy said.

"What happens when you get the aircraft towed back to the hangar?" asked Connor.

"If a work bay is open, we pull the aircraft in and get going on it right away and get it fixed," Andy said.

"And what if a work bay isn't open?" asked Connor.

"We have a holding area where we line up the aircraft in the order that they came in. When a work bay opens, we get the next aircraft in line and pull it in," Andy said.

Connor was nodding his head and asked, "On any given day, how many aircraft need to be taken to the hangar?"

"That varies quite a bit from day to day and week to week. I don't have the data right here with me, but if I remember correctly, it averages approximately 8 or 9 per day. I think approximately 40% can be fixed on the flight line. Of the remaining aircraft, 60% needs to come back to the hangar, and there is probably 60% of that total that can be fixed in 2 hours or less. The remaining aircraft need to stay longer, sometimes maybe 2, 3, or 4 days, depending on what might be wrong and depending on parts availability. The biggest problem with parts happens when we have a part that is Return To Vendor (RTV). Sometimes, that can take a while," Andy said. "It has happened where we can have four or five work bays with aircraft that are just sitting and waiting for new parts or RTV parts. It's difficult to just pull an aircraft out and put another one in because they've already been disassembled. It stops everything we are doing until parts are available," he explained.

Connor smiled and said to Andy, "I can only imagine that at times, your holding area can become overloaded."

"It has happened. There have been times when we just leave aircraft on the flight line because we don't have anywhere to put them in the holding area. It doesn't happen very often, but it has happened," Andy said.

Zeke said, "Hopefully, our new procurement process will help take care of many of the part shortages."

Joe spoke up and said, "When you think about the procurement side, you'll need to consider new parts and RTV parts for both scheduled and unscheduled maintenance. The buffer you determine will need to be adequate to accommodate both hangars, and not just one or the other," he added.

Andy looked at Zeke and said, "I've been a little worried about that. Jim and Agnes told me about the change to procurement and how unscheduled maintenance won't get first pick of the parts anymore. If that's the case, it will slow us down even more."

Marcia jumped in to explain to Andy about the data being collected to do a Pareto analysis to determine the most commonly used parts with the longest lead times. They were also looking at the RTV parts to gain the same understanding. Andy nodded his head as if to say he understood.

"Andy, when you have aircraft that are waiting in the holding area, how do you decide which one is next for a work bay?" Connor asked.

"We keep a running list by tail number of when they showed up. So, it's basically whichever one has been there the longest is next in line," Andy said.

"So, it's possible that an aircraft that could be fixed in a shorter time might have to wait for an aircraft that takes a longer time, just because of its place in line?" asked Connor.

"That's a very possible scenario. We try to watch it, but the truth is, everyone is waiting for their aircraft and the pilots wouldn't take kindly to moving someone else ahead of them," Andy said. "It's like taking your car to a garage to be fixed. You sit in the waiting room and keep looking through the window out to the shop area looking for your car, and then the service manager tells you somebody moved ahead of you," he said.

"What if your car only needed something like an oil change?" asked Connor.

Andy and the rest of the room sat silent for a minute and finally Andy answered, "I guess you'd be really mad. It would seem they change the oil fairly fast and you shouldn't have to wait that long."

"I'd just take my car to a Jiffy Lube. You can get in and get out much faster. That's why I don't go to a dealership, they just take too long," Jim said.

"What if the dealership had an express lane like Jiffy Lube and they could do it faster?" asked Connor, mostly to the group. Connor was scanning the room and noticed Brad shaking his head with a smile on his face. Connor kept looking at Brad and finally Brad spoke. "Most dealerships do have an express lane. The question I'm sitting here asking myself right now is why don't we have one?"

"That's a good question," Connor responded with a smile. "If you added just one more level of triage for aircraft coming to the hangar and determined which aircraft required minimal repairs or long repairs, you would have two lists and not just one. If you also designate one or perhaps two bays as express lanes, depending on the type of repair loads, you could move repairs through the system faster. All of the repairs that could be done quickly wouldn't have to wait for those that might take longer," Connor explained.

Connor continued, "There will still be a certain amount of uncertainty with each repair on the basis of not knowing for sure what needs to be fixed or how much testing needs to be completed to know what might be wrong. However, the uncertainty could be reduced by the dedicated work bays scheduling work on the basis of category and not just placement of when it arrived at the hangar. Another aspect of determining which aircraft will move next from the holding area is an assessment of what parts might be needed, if any. If a new part is required, do you have one? How long will it take to get one? If it's a possible RTV part, do you have a current replacement? If not, how long to get one?"

"I think I hear what you're saying. You mean not to clog the work bays with something that can't be completed and moved out quickly, is that correct?" asked Andy.

"That's correct," Connor said.

"The purpose behind the M-DBR concept is not to build and manage a work buffer, but rather to move as quickly as you can to take the work buffer to zero. In the case of a hospital ER or unscheduled maintenance, the very best buffer to have is zero. What you want to avoid is having a repair moving into a work bay and then just sit there. What you want to do is keep the work moving in and out," Connor said.

"This will require an exceptionally managed procurement system," Zeke said.

"It will indeed!" said Connor. "And up front you might stumble a bit before you get it all figured out. Getting your suppliers on board will be important. It won't all happen at once, but it will happen. I fully anticipate that Marsha, and her team, will be up to the task." Marsha smiled at Connor as if to say "Thank you."

Brad was sitting with his arms folded across his chest and head tilted to one side looking at Connor and finally said, "The common denominator for scheduled and unscheduled is the parts availability. It's not going to require any new investment for unscheduled maintenance for software, or equipment, but rather just changing our mind-set about how we distribute the work. Is that correct?"

"That's correct," Connor said. "In fact, in the future, it might even be possible, depending on the system loads and the variation of the work, that scheduled maintenance might even have some capacity to help unscheduled maintenance, if it's required." Connor looked at Collin and asked, "Collin, based on your past experience, what is the average time reduction for projects when CCPM is used?"

Collin thought for a moment and said, "It depends, but I think it could range anywhere from 40% to 60% reduction."

"OK, for the sake of discussion, let's assume you can achieve and maintain a 50% reduction in the time it takes to complete a scheduled maintenance project. In essence, that means you complete a project in half the normal time, or work is completed twice as fast as it was before. Remember earlier this morning that we talked about one of the outcomes from using CCPM would be exposing excess capacity?" Most were nodding their heads that they remembered the discussion. "We also talked about expanding your marketing effort to find and get new business to fill that excess capacity. The initial reaction that I'm sure all of you had was to look external to fill the capacity, but what if there was a way to look internal and use some of that capacity to off-load work from unscheduled maintenance, if required?"

Zeke was rubbing his hands together and thinking out loud when he said, "That means we could have additional resources available to help unscheduled maintenance if it was needed."

"If that were possible, we could complete the work for unscheduled maintenance even faster and get closer to having the work buffer to zero," Jim said.

"There are some days we could use the extra help," Andy said.

"Not all of your excess capacity would be required to support unscheduled maintenance. You would still have capacity to market for new business," Connor said.

"What will happen to revenues if more work comes in and is completed faster and on time, and unscheduled work can get completed faster?" asked Connor looking directly at Hal.

"We'll probably make more money," Hal answered in a low voice.

"How many more new employees will you need to hire to do twice as much work?" asked Connor, again, looking at Hal. However, Brad jumped in and answered this question saying, "None! We'll be able to do more with the number of employees that we already have. Plus the increased revenue will translate to increased profit." Brad was smiling and it seemed to be contagious, because everyone else was smiling as well, including Hal!

"It seems to me that shifting the overall strategy from 'saving money' to 'making money' will allow you to meet both of your desired objectives; maintaining the current contracts and getting new contracts," Connor said. "Now that you have the proper direction, it's time for you to apply the velocity to get there," he added.

"It looks like a win–win," Brad said. "It helps what we're doing now and also positions us for the future. I can visualize a time in the near future when we can be extremely competitive with our bids to get new work." His eyes seemed to be looking across the room and out the window as he visualized the possible future.

"Are there any questions?" asked Connor. No one raised their hand. They all seemed to be caught in the same euphoria as Brad, each imagining future events in their own area of expertise.

Connor turned and looked at Joe and Sam and said, "For the time being, I believe our work here is done!"

For a brief instant, Brad looked panicked and asked, "What do you mean you're done?"

"For the time being, I believe our work here is done," Connor said again. "You just need to go work the remaining issues and work your way up the learning curve. Figure out how all of this will best work for you and your organization," Connor added.

"But, what if we need your help again?" Brad asked.

"Then, just give us a call and we'd be happy to walk you through it, or make another visit if it is deemed necessary," Connor said. "Right now, you know everything you need to know to make this work. You have your plan and you know what actions need to be taken. The success of this effort is in your hands; you have to take ownership, and I have high confidence you will figure out the right way and make it work," he added confidently.

Brad understood what Connor was saying about accepting ownership, and though he didn't really want to admit it, he knew Connor was right.

Brad looked at Connor, Joe, and Sam smiling and said, "Don't get too far away from your phone." Everyone laughed.

"I want to thank you for everything you have done. I mostly want to thank you for helping us look at these issues through a different set of eyes. I was totally convinced up front that the only way to succeed was by implementing more cost cutting and trying to save more money and I had no idea how to do that. I now understand a different approach, which is making money. Thank you!" Brad said. Everyone else around the table was chiming in with their own "Thank you."

The discussions lasted for a while longer and then Connor, Joe, and Sam gathered their things, getting ready to leave. The entire management team walked them to the lobby for handshakes and good-byes.

23

The Finale

Connor, Joe, and Sam left Aviation Dynamics feeling very good about what had happened in both scheduled and unscheduled maintenance. They drove back to the airport, checked in, and waited for their flight. Sam was feeling a little disappointed that this might be the last time he is able to fly in a private jet. He had really enjoyed the convenience of the service and would miss it when he started flying commercial again. The plane arrived and before long they were in the air headed home. Everyone was buckled in their seats looking out the windows when Joe broke the silence.

"What are you guys doing this weekend?" he asked.

Sam replied, "I think I'm going to take my wife and kids swimming at the new water park. How about you Connor?" he asked.

Connor thought for a moment and then said, "I think Becky and I will probably just stay home and enjoy each other. I'll probably take her to dinner Saturday night to this new restaurant that just opened downtown. It will be kind of a celebratory dinner for everything we've accomplished both at Aviation Dynamics and at Saint Luke's," he added.

"What about you Joe?" Sam asked.

"I think my in-laws are coming in from Dallas this weekend for an extended visit, so I'll be entertaining them," he replied. "So Connor, how do you think Aviation Dynamics will fare going forward?" he asked. "Do you think they can continue with what they're doing in both hangars?" he asked in rapid-fire questions.

"That remains to be seen, but I think at least in the short term, they'll do extremely well. My concern is that if they have a leadership change, and someone new comes in and dismantles everything," Connor said. "They are set up right now to achieve huge gains in profitability, but if Brad gets promoted, that could all change," he added.

"Why do you think that a new site leader would change what they have in place Connor?" asked Joe.

"I've seen it happen too many times before. New leadership sometimes want to make a name for themselves and they have a tendency to inject new ways of doing business into a system that does not necessarily need fixing," Connor said.

"I hope that doesn't happen," said Joe. "What you helped them do has totally changed their entire approach to maintenance, repair, and overhaul (MRO). Both management and the union are working so well together now, and for me, that was really the major change that took place," he added.

"You're right Joe, that was one of the key benefits of the whole initiative. The message I hope management learned was that, if they want true and lasting improvement, then they have to listen to their true subject matter experts. It usually happens that, within organizations, the answers you need are there, if management would just take the time to listen and then act on those ideas," Connor replied.

The rest of the flight home was uneventful and all three of them actually got some needed rest. The flight landed on schedule and when they got off the plane and walked into the terminal, Connor was greeted by Becky. She ran to Connor and jumped into his arms telling him that she had missed him terribly as both Joe and Sam smiled and looked on. All three said their good-byes and drove home.

It had been 2 weeks since Joe, Sam, and Connor had returned from Aviation Dynamics and so far everything had been quiet. Joe and Sam had received only one phone call from Jim and it was an easy question to answer. Jim had also reported that everything seemed to be going OK. Everyone was very busy learning the new system. Collin had finished with the team creating the scheduling templates for the aircraft they worked on. There was only one template left and the team felt confident they could do it on their own when the need materialized. Collin and his trainers had left the end of the previous week but were on standby in case something happened and they were needed. Jim also reported they had put three more aircraft into scheduled maintenance and had a total of four that were using Critical Chain Project Management (CCPM). The first aircraft in the system had been there approximately 3 weeks and was approximately 60% complete and everyone was pleased with the results so far. Joe and Sam told Jim to call them when the first aircraft was completed so they could share the results with Connor. Jim agreed to do that.

Connor and Becky had disappeared for approximately 5 days. No one knew for sure where they had gone, but all suspected it was someplace to relax and play some golf. With everything that had happened over the last 2 months, they probably deserved some time away.

For Joe and Sam, things at Barton Enterprises were running smoothly. It was almost like the plant was on autopilot. When any issues did come up, the people on the shop floor seemed more than capable of handling the issue and getting things going again. The whole Barton operation was just humming like a well-tuned engine, and it was making a beautiful sound.

Joe was in his office when the phone rang. He looked at the display and it was Connor. He quickly picked up the phone and said, "Hello Connor."

"Hi Joe, how are you?" asked Connor.

"I'm doing well. I noticed you've been gone for a few days, how was your getaway?" asked Joe.

"It was fun. We flew to Florida and spent some time on the beach and played a lot of golf," Connor replied.

"Good for you! I wish I could get away for a while, but my in-laws are here for an extended visit and I guess I'll be homebound," Joe answered.

"Listen, the reason I called was when Becky and I returned, there was a phone message from Ron Parsons. He said he had called and talked with Brad, and Brad was feeling very good about what was going on. Brad wanted to thank Ron for making the contacts and getting everything set up, and Ron wanted to thank all of us for accepting the project and helping Brad," Connor said.

Joe said, "I'm glad we did it too. It was a fun project to get involved with."

"Have you heard anything back from them?" asked Connor.

"Jim called about a week ago and said things were going well. He said four of the work bays in scheduled maintenance had new aircraft in them, and all were using their new CCPM templates. Collin and his group left approximately 2 weeks ago, but were on standby if need be," Joe said.

"So, they didn't talk about any issues or problems?" asked Connor.

"No issues that he mentioned to us. Jim said he would call when the first aircraft was complete and tell us the results," Joe said.

"Let's see, that means the first aircraft will have been in approximately 4 weeks now, so I'm thinking it might be close to being finished," Connor said thinking out loud.

"I was thinking the same thing. We should give them one more week and then give a call and check in if we haven't heard from them," Joe said.

"I agree. Do me a favor and pass the information from Ron Parsons on to Sam, if you would," Connor said.

"Sam already knows, he was on the phone with us," Joe said. They ended the conversation and disconnected.

One week later, Jim called Joe to announce that the first aircraft was nearing completion. He also wanted to set a time for a conference call when they could talk. They set it up for early the next morning. Joe called Sam and Connor to pass on the information about the conference call. They all met in Sam's office the next morning at 7:00 to make the call. The phone number Jim had given Joe was not a familiar one, but he called it anyway. Joe dialed the number, and when the call went through, it connected directly to Brad's office.

"Good morning," Brad said.

"Good morning to everyone on your end. I've got Connor and Sam with me," Joe said.

"We have Zeke, Jim, and Marsha on this end," said Brad.

"So, I understand the first aircraft is almost through the system," Joe said.

"It is, and we are really quite happy," Jim responded. "This aircraft will finish in just 41 days. We've never come close to a number like that before," Jim said. Joe, Connor, and Sam could hear some hand clapping on the other end and they smiled at each other.

"In fact, we're thinking we did a really good job with this one. It looks as if the buffer penetration will stay in the green zone all the way to the end. We really didn't have any problems at all," said Jim.

"Wait a minute, your buffer penetration stayed in the green zone the entire time?" asked Connor.

"Yes it did. We kept watching it, but it stayed in the green zone. We thought it was because we were paying so much attention to the first one, that it just happened that way," Jim said.

"This is a problem," Connor said, with what sounded like a bit of concern.

"What do you mean it's a problem? We achieved almost a perfect score and you call it a problem?" asked Zeke.

"Well, it is a problem, but it's a problem in a good way," Connor said.

"As usual, I'm afraid you're going to have to explain yourself," Brad said.

"I know what you're seeing is an indication of very good results, and don't get me wrong, these are good results. But not having any penetration outside of the green zone is also an indicator of a problem. If I were you, I certainly wouldn't make any changes yet, after all it's only one data point.

But, what this indicates is that the project buffer might be too large. In the future, it means you could reduce the buffer size and do the aircraft even faster. Something like this could become an excellent marketing tool when bidding on new projects. I would estimate you might be able to reduce it by another 5 to 7 days," Connor explained. "You know, what happened with the green zone is not uncommon. Companies or, maybe more precisely, people tend to be very conservative with the project buffer when they start, and when they get these kinds of results, they are happy, just like you guys are, but it might be possible to reduce it even further and get even better results," Connor stressed. "If you look at the other three aircraft in the work bays, are they showing the same trend of not exceeding the green zone?" asked Connor.

"The others are not as far along, but yes they are all showing the same trend. I usually have a quick meeting with the supervisors every morning and we walk the aisle looking at the fever charts for any issues. So far, all of them are staying in the green zone. We used exactly the same template for all four of them, so I guess it's the same thing," Jim said. "All of this is still so very counterintuitive to me. I still haven't wrapped my mind around taking time out of the schedule in order to do it faster," Jim said.

"Frankly, I was totally amazed at 41 days, and to think that we might get it down to 36 or 34 days, it just seems unbelievable," Zeke said.

"Actually, I think you could get down to 25 or 28 days. When it gets that low, then getting new business will be mandatory," Connor said. "You'll need to be able to feed the beast! It is something worth keeping an eye on," Connor added.

"It's funny, but Collin told us the same thing and we all secretly laughed under our breath. Now with you also saying it, I guess it might be possible," Jim said.

"How was the parts availability?" asked Joe.

Marsha jumped in with the answer. "So far, the parts have been where they need to be when they are needed. We were able to meet the feeding buffer needs, except for one that was 2 days late. We are collecting the data to help us predict the future needs."

"Remember, if you start to reduce the project buffer times, it will increase the pressure on your parts buffers, which will increase the pressure on procurement. You'll need parts faster and faster," Joe said.

"We don't need any more pressure right now! We're still trying to figure this out," Marsha said with a laugh.

"Do we need to do it any faster than 41 days right now?" asked Brad. Connor, Joe, and Sam had heard the question Brad was asking on his end and waited for a response. There was a momentary silence on the phone.

"We have a backlog right now of seven aircraft, and we have more arriving soon according to the flight log data. The faster we can get them finished, the better it will be," Zeke said.

Brad took his hands and rubbed his face. "Let's think about this for a minute. I don't disagree that we need to do them faster, but for that to happen, we need a very streamlined procurement system with adequate parts buffers to handle the reduced time," Brad said. Connor, Joe, and Sam were listening on the other end of the phone and looking at each other.

"If we reduce the time too much and too fast, we could get ourselves in trouble by creating a parts availability issue. I think we need to stage our improvements to the same level that procurement and parts improve and keep monitoring the demand. I have no doubt we can reduce the repair time and find some new contracts based on an improved offering, but none of that will have the desired impact without the right parts. Procurement and parts availability have become the new constraint, and we need to subordinate everything else to the same drumbeat that procurement and parts can keep up with what we are doing. As that improves, everything else can improve right along with it. We have to do this in the right order," Brad said.

Connor and Joe were looking at each other and smiling. Joe reached up and put his finger on the mute button. "He does understand," Joe said.

"Indeed he does. That was an impressive narrative to distinguish between what you *must fix* and what you *can fix*. He can see the intrinsic order of where to start and what to do next. I think these guys will do just fine," Connor said. Joe removed his finger from the mute button.

"I can see your point. If we just reduce the days and the parts aren't available, then the buffer is consumed and the project is late," Jim said.

Brad smiled and asked Marsha, "Is there anything any of us can do to help with your efforts?"

"I think we understand the scheduled maintenance fairly well. That list doesn't change much from aircraft to aircraft, unless they find something during the inspection. The list that is causing the most problems now is the unscheduled maintenance. I think we need you guys to take a hard look at the Pareto analysis and see if it makes sense," Marsha said, looking at Zeke and Jim. "I know we'll need to make adjustments as we go, but you guys need to tell us what those adjustments are," she explained. "Right now, I have more worries about unscheduled maintenance than scheduled maintenance."

"We can do that. Let's get something set up and review your list one more time, especially for those items that have a long lead time," Jim said.

Brad had been thinking and said, "Let's do this. Let's remove 2 days from the three remaining aircraft in the CCPM system and monitor what happens to parts availability. If procurement seems to be able to keep up, then we'll consider a couple of more days. However, if we start to see issues with parts availability, then we'll focus our attention on that issue, quickly identify the problem, and resolve it. We won't remove any more time from the buffer until it is resolved. Each new aircraft that enters will use the template and project buffer from the aircraft that just finished," he explained.

"Connor, what do you guys think about that?" asked Brad.

Connor was looking at Joe and Sam and they we nodding their heads in agreement. "We think it's a good plan, and a good place to start," Connor said. "Your understanding that the constraint will move during your improvement efforts is essential to know where to focus your efforts and leverage your results," he added.

"Thanks!" Brad said. He looked at everyone in his office and asked, "So, does everyone understand the plan moving forward?"

Connor, Joe, and Sam could hear an audible "Yes" on the phone.

Sam jumped in the conversation and said, "Before we finish, I want to ask how unscheduled maintenance is doing?"

Zeke answered, "After our meeting with you guys, Jim and I went with Andy to help explain to the supervisors and team leads what was going on and the idea of an express lane. Neither one of the supervisors had a problem with the idea, nor did the team leads. They all thought it was a good idea. When the next bay came open, they designated it as an express lane and started reviewing the aircraft in the holding area with short repair and turnaround times. At the end of that day, Andy estimated they got three additional aircraft through, which otherwise would have had to wait in line. After about a week of doing this, Andy is thinking they probably got seven to eight additional aircraft through the system using the express lane. Andy is trying to define some criteria about when to open an additional express lane, so I think it's going very well," he explained. "The only real issue, which hasn't been a big problem yet, is the parts, as Marsha explained."

"That's good," Sam replied. "Keep up the good work!"

344 • *Focus and Leverage*

"Are there any more questions?" asked Brad. No one on either end of the call responded with anything.

"Connor, Joe, Sam, thanks for joining us today. I think we've got a good idea of what we need to do moving forward. We'll keep you posted on our progress, or let you know if we run into something that needs your help," Brad said.

"OK, that sounds good and good luck to you and your team," Joe said; they disconnected the phone call.

"It's pretty impressive how they have embraced this effort and made it their own. I think they've reached the point where they believe they can solve the problems now without our intervention," Joe said.

"I agree," Connor said. Sam was nodding his head in agreement.

Two days later, Connor was in his home office working on some things when his cell rang. He looked at the display but did not recognize the number. "Hello, this is Connor," he said.

"Hi Connor, this is Brad Carter, how are you?" asked Brad.

"I'm doing well. Is everything alright on your end?" asked Connor.

"It's going very well. Each day, we seem to make a little more progress. Even Hal is getting excited. He's been running some numbers forward and seems to be genuinely embracing what's happening. Listen, the reason I called was, I wanted to talk with you personally and express my deepest appreciation for what you and your group have done for us," Brad said.

"You are more than welcome, it's what we do!" Connor said.

"You guys and Becky of course have walked us through an incredible journey. It seems we really did know the answer, but we were asking the wrong questions. I'll never forget your reference to the water pump in the desert. I think it was at that moment that everything started to come together for me. I'm sure corporate will be happy with the results and their first question will be 'How did you do it?' They might want to spread this to some of the other divisional facilities when they finally grasp what is happening. Would you and the group be available to help if that happens?" asked Brad.

"We can be available, if you need us, but I think you are much better at this than you think you are. You might even consider doing it yourself and just getting with us if you need help with a troublesome issue," Connor said.

"Thanks Connor, I'll consider that. Anyway, thanks again for your help and mentoring us through this process. We are all feeling much better here and it's all because of you, Becky, Joe, and Sam," Brad said.

"Remember, we really did very little, other than point the way. You and your group did all the hard work to make it happen," Connor said.

"Thanks Connor. Take care of yourself and pass this on to the rest of the gang," said Brad.

"I'll do that, and you take care as well," said Connor.

They disconnected and Connor sat his phone down on the desk. He knew they would do well.

Joe was at his desk finishing up some reports that he had to submit when his office phone rang. "Hello, this is Joe, how can I help you?" It was Joe's wife, Jennifer, and she was in a state of hysteria. "Calm down honey and tell me what's wrong," he said to his obviously upset wife. Jennifer had called about her father, who was visiting. "Where is he now?" Joe asked.

"He's in bed right now, and he has chest pains," said Jennifer. "He told me that it feels like an elephant sitting on his chest," she added.

"I think you need to call an ambulance and get him to the hospital right away!" said Joe in a concerned voice.

"The ambulance is already on the way," said Jennifer. "He'll be going to Saint Luke's hospital … wait they're here … I'll see you at the hospital," and the phone went dead.

Joe's father-in-law, Bill Donald, was experiencing classic symptoms of a heart attack, which Joe knew could be life threatening. Joe also knew, from his conversations with Connor, that minutes mattered as far as damage to the heart muscle goes. Joe ran to the parking lot, jumped into his car, and drove to the hospital. Joe entered the emergency room at the hospital and checked with the receptionist to see where Jennifer's father was. Joe looked for his wife, but couldn't see her; apparently she was in one of the back rooms with her father. Joe began walking through the curtained area of the ER, looking for her. He finally found her behind one of the curtains.

"How's he doing?" he asked.

"They just wheeled him away to have a balloon inserted, of all things, inflated in one of his arteries," she said in an excited and concerned voice.

"He must be having a STEMI heart attack," Joe said.

"A what?" Jennifer asked.

"A STEMI heart attack is the most serious type and is caused when a blood clot suddenly forms, completely blocking an artery to the heart," Joe explained. "They treat the STEMI heart attack by inflating a very small balloon in the patient's artery to open up the blockage and let the blood flow better. And the reason I know about this is because the first improvement team that Connor was involved with here at the hospital was a team to reduce the 'Door to Balloon' time," he explained.

"Balloons, STEMI, Door to Balloon? What are you talking about Joe?" asked Jennifer with concern in her voice.

"The Door to Balloon time is a performance metric that the hospital is required to track that measures the length of time from when a patient enters the ER until a balloon is inflated in the patient's artery to free up the blockage," Joe explained.

"They will actually inflate a balloon inside my dad's heart?" she asked in disbelief.

"Not in his heart, but in the artery wherever the blockage is," Joe explained.

"Where is your dad now?" asked Joe.

"Like I said, they came and took him, I think they called it their Cardiac Catheterization laboratory, I guess to do the balloon thing," she replied. "They told me I had to wait here for him," she added.

"Wow! That was pretty quick ... how long did it take him to get to the lab?" Joe asked.

"We've only been here for 25 minutes, so I would guess that within 20 minutes, he was on his way," she explained.

"I remember Connor telling me that when he first started the improvement effort, the Door to Balloon time was around 90 minutes, but based on what you're telling me, it sounds like they moved very quickly," said Joe.

"Why is it so important to get the balloon thing done so quickly?" she asked.

"Connor explained it to me this way. For every minute the blood supply is cut off from the heart, heart muscle is damaged. So by reducing the time it takes to get this procedure done, the survival rate improves proportionally," he explained.

Just then, the curtain opened and there was Jennifer's father, Bill, on a hospital gurney. "Hi Joe, good to see you here," said Bill in a slurred voice.

"How are you feeling, Bill?" asked Joe.

"I'm feeling much better, thanks to this amazing team of medical folks," he replied. "I have to tell you, this is one of the best hospitals I've ever seen in my life!" he exclaimed. "From the time the ambulance pulled in, it was like everyone knew exactly what they needed to do to get me feeling better. I have to be admitted and stay here at the hospital for a few days, but they told me everything went very well," Bill explained.

As the technician was leaving, Joe decided to leave Jennifer alone with her father. He turned to the technician and asked, "What was the Door to Balloon time for him?"

"You know about Door to Balloon time? I'm not sure what the time was, so let's go ask the ER nurse in charge," he replied, as they both walked over to the nurses' station. The technician walked into the nurses' area and asked about the Door to Balloon time for Joe's father-in-law. He turned and signaled with his fingers, the number 31, indicating 31 minutes from time of entry to the ER to inflation of the balloon in his artery. That sounded like a pretty good time to Joe, so he decided to call Connor and get his take on it.

"Hello, this is Connor," he said as he answered his phone on the second ring.

"Hi Connor, this is Joe. Connor, I'm at Saint Luke's and I wanted to ask you something," said Joe.

"What's going on Joe? Are you OK?" asked Connor.

"I'm fine. We had to rush Jennifer's father to the hospital because he was apparently having chest pains and shortness of breath," said Joe.

"Is he OK Joe?" asked Connor.

"He seems to be fine, but I wanted to ask you a question about your Door to Balloon time team," said Joe. "I think you told me when you first started working with this team that the average time was around 90 minutes ... is that correct?" he asked.

"Yes, I think it was right around 91 minutes," said Connor.

"Well, whatever you did, it worked!" said Joe.

"How much time did it take?" asked Connor.

"It took only a total of 31 minutes!" said Joe. "The work you did may have just saved Jennifer's father's life, so thank you very much!" said Joe with a certain amount of emotion in his voice.

"I'm very happy for Jennifer and her dad, but it wasn't what I did, it was the team who did it all. All I did was point them in the right direction to help find the constraint and they did the rest," replied Connor. "I think tomorrow, maybe I'll go to the hospital and look up Dr. Price and Terry and let them know how proud I am of them," he added. "Did any of them mention me by name?" he asked.

"No, why do you ask that?" asked Joe, somewhat surprised by this question.

"I was just wondering if you received some kind of special treatment because they knew me and that might have been the reason your father-in-law breezed through the ER," Connor replied.

"No Connor, this ER looks like a well-oiled machine with everyone knowing their role and executing it to perfection," said Joe. "I'm sure they didn't see any connection between you and me and my father-in-law," he added.

"That's great because it means that the hospital is maintaining their new process," Connor said. Joe said he was going back to the room to find his wife and they disconnected.

The next day, Connor did make his trip to the hospital and had Dr. Price and Terry paged. Dr. Price was the first to answer the page and called the front desk where Connor was waiting. The receptionist took the call and then handed the phone to Connor. "Hello, this is Dr. Price, how can I help you?"

"Hi Jules, this is Connor and I was hoping to have approximately 10 minutes of your time and Terry's time," he replied.

"I'm free right now … where are you Connor?" he asked.

"I'm in the hospital lobby at the front desk," Connor replied.

"I'll be right there," Dr. Price said. "Wait!" Connor exclaimed. "Don't come to the front desk, just meet me in the executive conference room where all of the charts are posted." Connor also asked Dr. Price to call Terry and let him know to meet him there.

As is typically the case, Connor arrived well before Dr. Price and Terry. While he was waiting, he scanned the various graphs and charts that populated the wall of the conference room, but today he was looking for his favorite chart of all, Door to Balloon time. What he saw shocked even this experienced continuous improvement (CI) veteran. Not only had this team maintained their improved Door to Balloon times, they had continued to demonstrate time reductions. Connor knew that the last data point on this run chart probably belonged to Joe's father-in-law and he knew what the time was. It made him smile, and as he was standing there feeling like the proud father of a newborn baby, the conference room door opened and in walked Jules and Terry.

"Hi Connor, how are you?" they both said as Connor walked over and shook both of their hands.

"I'm doing great," he replied smiling broadly.

"What brings you to the hospital today?" asked Dr. Price.

"I wanted to come by and personally thank you two for the job you've done on Door to Balloon time. Yesterday I received a call from Joe Pecci, one of my business associates. It seems that his father-in-law, who is visiting from Texas, had chest pains and was rushed to the hospital by ambulance."

"How's he doing?" asked Terry.

"He's doing fine, thanks to the folks in the ER and the Cardiac Cath lab," said Connor. "His Door to Balloon time was an amazing 31 minutes," he said and pointed to the last data point on the run chart. "Not only have you guys reduced this time from the original 91 minutes, but you continue to reduce it! This is an amazing trend gentlemen!" Connor exclaimed.

Dr. Price and Terry acknowledged the newest data point with a smile.

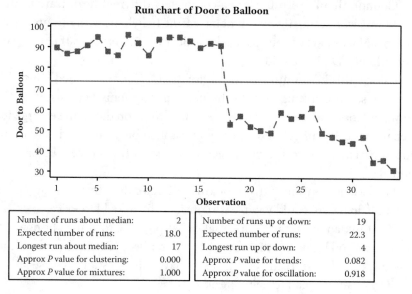

Run chart of Door to Balloon

Number of runs about median:	2	Number of runs up or down:	19
Expected number of runs:	18.0	Expected number of runs:	22.3
Longest run about median:	17	Longest run up or down:	4
Approx *P* value for clustering:	0.000	Approx *P* value for trends:	0.082
Approx *P* value for mixtures:	1.000	Approx *P* value for oscillation:	0.918

"I just wanted to come by and thank both of you personally for all you have done, because it's clear that your improvement efforts are really paying off in terms of patient care," said Connor.

"All of the teams are really doing well, but Connor, you are the one who we should be thanking," said Dr. Price as Terry nodded his head in agreement. "If you hadn't shown us a better way, we'd still be struggling like we were before we met you," he added. "And by the way, how is my favorite patient doing?" he asked.

"She's doing really well and told me to tell you hello," said Connor. "What about the overall wait times in the ER?" Connor asked.

Terry replied, "They're doing much better. The average wait times have been reduced by roughly 40% since Becky was here. The Multiple Drum–Buffer–Rope (M-DBR) system, with the express lane, is working very well.

So much so, that Dr. Price and I have been asked to present our results at an upcoming healthcare conference. It seems as if word is getting out about what we're doing here and we are more than happy to share," said Terry.

"Congratulations to both of you," said Connor. "Make sure you send me a copy of your presentation, I'd love to see it," he added.

"Connor, before you leave, I wanted to ask you about something," said Dr. Price.

"Ask away Jules," Connor answered.

"Connor, thanks to you, we're a completely different healthcare facility and I was wondering if you might have time to help us with our operating rooms? Not as part of your payback for Becky's illness, but rather as a paid consultant," Dr. Price said.

"I don't think you guys need me for that," Connor replied. "Just follow the same thinking and do the necessary systems analysis, map the flow, and look for the constraint, the same thing you did in the emergency department. It will get you where you want to be. Actually, it should be much easier, since you've both been involved in this process before," he added.

"I had a conversation with our board of directors and they have approved you to help us, so would you please consider it?" asked Dr. Price.

"I'll think about it, but I can't make that promise to you right now. I'll have to let you know another day," Connor replied. "But in the meantime, you guys need to start the effort. If you have any questions, please let me know. I'm always glad to help," he added.

Connor left, and on his drive home, he kept going over in his mind the impressive results he had just seen and heard about. Connor thought to himself that helping the hospital improve was very rewarding, because at the end of the day, it helped society improve and when society improves, it helps everyone improve. As he was driving, Connor said to himself, "Maybe I should help them with their operating rooms ..."

Index